HEAVEN'S WIND

HEAVEN'S WIND

THE LIFE AND TEACHINGS
OF NAKAMURA TEMPU

STEPHEN EARLE

North Atlantic Books
Berkeley, California

Published by   Cover photo provided by Robert Frager
North Atlantic Books   Cover design by John Yates
Berkeley, California   Book design by Brad Greene

Printed in the United States of America

Heaven's Wind: The Life and Teachings of Nakamura Tempu is sponsored and published by the Society for the Study of Native Arts and Sciences (dba North Atlantic Books), an educational nonprofit based in Berkeley, California, that collaborates with partners to develop cross-cultural perspectives, nurture holistic views of art, science, the humanities, and healing, and seed personal and global transformation by publishing work on the relationship of body, spirit, and nature.

North Atlantic Books' publications are available through most bookstores. For further information, visit our website at www.northatlanticbooks.com or call 800-733-3000.

Library of Congress Cataloging-in-Publication Data

Names: Earle, Stephen, 1949-
Title: Heaven's wind : the life and teachings of Nakamura Tempu / Stephen Earle.
Description: Berkeley, California : North Atlantic Books, 2017.
Identifiers: LCCN 2016027121 (print) | LCCN 2016055950 (ebook) | ISBN 9781623171148 (paperback) | ISBN 9781623171155 (ebook)
Subjects: LCSH: Tempu, Nakamura. | Martial artists—Japan—Biography. | Educators—Japan—Biography. | BISAC: BIOGRAPHY & AUTOBIOGRAPHY / Historical. | HISTORY / Asia / Japan. | SPORTS & RECREATION / Martial Arts & Self-Defense.
Classification: LCC GV1113.T45 E37 2017 (print) | LCC GV1113.T45 (ebook) | DDC 796.8092 [B] —dc23
LC record available at https://lccn.loc.gov/2016027121

1 2 3 4 5 6 7 8 9 United 22 21 20 19 18 17

Printed on recycled paper

North Atlantic Books is committed to the protection of our environment. We partner with FSC-certified printers using soy-based inks and print on recycled paper whenever possible.

In Memory of Sasaki Masando,
But for whose story that day in the coffee shop,
this book would never have come to be.

Nakamura Tempū (1876–1968)

CONTENTS

FOREWORD

This book is about the life and teachings of a great teacher and an extraordinary human being. Through his example and his teachings, Nakamura Tempū-sensei taught me invaluable lessons about the highest potentials of human nature. He also inspired over one million Japanese people, from college students to national leaders.

I first met Nakamura Tempū in 1965. A close aikido friend brought me to one of his lectures. There was an audience of two or three hundred people, and I was the only non-Japanese. My friend explained that new students could only study with Tempū-sensei if they were invited by one of his followers.

I knew that many of the senior aikido teachers had been students of Tempū-sensei. They found his teachings extremely helpful in comprehending the principles of aikido, as the founder of aikido was often extremely difficult to understand. The founder generally explained aikido using esoteric terms from the ancient Shinto scriptures. In contrast, Tempū-sensei related his ideas to modern psychology, comparative philosophy, and even nuclear physics.

The more I learned about Tempū-sensei, the more impressed I became. He had fought in the Russo-Japanese war and spent two years in Manchuria behind Russian lines. He traveled to the United States after the war and studied here for several years. Tempū-sensei also spent three years in an ashram in the Himalayas intensely practicing meditation and other yoga disciplines. On his return to Japan, Tempū-sensei enjoyed an extraordinarily successful business career. He devoted himself to assisting Japanese modernization, a process he understood because of his profound familiarity with Western culture and society.

In 1919 Tempū-sensei founded the Tempu Society. His ideas and practices became popular with many Japanese scholars, businesspeople, scientists, and politicians. Tempū-sensei also became the spiritual tutor to members of the Japanese imperial family.

Tempū-sensei gave a series of five evening lectures a month in Tokyo. He taught in other Japanese cities, but less frequently. At my first lecture, a distinguished older man sitting next to me introduced himself as a retired aeronautical engineer. Then he mentioned he had been the designer of the Zero, the famous Japanese fighter plane.

Tempū-sensei discussed the relationship of mind and body decades before Western medicine discovered the importance of mental attitude in health and healing. Tempū explained that the mind can affect the body far more than we realize. He stressed the power of the mind to increase our capacity for healing and also our resistance to illness. For example, Tempū students refused to use medication unless it was truly necessary. They knew the best medicine was their belief in their own health and capacity for self-healing. This made a deep impression on me, one that has lasted for over fifty years.

After my first trip to Japan, I returned to complete my PhD at Harvard. I taught psychology at Harvard, the University of California, Berkeley, and the University of California, Santa Cruz. In 1975 I founded the Institute of Transpersonal Psychology, now known as Sofia University. I had no endowment and minimal support, but I had a dream of a truly holistic approach to education, a dream based in large part on Tempū-sensei's teachings. I envisioned a university in which students would not only gain academic skills but would also develop themselves as human beings. I strongly believed that who we are is more important than what we know. This dream has flourished for over forty years, and Sofia University has transformed the lives of hundreds of graduates and thousands of their clients and students.

I never would have founded my own university if it wasn't for Tempū-sensei. One of the greatest lessons he taught me is that we all have the capacities to achieve whatever any other human being has achieved. This gave me the confidence to open my own school based on my ideals and my confidence in my ability to handle such a great challenge.

Tempū-sensei's teachings have kept me healthy, energetic, and inspired throughout the years since I first met him in 1965. I can't begin to express the debt of gratitude I owe him.

Robert Frager
Founder and President Emeritus, Sofia University
Aikido 7th Dan

ACKNOWLEDGMENTS

My acquaintance with the teachings of Nakamura Tempū began with two aikido instructors. The first, Tada Hiroshi-sensei, continues to be a beacon of both Ueshiba Morihei's aikido and Nakamura Tempū's *shin-shin tōitsu-dō* at the age of eighty-seven. The second, Sasaki Masando-sensei, to whom I have dedicated this book, passed away in 2013 at age eighty-four. Lessons learned from these exemplars not only inform these pages but continue to affect the way I live, and I am eternally grateful to each of them.

The Tempūkai's instructors, volunteers, and fellow students, all too numerous to name, have not only contributed to my understanding of *Tempū tetsugaku*, "Tempū philosophy," more than has all my readings, but have also provided me with many fond memories. In 2005, Aida Shūhei-sensei, then serving as Tempūkai chairman, encouraged me to think seriously about how best to present Tempū's teachings in English. The Tempūkai board of directors has most graciously allowed me to use a number of photographs from the Tempūkai's extensive archive.

Beginning in 2007, long before I was certain that this project would lead to a book, I posted a three-part preliminary exposition of the Naka-mura Tempū story online. Stan Pranin of *Aikido Journal* was instrumental in making these writings known within the aikido community by posting links to them on his blog, and I am deeply grateful to the many readers who subsequently contacted me by email; it was largely as a result of their encouragement that I decided to take the project to the next level.

One of the emails I received was from Robert Frager. Bob's name was known to me as a pioneer of aikido's dissemination in the United States; he is one of only a handful of American practitioners to have trained in Japan while the founder of the art, Ueshiba Morihei, was still alive and teaching. What I did not know was that during those same years he had also studied under Nakamura Tempū. Bob and I have subsequently cor-responded by email and spoken by telephone, and I am privileged and honored to be able to include his foreword.

One day in spring 2009 I returned home to find a message on our voice mail from Naoko Matsubara Waterhouse in Ontario, Canada; evidently her husband, David Waterhouse, had seen Stan's post in *Aikido Journal* and found our phone number through directory assistance. Naoko, I learned from both her message and our subsequent phone conversation, had studied under Nakamura Tempū during her late teens and early twenties and was excited to find that someone was finally writing about him in English. The timing of her phone call, however, was particularly uncanny, in that it came just three days before I was to leave on a road trip to Toronto, a city I had not visited in over thirty years. Just days later, Naoko-san treated me to her wonderful cooking and introduced me to her most extraordinary work as an artist at the Waterhouses' home in Oakville, Ontario.

Naoko-san's encouragement and her insistence that the project be made into a book, as well as her stories about studying under Tempū-sensei as a young woman, were critical to the project's completion. On top of this, she contributed an original woodcut for use on the book's cover; even though, in the end, the decision was made to use a photograph instead, her generosity is warmly received and appreciated.

Arlene Gehmacher of the Royal Ontario Museum in Toronto helped with piecing together Naoko-san's story as it appears in the book's final chapter.

David Waterhouse, a longtime judo practitioner with an encyclopedic knowledge of the art's history, was insightful with regard to the Meidōkan dojo and its relationship (or lack thereof) to the Kōdōkan. He also provided much needed advice regarding word selection and sentence structure in early drafts.

Martine Bellen's editorial comments and guidance, as well as copy corrections, on an early draft were an education and did much to improve my writing, both in composition and in style.

My visit to Gorkhey was only possible through the arrangements made by Navin Tamang in Darjeeling, and without Pemba, the guide provided by Navin, communications with the villagers would have been all but impossible. Bishal Maskey of Gorkhey also helped with communications and has continued to be of assistance via email since my departure. I am grateful to Nimesh Mittal in Kathmandu—to my knowledge, the only person in Nepal to research the question of Kariappa's identity—for his willingness to share by telephone and email what he has learned.

Longtime friend and publishing industry denizen Leonard Jacobs lent invaluable advice with regard to the volatile world of book publishers and, even more importantly, referred me to Richard Grossinger; Richard, in turn, graciously referred me to Tim McKee at North Atlantic Books. Thanks go to those on North Atlantic's acquisitions committee who voiced support for the *Heaven's Wind* project, and to all at North Atlantic for your willingness to take the risk. Louis Swaim, my project editor, and Christopher Church, my copy editor, deserve special mention.

Last but far from least, my wife, Akemi, has been my companion in this project from beginning to end. Akemi is, in many respects, a more earnest and committed practitioner of Nakamura Tempū's mind-body unification methods than am I, and she has read his writings and participated with me in several Tempūkai retreats and events. Her insights, observations, and advice have contributed invaluably to the pages that follow.

INTRODUCTION

Nakamura Tempū was both a spiritual giant and a significant player in the making of modern Japan. Tempū, written 天風, is composed of the characters 天, meaning "heaven," and 風, meaning "wind," thus giving us "heaven's wind." As the events of his epic story show, not only did he have the audacity to go by that name, he also had sufficient audacity to live up to it.

Sent off to war at an early age, he survived a harrowing mission behind Russian enemy lines as a spy during the Russo-Japanese War, only to contract tuberculosis and be handed a death sentence by his doctors. In search of a cure, he traveled first to New York, where he obtained a medical degree from Columbia University, and then on to London and Paris, where he met notable intellectuals and encountered a groundswell of new ideas shaping modernity; none of this knowledge and exposure, however, provided any insight into how to overcome his disease. Then, on his journey home, providence sidetracked him to the foothills of the Himalayas and the practice of yoga under a venerable master, wherein he discovered an essential truth that not only restored him to health but also brought about a mental and spiritual transformation.

Returned to Japan, he first ascended heights of financial success as a entrepreneur and then gave up his wealth to pursue a calling as a teacher of the principles of mind-body integration. His practical wisdom has saved lives, inspired greatness, and proven invaluable, in the wake of World War II, to the task of regenerating the spirit of a broken nation. And yet, the man, his story, and his legacy of teachings remain almost unknown outside Japan. This book is the first of its kind to address that void.

Nakamura Tempū was of my grandfathers' generation, so hypothetically, had I been in the right place at the right time, I could have met him: the last nineteen years of his life matched, almost to the day, the first nineteen of mine. As it was, half a globe came between us, and only after taking the initiative to travel to Japan at the tender age of twenty-two did I encounter first the name and then, after living there for sixteen years, the story.

My initial exposure to Tempū and his teachings came by way of aikido, a martial art I have practiced since 1970. A contemporary of aikido founder Ueshiba Morihei, Nakamura Tempū had a deep and lasting influence on the first generation of postwar aikido instructors, a number of whom, in the 1950s and 1960s, split their time between Ueshiba's Hombu Dojo (aikido's headquarters) and Nakamura's Tempūkai (the Tempu Society). Of these, the best-known was Tōhei Kōichi, who broke away from the Ueshiba family lineage in 1974 to found his own derivative art. Tōhei's aikido, which he called *shin-shin tōitsu aikido,* "mind-body unification aikido," is his synthesis of Nakamura Tempū's teachings with those of Ueshiba Morihei.

Tōhei, however, was not the only aikido instructor to be influenced by Nakamura. Tada Hiroshi, currently the most senior and highest-ranking instructor within aikido's Aikikai Foundation, and under whom I trained for six years in Tokyo during the 1980s, was a regular attendee of Tempū's lectures and was often called upon by Tempū to assist in demonstrations involving the use of *ki,* or vital energy. Tada-sensei has incorporated Tempū's breathing exercises and other elements of his mind-body discipline into the *ki-no-renma* ("energy training") practices with which classes begin in his dojos, and while Tōhei was critical of and took exception to some of Tempū's teachings, Tada has remained loyal to the man and to his work.

Sasaki Masando, another of my aikido mentors, served as a personal assistant to Nakamura for many years, accompanying him on visits to Tempūkai chapters in northeastern and western Japan. I returned to the United States in 1988, but from the mid-1990s until Sasaki's retirement from the Aikikai instructors panel in 2007, I made it a point to attended Sasaki-sensei's Saturday morning class at Hombu Dojo whenever I visited Tokyo—which, for work reasons, was typically several times a year. One morning in 1998, following a class during which he dropped, as he often did in the course of his immensely entertaining class-time digressions, the name Nakamura Tempū, I said to him as we seated ourselves in a Shinjuku coffee shop, "Sensei, I would like to hear more about Nakamura

Tempū." Sensei's eyes lit up. He settled back into his chair and held forth for the next hour to a spellbound audience of five or so of us seated around his table. Sasaki had heard Tempū tell his story so many times that he could repeat large parts of it verbatim, and I remember thinking then that this was as close as I was ever going to get to hearing it from the horse's mouth. To my great regret, Sasaki-sensei passed away in 2013, before I could show him this book.

While Sasaki-sensei's account that day in the coffee shop serves as the inspiration for the pages that follow, it is not my only source. The novelist Uno Chiyo wrote a wonderful little book called *Tempū-sensei Zadan* (Talks by Tempū-sensei), a copy of which a friend sent to my wife in the early 1990s when she learned we were in the midst of a midlife financial crisis; we both read it, and our circumstances took a turn for the better. Another writer, Ōi Mitsuru, has written a brilliant three-volume account of Nakamura's life that I have drawn upon liberally, both for narrative and for background. The Tempūkai's monthly publication, *Shirube* (Guidepost), has also been an invaluable resource, as has the Tempūkai's 2005 publication of *Zusetsu, Nakamura Tempū,* an illustrated account of Nakamura's life and times, filled with photographs, each worth a thousand words.

My association with the Tempūkai began during a second one-year-long Japan residence in 2004, and the excellent instruction provided at Tempūkai summer retreats, seminars, and workshops brought me closer to an understanding of Tempū's teachings. The Tempūkai has been helpful and responsive to a number of questions and requests with regard to this project. They have also graciously provided several of the photographs contained in *Zusetsu, Nakamura Tempū* with permission to publish them herein.

My primary sources, however, have been the transcripts of Tempū's 1950s and 1960s lectures, especially those published in the three volumes *Seikō-no Jitsugen* (The Realization of Success), *Seidai-na Jinsei* (A Prodigious Life), and *Kokoro-ni Seikō-no Honō-wo* (Mentally Kindling the Flame of Success). Additionally, the Tempūkai has made a number of recordings and film clips of Tempū from their archive available in CD and DVD format, allowing those like me who never met him to gain an appreciation of what it must have been like to see and to hear the man in person.

Unlike my telling of it herein, Tempū's account is given to us not as one uninterrupted autobiographical narrative but rather as isolated vignettes dispersed among his talks, each serving to explain or illustrate the particular principle or practice under discussion. Thus, in order to construct the fuller narrative, I have had to sift through these episodes and piece them together in chronological order. A number of his stories are recorded multiple times in the transcripts alluded to above but with minor discrepancies among them, and time and place are sometimes left undetermined. I have done the best I can with the information available but, in some instances, have had to make less than fully supportable judgment calls with regard to exact sequences of events. Where chronology is not critical, I have sometimes inserted events into slots that may or may not be historically accurate but serve the purpose of the narrative.

In so doing, I have also adopted a style resembling that of a historical novel; this, I believe, is befitting of the way his many stories come down to us through his telling of them. A consummate storyteller, Tempū is the only source we have for most of his story, the events of which happened more than eighty, some more than one hundred, years ago, and his account has almost certainly been embellished in the course of its telling and retelling. But then, he also gives us no reason to suspect that the events themselves are his invention; they dovetail with history and, in many cases, contain details that could only have been known to someone who lived them. Furthermore, his stories were told neither purely to entertain nor to boast. Tempū speaks of his past with great humility, and his story is important, he insists, only because it explains just how it was that he came to the conclusions he did regarding human health, happiness, and the importance of mind-body integrity. What is fact and what is fiction is ultimately a matter of opinion, and readers will form their own; in my opinion, the principle events are factual. They are also testament to the adage, Fact is stranger than fiction.

Consistent with the style of a historical novel, the story as I tell it contains conversations between characters. Those conversations, however, where they appear, are not my inventions; they are based on the words ascribed to the respective characters by Tempū in his accounts, allowing for small liberties taken in translating them into vernacular English.

Citations for directly quoted longer passages, as well as significant quotes attributable to historical figures other than Tempū, are included in the endnotes. I have forgone citations, however, for the bulk of the narrative; in almost all cases, my sources are those mentioned above, and a full list of references is included in the bibliography at the end of the book.

Unless otherwise noted, translations from Japanese into English are mine. As a gross generalization, translation comes in two colors: literal and interpretive. As I say, this is grossly general, since even the most literal translation is interpretive, and the most interpretive is still beholden to its literal source. All translation falls somewhere between those two poles. That said, I am more of the interpretive persuasion, inclined to first look for what it is the author or speaker wants to say and then to work backward from there to a semblance of the original text. While the risk of getting it wrong remains, I accept that risk and am prepared to defend my interpretations; better, it seems to me, to come down on the side of lucidity rather than word-for-word accuracy.

In the course of researching Tempū's narrative, I have encountered discrepancies here and there between his version of events and the historical record. Most of these are minor and of little consequence, whatever the explanation. Larger questions, like those concerning the identity of his teacher Kariappa, the yogi, and the nature of his involvement in Sun Yat-sen's Second Revolution, are addressed within the context of the narrative as they arise.

One of the more frustrating problems I encountered, however, is that of dates. If we are to take Nakamura at his word, we have him departing Japan in the spring of 1909 to go first to Shanghai and then, in May, to New York. The journey to New York takes him about three months, and I have inferred that he traveled the western route by way of the Suez Canal, since the Panama Canal was not completed until 1914, and he says nothing of crossing the North American continent by way of the transcontinental railroad. We are told that he stayed in New York just long enough to secure two degrees in medicine from Columbia University before traveling on to London and Paris, and that the entire duration of his sojourn in the West was about two years. We are then given a date of May 25, 1911, for his departure from Marseilles. So far, everything adds up.

Seven days later, however, he encounters the Indian sage Kariappa in Cairo, accompanies him on a ninety-day journey to India, where he remains, studying the ways of yoga, for two years and nine months. But upon departing India and before returning to Japan, he stops first in Shanghai, where he participates in Sun Yat-sen's Second Revolution, an event that occurred in July 1913.

Simple math tells us something is wrong. If we take his 1909 departure from Japan as a fixed starting point, then one of the following scenarios must be true. Either he arrived back in Shanghai at least nine months too late to have participated in Sun Yat-sen's Second Revolution, calling into question the stories he tells with regard to it. Or his departure from Marseilles was not in May 1911 but May 1910—in which case, his time in New York could have been no more than six months, thereby straining the credibility of his claims to have received two degrees in medicine. Or, if the May 1911 date is correct, then his time in India must have been not two years and nine months but one year and nine months—this despite his assertion of the two-year, nine-month figure many times over in his talks.

Needless to say, none of these explanations is satisfactory; for any one of them to be true, the credibility of his entire narrative suffers. To my additional frustration, the Tempūkai doggedly adheres to the dates given by Tempū in his accounts, despite the obvious problem with them. The Tempūkai timeline shows him leaving Japan in 1909, setting sail from Marseilles in 1911, and participating with Sun Yat-sen in his 1913 Second Revolution.

As I have already noted, Tempū almost certainly took liberties in the telling of his stories, embellishing them to entertain and circumventing details not directly pertinent to the particular lesson the story was meant to illustrate. But embellishment and falsehood are two different things, and I have no reason to suspect that he made anything up; not only would doing so have served him no purpose, it would also have been contrary to everything he taught with regard to the sanctity of truthfulness and human integrity. Consequently, I have chosen to accept Tempū at his word with regard to the main chapters of his story.

As a result, the only palatable solution with regard to dates appears, at least to me, to be to move the first one, the date of his departure from Japan, back one year. Nothing he reports ties him to late 1908 and early 1909 events in Japan, and were he to have departed in spring 1908, then everything afterward works out. Yes, it would mean his departure from Marseilles occurred in May 1910—not, as he says, in 1911—but that also appears entirely plausible. I am even supported in this hypothesis by Ōi Mitsuru, who, in *Yoga-ni Ikiru* (Living in Yoga), pegs, as I do, Nakamura's Marseilles departure to the year 1910.

Why the confusion in Tempū's accounts? For no better reason, I suspect, than the fallibility of memory. The published transcripts and recordings of Nakamura Tempū's talks all date from the 1950s and 1960s; in them, he is talking about events that occurred almost a half century earlier. Could he not simply have been mistaken?

Years are commonly numbered in Japan not by Common Era notation but by imperial reign; thus, the year given by Tempū for his departure from Japan is Meiji 42. The Meiji era ended with the death of the Emperor Meiji in 1912, and consequently, 1912 is both Meiji 45 and Taishō 1. Tempū would not have heard about the emperor's passing and the change of dating from Meiji to Taishō until his arrival in Shanghai, the date for which, if we assume 1913 to be correct, was Taishō 2. Taishō gave way to Shōwa in 1926, and Shōwa gave way to Heisei in 1989; as with the transition from Meiji to Taishō, each of the transitional years is counted under both the outgoing and the incoming monarch's reign.

The imperial dating system has its advantages. For one, it segments history into convenient blocks of time, each era assuming the colors of the popular mood, cultural habits, and major events within its span. Thus, for example, mention Meiji and images of a newly reinvented nation, vigorously engaged in playing catch-up with the industrial nations of Europe and America and throwing over many of its traditional habits for more modern, Western ones, come to mind. But the division of time into blocks of unequal and less-than-human-lifespan duration can also get in the way of simple reckoning and consequently obfuscate longer perspectives on the historical continuum.

This is not to suggest that Tempū was confused by Japan's system of counting years; he was educated and intelligent, and he would have been entirely capable of translating between Japanese dates and those of the Common Era. Nevertheless, were he, in looking back at events fifty years in the past, to have miscalculated the year of his departure from Japan by one year, such a miscalculation would be, I believe, forgivable. In the absence of a more satisfactory explanation, this is the one I have adopted.

Not only did Tempū live through and witness some of the more tumultuous chapters in the making of modern East Asia, he also participated in them. Among those chapters were the Sino-Japanese War of 1894–1895, the Russo-Japanese War of 1904–1905, Sun Yat-sen's 1913 Second Revolution, Taishō-era labor disputes, the 2-26 Incident of 1936, the 1945 air raid destruction and burning of Tokyo, and postwar Japanese reconstruction. He also brushed up against people of power and influence, both in Japan and abroad. Getting to know, through research, these events and characters—some, for the first time; others, as I had not known them before—has been an adventure all of its own, and perhaps my enthusiasm shows. To understand Tempū's role in these events and the relationships he maintained with the various characters that populate them, some framing of the historical context is necessary, and I have invested a fair number of pages to that endeavor.

Tempū's lifelong mentor Tōyama Mitsuru was and is a subject of controversy. I suspect the single most compelling reason for the failure of Nakamura Tempū's teachings to have gained more traction than they have heretofore outside Japan is his association with the Genyōsha and Tōyama's nationalist political agenda. Some of Tempū's admirers have either spoken of this association apologetically or avoided it. I have chosen to meet it head-on. What is important to know is that Tempū, to his dying day, never once spoke critically of Tōyama, and as someone engaged in telling Tempū's story, I cannot help but be fascinated by the question: Just what was it that Nakamura Tempū found in Tōyama to be so worthy of devotion? Tōyama Mitsuru is, at the very least, an extremely rich and complex character. If I have sounded revisionist in my estimation of him, it is only because I have sought to see him as Nakamura did and to answer the above question.

Likewise, with regard to observations and assessments made in chapter 15, it is not my purpose, nor am I qualified, to rewage World War II. However, I do believe it important, in order to understand Japan's postwar psychology, as well as Nakamura Tempū's contribution to the postwar reconstruction, to at least attempt to see that war from the Japanese perspective. This is especially so, since the prevailing interpretations of Japan's actions are the ones given us by the victors' historians.

The rise of Japanese militancy in the 1930s and the horrors and devastation it ultimately perpetrated on much of the Asia-Pacific region are matters of record—a record that weighed heavily on Tempū's conscience, as it did on the postwar conscience of the nation. At the same time, the accepted Anglo-American, Chinese, and Japanese versions of that dark chapter each differ significantly. Was, for example, Japan simply and categorically an unapologetic aggressor? Or were its actions more like those of a caged tiger backed into a corner? Was Japanese militarism motivated solely by dreams of empire? Or was it born of a desire to preserve national security and to free Asia of Western colonialism? Was the brutality of the atrocities committed by Japanese soldiers in the countries they invaded endemic to the national character? Or was it endemic to the war itself, comparable in kind to atrocities committed by Chiang Kai-shek and his Kuomintang regime, as well as to the United States' fire bombings of Japanese cities and its detonation of two atomic bombs? Arguments can and have been made on all sides. My personal opinion is that, in any war, it takes at least two to tango; that, with particular regard to the war in question, each side was both justified by and hostage to its particular cultural perspective and geopolitical world-view; and that each side made mistakes and committed crimes.

That said, by any rational analysis, Japan's actions were misguided and doomed to failure from the beginning. Like any good citizen of any country, Tempū lauded the bravery and resolve of the nation's young men going off to war, but he was also incensed by the pigheaded shortsight-edness of the country's leaders and their willingness to bet the future on a cause so poorly conceived and so unlikely to succeed. Furthermore, I venture to assert, he appreciated, in the War's aftermath, that the only spoils that war can possibly deliver are the lessons to be derived from it, and that, in that sense, the only potential winner in war is posterity—pro-vided only that posterity takes those lessons to heart.

Nakamura's story documents the trajectory of his development, through stages of self-centered rebelliousness in youth and ethnocentric identification with Japanese nationalism in his prime, to world-centric maturity, as a result of his suffering due to sickness and his travels abroad, and finally to a universal or cosmological perspective on life and humanity with the formulation and refinement of his philosophy and its methods of instruction. Likewise, his teachings are developmental by design, meaning they are meant to empower the individual on his or her unfolding journey toward mental, emotional, and spiritual maturity and to propel humanity along its evolutionary ascent toward greater goodness, truth, and beauty.

Those teachings are in a vast body of work, both broad and deep in scope. This book does not purport to be either thorough or authoritative in its exposition of Tempū's philosophy, but it is meant to serve as an introduction. In much the same way that he uses the stories of his past to explain where his philosophy came from and to illustrate how reali-zations he had along the way permanently changed him for the better, I have chosen to introduce the central tenets of his philosophy through the events giving rise to their formulation.

The exception is chapter 13, where I have attempted an overview of his mind-body philosophy and a general description of some of the practices that come with it. That said, it is explicitly beyond the scope of this volume to go into the details of the many practices that make up the "how to do" part of his system—the reason being that most of these practices are best learned firsthand from a qualified instructor, and to attempt to transmit them through the medium of the written page would, I believe, be futile and even counterproductive. The Lindler system of autosuggestion, *anjō-daza* meditation, and *kumbhaka* aside—for these I go into in some detail at appropriate points in the narrative—I have, for the most part, shied away from practical instruction.

This may, I am painfully aware, prompt the question, "Where do I need to go to learn more?" Painfully so, because there are not many options as yet available outside the Tempūkai's courses and retreats in Japan (although, the Tempūkai has, I understand, recently begun to conduct an annual retreat in Hawaii). Supply, however, usually follows demand, and hopefully this book will inspire more interest than has existed heretofore. To the extent I am able, it is my purpose to mentor such interest, and information regarding seminars or other programs related to Tempū's teachings in the United States and elsewhere, if and when they are made available, will be posted on the website www.heavenswind.com.

One resource worthy of mention is H. E. Davey's books *Japanese Yoga: The Way of Dynamic Meditation* and *The Teachings of Tempu: Practical Meditation for Daily Life*. Davey is a longtime student of Nakamura Tempū's teachings, and despite my reservations regarding the efficacy of attempting to transmit Tempū's practices through written explanation, he has done an admirable job of making many of these practices accessible to English readers.

* * *

In the writings that follow, I have gone beyond the role of dispassionate researcher to that of advocate. As a reader, you may wonder, just what have Nakamura's teachings meant to me personally? In short, how much skin do I have in the game?

In answer to that question, I shall tell the following story. In mid-February 2016, as I was bearing down on completion of the manuscript for this book, I was diagnosed with prostate cancer. The news came most unexpectedly, as I was feeling as well or better than I had at any time in recent memory. However, in December, as part of a checkup, a routine blood test had come back showing elevated PSA, and the urologist to whom I was referred ordered what is called a sonic biopsy, an unpleasant procedure I reluctantly agreed to undergo just to get the doctors off of my back. Thus it was that, in February, at 8:30 on a Friday morning, I went back to the urologist to receive the biopsy results, fully expecting to be given a clean bill of health and sent on my way.

Instead, he dropped the *c* word. My first response was to assume he was joking. But then, here I was in a doctor's office, and this was the doctor speaking. On second thought, he must be serious.

More important, however, was what occurred next. Had this been me even a couple of years ago, I would have almost certainly been subject to a rush of adrenalin and an onset of the kind of fear that rests in the pit of the stomach and causes shortness of breath. As it was, I experienced no such reaction.

Even though this book was long in the making, only for the last seventeen months had I been working on it full time. Moreover, during those seventeen months, that I might responsibly reflect Nakamura Tempū's teachings on the pages herein, I had immersed myself in his writings and applied myself to his instructions regarding the cultivation of mental positivity with a rigor that, admittedly, had been lacking from my practice before. And as a product of this conditioning—or so I assume, for no other cause seems likely—my second response was one of no more than mild surprise.

Oh, I thought to myself. *I have cancer.* The thought came as an acknowledgment that life had, yet again, thrown up the unexpected and was telling me I was to embark on a new adventure. More surprising than the news itself was the total lack of fear or concern it prompted in me; to the contrary, I felt a twinge of excitement. *How interesting,* I thought. *A new challenge.*

Neither is this a book about cancer, nor do I claim to have discovered in Nakamura Tempū's mind-body unification philosophy and methodology the cure for all disease. It is, however, a book about the relationship between how we conduct ourselves mentally and how life shows up as a result. What I can and will say without reservation is that the days, weeks, and months since that visit to the doctor's office have been nothing short of miraculous. Very shortly after returning home and discussing the news with my wife, Akemi, I was overcome by a feeling of empowerment and possibility. We both decided not to tell anyone—neither family nor friends—until after the storm had passed, and with the exception of one close friend, someone I was confident I could trust to see the news in a positive light, all will be learning of it for the first time from the words on this page.

Furthermore, Akemi and I agreed we were up for the challenge and would see it through. I say this not with the kind of teeth-clenching resolve I imagine soldiers take with them into battle—the "do or die" mentality—but with the kind of excitement one exhibits when engaging in a new undertaking or project. Three days later, I had a realization that I can only describe as spiritual in nature; it was the kind of all-at-once illumination that defies the subject-verb-predicate syntax of the linguistic medium, but the best I can do to put it into words is as follows. I saw that health is a state of mind before it is a state of body, and that, in one sense, I was already cured—that my body may or may not continue to harbor cancerous cells, but, either way, such was of no consequence to my ability to live this life to its maximum. And given that I was not going to allow cancer to win out over me mentally, the likelihood of my winning out over the cancer in my body approached a high level of certainty.

All of this has had a profound effect on the way I live. To paraphrase Samuel Johnson, nothing focuses the mind quite like the knowledge one is to be hanged in the morning, and coming face-to-face with one's mortality has a way of not only sharpening one's attention but also highlighting one's blessings, the number of which is far larger than I had ever before been aware. Each day and each moment of that day, I began to see, is possessed of its own, special magic. The flowers this spring have been especially beautiful. I have found myself enjoying the company of people more and being more receptive to what it is they have to say. People I meet and deal with, even if only over the telephone or across the counter at a checkout register, show up as familiar members of a shared humanity, and the world shows up as one filled with goodness.

Furthermore, many of my bad and more self-destructive habits have spontaneously fallen away. I am eating better, sleeping better, and rising earlier than I have in years. My consumption of coffee has fallen off dramatically, and my consumption of alcohol has all but disappeared.

Regarding this last, while my drinking habits have always been moderate, a couple of beers or glasses of wine in the evening, especially after any of my four to five evenings a week of martial arts training, is an indulgence I have cultivated over many years and one I have never been particularly successful at curbing through exercise of willpower. And yet, on the evening of the day I learned of the results of my biopsy from my doctor, and after two hours of aikido, not only did I abstain from alcohol, but I was not even tempted by the wine and beer plainly in sight in our living room. Furthermore, that lack of allure has persisted; while I have made up no rules and am following no prescribed regime, alcohol has lost its attraction. In testament to this, I have, on several social occasions, indulged in the company of friends but experienced nothing that would resemble falling-off-the-wagon syndrome: I stopped after the second drink and had no desire to partake the following day.

Two months after my biopsy, I went in for an MRI, and two weeks after that, back in for the results. Of the four locations in my prostate from where biopsy samples had tested positive for carcinoma, only one showed up in the MRI, and that was described by my doctor as "low-grade." That same doctor, who in February had recommended surgery, was now of the opinion that my choice to pursue surveillance instead constituted a "reasonable approach."

Among cancers, prostate cancer is relatively tame—a minor-league player when compared to some of cancer's more aggressive incarnations—and consequently, I do not wish to make too much out of this small miracle. Nevertheless, I have chosen to leave more cautious interpretations to the doctor and to take these results as proof positive that providence is working its magic.

In the meantime, without solicitation on my part, the one friend to whom I divulged my secret has given me the name of a naturopathic but clinically trained doctor in North Carolina; I have subsequently made contact with him by telephone, undergone some additional blood tests requested by him, and, on the basis of his advice, taken up his recommendations. Akemi has discovered an extremely simple exercise routine that is purported to have cured a number of people in Japan of cancer, and she and I are devoting fifteen minutes to this practice every morning. I continue to teach and to train in two martial arts and to otherwise carry on just as before my diagnosis. In general, life continues, but does so with more fullness and meaning than ever before.

All of life is an adventure. Whatever this particular adventure's outcome, it has been an extraordinary gift, one I would not choose to have any other way. After all, it has led me here, to the writing of this book. How lucky I am to have encountered the teachings of Nakamura Tempū and to be guided by his wisdom.

JAPANESE AND CHINESE
NAMES AND TERMS

Japanese and Chinese names appear in the Japanese and Chinese conventional order of surname first, followed by given name. Thus, in the case of Nakamura Tempū, Nakamura is the family name or surname, and Tempū a given name.

Romanization of Japanese names and terms is consistent with generally recognized practice. For the most part, Japanese words read as their Romanized spellings suggest; however, rules to remember are, all syllables are equally accented, vowels *a, e,* and *i* are always short, and there are no diphthongs: where an *e* and an *i* appear together, either as *ei* or as *ie,* they are to be read as two short, separate, equally stressed syllables. Examples are *sensei,* an honorific title usually reserved for a teacher, pronounced *sen-se-i,* and *sumie,* "ink painting," pronounced *su-mi-e.*

Macrons, or superscripted dashes, over *o* and *u,* like that over the *u* in Tempū, indicate long vowels, approximately double the marked vowel's usual length. Macrons have been dispensed with when the name or term is widely recognized in English; thus Tokyo, Osaka, and judo, as opposed to Tōkyō, Ōsaka, and jūdō.

In most cases, Chinese place-names appear in modern pinyin; thus, Beijing as opposed to Peking and Nanjing as opposed to Nanking. The names Sun Yat-sen and Chiang Kai-shek are not in pinyin but reflect the most widely accepted spellings outside China.

I.

ONE
IMPORTANT
THING

1.
THIRD MALE CHILD

They first named him Sango, written "three oxen," because he was born in the lunar sixth month on the tenth day at the noon hour, the month, day, and hour of the ox. The year was the ninth in the Meiji emperor's reign, making the date, by Western reckoning, July 30, 1876. Upon discovering he had come into the world with two front teeth, his parents took him to a celebrated fortune-teller and were told that, if they were not careful, he would turn out to be a worse character than Ishikawa Goemon, the quintessential sixteenth-century outlaw famously put to death by the shōgun Hideyoshi in a cauldron of boiling water.

He was the Nakamura's third born but second surviving son, and before he entered his third year, his father changed his name to Saburō, "third male child."

Nakamura Saburō's father, Sukeoki, was of *bushi*, or samurai, lineage, born into the Tachibana clan of Yanagawa, in what is now Fukuoka Prefecture, on the southwestern island of Kyushu. Growing up during the last years of the Tokugawa Shogunate, he was tutored from a young age in *bunbu*, "letters and martial arts"—that is, the Japanese and Chinese classics and the ways of war—and he learned to groom his hair into a topknot, don the wide pleated skirt-like riding pants known as *hakama*, and insert those quintessential symbols of the bushi prerogative, two swords, one long and one short, under the sash around his waist. He would, all assumed, live out his days in service to the Yanagawa fiefdom.

But such was not to be. Incursions by Western powers on the serenity of the national landscape had awoken some of the more visionary samurai to just how vulnerable their tiny island nation had become and how far behind it had been left by the march of progress. The country split sharply along conservative and progressive lines, leading to all-out civil war and the eventual ousting of the Tokugawa regime. The new regime asserted itself by "restoring" (a euphemism, as the Restoration had no true precedent) power to the imperial throne, an age-old institution long relegated to the shadows by a succession of military rulers. The Yanagawa fiefdom, due in part to its proximity to the trading port of Nagasaki, had been an advocate of openness to foreign trade and consequently aligned with the anti-Tokugawa faction during the civil conflict, landing itself firmly on the right side of history when the dust finally settled. Sukeoki and his clansmen were counted among the movers and shakers of the new age, the Meiji elite who engineered Japan's agrarian-to-industrial economic reinvention and who took on the work of integrating Western ideas and technologies into a society that, after centuries of isolation, had deeply imbedded traditional beliefs and cultural values.

The transformation that followed was one of the most dramatic political, social, and economic experiments of the nineteenth century. Before it was over, it would touch every family, institution, and aspect of the nation's way of life. But its new leaders recognized that between this experiment and any successful outcome stood enormous challenges and countless obstacles.

One such obstacle, in the way of economic reform, was the lack of a national currency. The secretary and staff of the newly consolidated treasury, when they undertook not only to mint coins but also to print the nation's first paper money, needed a paper stock strong enough to withstand the wear and tear of passage between many hands; and to discourage would-be counterfeiters, they also needed to be able to infuse the fabric of that paper with sophisticated watermarks. On the basis of the meager qualification that he had once apprenticed to a paper manufacturer in Nagasaki, Sukeoki was nominated and duly commissioned to acquire the requisite technology from abroad and to bring that technology into production. Facilities for a laboratory and factory in the town of Ōji, just outside Tokyo, were placed at his disposal, and he, his Tokyo-born wife, Teu, and their first son took up residence nearby.

Just three months before Saburō's birth, Nakamura Sukeoki was honored with a visit from His Excellency the Emperor Meiji, whom he guided through his plant, explaining its operations. And in 1881, when Saburō was five, the first five-yen notes, printed on paper manufactured by his father's mill, went into circulation.

Consumed by his work, Sukeoki, who turned fifty in 1879, was predominantly absent from the Nakamura household. When not away on buying missions or attending meetings in the city, he worked until late at his office. In the absence of paternal supervision, young Saburō cultivated a flare for mischief.

This flare was magnified when, upon his brother's entry into middle school, the family of five (including a daughter, two years older than Saburō) moved from quiet rural Ōji, where Saburō had spent his earliest years chasing insects and catching frogs in rice fields, to the city neighborhood of Hongō. Now part of central Tokyo, even Hongō was then semirural, with many of the households cultivating vegetables and even rice in their adjacent lots. But it also housed a sizeable population of school-aged children, and young Saburō quickly discovered its potential as an environment in which to run wild and to pick fights.

And pick fights he did. By the age of ten, Nakamura had established a reputation as the neighborhood terror, the kid no other boy his age wanted to meet on the street. Those who did were prone to return home not only well bruised but with torn earlobes or broken fingers, while his mother was to be seen scurrying from house to house, delivering offerings of sweets together with apologies.

Nakamura Tempū biographer Ōi Mitsuru tells the following story.[1] The time is now 1949, and the first signs of economic recovery are beginning to show on the streets of postwar Tokyo.

Yebisu Beer, a small brewery, now back in production and gainfully employing several dozen workers, has invited Nakamura Tempū to speak, and the employees are gathered in front of the company office building, listening attentively as Tempū delivers his message. He tells them how, in his early thirties, after surviving the perils of an earlier war, he contracted an "incurable" disease; how he then recovered from that disease through the discovery of an "important truth"; and how, after first making and then giving up a financial fortune, he has devoted himself single-mindedly to the transmission of his practical methodology for coordinating and unifying the agencies of mind and body. Louder than his words, his presence and the aura it projects are living proof of his contention that the attainment of health, happiness, and fortune need not be contingent on one's circumstances.

During the Pacific War, as the recent war is known to him and his countrymen, Nakamura had come under secret police surveillance for his criticism of the national leadership and their myopic decision to engage in a conflict that, he said time and again, could not possibly end favorably. But there is no mention of this recent past today; what is tantamount now is that the nation restore itself of its pride and dignity. And what better place to begin than with the one-by-one restoration of the physical and spiritual health of its citizens?

His talk now concluded, Tempū follows the company's president inside to his office, where the two of them settle into cushioned chairs and engage in light conversation over tea.

Minutes later they are interrupted by a knock on the door. The door opens and the president's secretary takes one step inside and bows.

"Excuse me for interrupting," she says, "but there is a man here asking to see Mr. Nakamura. It's Kuroda, the company security guard. He says that Mr. Nakamura is an old acquaintance."

Tempū can think of no one he knows by the name of Kuroda, especially a Kuroda working as a security guard, but is intrigued. "Show him in," he says.

A moment later, the door opens again and a stout man dressed in uniform enters; the man is similar in years to Nakamura but slightly hunched at the shoulders and looking a little the worse for wear. "It's me, Kuroda.

From Hongō. I lived two blocks up from you. We ran a small shop where we sold vegetables and dry goods."

Yes, Tempū does vaguely remember a family named Kuroda who operated a vegetable-stand and who had a boy his age.

"Look," Kuroda says with a broad smile. "You may not remember me, but I remember you."

Whereupon he turns his head to the left to show his right ear. A jagged edge covered by scar tissue is all that remains of what had once been an earlobe.

Nakamura, seldom at a loss for words, stares speechlessly at Kuroda and his missing earlobe, the look of mortification on his face answering for him.

Kuroda laughs heartily. "That was sixty years ago, and we were both just children."

Kuroda, it turns out, has lost his entire family to firebombs dropped during the last year of the war. Upon learning this, Nakamura insists on taking him into his own household, and it is there, under the same roof as Tempū and his family, that Kuroda lives out the rest of his days.

Nakamura Saburō's behavior had become so uncontrollable by middle school age that his parents were at a loss as to what to do. In particular, he had all but declared open rebellion against paternal authority, and his mother questioned the safety of her household should father and son continue living under the same roof. Young Saburō, meanwhile, wanted nothing more than to leave home, and his unruliness, Tempū tells us much later, was at least partially a premeditated ploy to that end. So, when a solution suggested itself by way of a family friend, for once, parents and son unanimously agreed.

The suggested solution was his removal to a school far away from Tokyo in Sukeoki's native Fukuoka. That school, called the Shūyūkan, was disciplined, as were most schools in this period, like a military academy; but then, in another respect, it was most unusual: most of the school's classes, other than those in the Japanese and Chinese classics, were taught in English. The Shūyūkan reflected the progressive ideals of Sukeoki's fellow Yanagawa clansmen and their recognition of the national shortage of men equipped to deal with, and to move freely within, the larger world. It is today one of the oldest continuously operating middle schools, as well as one of the most elite, in all Japan.

Furthermore, English, as the school was to discover, was not foreign to Nakamura Saburō. During the Nakamuras' residence in Ōji, Saburō's father had brought in a technical adviser from England, and the English-man and his wife had occupied a house next door. The couple, who spoke almost no Japanese, had no children of their own and adored the young Nakamuras, and Saburō, still a toddler, as well as his older brother, spent hours every day inside their home. Such circumstances, at a time when the majority of people in Japan had never seen a Westerner, much less spoken to one, were most unusual. The Nakamura children, however, related to these people only as neighbors, and Saburō was consequently exposed to the sounds and syntax of the English language just as he was learning to talk. This exposure continued until the Nakamuras moved to Hongō, a period of four years.

Children forget almost as quickly as they learn, but nevertheless, the sounds and voice patterns of English remained ingrained in the recesses of Nakamura's memory, only now to be reactivated. The Shūyūkan, having first adopted its all-English curriculum just five years prior to Nakamura's enrollment, had never before seen a student with his qualifications, and to the awe of his classmates, Nakamura's almost native English elocution outshined that of his instructors. For the first time in his life, he savored the sweet flavor of academic recognition.

Nakamura was thirteen when his parents sent him off to Fukuoka, a three-day journey by ferry. Upon arrival, he found his way to the house of the man with whom his father had made boarding arrangements, and who, not incidentally, was a reputed disciplinarian. His house was small, the man explained, and so he had secured a room for young Saburō with a neighbor. This neighbor's welcome, however, was short-lived, lasting only until Saburō threw the family cat down a well. Brought back to live under the man's roof, he was quickly taken under wing by the man's wife and included in the household as a new addition to their three children.

The man's name was Tōyama Mitsuru.[2] Head of a political association called the Genyōsha (Gen'yōsha), or "Dark Ocean Society," named after the Genkai-nada or "Dark Sea," the southwestern tip of the Sea of Japan separating Kyushu from the Korean Peninsula, Tōyama was still of only marginal reputation outside his native Fukuoka, but by the early twentieth century, popular wisdom would have it that "a Japanese schoolboy might not know the name of the prime minister, but he knows the name Tōyama Mitsuru."[3]

Born into a poor samurai family in 1855, Tōyama grew up amid the turbulent last years of the Shogunate and early years of Meiji. In 1876, at the age of twenty-one, he landed himself in prison for participating in a failed local uprising known as the Hagi Rebellion. That uprising—fomented by former samurai in protest of policies being implemented by the Restoration's new leaders, policies they believed to be part of a wider trend toward indiscriminate abandonment of traditional values in favor of Western ideologies, ethics, and morals—was a harbinger of the following year's larger and even more bloody Satsuma Rebellion, led by the great statesman and military leader Saigō Takamori. Saigō, whom Tōyama revered, died by his own hand in atonement for the rebellion's failure, and his demise occurred, as fate would have it, on the same day that Tōyama was released from prison. These uprisings and their ultimate suppression, as well as the death of Saigō, effectively sealed the coffin on the status of the samurai as a ruling class. In many respects, they also sealed the fate of Tōyama's subsequent political career, because, first, his prison record all but guaranteed his exemption from normal paths to power and therefore required him to chart a path uniquely his own; and second, his participation as a young idealist in the revolt brought him eye-to-eye with death and permanently relieved him of fear. Thereafter, regardless of the opposition or the risks, Tōyama never hesitated to pursue what he believed to be right.

The Genyōsha was but one of many similar societies or brotherhoods that sprang up around the country during this same period; however, it rapidly outgrew and ultimately outlived most others. Tōyama, in league with two like-minded associates with whom he had done his prison time, used the vestiges of an earlier organization to establish the society in 1880. Initially, it assumed the cause of civil liberties and civil rights as part of the nationwide Freedom and Peoples Rights Movement that eventually catalyzed the writing of the Meiji constitution and the institution of Japan's first parliament. However, partly due to Fukuoka's proximity to Korea and its consequent susceptibility to continental influences, the society also took up the cause of Korean self-determination, lending support to, and even engaging in, intelligence and paramilitary activities on the peninsula. Then, having once gotten its feet wet in the confusing puddle of continental affairs, the society soon became a leading proponent of pan-Asianism and cultivated an elaborate paramilitary network in the Russian Far East, Manchuria, and China.

The Genyōsha's charter was composed of just three clauses, all reflected in one slogan: "Revere the emperor, honor love of country, and protect the rights of the people." In light of twentieth-century history, that statement cannot help but evoke jingoistic connotations. When it was coined, however, the emperor to whom it pledged fidelity was not the Shōwa emperor, Hirohito, but the Emperor Meiji, the face of Japan's emergence into the modern age, and consequently, in the context of the times, it reflected the voice of progress. But then, as a tight-knit association of like-minded, like-spirited individuals, the Genyōsha also operated by Mafia-like codes of conduct, and in subsequent years, the yakuza crime syndicates to emerge out of northern Kyushu's coal mining subculture would emulate it organizationally and look upon Tōyama Mitsuru as something of a patron saint.

Just two months after Nakamura's arrival in Fukuoka, the Genyōsha came to national attention in connection with the attempted assassination of the foreign minister, Ōkuma Shigenobu. In coming to office, Ōkuma had inherited the thankless task of renegotiating unequal treaties with the United States, Britain, Russia, and Germany, and he had drafted a proposed extension of those unequal terms. In response the Genyōsha had launched an all-out nationwide campaign of opposition. Despite garnering widespread public endorsement, this campaign was snubbed, and Ōkuma's proposal was summarily passed on to the emperor for signing. One of Tōyama's associates, Kurushima Tsuneki, took it upon himself to throw a bomb into Ōkuma's carriage. In the aftermath, the Genyōsha leadership, including Tōyama, were rounded up and imprisoned. They were soon released: Kurushima, who impaled himself with a short sword immediately after the event, had formally resigned from the Genyōsha and left behind a statement to the effect that he was operating alone and under his sole initiative.

These were complicated times. The gunpowder that went into Kurushima's bomb was almost certainly acquired with Tōyama's help and through his network of connections. But then, nothing was found to implicate anyone other than Kurushima in the actual plot and its execution. More than one thousand guests attended Kurushima's funeral; Tōyama, always a man of few words, delivered a one-sentence eulogy; and eminent statesman and Restoration hero Katsu Kaishū wrote a plaque for Kurushima's grave. Even Ōkuma, who survived the blast but lost his right leg, later visited the grave and acknowledged that he bore his would-be assassin no hard feelings. General sentiment placed ultimate blame on the prime minister and his cabinet for failing to heed the voice of the people, and the incident was widely construed to have been an act not of terrorism but, albeit desperate and radical, political expression. It also achieved its purpose, for in the aftermath, the prime minister resigned and the treaty proposal was rescinded.

During the course of his long career, Tōyama, who never ran for public office or served in any official capacity, exercised inordinate influence over domestic and international Japanese policy. Sasa Hirō, one of Tōyama's earliest biographers, writes, "Tōyama's power stimulated, castigated, and compelled the statesmen who held power throughout the Meiji era. If those governments acquitted themselves without glaring faults it was largely thanks to the presence of so cool-headed a watcher and so daring a condemner. The political history of the Meiji era is largely the record of the activities of the *ronin* [disenfranchised samurai] behind the scenes. Theirs was hidden but active power."[4]

In the aftermath of World War II—an aftermath Tōyama did not live long enough to witness—the occupying Allied Command was quick to condemn the Genyōsha and its leader, Tōyama Mitsuru, as "ultranationalist" contributors to the rise of Japanese militarism. The charges were neither accurate nor fair. That Tōyama and his associates were nationalists is beyond question, but they were nationalists at a time when nation-building was a legitimate priority: most of Asia had succumbed to Western imperialism, and several of the Western powers, most notably Britain and Russia, were expressing disingenuous interest in the future of the Japanese archipelago; unless the nation was amply equipped and prepared to resist foreign invasion, all efforts to guarantee the rights of the common man at home would be for nothing. Moreover, the Genyōsha had little to do with the growth of the 1930s militancy that the Allied Command's indictments sought to redress. A product of the late-nineteenth-century political milieu, its influence by that time had waned and its activities all but suspended.

This is not to say that the hands of the Genyōsha were always clean. Its members had a reputation for mischief, and as the attempt on Foreign Minister Ōkuma's life indicates, they were not above the use of violence. Again, however, these actions need to be seen in the context of the times. Violence was rampant in nineteenth- and early-twentieth-century Japanese politics, just as it was in British and American politics, and not just fringe groups but even establishment politicians regularly resorted to it to further their agendas. The Genyōsha cadre, aware of the limits of gentle persuasion and schooled in the belief that the sword—an instrument that, as a symbol of both the warrior's responsibility and his prerogative, was equated with the samurai soul—was a legitimate tool of righteousness, practiced violence only when they believed their cause was worth fighting for and never for purposes of personal gain.

More telling than the Allied Command's assessment is Tōyama's reputation among his contemporaries. The few attempts made during Tōyama

Mitsuru's lifetime to implicate him in illegal wrongdoings all failed spec-
tacularly for lack of evidence. Among the rarest of distinctions within the
world of politics, he was known by all to be as good as his word—even
among his political enemies, few ever went so far as to challenge his integrity. His detractors were few, while his admirers, among whom Nakamura
Tempū may be counted, were many.

From all descriptions, Tōyama appears to have been neither an exponent of lofty ideals nor particularly skilled as a public speaker. He was,
however, a man of extraordinary mettle. Nakamura tells the story of
when, in 1914, a gangster, under hire by the Chinese embassy to eliminate
the exiled fugitive Sun Yat-sen, intruded on a small gathering at which
Tōyama, as well as Sun and Nakamura, were in attendance. Tōyama,
Nakamura says, took a long draw on the cigarette he was holding, and
with no change in countenance, looked the pistol-wielding gangster in
the eye. The young man's hand soon began to tremble so violently that he
was easily disarmed. Tōyama subsequently talked the young man down
and, after returning to him his pistol, sent him on his way.

As this story suggests, Tōyama's influence also extended into continental politics. Beginning in the 1880s and 1890s, out of concern over the
endemic instability of the nation's continental neighbors and the resulting
threat posed to Japanese security—in particular, because such instability played into the hands of Western interlopers and their colonial ambitions—the Genyōsha cultivated relationships and installed intelligence
operations in China and Manchuria. Tōyama and his associates could be
counted on to be ahead of the curve in their assessments of Asian affairs
and to point the way for Japanese diplomacy. Territorial expansion, however, was never part of the Genyōsha's vision. It advocated an "Asia for
Asians," and it encouraged and funded (the pockets that sourced these
funds included those of northern Kyushu's burgeoning coal industry barons, to whom Tōyama had ready access) a number of indigenous independence movements. And when these movements failed, as they invariably
did, and their leaders sought asylum, it was Tōyama and his Genyōsha
who took them in—often in defiance of national policy. The Genyōsha

watched over not only Sun Yat-sen but also the Korean republican Kim Ok-kiun and the Indian independence advocate Rash Behari Bose during their respective exiles in Japan.

Modest and soft-spoken, Tōyama had an uncanny ability to assess people, regardless of rank or position, by what they were made of on the inside, and in his later years, he counseled his young followers each to "become a man who is never lonely, even when alone." He led a frugal, almost Spartan personal existence, even while controlling and disbursing large sums of political funds, and in stark contrast with the times, never adopted Western habits; he dressed in plain kimonos and wore straw sandals under his bare feet, even when visiting the snow-covered northern provinces.

Tōyama was just thirty-four when Nakamura Saburō went to live with him, and their subsequent association spanned the most active years of Tōyama's career. Never once did Nakamura's esteem for the man waver. Tōyama was one of only two men—the Indian yogi Kariappa, the other—for whom Nakamura reserved the title *onshi,* "revered teacher." And when Nakamura was in his forties, it was Tōyama who bestowed upon him the name by which he would make his mark on the world. Tempū, which translates literally as "heaven's wind," was taken from two of the characters used to write *amatsukaze,* the name for one of the forms practiced in *zuihenryū-battōjutsu,* a classical sword school, of which Tempū was an adept.

In his later years, Tōyama was to remark that he had lived long and witnessed many strange and wondrous things, but nothing in his life had ever surprised him more than to see Nakamura Tempū become a teacher of spiritual virtue.

One early spring day, three years into his schooling at the Shūyūkan, while Nakamura and his classmates were outside at play, an army regiment from a garrison just down the road marched by on the other side of the schoolyard wall. The students, engrossed in their games, first failed to notice when a brash young sergeant appeared at the gate, livid with rage. A shard of roofing tile, it seems, had come sailing over the wall and struck one of his soldiers in the head. The boy who perpetrated this travesty was to come forward immediately and receive his just punishment, the sergeant bellowed.

A more rational assessment of the circumstances would have suggested that the projectile had been launched without mischievous intent. The wall blocked the view of the street, and the children had been too engrossed in play to have even been aware of the passing regiment. The far more likely explanation was that one of the boys, perceiving the tile shard to be a hazard, had lobbed it over the wall just to get it out of the way. But the sergeant is enraged beyond reason. And no boy, however guilty, is about to give himself up to this red-faced monster.

Apologies proffered by Nakamura's homeroom teacher, who has come running out to the gate, are to no avail. The young sergeant is ushered into the school building to be received by the director of studies and the school headmaster, both of whom implore him with apologies of their own. Still, he is unyielding. Refusing the chair offered him, he stands stiffly at attention and implacably demands that the young rascal who has so outrageously insulted his Imperial Majesty's Army be delivered up; short of this, no one is to leave the school grounds.

Headmaster and sergeant are now at an impasse. The army, the headmaster would have it, has no jurisdiction over school affairs, and under no circumstances is he going to turn over one of his boys to army justice; the army, the sergeant counters, has suffered an indignity and is not going to accept school jurisdiction as an excuse for impunity. Meanwhile, soldiers have taken up positions at each of the school's gates.

Shadows on the ground grow long, and as scents from neighboring kitchens waft into the schoolyard, the students are beset by pangs of hunger. Nakamura, too, is becoming increasingly wearied of the whole spectacle: on the one hand, whoever threw the tile is clearly too terrified to come forward, and on the other, unless someone owns up and takes the rap, none of them will be leaving the school grounds this evening. "What sort of punishment could the army possibly mete out that could be so bad?" he wonders. A scolding or even a caning, he calculates, drawing on past experience, seems but a small hardship to endure when balanced against the reward of a hot bath and warm dinner at home.

Enough, he decides. He will put an end to this nonsense. Nakamura marches into the room where the sergeant is still standing and declares himself the culprit.

The affair, however, is not to be so easily resolved as he has supposed. The soldiers remain in their positions even after he is led away to the garrison for questioning, and the school, the teachers are told, is to remain under lockdown, pending the results of Nakamura Saburō's inquisition. Concurrently, Nakamura is learning that the part he has chosen is more difficult to play than he had imagined: apparent to all is the lack of authenticity in his expression of guilt. Furthermore, the more his story does not add up, the harder become his interrogators' questions. Where did he find the tile? How big was it and what shape? Where exactly was he standing and in what direction did he throw it?

A lieutenant joins. After watching the proceedings for a couple of minutes, he intervenes. "You are covering for a classmate, aren't you?" he asks.

But having come this far, Nakamura is not about to quit. "It was me who threw that piece of tile," he insists.

"Can you prove it?"

"No."

"Well, if you can't prove it, then we can't charge you," the lieutenant says with a wry smile.

Nakamura, incensed by both the refusal of his captors to accept his admission of guilt and the realization that his plan is not working, can no longer contain himself.

"If you need me to commit a crime, that I can fix," he replies indignantly. He reaches for an ashtray sitting on top of the desk and throws it at the lieutenant. The lieutenant, in keeping with the dignity of his rank, does not so much as flinch, but his neatly pressed uniform is now adorned with ashes. Nakamura Saburō is thrown into the guardhouse.

Meanwhile, the schoolhouse standoff between sergeant and headmaster has escalated to a confrontation between the army and the prefectural administration. The army has no right to interfere with the education of our youth, the officials maintain. The army has every right to protect its honor and dignity, the regiment's commander retorts. In the end, cooler heads, including that of the governor of Fukuoka, by chance a childhood friend of Saburō's father, prevail from behind the scenes, and a negotiated settlement is reached. The headmaster will take the fall for the school and resign, while the commander will be reassigned to another garrison far away from Fukuoka.

The students spend one night inside the schoolhouse, and Nakamura spends two in the guardhouse. Upon his return home after release, Tōyama Mitsuru says nothing; he does, however, smile and give a small nod indicating his approval. Public opinion among the townspeople divides evenly over the question as to whether Saburō's conduct demonstrates guts or insolence, but either way, he has become something of a local celebrity. Such notoriety is but a small token of that soon to follow.

Fukuoka boasted an especially active martial arts training hall, or dojo (dōjō), called the Meidōkan, and every afternoon, Nakamura, like many of the boys in his class, went directly from school to the Meidōkan to train. With the collapse of feudalism and the advent of modern means of warfare, Japan's traditional martial arts had, by this time, fallen largely out of favor, and disciplines and skills that were once a mainstay of the samurai class were rapidly being lost to posterity. Their value, however, to the cultivation of character and spirit had not been lost on Tōyama Mitsuru and his Genyōsha associates: they established the Meidōkan both to provide a venue for the conservation of traditional martial training and to contribute to the physical and moral development of local youth. It was a singularly colorful institution. While contemporary martial arts schools, where they existed, typically operated under veils of secrecy and exercised extreme circumspection with regard to whom they allowed into their folds, the Meidōkan was open to anyone willing to submit to its austerity and enlisted participation from a wide cross-section of the community.

Training at the Meidōkan was conducted under the label of judo, but the legitimacy of that label is questionable. Among martial arts, judo was still new. It was largely a product of the efforts of one man, Kanō Jigorō, to make martial arts training and the physical and moral discipline afforded by these arts part of Japan's rapidly evolving educational system. Kanō, an educator, later to rise to a position of prominence within the Ministry of Education, studied and mastered a number of traditional grappling disciplines, often lumped together under the single heading of *jūjutsu,* and then synthesized what he learned into a curriculum and pedagogy of best practices. He also added rules of conduct and guidelines for moral behavior. This new synthetic discipline he called *jūdō,* from *jū,* meaning "softness" or "flexibility," and *dō,* meaning "path" or "discipline." The name was intended to distinguish his art, the purpose of which was to cultivate soundness of body and strength character, from traditional systems of self-defense.

At the time that Nakamura joined the Meidōkan, Kanō was in his early thirties, and his art still in the making. The total number of judo practitioners, almost all of whom were in Tokyo, was small, and the number of qualified teachers of the art was limited; neither is it likely that one of those instructors should have found his way to the Meidōkan, nor did Kanō's Kōdōkan recognize the Meidōkan as an affiliate.[5] If any relationship existed between what Kanō was teaching in Tokyo and what was being taught at the Meidōkan, it was tenuous at best and could only have derived from the influences of either one or both of two people. The first was Yamaza Enjirō, to be introduced in more detail below. At this time Yamaza was training at the Kōdōkan in Tokyo and was to ascend to one of the higher judo ranks before entering the diplomatic corps.[6] The other was Uchida Ryōhei. Born in Fukuoka, Uchida was three years Nakamura's senior and one of Tōyama's early Genyōsha protégés; he was also training under Kanō in Tokyo. Uchida was already well on his way to becoming both a renowned martial artist, highly accomplished in several of the traditional disciplines,[7] and an infamous advocate of Japanese militancy; we will encounter him again later in our story.

The immediate source of the methods taught at the Meidōkan, however, was almost certainly not Kano's judo but a classical jūjutsu transmission from within the former Fukuoka fiefdom called *jigō-tenshinryū*. Like all classical styles, jigō-tenshinryū was a comprehensive fighting system that included not only empty-handed grappling but also use of the sword, spear, and other weapons. Furthermore, in addition to jigō-tenshinryū, it was here, at the Meidōkan, that Nakamura received his initiation into the art of zuihenryū-battōjutsu, a four-hundred-year-old transmission of Fukuoka's Tachibana clan, the art from which his eventual name, Tempū, was to be derived.[8] *Battōjutsu*—literally, "the art of drawing the sword"—teaches the way of drawing the sword and cutting in one, uninterrupted movement.

Judo's reputation among Tokyo's cultural elite would likely have preceded the art's actual transmission to Fukuoka, and the Meidōkan may have chosen the label "judo" simply for its modern ring. But whatever the explanation, the training that Nakamura underwent at the Meidōkan, safe to say, bore little resemblance to judo as it is practiced today. It was rather a serious indoctrination into the fighting arts.

Nakamura was not new to martial discipline. He began his schooling in the way of the sword at the age of six, when his parents, in the hope of channeling his aggressions into an outlet more productive than neighborhood mischief, placed him under a respected jūjutsu instructor in Tokyo. Of this training, Tempū tells us that, for three years, he was not allowed to pick up a sword but was required instead to master the discipline's footwork: he first had to show that he could walk with impeccable balance and exact foot placement. Only then, for the next two years, was he given a wooden sword and allowed to practice strikes—and then, not at a target or toward an opponent, but into empty air. These strikes, he was instructed, needed to be clean and without waver. A weighted piece of silk thread was hung from the dojo's rafters, and he was told to trace the line established by the hanging thread with the tip of the sword. Without touching it but just by the air disturbance generated from the cut of his wooden blade, he was to cause the thread to move. As the fine silk thread was only visible when his eyes were exactly focused on the area of space just beyond the sword's tip, this practice required intense concentration. The sword, Tempū goes on to explain, is an instrument of mental discipline before physical; above all else, it demands clarity and focus of mind.

Nakamura and his friends receive most of their instruction at the Meidōkan from their *sempai,* or "seniors"; in this respect, the Meidōkan is not different from other dojos, where, as part of their own training, the sempai seek to uphold the reputation of the dojo by seeing to it that the *kōhai,* their "juniors," receive the full benefit of everything they themselves have learned. Although small in stature, Nakamura is agile and has a fighter's intuition. Furthermore, he is uninhibited by the larger size of most of his opponents. As a result, the senior students focus much of their attention on him—meaning they pull out all the stops when they go to throw him. His resiliency and readiness to always come back for more earns him their respect, as well as that of his classmates.

Following practice, sempai and kōhai linger in the dojo to talk about women and politics into the evening. And in this setting, too, Nakamura Saburō excels: he enjoys good company and is a natural conversationalist. Nakamura's associations with many of these young men will continue, through the auspices of the Genyōsha, for years to come and in ways unforeseen.

Over its years of operation, the Meidōkan counted among its members a disproportionately large number of future leaders in Japanese politics and industry, two of whom, in light of later roles they will play in the unfolding of Nakamura Tempū's story, warrant mention. The first, already introduced above, is Yamaza Enjirō, and the second is Hirota Kōki. Yamaza is ten years Nakamura's senior and one of the dojo's founding members. During the time Nakamura is in Fukuoka, Yamaza is in Tokyo, completing his studies and embarking upon a distinguished career in the Foreign Service; however, upon his occasional visits home to Fukuoka, he invariably calls on Tōyama, as well as the Meidōkan. Young Nakamura looks up to Yamaza as a role model, and Yamaza recognizes in Nakamura a mutual flare for impetuosity. Their paths will cross several times on different continents in subsequent years.

Hirota Kōki is two years junior to Nakamura, and the junior-to-senior nature of their relationship will continue beyond childhood, right through the unfortunate circumstances of Hirota's death in 1948. He will serve as foreign minister under three prime ministers and as prime minister between March 1936 and February 1937.

One afternoon about a year after the schoolyard incident, the seniors propose that the middle school judo club challenge a similar club in neighboring Kumamoto Prefecture. Nakamura and his friends rally behind this idea: not only will they get to test their skills against practitioners of another style, but they will also get a change of scenery. The arrangements are made, the date set, and the team, with Nakamura as its captain, sets off.

Matches such as this one are rough-and-tumble affairs. Supervision is nominal, and the competitions are unencumbered by more than the most basic rules. Contests are decided, more often than not, only when one of the two contestants acknowledges defeat. And while the Kumamoto team puts up a good fight, they lack the Fukuoka team's depth of training; the Meidōkan wins handily.

Flushed with the glow of victory, Nakamura and his friends return to the country inn where they are lodged. Nakamura, who is looking forward to an evening stroll through town following dinner, has just taken a bath and changed back into his school uniform when a maid comes up to the room to announce that someone is asking for him. Puzzled, he descends the stairs to find a boy from the defeated Kumamoto team standing in the entrance.

"Our captain," the boy says, "wants to meet with you to talk about scheduling another match."

Odd timing for such a request, Nakamura thinks. Odd, also, that the captain has not come in person. Nevertheless, he follows the boy out to the street.

They walk quickly through town. Dusk has fallen, and gas lamps burning inside the houses are the street's only illumination. The boy looks straight ahead and says nothing as they walk.

When they cross a wooden bridge over the river that marks the town limits, Nakamura senses that something is awry. Soon they are in open land obscured by tall reeds. The road widens slightly, and here, the boy stops. All at once, out of the shadows, the Kumamoto team captain and his teammates appear; Nakamura is surrounded.

Before he can say anything, the boys rush. He throws the first to reach him into the midst of the others oncoming, but the ensuing wave is greater than he can handle. He is brought to the ground and pummeled with fists and feet. When a wooden clog comes down on his temple, the world goes dark.

Nakamura awakens to the sound of morning taps from a bugle at a nearby army post. He is lying in a ditch, hair matted with dried blood and mouth filled with dirt. His aggressors long gone, the road in either direction is deserted. After getting up and brushing himself off, he makes his way back to town.

The maids are already up and about at the inn. He arouses the others, washes off most of the blood and dirt, and devours an early breakfast before setting out again. Despite entreaties from his teammates, he insists on going alone. "This is my score to settle," he says. "Don't make a coward of me."

One of the maids has recognized the boy at the door the previous evening and provides Nakamura with directions to his house. Still early, the household is asleep when he opens the front door and, without bothering to remove his clogs, steps up into the hallway. Startled figures sit up in each of the rooms as he throws apart sliding doors. In the last room, he uncovers the object of his search. He lifts the sleeping boy off the floor by his nightgown, throws him into the hall, and drags him into the backyard. There, he thrashes him until the boy has divulged names and addresses.

Following the boy's directions, he then proceeds from one teammate's house to the next. At each stop, much the same scenario is repeated: he intrudes on the sleeping household, finds the offending perpetrator, inflicts bruises, and exacts a satisfactorily level of pain. The fifth house is that of the team captain. Nakamura's thirst for revenge is all but satiated, and this stop, he decides, will be his last. But first, he needs to give the chief instigator his rightful due.

Entering the house as he has the others, he discovers the captain almost immediately. The boy is awake and sitting upright when Nakamura enters the room. "I have a score to settle with you," Nakamura says. "Follow me into the yard."

Nakamura steps back into the hallway, expecting his adversary to follow. But instead, the boy dashes into an adjacent room. Enraged by this display of cowardice, Nakamura pursues. The chase proceeds from room to room, until the boys reach the kitchen. Now Nakamura's adversary, when he finally turns around to face him, is holding a large kitchen knife.

"Put that thing down and fight me fairly," Nakamura yells.

The boy lunges.

What happens next falls subject to repression in Nakamura's memory and remains beyond recall for the rest of his life. The thrust, he remembers, but not what follows—except that, when the skirmish is over, the knife is now in his hand, and the boy is on the kitchen floor, bleeding profusely.

Receiving hastily delivered instructions from the boy's mother, Nakamura runs to fetch a doctor and the police. The doctor can do little; the boy has lost too much blood and expires within the hour. The police escort Nakamura Saburō to the city jail.

In the end, Nakamura is released after only a brief investigation. Disputes leading to bloodshed are not uncommon in these parts, and moreover, the local police cannot help but take an interest in the story; not every day do they get to arrest a young man who has overcome an armed assailant with his bare hands. But the evidence that clinches the case is the testimony of none other than the dead boy's mother. The only third-party witness to the entire incident and, undoubtedly, still in a state of shock, she responds to police questioning with unnerving honesty, her account corroborating everything they have already been told by Nakamura. The boy acted in self-defense, the local magistrate rules. Nakamura Saburō is free to go.

Back in Fukuoka, the consequences are more severe. Summarily expelled from both the Shūyūkan and the Meidōkan, Nakamura's contact with his classmates and dojo sempai and kōhai all but disappears. The same townspeople once entertained by the story of his conduct at the army garrison now utter his name in hushed voices and avert their eyes when he appears on the street. With nowhere to go and nothing to do, Nakamura Saburō passes time within the confines of the Tōyama household by helping with household chores and napping and reading in his room.

2.
IN SERVICE
OF COUNTRY

Weeks later, on a warm spring evening, Nakamura Saburō is interrupted from his daydreams by a summons. He is wanted, he is told, in the master's study.

Voices are audible in the corridor as he approaches: one, the familiar voice of Tōyama Mitsuru, the other, new. "He has a guest," Nakamura notes.

When he announces himself outside the closed door, Tōyama bids him to enter. Now inside, Tōyama, a mischievous grin on his face, beckons him forward and tells him to take a seat beside him on the tatami. The visitor, sitting opposite, is dressed in formal *haori*, or topcoat, and *hakama*, the traditional skirt-like pants worn over a kimono. Through squinted eyes, he looks Nakamura up and down, inspecting him in much the way a horse buyer looks over a horse.

Nakamura glares back.

The glare elicits the visitor's approval. Turning to Tōyama, he nods and says, "He will do."

Making no effort to conceal his displeasure, Nakamura also turns toward Tōyama. "What is it that you want of me, sir?" he asks.

Tōyama is still sporting the same mischievous grin. "How would you like to go where you can fight to your heart's content without worrying about the police?" he asks by way of reply. "A place where you can even kill people and not go to jail."

Nakamura stares back at his mentor in astonishment. What is he talking about? Is he joking, or is he serious? And if serious, how could it be that such a place exists? Slowly, however, his astonishment gives way to the more sanguine calculation that, whatever is being asked of him, it almost certainly beats the current agony of his boredom.

Nakamura Saburō, just shy of his seventeenth birthday, was being recruited, he discovered, into service of the nation's cause. He was to accompany the stranger, one Kōno Kinkichi, an officer of the Imperial Army, on covert assignment into northeastern China for purposes of military reconnaissance. Days after their introduction in Tōyama's study, Kōno and Nakamura, disguised as merchants, board a steamship in Shimonoseki, bound for Tianjin. From there, they travel first to the Liaodong Peninsula and then into Manchuria along the Yalu River on the Korean border.

The year was 1893, and the issue at stake, the future of Korea. The Prussian military strategist Jacob Meckel, employed by the Japanese Imperial Army as an adviser, had appropriately observed that, on a map, the Korean Peninsula resembled a dagger pointed straight at Japan's heart. That dagger, as long as it rested in Korean hands, posed no imminent threat; but Korean sovereignty, under the sunset rule of a decadent imperial dynasty besieged by popular uprisings, was at risk of implosion, and in response to this situation, Imperial Russia, whose Far Eastern territories bordered Korea to the north, was moving troops and battleships to Vladivostok.

This vulture-like Russian specter hanging over the Korean peninsula inspired among the Japanese a healthy measure of dread, especially as the Imperial Russian Navy, were it to descend upon Pusan, stood to effectively control the Tsushima Strait. However, within the framework of late-nineteenth-century East Asian geopolitics, the burden of responsibility for Korea fell not to Japan but to China. Korea had operated as a tributary vassal to China for centuries, and consequently, the Chinese would, they asserted, act on behalf of the failing Korean regime as the peninsula's rightful guardians.

But then, China's own sovereignty was also showing signs of distress. The Qing dynasty, itself in its twilight years, had managed to prolong its heavenly mandate only by making concession after concession to the West's imperial ambitions, so that, by now, all of the so-called Great

Powers had well-established interests, enclaves, and even garrisons on Chinese soil. In the eyes of most observers, China had neither the political will nor the military resolve to stem the tide of Western encroachment within its own borders, let alone those of an outlying vassal state.

Differences between Japan and China over the Korean question had sparked a series of incidents, standoffs, and skirmishes between Japanese and Chinese soldiers in Korea, and the Japanese leadership, their diplomatic patience exhausted, had become convinced that the solution would need to be military. Within the scheme of things, Kōno was but one among many cogs in a machine that was moving purposefully in the direction of war against the Qing regime; Kōno, an officer, was chosen over more junior enlisted men for the job of gathering field intelligence because he was expected to later lead soldiers into battle over the same terrain now under his survey.

Foreign diplomatic missions in Japan and China watched Japan's saber rattling with unconcealed amusement. A fledgling state of moderate means, Japan was, in terms of military resources, a David to the Chinese Goliath. The Qing dynasty may have been a dinosaur in a modernizing world, but like a dinosaur, it had the advantage of size. Even the Great Powers recognized China's geography, population, and military reserves as daunting impediments to conquest—especially given that the Qing rulers, in the interest of projecting a greater semblance of strength to the outside world than they actually possessed, had been dipping into their diminished coffers to outfit their navy with modern battleships and their army with modern guns and artillery.

But where the Chinese were long on military investments, they were short on discipline and intelligence, attributes quintessential to Meiji Japan's military, industrial, and commercial ascendance. Japan, in comparison with China, had been a far more serious student of the ways of modern warfare. Part of the reason for this was cultural. Military careers, among the highest of callings in Japan, were looked down upon by the scholarly and gentlemanly Chinese mandarins, and consequently not only were the Chinese men enlisted to this calling predominantly poorly educated, they also bore little affiliation with the mandarin-controlled national agenda. The Japanese Army and Navy, unable to match Chinese investments in ships and guns, invested instead in the acquisition of know-how by hiring foreign military advisers and sending their most promising young officers abroad—to England, France, Germany, and the United States—for training.

Furthermore, the Japanese had been doing their homework with regard to China for years. As Kōno's visit to Fukuoka would indicate, the Genyōsha, with its continental network, was an invaluable asset to the national enterprise. Additionally, however, army and navy intelligence had assembled their own sophisticated China networks and consequently had at their disposal exceptionally accurate information regarding China's military readiness and strength. The Japanese, in choosing to go to war, would not do so unprepared.

Such was the nature of the circumstances that plucked an adolescent Nakamura Saburō out of the Tōyama household and set him down on a foreign shore. The mission lasted through summer and fall, right up until the first snows of winter. Under Kōno, Nakamura learned to look at the contours of the broad continental landscape while imagining how its accesses and exits might lend themselves to troop movements. Chinese surveillance was lax, but the territory was fraught with bandits and largely under local warlord rule. The men traveled on horseback, breathing the crisp, dry air blowing in from the Mongolian and Siberian steppes and often sleeping out under the stars. For Nakamura, the broad horizons surrounding him day after day virtually sparkled with the promise of adventure, and he marveled at the immensity of the world.

One year later, in October 1894, now safely returned to his parents' home in Tokyo, a much matured Nakamura Saburō followed news reports of the decisive land battles being fought on the very terrain that he and Kōno had surveyed. Japanese troops, some under Kōno's command, moved quickly into positions of advantage, crossing the Yalu and driving the Chinese back, first to Mukden and then down the Liaodong Peninsula.

The knowledge that he had played a role, even if ever so minor, in these successes gave Nakamura enormous satisfaction.

He was not alone in his elation; the army and navy's victories precipitated a popular resurgence of pride and restoration of faith in the nation's destiny. On both land and the high seas, Japan had inflicted strategic defeat and grossly disproportionate casualties upon an adversary far superior in number and firepower, and had established itself as the dominant military power in East Asia. The same Western observers who had previously derided Japan's military capacities now recanted and published glowing accounts of Japanese prowess—tempered though those accounts were by parallel scathing indictments of the Chinese for incompetence.

Japanese victory was sealed on April 17, 1895, with the signing of the Treaty of Shimonoseki, under which Korea became a constitutional monarchy, Japan became its designated protector, and China ceded to Japan, in compensatory restitution for war losses, the island of Formosa, today's Taiwan. The treaty also irrevocably altered the balance of power in Asia and testified to the emergence, for the first time, of an indigenous Asian polity onto the modern world stage, thereby poking a hole in the Anglo-European narrative regarding their prerogative to colonize and to rule. But then, among some of Japan's military elite, victory also inspired colonial aspirations of their own that would play out in the coming century.

The Manchurian assignment had the effect of both repairing Nakamura's reputation and tempering his character. Following his return to Japan, as a reflection of both his record of national service and his father's social standing, he was admitted to Gakushūin, a prestigious college attended almost exclusively by aristocratic youth. His parents' delight, however, was short-lived, lasting only the few months up until a dispute with one of his teachers led to his expulsion. Instead, he entered and subsequently graduated from a technical school of military affiliation.

One of the more unusual features of this school's curriculum, implemented after the Sino-Japanese War, was an accelerated Chinese language program. Nakamura Saburō, whose natural facility for languages had asserted itself previously at the Shūyūkan, had acquired some Chinese in Manchuria and now cultivated that exposure into a competency, little knowing that it would soon prove invaluable.

Coincidental to Nakamura's return, Tōyama Mitsuru, to be closer to the institutions of political power, joined the Genyōsha's Tokyo cadre and established a second residence in what is now the capital's Akasaka district. Nakamura, although never formally inducted into the Genyōsha, demonstrated continuing fidelity to his mentor by serving him on errands and by attending to whatever odd jobs were asked of him. These years coincided with Sun Yat-sen's first Japan exile under Genyōsha subsidy, and Tōyama assigned Nakamura to the detail charged with protecting Sun from the long arm of the Chinese regime and its hired assassins, an assignment that earned Nakamura the nickname "the Genyōsha panther."

Six years after the end of the Sino-Japanese War, tensions were again mounting over the future of the Korean peninsula, and talk of war was again circulating in the streets. This time, however, the enemy was Russia.

Japanese contempt for the Russians had its origins in the early nineteenth century, when Russia made a grab for the Japanese northern territories of Sakhalin and the Kuril Islands. The ensuing land dispute was temporarily settled under a treaty executed in 1855, but the specter of a Cossack army descending upon the Japanese archipelago from the north was one of the concerns that precipitated the overthrow of the Tokugawa Shogunate and led to the Meiji Restoration. That concern was heightened in 1860, when Russia wrested away from Qing China the territory east of the Ussuri River, including a Pacific port they named Vladivostok, "the ruler of the East."

In historical hindsight, the Japanese archipelago was probably of little interest to the Russians. It had no significant natural resources and produced almost nothing, other than rice, of trade value; furthermore, its dense homogeneous population, the Russian's understood, would not easily be subjugated to colonial rule. But more sparsely populated and more resource-rich northeastern China and Korea were a different matter.

Like all the imperial powers, Russia, under the despotic Romanovs, lusted after empire, and having seen its ambitions thwarted in Turkey and the Balkans, it was pursuing the only other options available to it: it was expanding southward, into Afghanistan, and eastward, into the Far East. Afghanistan, as it was outside Japan's sphere of influence, was of little concern to the Japanese, but China and Korea were close to home. Continuing access to Chinese and Korean natural resources was critical to Japan's economic survival, and consequently, Japan harbored imperial ambitions of its own.

In 1891, Russia began laying track across its Siberian interior with the goal of connecting Vladivostok to Moscow, a distance of over 5,500 miles (9,000 kilometers). Czar Alexander III and his son and successor Nicholas II threw the weight of the empire behind the project, and the Moscow–Vladivostok connection—with the exception of an interruption at Lake Baikal, where railheads at either end of the lake were connected by ferry in summer and temporary rail over the ice in winter—was completed in 1898. Furthermore, in 1896, just two years after the Sino-Japanese War, the Qing granted Russia permission to build the Chinese Eastern Railway across northern Manchuria. Logistically, this concession was justified, for it provided the Russians with a second, more direct link to Vladivostok: the trans-Manchurian link was several hundred miles shorter than the original rail line running north of the Amur River. In terms of implications for Chinese sovereignty in Manchuria, however, the concession was a disaster.

As one of the spoils of its victory over China, Japan had gained a militarily and commercially strategic foothold on the Liaodong Peninsula, the jewel of which was an ice-free natural harbor ideally positioned for naval command of the Bohai Gulf. The Chinese called this port Lushun; the Japanese, Ryojun; and the English, Port Arthur, a name ascribed to it during the Opium War. The Russians, however, took exception to this Japanese acquisition, declaring it a threat to regional stability, and in 1895, with nominal support from the French and the Germans, sued for the return of the Liaodong Peninsula to China. Japan was ill-equipped for a showdown with international opinion, and with the Russian Pacific Fleet positioned menacingly just outside Japanese waters, the Meiji emperor, feigning magnanimity, acquiesced. Then, while the bitterness of this pill was still recent memory, the Russians sailed their own navy into Lushun and took up anchor. Japanese humiliation over this incident ran so deep that it would be remembered fifty years later by Meiji's grandson, the Shōwa emperor, Hirohito, in a monologue he delivered as his official statement concerning the events of World War II.

The duplicity of this maneuver earned the Russians lasting resentment from not only the Japanese and Chinese but also the other Western powers. Not that the Russians much cared; Russia had endured without ice-free access to the world's major oceans for far too long to pass up this opportunity—especially given that no one else in the region had the military wherewithal to contest it. Then, from the town of Harbin in northern Manchuria, they rapidly built a second rail line extending due south, through the central Manchurian plains and down the Liaodong Peninsula to Lushun. They also posted army garrisons intermittently along it and established a command headquarters in Mukden.

In 1900, China was beset by a widespread popular revolt the British named the Boxer Rebellion. The so-called boxers were a brotherhood of Chinese martial artists whose Chinese name roughly translates as the "fists of righteous harmony." They also famously believed that their religious purification rites and martial training would render them immune to the effects of firepower, a belief of which they were soon rudely disabused. Patriotically motivated, the boxers blamed all manner of evils, including a flooding of the Yellow River followed by a several-year-long drought, on the incursions of Christianity, Western technologies, and Western economic interests on Chinese society. Also exasperated by the Qing rulers and their failures to respond to foreign humiliations, they decided to take things into their own hands. The movement began with attacks on Christians and the burning of their churches in Shandong Province, but it quickly caught on, spreading to Tianjin and Beijing and escalating to include all manner of foreign concerns and their Chinese, as well as foreign, constituencies. It also drew to its cause, first, other secret societies and their militias; next, ordinary peasants; and finally, the Qing government and its army. In response to the massacres and general terror wreaked on their legations, the affected nations—England, Russia, Japan, France, the United States, Germany, Italy, and Austria-Hungary—dispatched troops, formed a coalition army, and brought the uprising and the offending Qing regime to its knees. And in the process, just for good measure, they also raped and plundered Tianjin and Beijing.

Although the rebellion failed, it had momentarily brought the Chinese nation together and chastised the foreign community. The rebellion showed, to those willing to see, the depth of resentment held by large sections of China's population for foreign incursions and the indignities those incursions perpetrated. Less obvious was its effect on a dormant popular appetite for revolution, an appetite that would awaken a decade later.

But then, it also showed the world how vulnerable and incapable of rule the Qing dynasty had become. Furthermore, it ultimately strengthened the hands of the Great Powers in China, as they exacted both substantial monetary reparations and rights to garrison large numbers of troops on Chinese soil.

The Japanese and the Russians awkwardly participated together in the suppression of the rebellion. By virtue of its proximity, Japan's contribution of troops to this effort was by far the largest: out of 55,000-plus coalition soldiers, over 20,000 were Japanese. The Russian contribution, in excess of 12,000, was second. But while Russian forces participated in the battles for Tianjin and Beijing, the major theaters of the conflict, the preponderance of their troops, brought into China via their railroad, remained in Manchuria. That Manchuria had been only marginally affected by the rebellion was beside the point; under the guise of protecting their investments and restoring order, the Russians placed the towns and cities along the Chinese Eastern Railway under Russian martial law.

This virtual annexation of Manchuria showed the true colors of Russia's intentions. And now that the Chinese Eastern Railway not only cut straight across northern Manchuria to Vladivostok but also extended down to the tip of the Liaodong Peninsula, the Russians effectively held the Korean Peninsula in the grip of their rail system like a walnut in a nutcracker. Russian propaganda professed the railroad to be in the economic best interests of both Russia and China, but the immediate use to which it was put was the transport of troops, armaments, and military supplies. On top of this, brazen statements made in Moscow gave credence to Japanese fears that Korea would be next on Russia's list of targets for conquest.

In Japan, hawkish diatribe sounded on the floor of the Japanese parliament, and patriotic societies, including the Genyōsha, lobbied and demonstrated in favor of war. The army and the navy, meanwhile, took careful stock of their resources and weighed the feasibility of conducting a successful military campaign against the largest standing army and one of the largest navies in the world.

The national mood thus consumed by a dark sense of foreboding, Nakamura Saburō receives a clandestine hand-delivered communication from the army's intelligence corps. The corps, he was informed, is seeking recruits. Applicants are by way of referral only—Nakamura's name has been submitted by a Fukuoka legislator with Genyōsha affiliations—and acceptance subject to successful completion of an examination. On the appointed morning, he joins some thirty other applicants in the lecture hall of a classified training facility in Tokyo.

Army Minister Terauchi Masatake delivers the welcoming address. Of noble birth, Terauchi has a prosthetic right hand, a souvenir of the Satsuma Rebellion. His appointment to the cabinet post of army minister will last for an unprecedented nine years, after which he will serve as annexed Korea's first governor-general and, later, the nation's ninth prime minister.

He wastes no time on formalities. "Thank you for your willingness to serve your country," he says. "But first, let me make something clear. Lest there be any misunderstanding, if you are accepted into this school, there will be no turning back. Upon induction, you will surrender all privileges.

You will belong to us. Should your father or mother expire while you are here, do not expect to be granted leave to attend the funeral.

"Furthermore, upon completion of your training, you will be immediately dispatched to Manchuria on an assignment from which the chances of your returning home alive are close to nil. If you think you are signing up to become a hero, you are badly mistaken. We are offering you a one-way ticket to hell. Please think about it overnight, and if you still wish to join, come back in the morning."[1]

Terauchi's address, in effect, is the entrance examination. When Nakamura reappears the following morning, the number assembled is a mere fraction of that the day before.

If showing up is all that it took to get in, the course of study soon reveals itself to be far more difficult. Nakamura's group is but one of many similar handfuls of men making up an entire class of about 3,000. Contrary to Terauchi's admonitions, the door is always open to anyone who cannot take what is dished out, the assumption being that a man who needs to be kept in training against his will is not likely to hold up in the field under fire. And indeed, the numbers soon began to dwindle. By the time of graduation, one year later, only 113 remain.

As promised, these men ship out soon afterward. Nakamura's parents first see to it that, as befitting a young man going off to war, he is properly married. A match is made with a nineteen-year-old woman from Fukuoka named Yoshi, and the ceremony hastily executed. The marriage will endure for fifty-nine years until Yoshi's death, and Yoshi will play a pivotal role in the making of the man that Nakamura Saburō is to become.

Nakamura is assigned to the Japanese embassy in Beijing in January 1903, just one year before the outbreak of the Russo-Japanese War.

The first major military contest of the twentieth century, the Russo-Japanese War of 1904–1905 has been largely relegated to footnote status on the pages of history only because it was so soon overshadowed by conflicts of such greater horror. All of the makings of those greater horrors,

Nakamura Saburō and Yoshi, just prior to Nakamura's departure for China and Manchuria

(with permission from the Tempu Society, a nonprofit public interest foundation)

however, were fully on display in this earlier conflict—the war served as a proving ground for armored battleships, heavy artillery, and trench warfare, for example—and combined military and civilian fatalities during just sixteen months of hostilities numbered in excess of 150,000.

It was also, until then, the most closely watched and accurately reported war ever fought. While military observers scrutinized the conflict for intelligence regarding deployment of modern weaponry, war correspondents fed on its news value, for the spectacle of an upstart Asian power taking on the Russian empire drew interest from around the world. Even so, many of the same errors committed on both sides—trench entrapment, cavalry deployment, misplacement of barbed wire resulting in hindrance of troop movements, and underestimation of the deadliness of machine guns and long-range artillery—would be repeated just ten years later on European soil.

During a state visit to Japan at the age of twenty-three, while still crown prince, the Russian czar, Nicholas II, had been attacked and severely wounded by a fanatic sword-wielding Japanese nationalist. He never forgot. In conversation and sometimes even in formal correspondence, he referred to the Japanese as monkeys. Russia's military establishment shared something of their ruler's disdain by way of their dismissive appraisals of Japanese military capabilities. The Romanovs, having not suffered English and French belligerence during the Crimean War lightly, had assembled a military commensurate to the size of their empire, and in the eyes of all—be they Russian, Japanese, English, German, American, or French—Japanese military strength was not even remotely equitable. So confident were the Russians of their military superiority that they failed to believe, right up until Japan's war declaration, the Japanese would be so foolhardy as to engage them.

Japan, on the other hand, was not acting rashly. Three decades later, Japanese leadership would fall prey, with dire consequence, to myopic and grossly inflated myths concerning their invincibility, but at the beginning of the century, neither the nation's political leaders nor its generals and admirals harbored any such delusions. To the contrary, both the army and the navy, informed as they were by the latest in military science, were all too well aware of their vulnerabilities. But then, given the imminence of the Russian menace, these same leaders could not, in good conscience to their emperor and the nation, allow the Russian advance to continue.

In early March, Nakamura and two subordinates, Hashitsune Wataru and Kondō Nobutaka, assigned to him in Beijing, head northeast from Beijing by train. Hashitsune, in particular, is an invaluable asset to Nakamura. Born and partly raised in Manchuria, he is fluent in a couple of local dialects and thoroughly familiar with the territory and its peoples.

The English *Manchuria* is derived from *Manshū*, the Japanese appellation for a territory that the Chinese refer to as their three northeastern provinces, the provinces of Liaoning, Jilin, and Heilongjiang. It also identifies this territory as the ancestral homeland of the Manchus, the racial minority that descended out of the northeast in the seventeenth century to conquer Beijing and, subsequently, the rest of China. But neither did the Manchus, whose hegemony over the region prior to their conquest of the national throne was brief, call their homeland Manchuria, nor had the territory ever been a sovereign geopolitical entity (that is to change in 1931 under the Japanese occupation with the conception of Manchukuo). Furthermore, the Manchus were not the only people to call this territory ancestral; it had always been racially diverse. And during the two and a half centuries since the Qing acquired the mandate of heaven, it had become even more so: the northeastern provinces, with their vast reserves of seductively open, flat, and fertile farmland, were magnets for the displaced and had been subject to several massive waves of migration. When Nakamura and his party enter Manchuria, the population is largely Han Chinese, as well as Korean, Mongolian, and, now, Russian. Even the Manchu dialect has all but disappeared, the Beijing dialect serving by default as the territory's common language.

Attired as common laborers, the party rides on the train's flatbed railcars, each aboard a separate car and snuggled between cargo and other laborers. The train takes them to the head of its line, the town of Xinmintun, where the Russians have a supply depot. Here they spend ten days surveying Russian installations. Then they set out for the city of Mukden, the longtime regional seat of power now under Russian control.

Mukden, the modern Shenyang, is some thirty miles (fifty kilometers) due east of Xinmintun. Chinese rail, narrower than the Russians' broadgauge, does not interface directly with the Chinese Eastern Railway, and while it goes to Mukden, it does so circuitously; furthermore, Xinmintun-Mukden traffic is almost exclusively military. Consequently, the party negotiates a purchase of horses outside the village and sets off on horseback across the still frozen snow-covered countryside.

Much of China's rural northeast, too remote to be ruled effectively by the central authorities, is subject to de facto governance administered by a complex collage of warlords and local power brokers, sometimes with overlapping domains, and bandits operate along the byways with relative impunity. Almost predictably, the party's first hostile encounter is not with Russian soldiers but with local highwaymen.

The bandits are also on horseback and three in number. They appear out of nowhere as the party passes through an aspen grove. Seeing that any attempt to outride them will be futile, Nakamura commands his men to dismount. The bandits, likewise, dismount and take up positions directly in front of them. They wear scarlet-colored gowns, identifying them ethnically as Manchu. Of the three, the largest steps forward, his broadsword drawn. Now he begins to swing the sword in wide circles around his head, each revolution eliciting a whistle as the sword's blade cuts into the still winter air.

"This is a job for Kondō," Hashitsune says from behind. Nakamura nods and steps aside. Kondō is a swordsman of no small accomplishment; he holds the rank of sixth dan within the *jikishinkage* school of the sword arts. Nakamura and Hashitsune are both nursing welts and bruises on their wrists and ribcages received from Kondō, who has made sparring partners of them, using bamboo sticks as weapons, during moments of free time.

Typical of Chinese laborers, the members of the Japanese party each has his belongings bundled and tethered to the end of a bamboo pole that he carries over his shoulder; their bamboo poles, however, have each been clandestinely fitted to sheath a Japanese short sword, their only weapons.

As Kondō unsheathes his sword and steps forward, the disparity between the two opponents is painfully apparent. Not only is the bandit a head taller and a hand broader than Kondō, but his sword, both long and wide, makes Kondō's short blade affixed to its bamboo handle look like a toy.

Kondō, standing right leg forward, left leg back, holds his sword with both hands and trains its tip on the spot between his opponent's eyes. Meanwhile, the bandit is closing the distance between them, one step at a time.

But something is not quite right. Kondō, Nakamura notices, appears to have lost all mobility. He is standing still, quite like a statue—but one that is precariously balanced and ready to topple at any moment. He has been literally, Nakamura realizes, petrified by his fear.

"This won't do," Nakamura says. He draws his own sword and steps forward. The bandit, broadsword still circling, turns away from Kondō and toward Nakamura. Now the point man, Nakamura sympathizes with Kondō, still standing in the same state of paralysis. Despite the cold, beads of sweat form on Nakamura's brow.

Meanwhile, the tempo of the revolutions of his opponent's sword, Nakamura observes, has slowed. As large as the man was, he is beginning to tire.

Then, in the intensity of the moment, something extraordinary happens. Eyes focused on the beast of a man in front of him and the regular cycle of his swinging blade, Nakamura falls, momentarily, into a kind of trance. And in that trance, out of the deepest recesses of his consciousness, an image arises. It is a face—that of an old man Nakamura remembers from early in his childhood—and the face is speaking to him.

Nakamura Saburō was four years old at the time. The man was a distant relative who lived alone, and in deference to family ties, Saburō's mother, with young Saburō in tow, would call on him now and again to cook him a proper meal.

A veteran of Japan's Boshin War, the civil war that toppled the Tokugawa Shogunate, the man had seen hand-to-hand combat in some of the bloodiest campaigns of this dark chapter, and nothing pleased him more in his old age than to recount his exploits. With Saburō's mother busy in the kitchen, the role of captive audience to the man's stories fell to young Saburō.

Seated cross-legged on the floor, the old man would place Saburō on his lap, sip his sake, and reminisce. His stories, always the same, were also always told in the same predictable order—at the end of which the man would swell up and declare with gusto and satisfaction, "I wasn't the most skilled man in the field. But what I lacked in skill, I made up for with guts."

Saburō, too young to be impressed by either skill or guts, was always pleased to hear these words, for they meant the old man was done with his story and would soon finish eating and retire. Then, and only then, would Saburō's mother appear out of the kitchen with his dinner.

More than twenty years have passed since Nakamura Saburō last listened to the old warrior's stories—almost as many since the man had gone on to his Valhalla—and neither the man nor his stories have entertained his thoughts in the interim. But now, standing in harm's way on foreign soil, the old man's face appears in front of him, like an apparition, and looks him in the eye. And once again, that ancient voice in its northern Kyushu dialect says to him, "Not skill but guts."

Hashitsune notices a change in Nakamura's demeanor. His posture straightens ever so slightly, and he seems to grow larger. He raises his sword to the position known as *jōdan*, his left hand in front of his forehead, the sword slightly tilted to point obliquely into the sky behind him. Then, with a piercing yell, he enters directly into the arc of the broadsword between its revolutions, at the same time cutting straight down on his opponent's head.

Many years later, Nakamura Tempū would tell this story to illustrate the power of memory and the mysterious workings of the subconscious mind. But in the immediate aftermath of the incident, the realization that he is still standing while his opponent lies toppled at his feet takes a moment to register. Meanwhile, the other two bandits have hastily remounted their horses and fled: according to local superstition, to bear witness to the blood of a fallen comrade is especially inauspicious.

Nakamura thinks to clean the blood from his blade but finds his hands, still closed around the sword's handle, unresponsive. Hashitsune steps in to help pry his fingers loose, one by one. Then, together, they coax Kondō, still standing as if carved from stone, back to the world of the living.

"Not to worry," says Hashitsune, who has seen live action during a previous assignment. "It happens to everybody the first time."[2]

3.
HARBIN

Japan declared war on Russia on February 11, 1904. By then, Nakamura and his cohorts, Hashitsune and Kondō, had been imbedded for almost a full year in the northern city of Harbin.

Harbin sits on the Songhua River, a major tributary of the Amur. Similar in latitude to Montreal—both are located on the 45th parallel—its summers are gloriously bright and warm, fostering prolific crop growth on the surrounding plains, while its winters, notoriously cold, turn those same plains into desolate repositories of windswept ice and snow.

Not long ago, Harbin had been a quiet country village. Then the Russians arrived with their railroad. After bridging the half-mile-wide Songhua, they chose Harbin, on the river's eastern bank, for the northern terminal of their secondary line running south through Mukden to Dalian and Lushun. They also made Harbin the seat of the railroad administration authority for the entire Chinese Eastern Railway zone.

The railroad and the work it provided attracted all manner of laborers, merchants, and entrepreneurs, and Harbin's burgeoning population included Europeans, Cossacks, Sikhs, Mongols, and Koreans as well as Chinese from every corner of the country. There was even a Japanese community of about three thousand; however, Nakamura and his party were under strict orders to avoid all contact with its members lest they be made targets of Russian surveillance.

In just five years' time, Harbin's Russian population had swelled from almost nothing to thirty thousand, and the Russian administrators had brought in a Polish architect to mastermind the city's Russification: broad avenues had been surveyed, and frenetic building of European-style

PERIOD PHOTOS OF HARBIN

(from the Urban Planning Society of Harbin archive)

Songhua River; the rail bridge appears in the background.

Harbin train station

View from in front of Harbin station; Nicholaevsky Cathedral can be seen in the background.

Street scene

edifices along them began. The highest point in the city was crowned with an orthodox cathedral named for Czar Nicholas II,[1] the spire of which could be seen from almost anywhere in the city.

British author Bertram Lenox Simpson, in his colorful Manchurian travelogue, *Manchu and Muscovite,* written during this same time period, describes the scene at the Harbin train station in September 1903, just six months after Nakamura's arrival, as follows:

> *The station at Harbin presented the most astonishing and bewildering activity the day we arrived. Dense crowds jostled one another, and shouted and cursed and laughed. Shantung [Shandong] and Chihli [Zhili] workmen coming and going formed the vast majority of this motley and odoriferous human concourse, but there was no lack of other varieties. Mongolian horse-dealers with long coats, rough top-boots, and queueless heads gazed dog-like at the puffing engines. Yellow-clad lama priests rolled strings of beads in their hands and muttered, possibly prayers, but most probably curses, on the heads of the lusty Chinese railway police, who, clad in semi-Chinese soldier attire, wielded unmercifully heavy sticks on all who did not keep moving. Buriat [Buryat] cavalrymen, with high Mongol cheek-bones and a purely Chinese aspect, swaggered about in their Russian uniforms. Red-turbaned Sikhs from down-town stores and godowns chanted Hindustani at one another; and Russian officers of every grade and size ran about looking for their wives or belongings, saluting and clicking their spurs endlessly at one another.*

> *Inside the station rooms and restaurants it was even worse. The crush was so great that at times one became hopelessly tied up in men, women, and children and could not move for minutes. It was a Thursday, and expresses had arrived from three directions, south, east and west, and a number of ordinary trains were about to start. Harbin was trying hard to keep up its reputation of a railway centre, and was succeeding admirably as far as I was personally concerned.[2]*

The city's diversity made Harbin an easy place in which to hide, but it also made it a treacherous place from which to operate: local police kowtowed to Russian officers before they did to Chinese administrators, while the laws of the street were largely made and enforced by gang leaders working on behalf of local warlords. The Russians paid handsomely for intelligence regarding informants and spies, and the diversity of interests operating on the same turf made it extremely difficult to know who to trust or just when a friend might become an enemy.

Even so, the Japanese intelligence network in northern Manchuria went largely undetected by the Russians through to the war's end. Among the more colorful of its operations was a camera store and photography studio in central Harbin operated by a Japanese agent and his staff. The agent, alias Kikuchi, made no secret of his nationality. He opened the store with his own money in the heart of the Russian quarter and operated it as a legitimate business; among the Russians were many avid amateur photographers, and consequently the store did well. More importantly, film brought in for development by the store's clientele provided a wealth of information on railroad and military installations; Kikuchi and his staff had only to make extra copies of the same prints for which they were being paid.

Like Kikuchi, Nakamura and his men retained civilian status; however, as all of the intelligence operatives in Manchuria reported directly to the Japanese military attaché in Beijing, a colonel named Aoki Nobuzumi, it was understood that the army was their ultimate authority. Nakamura's orders, as well as his reports, were transmitted through the medium of a local depot operated by an out-of-uniform army lieutenant and located behind an unmarked alley doorway. The lieutenant, who looked and acted his part so well that even the locals assumed him to be Chinese, traveled back and forth regularly between Harbin and Beijing, and his office was but one among many one-room dwellings lining the tangled web of narrow backstreets that harbored the thousands of transient laborers pouring into Harbin in search of work. Refuge to the most desperate fringes of Harbin's population, these squalid neighborhoods were shunned by the

Russians, thus providing the Japanese with a relatively safe haven from which to operate.

Exchanges between Nakamura and the lieutenant were exclusively verbal; nothing was ever committed to paper lest that paper fall into the wrong hands, and Nakamura and his men were forbidden to take notes even when in the field. Not that this was any surprise: as part of his training, Nakamura had learned to mentally record and retain large amounts of information, including lists and numbers. His findings he would recite to the lieutenant who, likewise, would commit them to memory and carry them in his head back to Beijing.

Through this venue also flowed news and gossip, allowing the men to keep abreast of developments among their comrades and to be informed of their achievements. The rumor mill thus created had the effect of promoting a rivalry among peers. And where rivalry was involved, Nakamura was not going to be easily outdone.

Period photo of the Russian Army headquarters building in Harbin. Nakamura entered the building through a second-floor window.

(from the Urban Planning Society of Harbin archive)

The Second Siberian Army's general headquarters were housed in an imposing two-story edifice located on West Dazhi Street in central Harbin.[3] Typical of Russian installations, Nakamura observes, the building is poorly guarded; the Russians are cavalier in their assessments of enemy capabilities this far north. One February evening, under cover of darkness, he climbs to the second story and picks open the lock on one of the windows.

Picking locks is an art Nakamura acquired during his training at the academy in Tokyo, where his competency in the art soon surpassed that of his instructors. It was a competency he was never to lose. Many years later, at any one of the Tempūkai summer retreats, he had only to declare "The lock I cannot pick has yet to be invented" to materialize a small collection of padlocks on the podium by the following morning. Then he would gleefully open them, one by one, as participants looked on.

Once inside the building, he quietly makes his way from room to room. Noises from below tell him that the ground floor is occupied, but the upstairs, given to offices, is vacant. Nakamura has mentally pieced together an approximate floor plan based on descriptions obtained from a Chinese craftsman brought into the building by the Russians to repair their office furniture. One of the doors off the main hallway opens into a conference room, and in the center of the room, just as the craftsman had said there would be, is a large round table surrounded by about thirty chairs. More importantly, the table is covered with a tablecloth that hangs down on all sides to less than an inch from the floor. Sliding under the table, Nakamura stretches out on the floor and goes promptly to sleep.

One afternoon two years earlier, as Nakamura Saburō was nearing the end of his training at the academy, and as part of what could be called his final examinations, one of his instructors handed him a hand towel and directed him toward a barracks.

"Go hide in the ceiling and don't come down for a week," he was instructed. "You are not to be discovered, and when you return, you are to give us a full report on everything that goes on and all that is said in the room below you."

Period Japanese ceilings were made of pine boards not designed to bear weight, and the slightest movement would cause the boards to creak, so when the room below was occupied, Nakamura would spread his weight over this surface as evenly as possible and lie perfectly still. The purpose of the hand towel soon became clear. Not to mention food rations, he was not carrying a canteen; to ward off total dehydration, he would urinate into the towel and then squeeze its contents into his mouth.

Nakamura distinguished himself by successfully passing the test; he was one of only three members of his class to do so. Thinking back to this ordeal, his current accommodations under the table are comfortable by comparison.

In the morning, a man comes in to light a fire in the heating oven. Then, sharply at ten o'clock, a group of officers stomp into the room and seat themselves around the table. Nakamura sees only the toes of their boots protruding beneath the tablecloth but recognizes several of the voices; by this time, he has also acquired a smattering of Russian.

The meeting lasts for two hours, after which the men leave and the room again becomes quiet. They return in the afternoon and then again the following morning. Under darkness of the third night, Nakamura slips back out through the window, locking it behind him, and climbs down to the street.

How much of value Nakamura was able to garner from the exchanges, all in Russian, conducted at these meetings is questionable. Nevertheless, he derives satisfaction from having proven the permeability of Russian security. The Russians never learn of the breach. Moreover, the story makes great fodder for the rumor mill.

The break-in escapade only days behind him, Nakamura Saburō and his two companions have embarked on reconnaissance of railroad installations and their defenses to the west. Disguised as soybean merchants and traveling on horseback, they follow a set of carriage tracks laid by previous travelers in a region more than sixty miles (one hundred kilometers) from Harbin. The tracks take them over terrain that in summer is grassland but in winter glistens all the way to the horizon.

The pathway is the closest thing to an actual road, so when a carriage, followed by two men on horses—local farmers, by all appearances—approaches from the opposite direction, the band is wary but not alarmed. Nakamura and his men steer their horses off the path to let the carriage pass. Just when it draws alongside them, however, the carriage doors fly open and the men find themselves half surrounded by five bandits bearing sickles and swords.

This time, unlike their encounter a year earlier, the Japanese are outnumbered. Nakamura, after quickly assessing the situation, orders his men to flee. In concert, each of the three men swings his horse in a different direction, acting on the assumption that the bandits, with only two horses at their disposal, cannot possibly pursue all three of them at once.

At this moment, a female voice from inside the carriage, evidently in response to Nakamura's command, calls out in their native tongue. "Wait! You are Japanese?"

Curiosity overtaking caution, Nakamura reins in his horse and turns to face the carriage.

The woman, they learn, is named Oharu. She is one of two renowned Japanese women in Manchuria commanding bandit militias; the two are unrelated and operate in distantly separate territories, but each has become a local living legend. Through quirks of fortune, each, having been married to a village leader, has succeeded her husband to power upon the husband's untimely death. As leadership in the villages is decided not purely by familial succession but by the council of village elders, Oharu had presumably already proven her competence prior to her husband's demise, for now she commands a force of about two hundred men.

The label "bandit" as it applies to Oharu's men and other similar bands is in need of qualification, for where a bandit is one given to lawlessness, these bandit militias, operating in the absence of any strong central authority, constitute the law of the land. During the growing season, the men are ordinary farmers. During the winter months, however, they scour the countryside—and especially the carriage paths that serve as highways—for supplemental income. Occasionally, one of these groups will clash with another when the fringes of their respective territories overlap, but, more often, honor among thieves makes for peaceful coexistence. When a leader of sufficient charisma and ability comes to the fore, a number of villages might unite under one warlord, and part of Nakamura's mission has been not only to observe the movements of the Russians but to gain intelligence concerning these local power structures. During the hostilities about to commence to the south, the Japanese will recruit—through promise of just reward, of course—some of the most powerful of these militias to fight alongside them against the Russians. Furthermore, the Genyōsha, as we shall see later, is to play a central role in that recruitment.

Consequently, Nakamura and his comrades are delighted when Oharu invites them back to her village. They are received as honored guests; an entire house is placed at their disposal; and it is impressed upon them that they are welcome to stay for as long as they wish.

Little is known about Oharu or her background. Nakamura guesses her to be several years older than his own twenty-seven years. She was also, according to him, stunningly attractive. Ōi Mitsuru writes that Tempū was guardedly circumspect with regard to the subject of Oharu, and he speculates that the nature of their relationship—one that lasted only several days—may have been romantic.

One evening, as the men are returning to the house, a wizened old guard with a toothless smile is waiting. "I have brought you a gift," he says.

From the backs of two horses, he hoists down two sacks; the sacks appear to be reasonably heavy, and their contents animate. "Please enjoy yourselves this evening," the old man says with the same toothless smile. When the men cart the sacks inside and open them, they find in each a young woman.

One of the girls appears to be in her teens, the other perhaps several years older. From the way they are dressed and the way they interact, the men discern that the younger woman is from a well-to-do household and the older is her servant. The girls huddle together in a corner, sitting on top of the sacks they came in, hugging their knees and trembling with fear. Attempts by the men to discover where they are from are to no avail; the women are too terrified to speak.

Spoils from a recent raid, Nakamura guesses. "We've got to get them home," he says. The day is late, so the men feed them and allow them to sleep.

In the morning, they call the wizened guard. He listens incredulously as the men explain their intentions. But then, he concedes, the women now belong to them, so they are free to do with them as they wish. His demeanor changes when Nakamura presses a reasonable sum of coins into his hands. Overcome by this unexpected generosity, he bows low and vows to do anything in his power to repay the kindness.

"In that case," Nakamura says, "you can lead us to where you found them."

That alone, the man insists, he cannot do. The villagers will recognize him from the day before and quickly put him to death. "However, the carriage driver knows the way," he informs them.

The carriage driver and his carriage are called. Nakamura mounts the carriage beside the driver, while Hashitsune, Kondō, and the two girls seat themselves inside. They travel for close to four hours before coming to a temple to Guan Yu, patron god of military prowess, on the outskirts of a village. The young women had been making an offering at the temple when they were captured, the driver explains.

Nakamura asks the girls if they can find their way home from the temple, and they nod affirmatively, eyes filled with tears. But when the men encourage them to leave, they do not move.

"First, tell us your name," the younger girl says to Nakamura.

Nakamura explains that they are Japanese, that the Japanese and the Russians are about to go to war, but that the Japanese have no quarrel and mean no harm to her people.

The girl is not satisfied. "If you can't tell me your name, then give me something to remember you by."

This is a difficult request. Nakamura feels his pockets but comes up with nothing. Thinking for a moment, he reaches into his shirt and pulls out a sheathed dagger. "Take this," he says. "Use it to protect yourself in the future."

Arms are in short supply, and Nakamura's companions protest; but, he assures them, his short sword, back at the house, is all he needs. The girl thanks him and clutches the dagger to her breast. Even so, however, she refuses to leave. Looking back over his shoulder after they have turned the carriage around and are headed for home, Nakamura sees the women still standing in the same spot, their eyes fixed on the carriage until it disappears from view.

Hostilities began on the high seas, followed by a fierce but indecisive naval attack on Lushun. The Japanese land offensive does not begin until spring, but predictably, the invasion occurs where the Japanese had met the Chinese ten years earlier, at the Yalu River separating Manchuria from Korea. Although outnumbered, Japanese infantry divisions prevail, and crossing the Yalu in early May, they follow the Russian retreat into Manchurian territory.

In February, however, life in Harbin, far removed as it is from the Russian lines of defense, is little affected by action in the south. The Russians assume their comrades to the south will make quick work of the Japanese offensive and the war will soon be over. Nevertheless, Nakamura's party is now deep inside enemy territory, and the new sense of urgency associated with their mission, as well as the heightened risk, is palpable.

The focus of their mission is the railroad. The Chinese Eastern Railway is the Russian Army's lifeline; it is what feeds troops, munitions, and supplies into the front, and with so much riding on this thin ribbon of steel, already tight security is tightened further. But if the railroad is the Russian's lifeline, then sabotage is their greatest vulnerability, for the length of exposed track is more than any army can possibly watch all the time. Nakamura and his men are charged with assessing this track, its traffic, and the weak points in its defense in preparation for a concerted guerrilla operation to follow.

The first station to the west, at a distance of about twenty miles (thirty kilometers) from Harbin, lies near the tiny village of Duiqingshan. That the Russians should choose this location over larger towns in the same region for a train station underscores how little the local economy figures into their planning; the real purpose of the station is to control a siding that allows trains traveling in opposite directions to pass. The Cossack regiment assigned to protect this installation has taken up residence in the village and has confiscated some of its better houses for conversion into barracks.

About a mile and a half (two kilometers) from the station, a small hill with a wooded summit provides a lookout from which, through binoculars, Nakamura and his subordinates can observe the railroad and take inventories of rolling stock and cargo—including human cargo: inbound troops number in the order of, they estimate, about five thousand per week. With the surrounding farming households locked down in winter hibernation, the men occupy this hill and go about their business without fear of detection.

One mid-February afternoon, as Nakamura and Hashitsune are making their way up the hill, they come upon three bodies in the snow. They are women, and from their clothing—kimonos—the men recognize them to be Japanese.

The Japanese population of Harbin, made up of merchants, traders, entrepreneurs, and criminals on the run from Japanese law, was predominantly male. But there were also prostitutes. Houses of prostitution were ubiquitous to Japanese settlements in not only Manchuria but also China and Southeast Asia. Not unlike many victims of the sex trade in underdeveloped countries today, the women in these establishments were predominantly daughters of poor farming communities, where conditions of chronic malnutrition and outright starvation spawned lucrative human trafficking opportunities. Sometimes the women left willingly, out of desperation, but most were sold into servitude by their families to put food on the table for those remaining. Many a family survived total starvation by sacrificing their daughters in this manner, with the result that thousands of these uneducated and hapless women, enslaved to underworld bosses, ended up in urban entertainment districts, while thousands more were shipped overseas.

Nakamura and his comrades have not failed to notice that, since the beginning of the year, much of the Japanese community—with whom they have faithfully avoided direct contact—has chosen to pack up and leave while leaving is still an option. Many of the women, however, are left behind: as investments, they have already paid for themselves and, in the eyes of their masters, now amount to no more than excess baggage.

The women in the snow belong to this forsaken lot. Furthermore, the story of their gruesome demise is painted in broad stokes by the evidence surrounding them. Trampled snow bears the imprints of Cossack army boots, and empty vodka bottles lie strewn around the remains of a campfire. The first woman has been disemboweled. The second has a long, straight Cossack sword planted in her crotch. The third, stripped naked from the waist, has been buried head first in the snow, her flailing legs evidently serving to entertain the soldiers while they drank.

Using farm implements borrowed from a barn at the bottom of the hill as shovels, Nakamura and Hashitsune dig a single grave in the snow and inter the three bodies—the best they can do, as the ground is rock-hard. Placing a stone on top, they bow and say a silent prayer.

By now, it is dusk. After returning the borrowed tools, they mount their horses. Nakamura has retrieved and is carrying the Cossack sword. With few words between them—each knows the other's mind—they set out. The men are explicitly forbidden to engage with the enemy, but this time, orders be damned. The indignity of this carnage calls for revenge.

They ride to the outskirts of the village and wait, in an empty shed large enough to accommodate both riders and horses, for the still of night to descend. Then, silhouetted by the star-filled sky, they remount and ride into the village along its main street.

Nakamura intuitively stops in front of one of the houses. The riders dismount and circle to the rear, where, sure enough, a Cossack saddle rests carelessly propped against the stable door. They tether their horses and walk quietly to the back door of the house. Unlocked, it slides open.

Inside, darkness is complete. Stepping gingerly, and with hands crossed and extended in front of them to feel for obstacles, they make their way. Rounding a corner, the outline of a closed door, drawn by flickering lamplight from the room within, appears at the end of a short hallway. Nakamura gently tries the door but it is latched. He puts his shoulder to it and shoves; the door pops easily off of its hinges and crashes onto the floor of the room inside.

The room, lit by a single lamp, has two beds, the occupants of which, as evidenced by empty bottles on the floor, are sleeping off the effects of their liquor. Startled by the crash of the door, one of the men rolls over and looks up with wide eyes. Nakamura raises the Cossack sword and, without hesitation, plunges it through the man's heart.

The second man sits bolt upright in his bed. Hashitsune, with a single stroke, cuts clean across the man's throat with his short sword; blood from his jugular spurts across the room to where Nakamura is standing.

Mission completed, Nakamura and Hashitsune retreat. Before they reach the back door, however, noises in the street inform them that their presence has been detected.

Mounted and back on the street, they follow agreed procedure by pointing their horses in opposite directions—Hashitsune facing back the way they had come and Nakamura toward the other side of town. "Harbin, tomorrow," Nakamura yells over his shoulder. He nudges his horse with his heel.

But dark forms close in from both sides. Too late, he realizes that he is riding into a semicircle of men armed with rifles. A single shot rings out and Nakamura's horse goes down, throwing him hard against the ground. He staggers to his feet.

The horse, likewise, rights itself. "Perhaps he has enough left in him to get me out of here," Nakamura thinks. But as he attempts to remount, he is buffeted by what feels like a wad of string, and his head, arms, and legs are immediately entangled. The Cossacks have thrown a large net, the kind the locals use to fish the river in summer, over his head, and with this, they pull him to the ground.

The men descend on Nakamura, now thrashing about inside the mesh, and after gathering up the net by its corners, they bale it, catch and all, with a rope. One of the soldiers then ties the end of the rope to his pony's saddle and jumps on; to the whooping and cheering of his comrades, he spurs his horse into a gallop, the bundle in tow bouncing along behind him. At the end of the street, horse and rider turn and, to continued whooping, gallop back to the point from which they began. Nakamura is vaguely conscious of being lifted up and thrown into the back of a wagon. After that, his world goes dark.

When consciousness returns, his first sensation is that of cold. He is lying on a dirt floor inside some kind of enclosure, the air in which is infected with a pungent odor. Darkness is complete, but, groping across the floor on all fours, he discovers a stack of coarse straw matting, the kind used to transport cargo. He inserts himself into this stack, between its layers, and promptly falls asleep.

He is awakened by tugs from Cossack guards separating him from his impromptu bedding. The guards place him on his feet and lead him into the daylight.

His prison, he can now see, is a storehouse—one among several, set in a row, housing large barrels of *doujiang*, the northern Chinese equivalent of Japanese miso, fermented soybean paste. This, then, explains the smell. The Russians, he subsequently learns through observation, use these storehouses to incarcerate their own when they get out of line, which is often. In addition to women and liquor, the Cossacks have a penchant for fights.

The merchant owner of the doujiang establishment is evidently wealthy, for his is the biggest house in town; the regiment's captain has consequently appropriated it as his residence and command post.

Nakamura is taken to a room in this house and seated in a chair. The army has even gone to the trouble, he is flattered to learn, of procuring a Russian-Japanese interpreter.

Nakamura's inquisition continues for close to a month, during which time the daily walks between his make-do cell in the storehouse and the interrogation room in the large house afford him his only view of the outside world. Understandably, the Russians are intrigued by this stray Japanese saboteur. They want to know what induced him to strike, so impetuously, when and where he did: what military purpose could his actions have been in service of? Nakamura is equally determined to give them nothing. The sessions begin early and go late, the inquisitors working in shifts. Their plan is to wear him down, and in this they succeed. From time to time, the faces of his tormentors blur in front of his eyes, but each time his head drops, the guard standing beside him slaps him sharply on the side of the face.

Nevertheless, Nakamura says nothing. Whether or not he gives them information is, he knows, immaterial to his own fate; either way, he is going to be executed, and transitory physical pain is but a small price to pay for the integrity of the Japanese intelligence network and the security of his comrades.

In the morning and evening, his captors bring him water and a couple of pieces of *mantou*, a regional dietary staple best described as steamed bread. At night, listening to the sound of his breath as he inhales the musty odors of fermenting doujiang, he falls asleep quickly and sleeps soundly.

One evening, not long after he retires, the storehouse door slides partially open and a hushed voice calls into the darkness in Chinese. "Japanese man, are you in there?"

Nakamura reveals himself, whereupon his visitor explains that he is there on behalf of the owner of the doujiang establishment and motions for him to follow. Boisterous laughter coming from the other end of the compound tells Nakamura that the guards are drunk and shirking their duties. Following the man on a circuitous route between the storehouses, he is ushered into a small dwelling with a carpeted, amply furnished, and delightfully warm sitting room.

"Wait here," the man instructs him. Nakamura settles into a large, cushioned chair of the Chinese variety with a deep, wide seat, and a straight back. A well-stoked heating oven in the corner is responsible for the delicious heat; this is, he reflects, the warmest he has been in many months, let alone the two weeks of his captivity.

Minutes later, an elderly, well-dressed Manchu gentleman enters from an adjoining room and bows. He is the owner of the doujiang establishment, he explains. Upon learning that the Russians were holding a Japanese prisoner, he felt compelled to meet the man. He is indebted to the Japanese. Just recently, his granddaughter, who had the misfortune of being kidnapped by bandits, was rescued and returned to him by a group of Japanese men.

At that moment, the door from the adjoining room opens again, and a young girl sticks her head in. She looks at Nakamura, gasps, and runs to him, throwing her arms around his waist. "Grandfather," she says between sobs. "It's him. This is the man who saved me."

Looking down into the girl's face, Nakamura recognizes her as the younger of the two women he and his men had returned to their village. He realizes also, for the first time, that the distance and direction in which they had traveled that day would have, indeed, put them in the vicinity of this village, the same village behind the train station where he was captured.

The old man promptly prostrates himself before Nakamura. "I can never repay you for the kindness shown my granddaughter," he says. "Anything in my power that I can do for you now, I'll gladly undertake. The soldiers are currently drunk and enjoying themselves, so you must flee immediately. We'll provide you with a horse. Please hurry; you don't have much time."

But Nakamura does not move. What will become of these good people when the Russians discover their prisoner gone and all signs pointing to them as accomplices?

Sensing what Nakamura is thinking, the old man seeks to reassure him. "Don't worry about us," he says. "We know how to take care of ourselves."

The opportunity for flight, however, has already passed. The sound of approaching soldiers comes from outside.

"Quick," Nakamura says. "Go back inside and lock the door."

The man and his granddaughter disappear into the rear of the house without time to say good-bye. When, moments later, a soldier enters from the street, Nakamura is seated comfortably in the chair with his hands to the oven and a look on his face that says, "Just trying to get warm."

Nakamura is moved to a different storehouse with a heavier door, and his right leg is shackled with an iron ball and chain. He is pleased to discover, however, that a Manchu guard assigned to him has worked for several years at the docks in Yokohama and speaks some Japanese. The man's assignment is obviously intentional: Nakamura's captors are hoping he will divulge in casual conversation what they have been unable to extract through interrogation. Nakamura and the guard cultivate a rapport and kill time talking about things of no intelligence value.

One evening after Nakamura is returned from the usual long day of questioning, and after he has washed down the evening ration of mantou with water, the guard approaches him. Is there anything that his prisoner wants, he asks with a long face. An odd question, Nakamura thinks, given his circumstances. But when he assures the man that he is well fed and reasonably comfortable, the guard persists.

"No need to hold back," the guard says. "Just tell me what you want."

Sensing that something is wrong, Nakamura presses him for an explanation.

With only a little coaxing, the guard confesses. "I'm sorry to be the one to tell you," he says, "but you are to be executed in the morning."

If the guard is expecting surprise, he is disappointed. Since his capture, Nakamura has been resigned to this outcome, and lately, he has been thinking, "Any day now." He accepts the guard's news with a nod and responds, "Is that so?"

Now it is the guard who shows surprise. "'Is that so?' I'm telling you that you have only a few more hours to live, and all you have to say is, 'Is that so?'"

"Everyone has to die sometime," Nakamura responds. "It just so happens that my day is tomorrow."

The guard looks at him incredulously.

Nakamura continues. "But if you really want to do something for me, then let me get some sleep. I have a big day tomorrow and want to be well rested."

The guard shakes his head in disbelief. This inscrutable prisoner wishes, he is being told, to use his last few hours alive to catch up on his sleep. Before he allows Nakamura to retire, however, the guard extracts verbal entitlement to Nakamura Saburō's few possessions. These consist of no more than the clothes on his back and some loose change in his pocket, but Nakamura is wearing a leather vest that the guard has had his eye on for some time.

This agreed, Nakamura turns in and sleeps soundly. He is awoken as usual at five the next morning; only this time, three Cossacks instead of the usual one, together with the interpreter, stand outside the door. Nakamura is to be executed, he is informed by way of the interpreter. Before that, however, he is invited to share breakfast with their captain.

Nakamura is acquainted with the captain. The man has taken an interest in the interrogation and has shown his face in the interrogation room several times. He is a tall, strong Russian of about Nakamura's age—or perhaps, Nakamura guesses, slightly younger.

At the captain's residence, Nakamura, still wearing his ball and chain, is instructed to sit across from the captain at a table liberally laden with sumptuous Russian fare. Having survived for a month on nothing but mantou, Nakamura surveys this spread with ravenous eyes and, when so invited, helps himself generously. The Cossack guards standing at attention behind him and the interpreter at his side look on.

Is there any message that Nakamura wishes to send home? If so, the captain says, he can arrange it through the Red Cross.

There is not.

The captain is acting under orders, he explains. He bears no grudge against Nakamura and will carry out his orders with a heavy heart. "Are you saddened to know that your life is coming to its end?" he asks.

Nakamura is not sad in the least. He has served his mission and will be dying for the national cause.

"What of your mother," the captain asks. "Won't she be sad?"

"Of course she will be sad. But she will also be proud," Nakamura answers. Nakamura's mother, when she saw him off, had told him that she expected him to fulfill his duty to the nation, no matter what the cost. Nakamura has lived up to her expectations. The one regret, one that he does not express to the captain, is that his mother will never know just how he died; she will never have the satisfaction of knowing that he had upheld his honor and dignity to the end.

Four years later, in New York, Nakamura would be asked by the prominent New Thought exponent Orison Swett Marden, "So, are you one of those Japanese who would willingly lay down your life for the emperor?"

Nakamura readily responds, "Of course."

"Did the emperor ever promise you anything for your service?"

"Never."

"How about praise?"

"No, never. No reward and no praise."

"Nothing?"

"Nothing, on all accounts."

"And for this emperor, you are willing to lay down your life. Are you mentally sane?"

When Nakamura Tempū recounts this incident, in 1957, his audience belongs predominantly to generations for whom the Meiji era is either a childhood memory or no memory at all, and to whom the mindset of that era is almost as alien as it was to Marden.

"When I first told my mother that I was going to risk my life for my country," he goes on, "she jumped for joy. In this age of nationalism, such a reaction was not unusual. It was quite normal. 'Banzai! Banzai! Banzai! The son I brought into the world is finally living up to my expectations of what it means to be a man. From this day forward, you no longer belong to your mother and father. You belong to your country and your emperor.' That is the way our mothers responded.

"Would a mother today say something like that? I don't think so. More like, 'Come here and sit down. You are all I have in the world. If you go get yourself killed, what is going to happen to me?'

"But in our day, it was different. And, of course, we too were delighted. For we went off to war with the confidence of knowing that we were fulfilling our parents' dreams as well as our own."[4]

"I will never understand you Japanese," the captain says. Producing a handkerchief and a fountain pen, he asks Nakamura to sign it.

Nakamura writes his name in capital Roman letters.

"In Japanese too," the captain requests.

Nakamura complies, writing his name in clear, bold strokes.

What becomes of the handkerchief, Nakamura never discovers, but the following day, he will reflect upon the irony of this exchange; although Nakamura Saburō has as yet no inkling, the meal they have just shared is to be not his but the captain's last.

Nakamura is unshackled. Hands tied, he is mounted on horseback and led out of the village. After a short journey into the frozen countryside, the procession comes to a spot where the soldiers have built a pitch on which, during the summer months, they play a Russian version of cricket. In the middle of the field, a single birch pole has been planted in the snow and frozen in place. The soldiers lift Nakamura off of his pony, untie his hands, lead him to the pole, and retie his hands, this time, around the pole behind him. In front of him, at a distance of thirty paces, stand the captain, the interpreter, and three Cossack soldiers.

"What a shame," Nakamura thinks. The shame is that, here on this desolate, windswept landscape, there will be no one other than these five to bear testament to his death.

The captain steps forward. He reads the charges and the sentence, and the interpreter faithfully renders them word for word into Japanese. Upon finishing, the captain asks, "Do you have anything to say?"

Nakamura remains silent but shakes his head.

One of the Cossack guards comes toward him holding a piece of white cloth.

"What are you doing?" Nakamura asks angrily.

The interpreter approaches. "This is a favor granted by our captain. The prisoner is to be blindfolded so that he doesn't see when the command to fire is given."

But Nakamura will not have it. "I want to see with both eyes exactly where the bullets hit," he says.

The captain concedes, and the Cossacks take up their positions. One lies prone, rifle supported by his elbows; the second kneels, left elbow resting on his advanced left knee to provide steady aim; the third stands. To Nakamura, the barrels of the three rifles are hidden, each behind its muzzle; all he can see is three black circles. Those circles, however, project the illusion of advancing toward him, their diameters expanding ever larger within his field of vision. Years later, Nakamura will flinch involuntarily whenever he views a movie scene depicting the muzzle of a rifle pointing at the camera.

"Aim for the heart," Nakamura yells at the men. "I don't want you to leave the job half finished."

The interpreter steps forward again. The prisoner's life is now in the hands of fate, he explains. Should all three bullets miss, his captors will interpret this as a sign from God and will release him unconditionally. This is a formality, Nakamura understands; indeed, nothing short of divine intervention is going to cause three trained riflemen to miss from thirty paces.

This final message delivered, the interpreter steps back, and the captain raises his saber; the falling of the saber will be the soldiers' signal to fire.

All is quiet. But just at that moment, the winter tranquility is torn by a deafening roar—followed, a split-second later, by a shockwave so forceful that it knocks Nakamura over backward, pole and all, onto the snow.

Stunned, Nakamura opens his eyes to find himself enveloped by a dream-like haze. "Could this be the afterlife?" he wonders. But then, his head hurts, his ears are ringing, and the cold of the snow is pressing against his back, while the haze smells distinctly like smoking gunpowder. Unlikely, then, that he is dead.

Seconds later, Hashitsune is lifting him to his feet and yelling into his still ringing left ear. "Are you all right?"

Nakamura does not attempt to make sense of this turn of events; that can wait.

"Run," Hashimoto says.

"You have to cut me loose first," Nakamura reminds him.

The cords binding him to the pole severed, the two men run for the cover of a nearby aspen grove. While they run, a second explosion, more muffled than the first, sounds from the edge of the field, but they do not stop to ponder its meaning. "This way," Hashitsune says. "We have horses waiting."

Advancing a couple of steps, however, Hashitsune suddenly stops. "Wait," he says. "We can't leave. I forgot the girl."

"What girl?"

"The girl we rescued that day from the bandits. I told her it was too dangerous, but she insisted on coming along."

They run back toward the field, one edge of which slopes suddenly away; this embankment is what provided Hashitsune with the cover he needed to approach the firing squad. There in the snow, the girl's body lies lifeless, half-buried by frozen rubble from above. In her hand, she clutches the keepsake dagger.

Not until they are back in Harbin does Nakamura learn the whole story. After several weeks of patient investigation, Hashitsune determined where Nakamura was being held. One evening he slipped into the dou-jiang establishment, where he encountered the girl, whose name was Yuling, and her grandfather. Not only did they confirm Nakamura's pres-ence, but they also informed him of the scheduled time and place of his execution.

By breaking into a Russian powder magazine, Hashitsune secured a substantial amount of gunpowder and fashioned a small arsenal of gre-nades. These he and Yuling, who insisted on accompanying him, carried out to the cricket field the prior evening. The two of them spent the night in the open field, the embankment serving as their only protection against the elements.

Once the firing squad had assembled, Hashitsune made his way down the length of the embankment to the point closest the soldiers. Then he lit the fuse of a grenade and lobbed it into their midst.

Meanwhile, Yuling, farther away and hidden from Hashitsune by a bend in the embankment, was left guarding the remaining explosives. In the confusion following the blast, she evidently looked out onto the smoke-filled field to see Nakamura lying in the snow and assumed that the plan had failed. She then lit one of the remaining grenades and attempted to throw it onto the field, but her throwing arm was not strong enough to clear the embankment's lip; the bomb lodged above her and brought down the side of the field with it when it exploded. It was this muffled second explosion that the men had heard while running for cover.

In the spring of 1906, following the end of the war, Nakamura took leave from his post in Korea to visit Manchuria and the embankment one last time and to offer a silent prayer to the spirit of the young girl whose fate had become so mysteriously entwined with his.

Many more years later, Nakamura Saburō's younger brother—younger by twenty years—wrote a novel based on Saburō's stories of his escapades in Manchuria. The novel, published in 1931, was subsequently turned into a play, and the play, titled *Manshū Hibun*, "Secret Stories from Manchuria," opened the following year to favorable reviews and capacity audiences at the national theater in Tokyo. In the play, Nakamura Saburō's character is called Fujimura Yoshio to protect his identity. The character of Yuling, however, retains her actual name, as do those of Hashitsune and Oharu.

4.
WAR'S TOLL

Other Japanese agents met with fates less fortunate than that of Nakamura Saburō. Caught in the act of espionage or sabotage, some were killed on the spot; others were captured, tried, and executed, much as Nakamura Saburō would have been, far away from outside scrutiny. Either way, the majority of their stories went unrecorded, and just where and how they died, no one will ever know.

One known incident, as it was widely publicized at the time, involved a Japanese colonel named Yokogawa Shōzō and a captain, Oki Sadasuke. The two, traveling in disguise as Mongolian lamas, were apprehended near Harbin by a Russian patrol. The incident attracted international attention when, under questioning, they proudly stated their names and military ranks. Yokogawa and Oki's execution was staged on April 21, exactly one month to the day from Nakamura's would-have-been execution. Like Nakamura, these men were tied to birch poles and read their sentences. They faced death with pride and equanimity, earning the respect not only of their Russian captors but also a German military observer and several other European witnesses. The story was picked up and distributed by the Associated Press.

In deference to their military standings in life, the bodies of Yokogawa and Oki were cremated and preserved by the Russians. As the story was to play out, when the Japanese learned of this and also learned where the remains were being held, the task of retrieving those remains would fall to Nakamura and his party. They would break into the army compound and steal the vessels containing the ashes of their fallen comrades out from under Russian guards, and the ashes would be returned to Japan and interred by their respective families.

At the time of Yokogawa and Oki's execution, however, Nakamura and his men were far from Harbin; no sooner was Nakamura Saburō back in the land of the living than he and his party, which now included three local Chinese recruits, making them six in all, were dispatched again on assignment. The men set out in late March, first veering south to distance themselves from the railroad, and then heading due west. Laden with supplies and leading an extra set of horses, they traveled overland for ten days.

Spring was still far off, and the farther into the interior they traveled, the lower the temperature dropped. For much of the journey, they were trailed by a lone wolf, evidently intent upon singling out one of the horses if allowed the opportunity. Wolves were a constant threat in these parts, their packs sometimes numbering one hundred strong.

Nakamura was all too familiar with wolves. Several months earlier, during an assignment east of Harbin to where the railroad crossed the Mudan River, he and a local man serving as his assistant were run up a tree while wolves took down their horses. The pack, averse to eating fresh kill, posted a sole sentry while they allowed the horsemeat to cure. Nakamura outwaited the wolves for three days and three nights. His assistant, however, ran out of patience on the afternoon of the third day; climbing down in an attempt to escape, he was torn to shreds at the base of the tree.

Crossing from Manchuria into Mongolia, they came to the Greater Khingan Mountain Range (Da Xing'an Ling) at the edge of the Mongolian Plateau. Here they turned north, following the baseline of the mountains until they came, once again, within sight of the Russian railroad. Tufts of smoke rising into the clear blue sky alerted them to the railroad's presence long before it came into view. To meet the call for troops, munitions, and supplies in the south, and to avoid the delays incurred by oncoming traffic and its diversion onto passing sidings, the Russians were sending an almost continuous stream of trains one-way to the east. Nakamura and his associates had not failed to notice the huge inventory of rolling stock parked in Harbin's yards and the frantic construction of additional siding to accommodate more.

Nakamura's party was but one among many similar parties spread out along the Russian railroad from as far inland as Lake Baikal to as far east as the Russian Maritime Province and as far south as Mukden and the Liaodong Peninsula—all part of a strategic plan, hatched in Tokyo by Generals Kodama Gentarō and Fukushima Yasumasa, to incapacitate the Russian supply line. The war room planners chose April 3, a holiday honoring the legendary first emperor, Jimmu, for the launching of this guerrilla blitzkrieg; but in the end, because coordination of so many parties, most of them nonmilitary, over such a wide geographical area proved logistically infeasible, the attacks occurred over a two-month period.

Nakamura and his comrades survey their target from a wooded slope overlooking the point at which the railroad disappears into a tunnel under the mountains. The Russians, in laying down their railroad, had chosen not only to use a gauge wider than that used by most other European nations but, in the interest of economy and of laying many kilometers of track as quickly as possible, wider spacing between the ties. The resulting construction is flimsy—easily warped and easily damaged—and the Russians are acutely aware of its vulnerability to sabotage. They have allocated 80,000 troops solely to railroad protection east of the Urals, and one-third of these are stationed in Manchuria and Mongolia. These troops are stationed in garrisons spaced along the railroad's entire length, and mounted Cossack patrols ride up and down each of the in-between sections of track at regular intervals. During the day, when visibility is good, the threat of sabotage is low, but during the night, these patrols pass by every thirty minutes.

Thirty minutes, then, is the window within which the Japanese have to work. Under the cover of darkness, they slip down to a gully close to the tracks and wait until a patrol passes. Once the riders are past, the men spring into action. Using pickaxes transported with them, they hack their way through ice and into the frozen earth between two ties. Into this shallow trench, they then lay the explosives that Hashitsune and Kondo carry wrapped in puttylike cords around their waists. From his own waist, Nakamura unwinds a length of fuse and inserts it. Next, they cover their work with the extracted frozen earth. Only Nakamura is trained in demolition and the use of explosives—training acquired at the academy in Tokyo—but he has gone over and over the plan with his men, and each knows his part.

Hashitsune sights the lantern of an approaching patrol. Nakamura instructs the others to depart. From his vest, he takes a perforated metal box that produces a still smoldering cigarette; in this snow-laden wasteland, the light from a single match can be seen for miles, while a cigarette ember is all but invisible. Nakamura resuscitates the cigarette by puffing on it and then touches it to the exposed end of the fuse; the operation requires focus and a steady hand, even as the enemy is approaching. Once sure the fuse has lit, he turns and runs in the tracks of his comrades. Less than a hundred yards (ninety meters) out, a brilliant flash of light casts his shadow in front of him. It is followed almost immediately by a thunderclap and a shockwave. He is sent flying, headfirst, into the snow.

Recovering their horses and gear from where they had left them, the men retreat into the forest. All has gone according to plan. Moving farther west, they conduct one more successful attack before turning around and beginning the trek back.

According to official Russian tally, enemy sabotage between the February outbreak of the war and the end of May resulted in thirty-seven instances of damaged track and twenty-four instances of damaged bridges. The attacks also generated casualties in excess of bed capacity in the only hospital in Harbin.

Nakamura and company's retrieval of the remains of Yokogawa and Oki took place in May. They came away from this episode after surviving an animated chase by Cossack guards, during which all but small dustings of the ashes were spilled; even so, the operation was deemed a success. Then, in June, the three said good-bye to Harbin and headed south to meet up with the Japanese forces.

In June, Nakamura was given leave and returned to Japan for a much-needed and well-deserved rest. But by fall, in time to participate in the battles for Liaoyang and Mukden, he had returned. His part in those operations remains shrouded, but it almost certainly involved the paramilitary Manshū Gigun, the "Manchurian Righteous Army."

The Manshū Gigun owed its inception to the Genyōsha and its affiliate, the Kokuryūkai, the "Black Dragon Society." Prior to the outbreak of the war, the Kokuryūkai had infiltrated Siberia and the Russian Far East, including Vladivostok. Now in Manchuria, Kokuryūkai operatives courted local warlords, enlisted them to the Japanese cause as mercenaries, and with army sanction, targeted Russian communication lines. The Genyōsha, through Tōyama Mitsuru's friends among the military elite, and through Yamaza Enjirō in the Foreign Service, brought to the army a proposal to create what might be called a joint venture between the army, whose responsibility it would be to provide leadership, training, and armaments, and the Genyōsha, who would enlist mercenary forces through its local warlord connections. The special duty corps that emerged from this proposal, the Manshū Gigun, ultimately mustered twelve hundred troops and participated in many of the major land campaigns of the war.

It was also successfully kept under wraps and out of public scrutiny by the military. The army imposed this cloud of secrecy out of concern for the national image, since the paramilitary status of the Manshū Gigun was legally gray at best under international convention. As a result, no documentation concerning it was kept, and its stories survive only through rumor. The only solid record of its existence is a stone monument to the "warriors of the Manshū Gigun" that stands in the Genyōsha cemetery in Fukuoka. Perhaps in deference to promises made at the time, Nakamura also never spoke of the organization or his part in it.

The Japanese siege of Lushun, lasting five months and resulting in close to 100,000 combined casualties, was the single most horrific battle the world had so far ever witnessed. But in the end, the Japanese prevailed. The war ended, as it had begun, at sea—this time in the Tsushima Strait, where the Japanese defeated the Russian Baltic Fleet on May 28, 1905.

The Russians' defense, in retrospect, had been uninspired and poorly managed. It had also been severely disadvantaged by logistics. They were, after all, fighting a major war on the farthest thrown fringes of their empire against a determined enemy close to home. But they were also at fault for having underestimated that disadvantage.

Nevertheless, it was an extraordinary accomplishment. The Japanese had exhibited tactical superiority; they had outwitted the enemy where they could not outgun them. They had also shown uncommon military valor and resolve, and their victory over a major European power catapulted them to stardom in the eyes of the world.

Japan's military prowess, however, was not matched by its diplomatic skills. Outfoxed by the Russians in treaty negotiations at Portsmouth, New Hampshire, the Japanese came away with coveted leaseholds on Lushun and Dalian but failed to exact the financial retribution they were counting on to repay their war debts. The war left them both militarily and financially spent.

Nevertheless, they were to remain in Manchuria, even acquiring the southern part of the Chinese Eastern Railway that the Russians left behind. The savor of these spoils, combined with the humiliation suffered at Portsmouth, were to contribute to their policies during the coming decades and a less glorious phase in their history. But that is getting ahead of our story.

Following the end of the land campaigns and the Russian army's final capitulation, when all of the special agents were called in from the field, Nakamura answered to roll call in Mukden. This was in March 1905, a full year after Nakamura had been stood in front of a firing squad. Of the 113 intelligence agents dispatched two years earlier, only seven mustered. Where the other 106 came to rest, no one knew: most lay buried without so much as a marking to indicate the presence of a grave.

For most of Nakamura's three years in the enemy's shadow, he lived in squalid conditions and on the most meager of rations. "We were infested with lice," Tempū would later say. "You couldn't get rid of lice; they were permanently ensconced in your hair. If I were to appear before you now as I was then, you would all get up and leave the room.... Filthy, lice infested, and dressed in the shoddiest clothes—peasant's clothing. We used to soak our clothes in a broth we concocted from garlic and chives, just so we would smell like everyone else."[1]

He had also sustained multiple injuries, including a gunshot wound— this with great loss of blood but somehow without damage to any of his vital organs, despite the fact that the bullet had pierced his abdomen and exited from his back—the loss of most of his teeth, partial loss of eyesight due to shrapnel, and a concussion that left him unconscious for several days and caused him recurring headaches for years afterward.

The war had taken a psychological toll as well. He could not help but to have been affected by the depravity of the war, including his participation in and contribution to its bloodshed, and when, more than half a century later, Tempū speaks of the incidents described in this and the preceding chapters, he does so with the humility of someone who is still excising demons and doing penance.

"Espionage is nothing more than thievery," Tempū remarks:

I killed plenty of people, but only out of necessity. The object of espionage is to steal the enemy's information, not to kill.... If the people we were stealing from could only have put their secrets somewhere convenient, like under a pillow, before they went to bed, we would have taken what we needed and left without killing them. A tickle on the cheek with a handkerchief and most people will roll over. As long as the fellow doesn't wake up, then all is well. But if he wakes up, unfortunately, you have to make him quiet.

Of course, the more valuable the information, the more determined he is going to be to keep it safe. In that case, you have to put him down.

He may be a good man. But you can't very well go up to him and ask, "Would you mind lending me the brief you are carrying? I would like to take a look at it and then return it. In ten days. I promise." It doesn't work that way. You are beholden, by the rules of war, to see the job through. Too bad, but there is no other way.

Many years ago, the head of the naval college said he wanted to study under me. He heard about me from Yamamoto Gombei [Yamamoto Gonnohyoe, naval admiral and prime minister (1913–1914 and 1923–1924)]. Seems he thought highly of me for what I did during that war. But there was nothing noble about my war record. I was sixteen when I first left Japan, and it wasn't for love of country that I left: I was sent away because I was a misfit. Had I stayed, I would probably have brought unpardonable shame to my parents and family. Everyone just figured it better I be entrusted to Manchu bandits than be allowed to continue to cause trouble at home. It's just that, somehow, I survived.[2]

When Nakamura Saburō's intelligence service commission renewed in February 1906, he was deployed to the Office of General Command in Korea as a senior-level interpreter. One morning, after only three months at this post, he coughed up a wad of blood. He had the "galloping consumption," his doctors told him—so-called because it was said to consume the body with the speed of a runaway stallion. It was tuberculosis, and the doctors gave him between six and twelve months to live.

5.
A CRISIS OF MIND

At the start of the twentieth century, tuberculosis was the world's single deadliest communicable disease. Reliable statistics are lacking, but tuberculosis-related fatality appears to have been at least as high in Japan as in Western Europe, where it accounted for between 20 and 25 percent of all nonviolent deaths, and worldwide, before the century was half over, it would claim the lives of almost 100 million people. In 1905, the same year as the signing of the Treaty of Portsmouth, a German physician named Robert Koch was awarded a Nobel Prize for his 1882 identification of the bacillus responsible for tuberculosis, but his discovery had no immediate remedial implications; the disease remained as resistant to treatment as it had during the Middle Ages. Not until the 1946 discovery of streptomycin did tuberculosis-related fatalities begin to decline. And while this and subsequent advances have brought the disease under control, it continues to plague populations in less developed regions of the world today.

Nakamura was summarily relieved of his post in Korea and returned to Japan, where, under quarantine, he receded into the confines of his home. The transition from a life of high drama to one of obscurity and convalescence was abrupt and disorienting; Tempū does not say as much, but he was almost certainly suffering the effects of post-traumatic stress, effects that, in that day and age, went unrecognized and exacted no sympathy. For the first time in his life, he fell into a state of severe depression.

Nakamura's illness was physical, but his crisis was existential. In war, the prospect of death under fire had been part of what had given his life meaning; were he to die, he would do so with honor, in the line of duty, and for love of country. But the imminence of a gradual death that served no such purpose, one brought on by physical degeneration through a debilitating fever and an unseemly cough, rendered life utterly meaningless. And the thought of not just dying but dying without meaning was terrifying. Retrospectively, Nakamura Tempū would characterize this period as one of unconscionable self-indulgence and self-pity. Indeed, even his mentor, Tōyama Mitsuru, told him to his face that he had become a disgrace.

Just what was the mechanism that allowed the same man who had exhibited fearlessness even when standing before a firing squad to shrink to such a pathetic state? In hindsight, Tempū attests to a threefold cause.[1] First, for all of his wartime bravado, he says, his mental outlook had already been infected with a subconscious negativity. Over the course of his childhood, he had acquired and internalized a litany of basic assumptions regarding the randomness of fate, the unworkability of life, and the repugnant nature of death. Short of addressing these fundamentally pessimistic assumptions, he could not be expected to consciously embrace his current predicament or to see it as other than cruel and undeserved.

Second, when the fact of his declining health forced him to confront the reality of his mortality, he allowed automatic and unexamined thoughts and emotions that arose in response to that reality to take over; the fact of his mortality and the thoughts and emotions that fact evoked in him all became rolled into one. Were he to have detached himself from his predicament, he would have seen that his thoughts and emotions were separate from and not necessarily dictated by his physical condition. The vigilant practice of mindfulness is essential to understanding and gaining control over the mechanism of rational and emotional response, Tempū advises. By bringing cognizance to bear on one's psyche, one can dispel negativity and condition oneself to respond constructively to all circumstances and in all situations.

But if his psychological negativity could be attributed to a lack of vigilance, it also had a physiological dimension. The third cause, he says, was the weakened state of his nervous system. Lack of nervous fortitude and stamina put him at the mercy of his discomforts and anxieties, consequently paving the way for physical fragility to debilitate him psychologically and spiritually as well. Preemptive training and conditioning of the nervous system, Tempū goes on to say, is key to the restitution of unity between mind and body. The essential practice here is the regulation and control of the central nervous system's response mechanism through centering. The methodology he prescribes, called kumbhaka, from yoga, is introduced later, in chapter 8.

More than the degeneration of his physical health, Tempū is saying, it was the collapse of his self-esteem and emotional stability that precipitated the crisis with which he found himself confronted. But for that crisis, however, he would never have begun the quest that led him abroad and caused him, eventually, to reexamine all of his assumptions about what it meant to be alive.

The medical profession, by its own admission, could do nothing more for him; his fate, his doctors told him, was out of their hands. So if not science, then perhaps religion. Tōyama introduced Nakamura to Nakahara Tōjū, otherwise known as Nantembō, a Rinzai abbot renowned for his hard, often physical, discipline. Nantembō was, famously, spiritual mentor to generals Nogi Maresuke and Kodama Gentarō, the two most celebrated army heroes of the Russo-Japanese War.

The abbot, upon meeting Nakamura and listening to his plea for help, delivered an opinion similar in content to that already delivered by Tōyama. "Imbecile!" he shouted. Nakamura looked on in stunned silence as Nantembō stomped out of the room.

Nakamura also called on the Christian theologian Ebina Danjō, then pastor at a nearby Congregational church. A native of Fukuoka, Ebina was a friend of Nakamura's father. He had discovered Christianity as a teenager by way of a U.S. Civil War veteran turned evangelist named Leroy Lansing James, and after graduating from Dōshisha English School in Kyoto, where he studied directly under the school founder and prominent Christian educator Niijima Jō, he became one of the founding members of the Congregational Church of Japan. In his later years, Ebina would be called back to his alma mater, now formally recognized as Dōshisha University, to serve with distinction as its eighth chancellor.

Ebina recognized the many theological similarities between Judaism and Japan's indigenous Shinto, and these similarities, he passionately believed, were argument enough for the relevance of Christianity to Japanese culture; if Christianity was, as he credited it to be, the pinnacle and culmination of the Judaic tradition, then it could serve the same superlative and culminating purpose in a society whose moral codes were based on Shinto. Among religious leaders, he was a modernist, and his advocacy of Christianity was founded on a desire to bring Japan into the modern world.

Nakamura listened to the pastor's ideas with interest. But even if more hospitable than Nantembō, Ebina had nothing to say that immediately addressed his problems.

After the disappointments of these two excursions, Nakamura retreated to the confines of his study. There he read prodigiously, searching the annals of philosophy, religion, and medical science for anything that might shed light on his predicament. Meanwhile, in spite of his doctors' prognosis and sustained in large part by the strength of his genetic constitution, the months stretched into a year, and one year stretched into the beginning of a second.

Tsuruko, Nakamura's daughter, conceived during his 1904 leave and born the following year while he was back in Manchuria, said later of this time that her father seemed out of place in his own household. "If I wanted to talk to Father, I would seek permission from the corridor before opening the door to his room," she said. His constant but seldom seen presence was, to her, both baffling and frightening.[2]

One day, a friend left him with a copy of a book by an American author named Orison Swett Marden. Tempū identifies the book as *How to Get What You Want*, the earliest extant edition of which, as it is copyrighted 1917 and contains references to the World War, could not have been the one he saw; there may, however, have been an earlier edition.[3]

Marden was a leading proponent of New Thought, a progressive Christian doctrine that allowed for rational speculation regarding the relationship of God to man. In Marden's writings, for example, Christ is discussed as a human thinker and teacher rather than a divine savior, and in addition to the Gospels, Marden extols the writings of Ralph Waldo Emerson, Oliver Wendell Holmes Sr., and William James. His success, however, derived from his ability to make transcendental ideas accessible to the common man through simple and clear prose.

Marden had raised himself out of poverty and into a position of considerable wealth after reading a book by the Scotsman Samuel Smiles titled *Self Help*. Having thus validated the efficacy of self-help and positive thinking to his own satisfaction, he made it his mission to proselytize that efficacy to the world. And in the process of making it known to all who would listen that anyone could achieve whatever he or she most wanted to achieve by exercising unwavering faith in his or her own abilities to do so, he became even wealthier and more successful. His first book, *Pushing to the Front*, published in 1894, was translated into twenty-five languages. The Japanese edition alone sold over 1.5 million copies and came to be held in such high esteem that the Meiji Bureau of Education approved the English edition for use in English-language classrooms.

Marden, a voracious reader, thrived on the stories of self-made men, and these stories he ingeniously molded to fit his message and to demonstrate that the weight of history sided with his ideas. He authored over sixty books and published a widely read periodical called *Success* magazine, all infused with an almost over-the-top enthusiasm. Like all of the best motivational writers, his optimism is infectious, and it survives him in the work of the next generation of New Thought understudies: the spark that Samuel Smiles ignited in him, he passed on, if indirectly, to the likes of Napoleon Hill, Dale Carnegie, Norman Vincent Peale, and Earl Nightingale. That transmission continues, and doctrines core to New Thought persist, exerting influence on ever more people today in the guise of motivational, human potential, and New Age teachings, workshops, and programs.[4]

During his climb out of poverty, Marden attended, among other academic institutions, Harvard Medical School. His views regarding health and wellness, however, appear to have been strongly influenced by Mary Baker Eddy and Christian Science, for his writings advance the proposition that faith and creative visualization have more power over disease than does medical science.

The optimism expressed in Marden's writings was unlike any Nakamura had so far encountered, and he fell readily under its spell. As indicated by his decisions to visit the Zen abbot Nantembō and the Christian pastor Ebina, he was as much in search of mental and spiritual relief as he was relief from physical symptoms; and where both those men of conventional religion had failed to inspire in him either hope or solace, the bold prose of this American ideologue succeeded.

Then again, it could also be said that almost all of the new knowledge and technologies of the day were coming from the West: if an answer to his quandary did exist, the place to look for it, almost certainly, would be on the other side of the world. Nakamura could no longer rest until he had pursued that possibility to either its validation or its elimination. He would, he decided, meet this man, Marden. But in order to do so, he would first need to travel to the United States.

Nakamura Saburō was pale, gaunt, and physically drained. He exhibited the classic symptoms of a tubercular patient, including a low but persistent fever and a stubborn cough that occasionally brought up blood. To leave home and country in this precarious state of health was to tempt fate; it was an act to be interpreted as either extraordinary bravery or out-and-out folly, and family and friends, he well knew, were more than likely to be of the folly persuasion. Consequently, he kept his plans to himself until the last minute.

Tuberculosis is contagious, and Nakamura was an acknowledged public health liability. Restrictions had been placed on where and how he could travel internally, let alone internationally, and upon his return from Korea, the authorities had reclaimed his passport.

The Genyōsha, however, had ways of dealing with such inconveniences. Availing himself of the society's assistance, he smuggled himself out of Japan aboard a freighter to Shanghai. His family was not to hear from him for another five years.

During a monthlong hiatus in Shanghai, Nakamura purchased a Chinese identity and obtained a counterfeit Chinese passport under the name Sun Yilang. The characters 孫 (sun) and 逸 (yi) are the same first two characters in the name Sun Yat-sen (yat is the Cantonese reading of the Mandarin yi), while the final character, 郎 (lang), is the rō in Saburō, a character commonly used in Japanese names but rarely in Chinese ones. The story line under which he was to travel was that he was a half-brother to Sun Yat-sen, born to one of their father's concubines, and that he was traveling to the United States to learn the cigar trade.

The alias and the story may well have been granted with Sun's blessing; Nakamura had, after all, once served as Sun's bodyguard, and the Genyō-sha continued to support Sun's revolutionary activities. In any event, the name is to merge uncannily with destiny five years later when, under the most unpredictable of circumstances, Sun and Nakamura meet again.

In May, Nakamura boarded a steamship bound for New York. He gives the year as 1909 but, for reasons explained in my Introduction, it was probably 1908.

The journey, Tempū tells us, lasted ninety-three days. Details are sparse, but given his condition, it must have been an excruciating ordeal. The voyage would have taken him across the South China Sea and through the Strait of Malacca to the Bay of Bengal. He would have then crossed the Arabian Sea and the Red Sea to the Suez Canal, from where he would have sailed the length of the Mediterranean to the Atlantic. And finally, he would have crossed to the American continent. He would have, I imagine, spent most of the voyage below deck in his bunk, although I also envision him wandering ashore, curiosity winning out over discomfort, in ports of call, the list of which almost certainly included Hong Kong, Singapore, Penang, Colombo, Goa, Port Said, Marseilles, and Liverpool.

Soon after arriving in New York in August, he made contact, Tempū informs us, with the diplomat Yoshizawa Kenkichi. At face value, this statement appears relatively benign, for Yoshizawa was both an acquaintance and a distant relative. But what Nakamura does not say in so many words is that Yoshizawa was not in New York. He was in Tokyo, serving as secretary to the policy bureau in the foreign ministry; this we know from Yoshizawa's meticulous memoir, *Gaikō Rokujū-Nen* (Sixty Years of Foreign Service). Thus, communications between the two could only have occurred by way of the embassy in New York over the embassy's telegraph, and Nakamura does allude to the embassy and embassy channels.

The terms of Nakamura and Yoshizawa's association, inhabiting, as they did, opposite sides of the law, must have been delicate and a little strained. Then again, the Japanese foreign ministry had no legal jurisdiction over Nakamura or his movements as long as he remained on foreign soil. Furthermore, scrutiny of national borders was far laxer than today, and Nakamura, as long as he abided by local laws, was in no great danger of deportation.

That said, Nakamura's relatively unencumbered access to diplomatic channels, despite his impaired legal status, is one of the enigmas of his story. Was the Genyōsha's involvement, perhaps, partly to answer for this? I suspect so. Yoshizawa was not a member of the Genyōsha; however, his father-in-law, the senior statesman Inukai Tsuyoshi, numbered among Tōyama Mitsuru's closest political associates. Furthermore, Yamaza Enjirō, Nakamura's judo sempai at the Meidōkan, was one of Yoshizawa's seniors within the Foreign Service, as well as one of its most prominent rising stars.

Just two years older than Nakamura, Yoshizawa had already served two diplomatic assignments in China and one in London. During his China postings, he had contended with the Boxer Rebellion and observed, first-hand, the Japanese siege of Lushun during the Russo-Japanese War. Again, I can only speculate, but it seems probable that Nakamura and Yoshizawa crossed paths at least once at the Japanese legation in Beijing. Yoshizawa was married to Inukai Tsuyoshi's eldest daughter, and in 1929, twenty-one years after the current point in our story, his father-in-law, upon becoming prime minister, would appoint him foreign minister; in that capacity, he was to voice his principled but highly unpopular opposition to the Japanese creation of Manchukuo. Then, in 1945, as a privy councilor, he would be among the inner circle of rational moderates who prevailed upon the emperor to accept Allied demands for unconditional surrender. His diplomatic career would span sixty years and would include appointments as consular general to Beijing and as ambassador to France, Indochina, and Taiwan.[5]

Upon seeking out Marden, Nakamura discovered that the man did not grant audiences easily. While he waited for his persistent entreaties to take effect, he rested, explored New York, and acclimated himself to his new surroundings. In September, on Yoshizawa's recommendation, he traveled to Philadelphia to undergo an alternative therapy that, from his description, appears to have been osteopathy; if so, the institution he visited would have been the Philadelphia College and Infirmary of Osteopathy, predecessor of today's Philadelphia College of Osteopathic Medicine. But whatever the therapy, it had little effect on his condition, and he came away unimpressed.

Finally, in November, Marden agreed to see him. The meeting took place in Marden's uptown office at Success Publishing. It lasted for less than one hour.

Nakamura had traveled a long way in the hope that Marden could counsel him on how to deal with his illness, he explained. Marden had written that faith and the power of the mind were sufficient to deal with any affliction, even those beyond the current reaches of science and medicine; Nakamura needed to know if Marden believed that the same principle might apply to his condition, and if so, what he needed to do. What were the practical steps that he needed to take in order to begin his journey back to health?

"How many times have you read my book?" Marden asked.

"At least ten," Nakamura replied.

"Then keep reading it until you know it by heart. Read it until you can recite it from cover to cover. Read it until you can say what is written on any given page."

"But I don't have that kind of time," Nakamura objected. "Were I to undertake such a task, I should be dead long before I finish."

"Ah! In that case, all the more reason to do as I say. For then, even though you may die trying, you will die a happy man."

Nakamura questioned his own ears; perhaps he had misunderstood what the man had said. "No," Marden insisted, "you understood correctly. This is the best advice that I can give you, and if you take it, I can assure you that either you will be cured, or you will die in the knowledge that you had restored yourself in the eyes of God and to the harmony of His universe."

Nakamura departed Marden's office rudely disillusioned. Having finally met the author whose book had induced him to travel halfway around the world, that man had proven himself to be no more than a hollow prophet. His method, it seemed, when stripped to its essence, promised not tangible results but religious salvation. "Is this, then, how Marden gets what he wants?" Nakamura wondered.

Tempū is harsh in his assessment of Marden, but the longer view suggests that several forces may have been at play. Marden is known to have been far more effective as a writer than as a speaker, and he is also known to have been somewhat reclusive, a man most comfortable when holed up in the citadel of his ideas. Furthermore, Marden may have found Nakamura's story—the story of how he, a Japanese man in failing health, had, after reading Marden's book, traveled all the way to New York just for this interview—difficult to swallow whole. Then again, Nakamura's expectations, inflated by his own sense of urgency, may also have been too great. Suffice it to say that, for whatever reason or combination of reasons, the chemistry between the two of them was nonbonding; Marden and Nakamura did not click.

Nevertheless, Marden's message, we can see from Tempū's later teachings, was not entirely without effect. Nakamura Tempū's mind-body philosophy espouses a form of "mind over body" and "power of positive thinking" doctrine that appears, at least superficially, to echo Marden, as well as others of his lineage. Tempū's teachings regarding the primacy of mind, however, are qualified in a way that Marden's are not. He emphasizes the importance of the mind leading the body in any endeavor, insisting, for example, that the restoration of the body to health can only be achieved when the mind is not only open to the possibility of health but has unshakable faith in the body's ability to heal itself—a proposition with which Orison Swett Marden would almost certainly have agreed. But he also insists that the body needs to be trained and conditioned in order to respond to the mind's suggestions. Positive thinking, in other words, is necessary but insufficient to the restoration of sympathetic agreement between mind and body; life practices that engage the body and that strengthen and encourage physical sensitivity toward the natural order constitute an equally important part of the puzzle.

The candle of hope he had pursued all the way to America now extinguished, Nakamura's physical condition worsened. Not only was he sick and alone in a foreign land, but having to contend with New York costs of living, he was also running out of money.

Even so, acting upon another introduction provided by Yoshizawa,[6] he took it upon himself to visit Boston and to call on Hereward Carrington, a prominent investigator of psychic phenomena. English by birth, Carrington was four years Nakamura's junior. His first book, *The Physical Phenomena of Spiritualism,* published the year before, had caused a minor sensation for its ruthless exposure of fraudulent practices associated with Spiritualism and some of its better-known psychics. Carrington was a healthy skeptic: as a prominent member of the American Society for Psychical Research, he advocated research into what could be identified as genuine psychic phenomena while also stressing the need to winnow the wheat from the chaff. He went on to become a prolific writer, publishing over thirty-five major works and many more articles and pamphlets during the course of his career.

Still reeling from the disappointment of his meeting with Marden, Nakamura was pleasantly surprised by Carrington's sympathy for his cause. Carrington listened with interest to Nakamura's story and praised him for his sense of purpose. "America's young men and women would do well to learn from you," he said. "All they care about is the pursuit of wealth and the acquisition of material comforts, while you are risking all to understand the nature of the mind. I tip my hat to you for the laudability of your endeavor."

Carrington's praise, Nakamura recognized, was genuine. But he was also conceding that answers to the questions Nakamura was asking were beyond the scope of his own research. It was not the message that Nakamura had hoped to hear.

Relief from Nakamura's financial concerns came, just when his money was almost gone, by way of the embassy, in the form of an introduction to a young Chinese man named Li Zongshun. Li was in New York under instructions from his wealthy Cantonese father to secure a medical degree from Columbia University's school of medicine. The problem was, he spoke only rudimentary English. He had contacted several foreign embassies, including the Embassy of Japan, to let them know that he was looking for an interpreter, and Yoshizawa, when he saw the posting—evidently forwarded by telegraph to Tokyo—thought immediately of Nakamura.

Li, Nakamura quickly gathered, was uninterested in academic pursuits. Secure in the knowledge that he stood to someday inherit his father's enormous wealth, he harbored no intention of pursuing medicine as a career. But then, he was also far from ill disposed toward life in New York, and together with three concubines, he had taken over a block of rooms in one of New York's better hotels and was actively participating in the city's nightlife and entertainment scenes.

Li's original offer, by Nakamura's account, was a retainer of $500 per month to help him with his homework. But Nakamura struck an even more lucrative deal: for $1,000 per month, he would attend all classes and take all exams on Li's behalf. After all, to the school faculty and administrators, all Orientals looked alike. Given that $1,000, at this time, was more than most middle-class American families made in a year, the accuracy of the amount warrants skepticism. When Nakamura cites his figures, he is speaking some forty-plus years after the fact; possibly, he is exaggerating to match 1950s price indexes, or possibly, his memory is simply in error. Whatever the actual amount, however, it was enough to make money the least of Nakamura's concerns.

The Chinese man's elected field of study was ear, nose, and throat, for which Columbia had a separate college. Once inside this center of learning, however, and while fulfilling his obligations to his mentor, Nakamura also enrolled in the school of general medicine under his own assumed Chinese name so that he could pursue studies more directly relevant to his condition.

Columbia's laxity over admissions, as well as the brevity of the programs offered, point to just how new the field of medical science was. Enormous strides were being made in physics and chemistry, but an empirical science of health, disease, and the human body, stripped of superstition, was still something of a new frontier. Consequently, Nakamura Saburō was able to successfully complete Li's courses by the end of the following summer, and his own courses three months later. By Christmas of the following year, he had come away with two degrees: a master's in ENT, this in the name of his benefactor, Li Zongshun, and a PhD in general medicine under his assumed name, Sun Yilang.

In the 1950s, a Tempūkai member introduced Tempū to a visiting Chinese man, a Columbia professor of Eastern religions, and the ensuing conversation inevitably touched on Nakamura's attendance of the university's medical school more than forty years earlier. Nakamura's doctorial certificate had not survived the remainder of his travels abroad, and he asked the professor if he would check the school's records when he returned to New York. Several months passed before a letter arrived in the mail; the professor had visited the medical school and found that, sure enough, a doctorate in general medicine was on record as having been issued to one Sun Yilang.[7]

Regardless of the infancy of medical science or the brevity of the courses of study, for a nonnative English speaker of no exceptional academic qualification to have achieved this distinction, especially given that all the while he was also dealing with the symptoms of advanced tuberculosis, was an extraordinary feat. Nothing focuses the mind, it is said, like the realization of one's mortality, and Nakamura appears to have exemplified that rule: he had pursued his study of medicine as though his life depended on it.

His achievement, however, was of little personal consolation, since what he did not come away with was a renewal of hope or any suggestion of a possible cure. Studies at an American citadel of learning, supposedly representative of the forefront of human knowledge, had revealed to him no more than what he had already been told many times before: tuberculosis was incurable, and the prognosis for those afflicted with tuberculosis, whether stated in months or in years, was death.

The person most delighted with Nakamura's achievement, however, was Li Zongshun. Upon receiving the diploma that Nakamura had earned for him, Li paid to Nakamura a bonus equal to, we are told, the eight months of wages Nakamura had already received, or an additional $8,000. If correct, Nakamura's total gain of $16,000 from this affair would have made him a wealthy man—wealthy enough, for example, to afford the purchase of prime Manhattan real estate. While reserving judgment, I remain skeptical. Easier to accept is the claim that the amount, whatever it was, proved sufficient to keep him solvent for the subsequent duration of his travels abroad.

With nothing to keep him in New York, Nakamura crossed the Atlantic again. His decision to go to London next may have been prompted by news he would have received in February 1910 that Yoshizawa was to be posted to London for a second time. If so, however, Yoshizawa's mid-April arrival, by way of the Trans-Siberian Railway with family in tow, was to miss Nakamura by a month, for by then, Nakamura had already moved on. But Nakamura's judo sempai Yamaza Enjiro was already settled in

London as embassy councilor; he and Nakamura would have almost certainly broken bread together and shared stories late into the evening. This would not be the last time their paths were to intersect.

In London, Nakamura attended a lecture on the relationship between the nervous system and the mind given by a Canadian-born U.S. journalist named H. Addington Bruce. While Bruce had no academic credentials in medical science, he had written a popular introduction to the new science of psychology titled *The Riddle of Personality*. The book had sold well, and he would go on to write a series of books in the same vein with titles such as *Scientific Mental Healing* (1911), *Adventurings in the Psychical* (1914), *Sleep and Sleeplessness* (1915), *Psychology and Parenthood* (1915), *Nerve Control and How to Gain It* (1918), and *Self Development, Handbook for the Ambitious* (1921).

One of the ideas Nakamura took away from Bruce's lecture, the concept that the nervous system serves as the bridge between mind and body, was to figure, years later, in the formulation of his mind-body philosophy. Following the lecture, he sought out the lecturer, and the two men conversed. The conversation was to fuel yet another disappointment.

Bruce, at thirty-eight, was two years Nakamura's senior, but in terms of maturity by way of experience, he was no match. Nakamura Saburō, having lived most of his adult years in close proximity—first in war, now in sickness—to the specter of death, was by far the more seasoned realist of the two. Bruce's work, which was also influenced by New Thought philosophy, was largely journalistic; he was reporting on newly emergent trends and providing commentary on these trends without having fully tested them himself.

"Don't think about your problems," was Bruce's advice. "Just forget."

Nakamura was well enough aware of the mechanics of mind to recognize that this injunction, just in its formulation, was counterproductive: to tell the mind to forget is only to reinforce the image of that which is to be forgotten.

"Easy for him to say," Nakamura thought. "Just how does one go about forgetting the fact that he is dying? Especially when the fever and cough he carries serve as constant reminders."

One day, while reading a newspaper inside London's Japan Club, Nakamura fell into conversation with a physician of some status within Europe's expatriate Japanese community. The man, named Kimura, took an instant liking to Nakamura and insisted that his travels include Paris. Paris, after all, was the acknowledged cultural and intellectual capital of the world; it would be a shame were Nakamura, having come this far, to miss it. Kimura had lived in Paris prior to London, and his outgoing and entertaining personality had endeared him to a substantial network among the city's elite. The plan was sealed when he provided Nakamura with a letter of introduction to none other than the actress Sarah Bernhardt.

Mark Twain is said to have said, "There are five kinds of actresses: bad actresses, fair actresses, good actresses, great actresses—and then there is Sarah Bernhardt."[8] Sixty-five years old when Nakamura Saburō met her, Bernhardt was legendary. Having achieved fame at the Comédie Française while in her early twenties, she had gone on to become perhaps the first global entertainment superstar, touring Britain, the United States, South America, and Australia, as well as the rest of Europe. Everywhere she went, she mesmerized her audiences, and kings, emperors, presidents, intellectuals, inventors, and financial barons all sought her company.

Almost as legendary as her acting ability was her lust for life. By even the most modern standards, she was a liberated woman, her lovers including a staggering lineup of actors, artists, intellectuals, financiers, and nobles, and the stories circulating around these liaisons providing delightfully scandalous material for the tabloids in Paris, London, and New York.

As to be expected of a renowned actress and courtesan, Bernhardt was also a shrewd judge of character, and so, despite Nakamura's sickly appearance, she immediately spotted both his strength and his charm. One who made her living by putting on the roles of others, Bernhardt recognized sincerity when she saw it. Nakamura may have been carrying the angel of death on his shoulder, but he was also engaged with the mystery of life, and the intensity of that engagement showed.

Moreover, a traveler of the world herself, she was better equipped than most of her contemporaries to appreciate not only the physical distance but also the social and cultural distance he had traveled prior to reaching her doorstep. He was welcome, she graciously insisted, to call her dwelling at Boulevard Pereire home for as long as he wished.

Paris at the end of this first decade of the twentieth century was ranked by almost everyone who knew it as the most vibrant metropolis in the world. Lavished with the accumulated prosperity of almost forty years of relative peace under the auspices of the French Third Republic, it was the acknowledged center of European culture and a magnet for artists and intellectuals. It was also the intellectual clearinghouse for the plethora of new ideas being generated within the greater European community.

The march of human progress tells us that even the best of ideas are impermanent and largely beholden to the historical context within which they occur. Furthermore, the culling of ideas by society can be a messy affair, and all too often, much of value gets discarded for less than well-thought-out reasons. Many such ideas, however popular in their day, fail to make the cut into longer-term mainstream currents of intellectual development.

One such body of ideas is contained in the work of the German biologist and philosopher Hans Adolf Eduard Driesch. Driesch, in antithesis to the Cartesian worldview and the mechanistic trajectory of scientific inquiry that it spawned, advocated a "vitalistic" approach to biological science: that is, in the tradition of Aristotle, Kant, and Hegel, he proposed that the phenomenon of life, because it was inherently self-organizing, could best be explained by the existence of a unique force, an élan vital that he called "vril." This vril, he posited, was inherently intelligent and teleological; its function was similar to that of the vital energy the Indian sages called *prana* (Driesch had spent time in India), the Chinese *qi,* and the Japanese *ki.*[9]

Bernhardt recommended Driesch to Nakamura and provided him with a letter of introduction, and Nakamura embarked on the short journey to Heidelberg in eager anticipation. Driesch, after having established his reputation as one of the foremost biological researchers of his day, was now focused almost solely on the pursuit of academic philosophy; surely, this great man of learning, Nakamura thought, could shed some light, based on new knowledge, on the questions confronting him.

Driesch met Nakamura graciously and as an equal. "The questions you are asking," he said, "are of importance, not just to you but to all of humanity. Who is first to answer them, whether it is you or I or another, is not nearly of as much consequence as the contribution to be made by them to the greater common good. Let us agree to the continued pursuit of these questions, each in his particular way. I shall be anxious to hear of any progress you may have made."

If warmed and flattered, Nakamura also understood he was being told, once again, that the cutting edge of Western thought fell far short of his needs.

Nakamura's meeting with Driesch, however, was to have a sequel. Many years later, in the 1930s, Nakamura would meet Driesch twice again, during visits by Driesch to Japan. At the second of these meetings, through an interpreter arranged by the German embassy, Nakamura explained the tenets of his practical method of mind-body unification. Driesch listened with riveted attention. After all, the simple fact that Nakamura was alive and well was proof enough he had successfully answered the questions they had discussed that day so many years before. Shortly afterward, Driesch saw to it that Nakamura was awarded an honorary degree in philosophy from the University of Berlin.

Bernhardt's house was host to a stream of her eclectic friends and notable admirers, and through the animated living room discussions sparked by these visitors, Nakamura was exposed to a number of ideas and intellectual currents then in circulation. Bernhardt told Nakamura the story of how Immanuel Kant, as a child, suffered a debilitating and painful skeletal deformity, and how he was told by the family physician that, while his pain was real and could not be ignored, to complain of it served no constructive purpose and only caused his parents to worry—that rather than directing his attention toward his suffering, he would be better served to be thankful that he was alive. Kant took this advice to heart and made a practice of counting his blessings over his discomforts. His adoption of this practice was, he would later say, an important early step on the path that eventually lead him to academic discourse and made of him one of the leading philosophers of the nineteenth century. The story made a strong impression on Nakamura, for it appears often in his talks. Tempū, like Kant, was to take issue with the assumption plaguing Western philosophy that the domains of mind and body somehow inhabited opposite sides of an unbridgeable divide.

While at Bernhardt's, Nakamura also learned of the work of Max Planck. Planck, in 1900, had applied statistical mechanics to problems associated with black-body radiation and observed that electromagnetic energy emissions occur in multiples of a mathematical constant, the value of which he symbolized with the letter h. Five years later, in 1905, Planck's constant would be put to use by an obscure patent office clerk in Bern, Switzerland, to explain the photoelectric effect, the publication of which explanation would give birth to quantum theory and quantum mechanics.

Paris, like the rest of Europe, was abuzz with talk of these developments, and Nakamura absorbed what he heard with great interest. Quantum theory, as well as the special theory of relativity, also published by Einstein in 1905, relied on mathematics sufficiently sophisticated to place them beyond the grasp of most ordinary mortals, and Nakamura was no exception; his explanations of the significance of Planck's constant as recorded in transcripts of his talks portray a muddled understanding. Nevertheless, taken in context, these explanations serve a purpose. Energy, he asserts, is that which mind and body hold in common, and the discovery of a universal constant behind energy's manifestations as both wave and particle, he further implies, constitutes evidence for the existence of a primordial, vital energy—Driesch's vril and the yogis' prana.

Another set of new ideas causing waves at this time were those emanating from the work of Sigmund Freud, and Bernhardt introduced

Nakamura to a professor of psychological science at the University of Lyon named Lindler.[10] Like Marden and Bruce, Lindler was intrigued with the impressionability of the subconscious mind and the implications that impressionability held for the development of human potential. He was almost certainly influenced by and may even have been a student of Émile Coué, the popular proponent of autosuggestion,[11] for Lindler explained to Nakamura the concept of autosuggestion and taught him how to apply it. Tempū would later incorporate what he learned from Lindler into his litany of mind-body unification practices as what he called the "autosuggestive command method" (meirei anji-hō). It works on the principle that the subconscious mind is most impressionable when the conscious mind is least active, and that window of inactivity, in the normal course of the day, is during the moments just before and just after sleep.

The method works as follows.[12] The first step is to identify some positive change you wish to effect or some goal you wish to achieve. These changes or goals are best conceived in terms of the emotional and psychological gratification their achievement will bring rather than a specific, real result. For example, if the issue is wealth, then the goal is best stated in terms of feelings of abundance and self-sufficiency rather than a specific monetary sum (monetary gain is, after all, relative and not guaranteed to satisfy someone convinced of their own state of insufficiency).

The next step is to summarize your goal or desired effect in a one-sentence, second-person command. Thus, if my goal were to overcome some dissatisfaction with my circumstances, I might summarize this by saying, "You will have the energy and perseverance to overcome [a particular challenge]." Other examples are "You will be secure in the knowledge that you can achieve [some desired goal or outcome]" or "You will be competent and successful at [your work]." To elicit positive results, these statements should strictly avoid the use of negatives. Also, your wish should be described not as a present reality but as something to be realized or achieved in the future—thus "you will" or "you shall" as opposed to "you are."

The third step, just before going to sleep, is to look at yourself in the mirror (you may wish to keep a small mirror at your bedside for this purpose), to address yourself out loud and by name, and to deliver the command you have decided to use. So, I might look at myself in the mirror and say aloud, "Steve, you will have the energy and perseverance to overcome [what is challenging you]."

Finally, upon waking the following morning, immediately affirm to yourself, silently, and in the first person, that you have achieved your desired outcome. So in my case, I might say to myself, "Yes, I now have the energy and perseverance to handle [all of life's challenges]."

Continue this practice daily until you are satisfied that you have achieved the results you desire; then identify a new goal or an intended result and start over again.

In my experience, results may come as early as the third day but are more likely to occur within the first two weeks of practice; ultimate fulfillment may take longer. And, of course, the more abstract and open-ended the nature of your stated outcome, the longer that statement will serve. Tempū is said to have told himself every night for more than forty years, "Your faith [in the universal order] will become stronger" (*shinnen-ga tsuyoku naru*).

The method's effectiveness is also cumulative, since each success— each realization of an intended result—reaffirms and strengthens your confidence in your ability to produce results. And the greater your confidence in your ability, as well as in the effectiveness of the method, the faster and more complete your results are likely to be. Thus, while it is useful in the realization of practical goals, more importantly, the autosuggestive command method also demonstrates something of the power of human intention, a power that we usually exercise unknowingly and, all too often, toward the enforcement of negative images and the realization of undesirable consequences.

The practice is malleable to almost any purpose, grand or minor, and it invites experimentation and originality. One of my favorite examples, one given me by a young Tempūkai member, is "You will become lucky."

As luck is in the eye of the beholder, this statement is almost guaranteed to become self-fulfilling.

In spite of all the wisdom and encouragement shared by Bernhardt and the learned men to whom she introduced him, Nakamura's health continued to decline. By spring, even menial tasks required all his strength to complete. He was coughing blood with greater frequency and spending more hours in bed. The miles he had traveled in his search for knowledge and his encounters with accomplished people had all been for naught; the time had come to throw in the towel. "Better to die at home than in a foreign land," he thought. He would return to Japan.

Bidding good-bye to Bernhardt over her entreaties to stay longer, he booked passage on a freighter from Marseilles that would take him as far as Penang. From there, he would find further passage to Shanghai, where he would join up, once again, with his Genyōsha associates and wait out the remainder of the five-year statutory limit on his contravention of quarantine before returning to Japan. Thoughts of the torturously long ocean voyage ahead, to be followed by even longer months and years in exile, weighed heavily on his spirits, and the odds on his ever seeing Japan again, he well recognized, were long indeed.

The date Nakamura gives for his departure from Marseilles was May 25, 1911, but, for the reasons given in my Introduction, was almost certainly 1910. The day was dark and rainy, and as he boarded the ship, he felt, he says, lonelier and more forlorn than he had at any other time. Had the voyage proceeded as planned, there would be no more story to tell.

Providence, however, had other plans. Ten days into the voyage, as they rounded the island of Sicily, the captain received word by wireless that an Italian freighter had run aground in the Suez, and consequently, they docked in Alexandria to wait out the estimated five-day delay. That delay would make all the difference in the outcome of Nakamura's story.

6.
"CERTAINLY"

Aboard ship, Nakamura is befriended by a Filipino seaman with the entreaty that "We Asians understand each other. We should stick together." When Nakamura is too weak to make it to the ship's canteen, the seaman brings food to him in his bunk. And when they dock in Alexandria with time on their hands, he prevails upon Nakamura to accompany him to the pyramids of Giza.

Arriving in Cairo late in the afternoon, they put up at an inn for the evening. During the night, however, Nakamura suffers a massive hemorrhage, coughing up a small basinful of blood. Too weak to rise in the morning, he sends the sailor on to the pyramids alone.[1]

The hotel's owner and staff are Indian, and midmorning, the manager, out of concern, arouses him and encourages him to eat something. At the manager's insistence, he makes his way down to the dining room and orders a bowl of soup.

The dining room is empty but for one other table, occupied by a slight dark-skinned man with a long white beard. The man is wearing a dark purple gown over a white sari, and he is attended by two young Indian boys from the hotel staff, one waiting at his knee while the other waves a large peacock-feather fan over him in an attempt to lessen the effects of the desert heat.

As Nakamura sits, sullenly sipping his soup, their eyes meet, and the old man's face twinkles.

"Won't you join me?" he asks, in English. "No need for you to eat alone."

Consenting, Nakamura moves himself to a seat across from him at his table. The man asks where he is from, where he has been, and where he is going; Nakamura replies with simple, one sentence answers. Then, as the conversation lulls, the man's gaze becomes serious.

"You have a large, dark spot in your right lung," he says.

Nakamura is startled. He has said nothing of his physical condition. The man, still holding him in his gaze, continues.

"If you return to Japan in your current condition, you'll be digging your own grave."

The admonition, spoken with unassuming candor, draws Nakamura into the man's confidence. "Yes, you're quite right," he responds. "But unfortunately, my condition is incurable. I'm returning to Japan because I would prefer to die at home rather than abroad."

After a reflective pause, the man picks up again in the same unassuming voice. "Why do you say that you can't be cured?"

Nakamura elaborates. He has tuberculosis, and tuberculosis has no cure. This he knows, because he is versed in medicine: he carries a medical degree from New York's Columbia University.

"So the doctors can't help you?"

"Yes, that's right."

Again, the man pauses. "And why do you assume that theirs is the last word?" he asks.

Nakamura stares blankly back.

"What I mean to say is, are you ready to make up your mind just on the basis of what the doctors say? Or, as you say that you, yourself, are a doctor, maybe the opinion of which you speak is your own, isn't that so?"

Nakamura is dumbfounded. Where this man is from, he does not know, but wherever it is, tuberculosis most certainly exists and is just as incurable there as it is anywhere. What is he suggesting?

The man gently but persuasively continues. "You may think that an early death is the only choice you have left, but from where I sit, I see someone who has yet to discover something important. If you discover that one truth, then there is no reason for you to die before your time. You had better follow me."

According to Sasaki Masando, Tempū would, at this juncture in his story, always pause to dry his eyes and clear the lump that had formed in his throat. He was retrospectively acknowledging that at that moment, years ago in Cairo, his life had hung in the balance of his answer.

Nakamura Saburō was nobody's fool. Schooled in the arts of espionage and serving with valor as a spy, he had looked death in the eye more than once and survived a war by taking the lives of others; now, in the course of his travels, he had also become a man of some academic and intellectual achievement. Yet here he was, sitting with a complete stranger in a foreign land, being asked to unconditionally interrupt his journey and to follow that stranger to an undetermined destination in order to learn who knew what. Under the circumstances, he could be expected to have asked a few discerning questions. Questions such as, "Who are you?" "Follow you where?" "For what purpose?" And, "For how long?"

But Nakamura asked none of these. For the first time since becoming ill, he had just heard someone say to him that all was not lost, that against all hope there was still hope, and that the number of his days may not, after all, be a forgone conclusion. He allows his instincts to answer for him. And this answer makes all the difference.

"Certainly," he says.

Much later, the man, soon to become his mentor and teacher, will tell Nakamura that, above all else, it was this answer that had won him a permanent place in the man's heart. Even so, not until years later would Nakamura come to fully appreciate the extent to which that single word, *certainly*, had determined his future.

"Why I answered as I did, I really can't explain," Tempū would say. "I was moved beyond words. Here I was, an invalid, the kind of ghastly shadow of a person even blood relations will seek to avoid. Just that morning, I had hemorrhaged enough blood to fill the soup bowl in front of me. One look at me would have told anyone that I was not long for this world. What sane person, knowing full well that their charge might croak on them at any time, would invite a man in my condition to accompany them on a long journey? But here was this strange old man with a beard, sitting in front of me, insisting that I follow him so that I might be cured. It was more than I could comprehend. Now that I think about it, the single word that came from my mouth, 'certainly,' was all I could say. It was an expression of shock and amazement."[2]

From the hotel staff, Nakamura learned something of the man and his provenance. His name was Kariappa, and he was a yogi, a revered Indian sage.

"How lucky you are to have been chosen to follow him," he was told. Nakamura reserved judgment: he knew nothing of either India or yoga, nor was he so sure of his luck.

Kariappa's presence in Cairo, Nakamura was also told, was but a stopover on his return from a visit to England, this by invitation from an English nobleman with an interest in Indian philosophy. He had also stopped in Rome, where he had had an audience with Pope Pius X.

Nakamura would also be told, after reaching their destination on the Indian subcontinent, that Kariappa was over 140 years old. Yogis, it was further explained, commonly lived to advanced ages, some as old as 360 years, and in a recording of a talk delivered in 1966, Nakamura Tempū mentions that he understands Kariappa to be alive and well at close to 200.[3]

Kariappa's identity—just who he was and where he fits into the landscape of the Indian spiritual tradition—is an enigma I shall address later; for now, let us continue with the story as Tempū tells it.

Neither did Nakamura know where they were going, nor did he ask; were they to tell him, he reasoned, he would not recognize the place-names given. The journey lasted three months. Kariappa was traveling with a small entourage aboard a yacht placed at his disposal by an Indian maharaja, and the vessel took them through the Suez Canal to the Red Sea, around the Arabian horn, and across the Arabian Sea to Karachi.

In Karachi, they anchored the yacht and ascended the Indus River on a barge drawn from the shore by camels. Then, on camelback, they traveled due east across what is now Rajasthan and Hindustan to Bengal. While Tempū does not say, they probably passed through Jaipur, Agra, and Allahabad. They would almost certainly have visited Benares on the Ganges. From there, they would have journeyed southeast to arrive in Calcutta.

From Calcutta, they headed due north into the foothills of the Himalayas and up to the English hill station of Darjeeling. Again, Tempū does not say, but they probably arrived by rail, for the Darjeeling Himalayan Railway—ranked for close to a century, until the Chinese completed their rail line into Tibet, as the highest railroad in the world—was already in service, and Nakamura, in his condition, would have found the long climb to Darjeeling exceedingly difficult to manage on horseback, let alone on foot.

Tempū alludes to the grandeur of Kanchenjunga, the world's third highest peak, and Ōi Mitsuru, in his account, imagines Nakamura taking in this view from the hills surrounding the village of Gorkhey, their final destination. This, however, is categorically impossible: the hills in question are neither high enough nor close enough to allow a view of the Kanchenjunga massif. The more likely explanation is that he saw the mountain from one of the high points near Darjeeling—perhaps Ghoom, or Tiger Hill.

From Darjeeling, they probably made their way west along ridgetop mountain roads to Pashupatinagar and then descended steep paths into the valley to arrive in Gorkhey. Enfeebled by his sickness, Nakamura would have managed this journey in a state of dazed exhaustion. Furthermore, when he looked around to see where the journey had brought him, his heart must have sunk. He had, it appeared, been delivered to the fringe of civilization.

The village of Gorkhey consisted of a few single-story dwellings arranged along one main street running parallel to a river. Hemmed by high hills—mountains, by most standards—this village and valley were insulated from the forces of history; life there had remained unchanged for centuries and, for all anyone could have foretold, would presumably continue unchanged for centuries to come. Nakamura was no stranger to privation, having survived winters in the hinterlands of Manchuria, but his arrival in this cultural backwater by way of New York, London, and Paris must have caused him to wonder what Gorkhey could possibly offer that those centers of progress could not? Could it really be that, as Kariappa had intimated, this remote hamlet would be the last stop on his search for a cure?

Kariappa's abode, a thatch-roofed hut, sat on a grassy piece of ground just larger than a tennis court, the edge of which fell away abruptly into the river. Nakamura, however, was shown to a nearby stable, the other occupant of which was a goat. This was the first among many rude awakenings. The Indian social order, he learned, was made up of castes, and Kariappa, a Brahmin, belonged to the priestly elite at the high end of that order—whereas Nakamura, a foreigner with no birth-claim to status of any kind, was placed by default on its lowest rungs, along with the Shudra, the caste reserved for servants and slaves. Other than one old man, the man to whom Kariappa had entrusted Nakamura's care, the community took little notice of Nakamura's existence; he and the goat were treated more or less as social equals.

Kariappa, after assigning the duty of looking after Nakamura to the old man, so chosen because he spoke a few words of English, took his leave. Nakamura was told to undress, and his clothes were folded and taken away. To replace them, he was given a sheet of light blue cloth and shown how to wrap and tie it around his waist.

During their journey from Cairo, Nakamura and Kariappa had conversed informally in a manner befitting fellow travelers, but now the rules of their engagement changed. The old man explained to Nakamura that, henceforth, whenever Kariappa came into sight, he was to sit and to bow, as did all Kariappa's students—not the kind of bow with which Nakamura was familiar from his Japanese upbringing, but more a prostration, where one's forehead touched to the ground and one's arms were extended along the ground in front with palms facing down.

Meals consisted of a gruel made from raw millet—wetted in cold water, the millet became soft enough to chew—complemented by a few cooked mountain vegetables. The surrounding fields, Nakamura observed, were given predominantly to the cultivation of rice, but that crop was not for local consumption: it was the village's principle trading commodity. Most of the villagers, he learned, did not even know the taste of rice. With only slight seasonal variation, this standard meal was served twice each day, once at mid-morning and once again in the evening.

The morning following their arrival, Kariappa stopped at Nakamura's stable to ask how he had slept. Nakamura took the opportunity to register a complaint regarding the food. The standard regimen in the sanatoriums of both Europe and Japan, he advised his mentor, included generous portions of animal protein—meat, fish, and dairy. After all, a sick man's body needed to be properly fueled in order to stand up to the disease. Such knowledge may have yet to make its way into these hinterlands, but, clearly, an exception was going to need to be made. Nakamura had lost a full fifty-three pounds (twenty-four kilograms) of body weight since becoming ill. What little resistance to the disease he had left, he needed to keep, and to that end, proper nutrition was key.

Kariappa listened to Nakamura with faint amusement. "Look," he said, pointing to an elephant standing just across the river in the shade. "See how much bigger and stronger he is than you are. Yet he does just fine on a diet of straw.

"Look at the people living here," he continued. "They never get sick. Yet they are all eating the same food we are giving you; in fact, they know nothing but this kind of food."

The argument was less than persuasive; but then, Nakamura understood, the subject was also not open to debate. Furthermore, upon reflection, he realized that he had consumed almost nothing in the way of animal protein since leaving Egypt; this privation he had thought to be a consequence of the journey but now understood to have been intentional.

This was Nakamura's last verbal exchange with his master for some time. He would see Kariappa only from a distance, and when he did, he would bow as the others did until the master passed from view. By day, Nakamura had not the strength to wander far from his hut and passed the time sitting sullenly in the shade. By night, plagued by fever, he slept fitfully. What was he doing here, he wondered. How could he have been induced to come to this godforsaken place?

In this way, a full month passed. Kariappa had yet to say anything to him about his course of study or the all-important truth he was meant to discover. Had he been forgotten? Or perhaps Kariappa had had second thoughts. Perhaps he had discovered another truth, the truth that Nakamura's condition was far more serious than he had originally thought. Perhaps he had decided to let nature take its course.

Nakamura began to weigh his options. Could he get himself to Darjeeling? If so, he could probably make his way back to Calcutta, from where he could secure passage on a steamship headed somewhere—anywhere, as long as it was to the east. But just the mental exercise of constructing this plan was exhausting; its execution, quite out of the question. Like it or not, he was hostage to this valley.

As the second month of his sojourn waned toward a third, Nakamura's patience gave out. He would, he decided, bring matters to a head. Each morning, Kariappa appeared at his door to address the ten or so yogis studying under him, and each morning, when he appeared, the yogis would sit on the green and bow in the prescribed manner. On this particular morning, Nakamura strategically places himself near the path leading from Kariappa's door. When Kariappa walks from his door, he bows, just as the others do. But when the master passes in front of him, he defiantly bobs back up.

Kariappa, who cannot help but notice, stops and turns. But as he does so, the twinkle from his eye throws Nakamura off his game; none of the words he has planned to say come out of his mouth. Instead, he glares at Kariappa like a surprised animal.

"What? You have something to say to me?" the master asks.

Nakamura finds his voice. His stay is going on two full months, he bursts out. What of the promise that Kariappa had made to him in Cairo?

"Did I promise you something in Cairo?" Kariappa answers absentmindedly.

Nakamura skips a breath in astonishment.

"You told me that it was not my time to die. You said that, if I followed you, you would teach me something important—something that I didn't know, but that, if learned, could save me. I have been waiting, day after day, but you have said nothing. What is it that you want from me? How am I to learn without instruction?"

Kariappa exhibits no change in his composure.

"Oh, that," he responds. "Yes, I did say that to you in Cairo. And it's still true. If you learn but one simple truth, you needn't die so soon. I've been ready to begin teaching you since the evening we arrived. But you haven't been ready to learn."

Nakamura gasps. "But that isn't true. This whole time, I have been waiting. Every day, I've wondered, when will my instruction begin? Will today be the day? But each day goes by, and still you say nothing."

Kariappa smiles a faint smile but remains firm. "Evidently I know you better than you know yourself. You think that you're ready to learn when clearly you're not."

Nakamura objects again. His time, he says, has been spent in anticipation.

"Let me show you," Kariappa says. "Go fetch a jug of cold water."

By now, Nakamura's indignation has given way to confusion. Just what is this old man telling him? Gingerly, he steps over and around the still supine backs of the other yogis and makes his way to the edge of the field, where an open fire pit and a roofed preparation stall serve as the yogis' communal kitchen. Under the roof is a large earthenware urn, narrowed at the top, where water is kept. The urn has a detached lining, allowing it to function much like a thermos; Nakamura has noted with interest just how effectively it keeps water inside cool, even during the hottest part of the day. From this urn, he ladles water into a jug, returns, and sets the jug down in front of Kariappa.

"Good. Now fetch a jug of hot water," the master says.

Again, Nakamura obeys. Over one of the fire pits is a simmering iron cauldron; borrowing another earthenware jug, he ladles steaming water from the cauldron into the jug and returns to Kariappa.

"Now," says Kariappa, "pour the hot water into the jug containing the cold water."

Nakamura is incensed. Is he being made fun of?

"You can't be serious. The one jug is already full. Anything I pour into it will just spill over onto the ground."

"Ah. So that much you understand," Kariappa replies.

Nakamura flushes with anger.

"Don't you see," Kariappa continues. "You're just like the jug of cold water. You're so full of your own ideas about what is wrong with you and what it is that you need in order to be cured that anything I tell you will only spill out onto the ground. You're just like the cold water that rejects the hot water from the second jug. You say that you are a doctor. If you're really a doctor, then why are you sick? Would you have me believe that all of your learning has some value when you appear before me in such a sorry state? If I were the patient, would you honestly expect me to trust you, the doctor, if you are unable to cure yourself?"

This is a perspective that Nakamura Saburō has never considered, but he cannot deny its logic. He hangs his head.

"That's better," Kariappa says quietly. "Come to my house this evening. But when you do so, leave your learning at the door. Come to me to like an empty jug. Come to me like a newborn baby, so that neither my time nor yours will be wasted."

So began Nakamura Saburō's formal training in the ways of yoga. That evening, Kariappa gave him some brief instructions and sent him away. The following morning, he arose before dawn and set forth with the other yogis to the river.

The river, even during the hottest months of the year, was icy cold. But each morning, regardless of season or weather, the yogis would wade into the shallows of one of the river's many pools. Each had his own spot in these shallows, a spot where he could sit comfortably, cross-legged, with the waterline at midpoint on his chest. Now, Nakamura too steps gingerly into the cold current and makes his way over the slippery stones in search of a spot to claim as his.

The air temperature is rising almost as quickly as the sun in the sky, but settled into the pool, Nakamura feels the cold of the water penetrate to his core. Nevertheless, through sheer willpower, he remains seated, until, one by one, the other yogis stand up and begin walking toward the shore. The time elapsed, perhaps twenty minutes, has felt like an eternity. Nakamura, lips blue and trembling, follows the others back to the village.

For several weeks, this is the full extent of his practice. The journey to the river and back uses all the strength he can muster, and he spends the remainder of each day in the shade of a huge linden tree.

Then one morning, upon returning from the river to the village, Kariappa beckons him.

"Follow me," he says.

Kariappa, mounted on a donkey, begins up a steep mountain path; Nakamura, on foot, straggles behind.

Each step is painful. From time to time, when Nakamura falls too far behind, Kariappa pats the donkey on its withers and the animal promptly halts. Man and donkey wait until Nakamura catches up. Then Kariappa nudges the donkey with his heel and, in silence, continues on up the path.

As they gain altitude, they are treated to panoramic views of green hills sided with terraced fields. Even in his exhaustion, Nakamura is awed by the spectacle's majesty.

Continuing on, he becomes aware of a dull roar.

"A waterfall," he thinks. The roar grows gradually louder until, upon rounding a corner, the waterfall comes into view. Water hurdles through a notch at the top of a sheer rock wall and falls a hundred feet (thirty meters) into a basin below, rainbows playing in the spray rising off the basin's edge.

Kariappa leads Nakamura to a rock outcrop beside the basin.

"Sit here," he says, putting his mouth to Nakamura's ear. "Just stay put. Don't wander off. I will come back for you in the evening."

The waterfall, Nakamura Saburō is told, was to be his designated place of practice, and by the third morning, the climb had become routine. A couple of weeks later, Kariappa outfits him with a rope harness, into which he then places a large rock; this, Nakamura is to transport on his back in both directions. Each day, he follows Kariappa up the path to the waterfall, unstraps the rock from his back, and takes his seat on the ledge. Each evening, when Kariappa returns, he lifts the rock in its harness onto his back for the return trek to the village.

"While you are sitting, think about whatever you want to think about," Kariappa instructs him. "But you must stay seated until I return." In the beginning, the roar of the falls is such that Nakamura is unable to think about much at all. Soon, however, his thoughts begin to wander. He thinks of his past. He thinks of home. He wonders, will he ever see his family

Tempū, in his eighties, demonstrating how he sat beside the waterfall in the Himalayan foothills.

(with permission from the Tempu Society, a nonprofit public interest foundation)

again? Seated amid these starkly beautiful surroundings, he feels naked, helpless, and excruciatingly lonely.

One morning as they set off, Kariappa remarks, as is his habit, on what a beautiful day it is. The teacher's comment, as Nakamura understands it, is a pleasantry, a nod to social convention.

"It would be nicer," he replies, "if my head did not hurt so much."

This answer, or something in the same vein, has also become something of a matter of habit, but for the first time, Kariappa does not let it pass. From atop his donkey, he turns and looks down sternly into Nakamura's eyes. "I wasn't asking about your state of health," he says. "I can see that you don't feel well just by looking at you; you don't need to remind me. Nevertheless, don't you agree that it is a beautiful day?"

Nakamura is not persuaded. "For you," he says, "the day may be beautiful. But for me, it could be better."

Kariappa persists. "Fool," he replies, curtly. "Don't you see that whether or not the day is beautiful is up to you? It's your choice. You can have beautiful days, or you can have ugly ones. You can have good days or bad days. And yet you insist on choosing to have bad days over good."

Nakamura protests. Surely the master does not mean to say that his sickness is of his own choosing. If that were so, he would have given up on being sick years ago.

"Look," Kariappa says. "Every morning, I ask you, how are you this morning? And every morning, you tell me your head hurts. Or you didn't sleep well. Or your fever is higher than usual. But don't you see, all of those things are sensations that originate in your body. Why do you need to allow physical sensations associated with your disease to affect you emotionally and mentally? That your head should hurt is no excuse for the day to be anything less than beautiful.

"Do this," he continues. "Whether or not you believe that the day is beautiful is unimportant; from now on, when I say that the day is beautiful, just agree with me. When I ask you how you are, just answer, 'Very well, thank you.'"

This is an order, and Nakamura understands the conversation to now be over. Reluctantly, as they set off up the path as usual, he decides to give the old man the benefit of the doubt. The next morning, when Kariappa greets him and asks how he feels, he musters the strength to reply, "Quite well, thank you." And when the master comments on what a beautiful day it is, Nakamura, if less than enthusiastically, agrees.

"That is better," his teacher says.

"You are afraid of dying, aren't you?"

They are seated along the path on a bright, clear morning. Kariappa has a way of asking him difficult questions, Nakamura reflects, just when he least expects them.

Not so long ago, Nakamura had thrived on beginning each day not knowing if he would still be alive by evening. He had even refused the blindfold offered him by his captors when facing a firing squad. Danger and proximity to death had been a source of strength, inspiring in him the will to fight.

But tuberculosis is a different kind of enemy. It has sapped him of his physical resilience, reducing him to a ghost of the man he once was and claiming his pride and dignity. Once again, Kariappa has seen into his heart with uncanny accuracy. The source of Nakamura's existential malaise is not his miserable fever and cough but fear—its grip and the power it exercises over him.

"What is it about death that you find so frightening?" An obvious question, but not one that Nakamura, until now, has ever considered. The only answer apparent is, he is afraid of death because death is frightening.

"When you go to sleep at night, do you fear you may not wake up in the morning?"

"Of course not."

"And while asleep, are you aware of the passage of time?"

"No. Not at all."

"So when you're asleep, are you not, in fact, dead to the world?"

Those last words take Nakamura momentarily back to Manchuria. After leaving Harbin and before his return to Japan on leave, he had been posted with Hashitsune and Kondō to the front, south of Mukden. They were stationed in a small city enclosed by ancient fortress walls, and atop these walls stood a lookout tower. One day, Nakamura climbed to the top of the tower.

No sooner did he reach the top than a bullet whistled past his ear. The tower was fully exposed and offered him no place to hide. Quickly assessing his options, he did what he had to do: he jumped.

The next instant—what he assumed to be the next instant—he opened his eyes to find himself on an army cot in a dark room with Hashitsune seated beside him.

Seeing that he was awake, Hashitsune expressed relief. "We were afraid you weren't coming back," he said. "You've been out for three days."

Just as Kariappa was now saying, Nakamura had, for all intent and purposes, been dead to the world for those three days. Now conscious, his head throbbed from a concussion; but, for those three days, he had felt nothing—not pain, not even lack of pain.

"Yet the idea of falling asleep does not frighten you in the least, does it?" Kariappa recalls him from his daydream. "In fact, from what I have seen, you are more than eager to bed down by the time that evening comes. Isn't that so?"

"Quite so," Nakamura admits.

"So if you aren't afraid of going to sleep at night, then why are you afraid of dying?

"More importantly," he continues, "when you wake up in the morning, why are you not filled with joy to discover that you are still alive? Has it never occurred to you that the very fact you wake up each morning is nothing less than a miracle?

"Do you not consider the possibility that, because you are so concerned with the prospect of dying, you are missing out on the joy of being alive? Do you see?"

For a split second, Nakamura Saburō does see, and evidently this shows in his face, for Kariappa smiles.

"Good, then. From now on, as you sit, meditate on the following questions: Why were you born into this world? And what is the purpose of living? Seriously focus on them. Make it your mission to discover the answers. And in the evening, when I return, I want you to report to me what you have discovered."

Here was a new kind of challenge. Nothing in Nakamura's academic experience had prepared him for inquiry of this nature, and in the beginning, he had no idea how even to begin. Clearly, however, anything less than an answer that was entirely honest, one that came from the heart as well as the head, was not going to pass his master's scrutiny.

INTERLUDE: THE SEARCH FOR KARIAPPA

Nakamura Tempū's story hinges on his encounter with Kariappa in Cairo. But for this fateful meeting, there may well have been no story to tell. So, then, who was this man Kariappa?

By Tempū's description, Kariappa was wise and venerable, an old man who had arrived at a profound understanding of the relationship between the mental, spiritual, and physical aspects of the human condition through long years of ascetic training in the ways of yoga. But Kariappa's education involved more than just yoga; this we know because he spoke English, an almost sure sign that he had received colonial schooling. And as access to such schooling was limited to people of privilege, we can also reasonably assume that Kariappa was from a family of social standing.

The circumstances of his presence in the hotel in Cairo would support these assumptions. Egypt, we are told, was but a stop on his return voyage from England, a journey the likes of which could only have been undertaken with the assistance of people in high places. The most plausible scenario would have involved sponsorship by one of the British administrators in India, almost by definition a person of aristocratic birth, and Nakamura, you will recall, tells us that Kariappa was invited to England by a member of the English nobility.

The story of subsidy from an Indian maharaja, including the loaning of his yacht, also rings true, for the wherewithal to travel to the other side of the world would have been well beyond the means of a lone Indian fakir who had long ago forsworn the accumulation of worldly possessions. The two visits of Swami Vivekananda to the United States and Europe

(1893–1897 and 1899–1902), seminal events in the history of Vedanta and yoga in the West, were largely financed by such persons of wealth, and the hatha yoga system developed by B. K. S. Iyengar's principal teacher, Tirumalai Krishnamacharya, beginning in the 1920s and 1930s, occurred under the sponsorship of the Maharaja of Mysore.

All the more mysterious, then, that no record of a man answering to Kariappa's description should appear in any of the histories I have seen of yoga's early dissemination in the West. Historical and geographical context would point with almost certainty in the direction of the followers of the revered Ramakrishna and his principal disciple, Vivekananda; yet none of Ramakrishna's disciples of record or Vivekananda's associates are suggestive of the man described by Nakamura Tempū.

Another more tenuous but nevertheless possible link to England is the Theosophists. Here again, however, Theosophy's Indian membership during the period in question is well documented, and I am unable to find among it anyone answering to Tempū's description of Kariappa—nor do I see anything in his descriptions of Kariappa's teachings suggestive of Theosophist doctrine.

A resource worthy of note is Paramhansa Yogananda's classic, *Autobiography of a Yogi*. Yogananda hailed from a privileged family and received just the sort of English education Kariappa must have shared. He was raised in Calcutta, the principle city of Bengal. Gorkhey, as we shall see, is located close to the border between West Bengal and eastern Nepal at a distance of approximately 400 miles (600 kilometers) from modern Kolkata (Calcutta)—not close, but also not far, relative to the scale of Indian geography; in terms of ease of travel, Kolkata is far more accessible to Gorkhey than is Kathmandu. Furthermore, the years of Yogananda's education and early training as a yogi overlap those of Nakamura's internship in Gorkhey under Kariappa.

Yogananda's stories of the saints and adepts with whom he came into contact bear witness to just how rich and alive India's spiritual culture was in his day. Kariappa must certainly have known of, and perhaps even have had contact with, some of these same saints and sages. Nevertheless, by my reading, Yogananda's account offers no clues regarding either the person Nakamura calls Kariappa or the provenance of his teachings.

So again, just who was Kariappa? In the late spring of 2014, in search of answers to that question, I visited the village of Gorkhey.

At the time, I was living and working in Beijing. To put distances on the Asian continent into perspective, Beijing to Delhi is a seven-hour flight, and Delhi to Bagdogra, the airport closest to my destination, another two hours due east; even if it was on the same side of the world, I still had a long way to travel.

Tempū identifies the village that hosted him by name as Gorkhey and describes its location as within the long shadow of Mount Kanchenjunga, the world's third highest peak, and also as proximate to Darjeeling. Poring over Google Maps, I was delighted to discover that, not only was there indeed a town of Gorkhey located not far from Kanchenjunga, but that it was also on the popular Sandakphu-Phalut trekking route. What better antidote to the long winter months of notoriously polluted Beijing air than a five-day trek with Himalayan views, culminated by a descent into Gorkhey, where I could then ask after Kariappa. I contacted a trekking company in Darjeeling and began planning a ten-day, late April–early May trip to overlap China's three-day May Day holiday.

I also contacted the Tempūkai in Tokyo and was kindly emailed a three-part account of a thirty-six-member expedition to Gorkhey in 1993, led by a former Tempūkai director named Shimizu Eiichi; the account is published in the July, August, and September 1993 issues of *Shirube*, the Tempūkai monthly journal. Shimizu and his group came away with strong circumstantial evidence for having successfully identified Nakamura's Gorkhey, not the least of which was their encounter with a ninety-two-year-old man who recalled, when he was about ten, seeing an East Asian man who was living in Gorkhey and studying under the tutelage of the local fakir.

In the meantime, however, Navin Tamang, my trek organizer, to whom I had explained the nature of my interest in Gorkhey, had made some inquiries in the village and now emailed me to say that responses to those inquiries had come back stone cold: no one had ever heard of anyone even remotely matching the description of Kariappa or of any association of the village with yoga or yogis. I took a closer, second look at the 1993 *Shirube* account. The Gorkhey that the Tempūkai group had visited was not in West Bengal but in eastern Nepal. And sure enough, Google Maps did show another town of Gorkhey (or Gorkhe, as it is spelled in Google Maps) just over the India-Nepal border. Furthermore, when Navin made similar inquiries in the Nepali Gorkhey, the response was immediate: Kariappa? Japanese visitors? Yes, of course; these were matters they knew all about.

The date of my departure by now quickly approaching, Navin hastily rearranged my schedule. He would also provide, I was assured, both an English-speaking guide and a car and driver.

This tale of two Gorkheys has a final chapter. After my visit to eastern Nepal, I returned to West Bengal to complete the Sandakphu-Phalut trek and thus ended up also spending a night in the other town of Gorkhey. It is a tiny hamlet, completely inaccessible by motor vehicle, located on the Phalut descent (or ascent, depending on which way you are going) at the floor of a narrow valley where two swiftly flowing rivers converge. The hostel accommodations were comfortable, including the first flush toilet I had seen in a number of days, and the food was outstanding: potatoes and other vegetables came directly from the terraced fields above the village; milk in my afternoon tea was less than an hour old (I watched the young mother of the hostel, with two small children in tow, milk the cow); and dinner included river fish—perhaps trout—caught that morning, as well as a locally raised goat-meat curry.

Both of the rivers have numerous pools of varying depths where the local children, and sometimes trekkers, swim, thus easily fitting the description of the river in which Tempū says he sat every morning. The river to the north of the village is also the Sikkim border; it is spanned by a simple footbridge without any kind of border control, let alone even a sign, and in the morning I took a leisurely stroll across the bridge and up the Sikkim side of the river.

The peacefulness and pristine beauty of Gorkhey in West Bengal is naturally conducive to meditative self-reflection, and I could easily imagine a yogi choosing it as his place of practice. Inquiries revealed, however, that the village was founded in 1935, long after Nakamura's sojourn, and that, one hundred years ago, this valley was almost completely uninhabited. These facts alone do not necessarily preclude the possibility of a yogi choosing this spot, precisely because of its remoteness, for the location of his retreat; however, had such been the case, Nakamura would not have referred to it as Gorkhey, since the name arrived with the first settlers—Nepali immigrants who may even have come from the Gorkhey in eastern Nepal—in 1935. Safe to say, then, the Gorkhey in West Bengal is not the Gorkhey visited by Nakamura Tempū between 1910 and 1913.

But then, if the Gorkhey of Nakamura Tempū's three-year sojourn is in Nepal, not India, why does he not say so? Tempū speaks often of India but never once of Nepal. Does not that discrepancy disqualify the Nepali Gorkhey as a possible location for the events of his story? I do not think so.

At the time of Nakamura's visit, the peoples of both India and Nepal, both then under the British Raj, had little sense of national identity. As poignantly described by Ramachandra Guha in his seminal *India after Gandhi: The History of the World's Largest Democracy,* India, even after its 1947 independence, consisted of a most unlikely confederation of ethnicities, religious affiliations, linguistic groups (twenty-two officially recognized languages), principalities (more than five hundred in 1947), castes, and social classes. The pull on identity by any one of those markers—ethnicity, religion, language, local polity, social strata or substrata—was stronger than that of nationality, even to the extent that the nation's postindependence survival is, in Ramachandra's analysis, nothing short of a modern miracle.

The same sort of ethno-cultural diversity applied to Nepal—on top of which, nothing makes for the segregation of cultures like mountains, and mountains Nepal has: not just the sparsely populated Himalayas, rightfully known as the roof of the world, but also the surprisingly densely populated foothills and deep valleys of the country's temperate middle zone, where small farms cling precariously to steep hillsides. While the explosion in Nepal's population is relatively recent, most of the valleys of this middle zone have been inhabited since long before Tempū's day, and they include a wide array of ethnicities made up of different tribes and subtribes, each with its own language and dialect and culture and subculture, making social intercourse among the towns and villages in these valleys a complicated affair.

My guess is that the people of Bengal one hundred years ago would have been no more likely to call themselves Indian than the people of Gorkhey to call themselves Nepali. Nor was there much in the way of border control between the two countries; if the Gorkhey in Nepal is indeed, as I believe it to be, Kariappa's and Nakamura's Gorkhey, then Nakamura was probably oblivious to the fact that he had crossed a national border to get there. The India to which he refers, I therefore contend, is the geographical one, the Indian subcontinent, not the national entity.

The Gorkhey in eastern Nepal is located just four miles (seven kilometers) by foot from the high ridge that marks the Indian border. The closest border crossings are at the towns of Pashupatinagar and Manebhanjang (there is even a road between Pashupatinagar and Gorkhey; I was told, however, it is in such an advanced state of disrepair that it is impassible by motor vehicle), and the border is crossed freely by Indian and Nepalese nationals. My driver and guide, both from Manebhanjang, had friends in and around Gorkhey, and the driver in particular was greeted as an acquaintance by a number of people we met on the street; this because he and his car routinely ferried them, along with their produce and cottage-industry wares, between Manebhanjang and the market in Darjeeling.

Upon locating the Nepali Gorkhey on the map, I naively assumed that I too could make a day trip of the visit by walking down and back from

Manebhanjang. Not so, Navin advised me. Since there are no Indian or Nepali immigration offices at either Manebhanjang or Pashupatinagar, I would need to enter from Kakarbhitta at the southeastern corner of Nepal, a diversion that would add a full two days to my itinerary.

The flight from Beijing to Delhi arrived in the wee hours of April 28, and after several hours of sleep in an airport hotel, I caught a midday flight to Bagdogra, just outside Siliguri in West Bengal. There, I was met by my guide and driver, and after a forty-minute drive on relatively good roads through flat landscape blanketed by tea plantations, we reached Kakarbhitta, where we signed me out of India and obtained my entry visa into Nepal—a procedure of sufficient bureaucratic complexity to have rendered me lost had I been on my own. The same flat landscape continued for another forty minutes or so into southern Nepal, and with the temperature in the high thirties Celsius (high nineties Fahrenheit), the mountains remained hidden under a steamy haze until we were at their base; whereupon they appeared suddenly and like a wall. My driver downshifted to the lower gears of his Indian-made four-wheel-drive Tata. This beast of a vehicle virtually ate up the endless switchbacks in front of us; anything less than its ilk, I was soon to discover when we exited the paved surfaces, would never have brought us to our destination.

Relative to road conditions, the easier but longer approach to Gorkhey is a roundabout route that avoids high climbs and comes into the valley from the west. We chose the more direct route, taking us to the top of a high ridge and through acre upon acre of tea plantations. The township of Kanyam produces some of the finest tea in the entire region, and this part of the drive was still on relatively well maintained paved roads; but at a point several miles beyond Kanyam, we dove off the side of the mountain onto a dirt path, the likes of which I have never driven before. The final six miles (thirteen kilometers) of the journey took over an hour and a half to navigate, as we bounced off boulders, in and out of bathtub-size pot-holes, and through streambeds. Having watched, between passing tree branches, the sun go down behind the line of hills to our west, we finally arrived in Gorkhey at dusk.

Village of Gorkhey,
main street

The roads into Gorkhey by either approach are unpaved and consequently non-navigable for about three months of the year during the monsoon. The village is inaccessible during that period, other than by horse or on foot, and more than one person told me that nothing would do more for the economic landscape of the valley than better roads: a paved road in from the west would give the village better access to the rest of Nepal, and a navigable road—even a dirt one—to the Indian border would greatly facilitate cross-border trade. So far, however, the central government in Kathmandu has lent a deaf ear to Gorkhey's petitions, and the town's allowance for road maintenance is marginally adequate for repairs, much less improvements.

The entire population of Gorkhey is about 7,000. The town consists of one- and two-story wood-frame buildings arranged along a single cobblestoned street running parallel to the approximately east-to-west flowing river at the base of the valley. The houses are served with electricity—although, as in much of Nepal and even in West Bengal, power failures and deliberate power outages are a common, even daily, event. When I asked about a small shed-like building carrying the Red Cross logo, I was told it was stocked with basic medical supplies, but that there were no doctors, nurses, or even paramedics in the village to dispense or administer those supplies. The closest medical facility is several hours away in the town of Ilam—provided, of course, that the roads are passable. The villagers rely largely on local herbal lore for the treatment of common ailments, and as for serious injuries or life-threatening diseases, as one man told me, "All we can do is pray to the gods."

Gorkhey has not always been such a backwater. Up until the 1980s, the town, by virtue of its proximity to the Indian border, hosted the central bazaar for the surrounding region, and indeed, just six weeks prior to my arrival, after a hiatus of twenty-five years, a Wednesday bazaar had been reopened and was drawing several thousand people. Furthermore, Gorkhey also once profited from the tourist trade, as it was the starting place for the Sandakphu trek: Sandakphu is the only point in either India or Nepal where the Himalayas from Bhutan in the east to Dhaulagiri and Annapurna in the west, and including four of the world's five highest peaks, are visible in one unbroken panorama. The Sandakphu gateway function, however, has long since been usurped by Manebhanjang, an inevitable consequence of better road access and closer proximity to Darjeeling.

When we reached Gorkhey, I was shown to a tiny guestroom in a small shopkeeper's house; the room's single window looked out on the town's main street. Later, we walked some fifty yards (fifty meters) up the street to another small storefront and invited ourselves into the kitchen. We ate all of our meals in this same kitchen—that evening; the morning, noon, and evening of the following day; and the morning of our final departure. Each meal consisted of rice with *dhal* (lentils) and some sort of curry—vegetable, chicken, or egg. Of moderately vegetarian persuasion by habit (a vegetarian who cheats, as I like to say), I found this food both tasty and satisfying.

That first evening, several of the locals joined us in the kitchen. English was limited, and while I relied upon my guide for interpretation, far more was being said than what was filtering down to me. I gathered, however, that because foreigners of any kind, and Westerners in particular, were a rarity in their village, they were genuinely curious as to what should have brought me there.

When it was explained that I was doing research on Kariappa, they responded with knowing nods. In all, four Japanese groups from the Tempūkai had visited Gorkhey—three since the first one in 1993—and the most recent one, in December 2013, had hosted a picnic dinner at the edge of town that attracted hundreds, maybe even more than a thousand people. Furthermore, just one month prior to my arrival, a Japanese cameraman and his crew had arrived by helicopter with an eye to later do a documentary. Now, they were being lead to believe, Kariappa had caught on with not only the Japanese but also the Americans. This Kariappa of theirs was undeniably a most valuable asset.

Upon prying only slightly further, however, I discovered that the name Kariappa had arrived with the Japanese: prior to the arrival of Shimizu's group in 1993, no one in Gorkhey knew anything of a man named Kariappa.

What they did know was that, up until 1950, a hermit or fakir, known by the name Koribaba, had lived on a grassy patch of riverbank located just below the village. Koribaba was said to have spent long hours in meditation each day atop a huge boulder beside the river.

This marked the beginning of my inquiry into the origins of a name. As that inquiry involves the workings of a language with which I am unfamiliar and was conducted through the medium of my guide and one other young man from the village who spoke good but imperfect English, I can be only moderately confident of its result. But what I understand to be so regarding the name is as follows. First, *kori* is a derivative of *kora*, the Nepali word for river. Second, *baba* is the common term for father or grandfather, and by extension, a tittle of respect applied to any elder male fulfilling a fatherly or grandfatherly role; *baba* is used in this way by not only the peoples of Nepal but also most of the peoples of North India. Taken together, then, "Koribaba" was, evidently, a title of reverence and endearment conferred on the fakir, the old man sitting by the river, by the villagers.

That, however, is not all. The Nepali script is syllabic, and within this script, as it was explained to me, the syllabic character for *ka* is sometimes read not *ka* but *ko*. That is, the alphabetical renditions of the Nepali characters used to write what sounds like *kori* and *kora* are, in fact, *kari* and *kara*. Furthermore, *appa*, as in Kariappa, can have exactly the same meaning as *baba* in Koribaba. In many of the languages and dialects of South India, for example, people call their fathers and grandfathers "appa" in just the same way that North Indians call their fathers and grandfathers "baba." Kariappa and Koribaba, then, appear to be names of the same derivation but as rendered by different dialects.

But if so, why then does Nakamura refer to his teacher as Kariappa when this was not the name used by the people of Gorkhey? Was Kariappa, perhaps, originally from South India? No one in the village had an answer.

Later, while in Darjeeling, I also learned that the title *appa* is not entirely foreign to Nepal. Navin Tamang, the man who so capably organized my trip, belongs, as his name indicates, to the Tamang tribe or clan, one of several Nepali tribes said to have inherited genes from Genghis Khan and his warriors when they invaded Tibet in the thirteenth century; the Tamang are among those tribes that, collectively, make up the Gurkhas, the acclaimed soldiers of mettle employed by the British Raj from the early nineteenth century through the end of World War II. In the Tamang dialect, Navin told me, fathers and grandfathers are addressed as "appa," not "baba."

To be clear, not all of the Gurkhas call their fathers "appa"; but at the very least, one tribe, the Tamang, does. Furthermore, Gorkha, from which the town of Gorkhey derives its name, is an alternate spelling of Gurkha; Gorkhey is a name for a town that was originally inhabited by Gurkhas. Were there people in Gorkhey when Tempū visited who might have referred to their fathers as "appa" rather than "baba"? Not likely, was the general consensus; the village has changed little ethnically for generations.

Then there is the provocative claim by Tempū in at least one of his talks that Kariappa is of Lepcha ethnicity. The Lepcha are a mountain people with distinctively oriental features and inhabiting the regions surrounding Kanchenjunga, including Sikkim, northern parts of West Bengal, and the Ilam District of eastern Nepal in which Gorkhey is located. They also, I am told, address their fathers and grandfathers as "appa." As promising as this lead appears, it is also problematic. The Lepcha are reclusive and predominantly Buddhist; the likelihood that, in the nineteenth century, one of them would have had either the motivation or the wherewithal to pursue an English education—and moreover, then to pursue yoga, presumably under a Hindu master—is, my Gorkhey associates agree, so remote as to remove it from contention. Most probably, Nakamura misunderstood something he was told or overheard.

Whatever the explanation for the apparent difference of dialect, the etymological match between the two names is reason enough to assume, I believe, that Kariappa and Koribaba are the same man. But whether Kariappa or Koribaba, the name is no more than a nickname given him by the villagers; the sage in question must have also had a proper name. As I have already noted, the circumstances of Nakamura's encounter with Kariappa in Cairo tell us that Kariappa enjoyed some kind of reputation among the British community in India as well as among Indians, and the absence of any record of a yogi named Kariappa from this time suggests that he was known outside Gorkhey by another name. The greater mystery is still, just who was Kariappa-Koribaba? Where did he come from? From what teacher or in what lineage did he derive his knowledge of yoga?

Not only were the people of Gorkhey unable to shed light on these questions, but even the notion that their beloved village fakir had, on at least one occasion, traveled to Europe and North Africa was news. This is all the more remarkable given that, in at least one of Tempū's talks, he asserts that Kariappa's visit to England was not an isolated occurrence but one of several, perhaps many, such visits.

But then, as a Brahmin, the uppermost caste in Indian and Nepali society, Kariappa may have had little actual contact with the villagers. The villagers, while charitably providing Kariappa and his disciples with grain and vegetables, would have been preoccupied with their own concerns and livelihoods and may have otherwise left him alone. Furthermore, if Kariappa was not native to Gorkhey, as the name Kariappa, as opposed to Koribaba, suggests, then he may also not have spoken the local Gorkhey dialect.

Memory is fallible, and memory across generations is more fallible still. I met no one in the village with firsthand knowledge of Koribaba; he departed Gorkhey in 1950, so anyone with such firsthand knowledge would have been at least seventy years old at the time of my visit—and even then, that memory would have been an early childhood one. What people in Gorkhey know today is based, almost exclusively, on what they heard from their parents and grandparents, and what those parents and grandparents remember is largely dependent upon how much interest they took in Koribaba's existence at the time.

The villagers did tell me the story of Koribaba's departure. In 1950, there was a flood. The river rose so high as to cover the top of Koribaba's rock, a height of at least twelve feet (four meters) above the river's normal level. The flood caused considerable damage to the village and also washed away Koribaba's hut on the riverbank. Koribaba, it was said, waited patiently by the river while the flood raged, expecting that someone would come to his assistance. But when no one did—the villagers were, undoubtedly, preoccupied with the effects of the flood on the village—he simply picked up his things and moved on.

Where he went, no one in the village knew. By telephone, however, I was introduced to a man who had grown up in Gorkhey—his older brother was one of the people who joined us in the kitchen the evening of our arrival—and who currently ran a small retail business in Kathmandu. The man spoke good English (his older brother did not) and explained to me over the phone how he has been availing himself of historical archives in Kathmandu to research the story of Kariappa-Koribaba and how he has even aroused interest on the part of the Nepal Archeological Society.

The man called Koribaba, he asserts, shows up in Kathmandu several years after his disappearance from Gorkhey and lives there for some time

Koribaba's boulder

before disappearing again. More intriguing, the temple at which he is said to have resided, Pashupatinath, venerating the god Shiva, is of South Indian provenance and, even today, is largely maintained by South Indian Brahmins. I have subsequently been in touch with this man by email and have confirmed that he escaped injury during the April 2015 earthquake; the earthquake has, however, postponed tentative plans on my part to visit.

The morning after our first night in Gorkhey, I was shown the boulder upon which Koribaba is said to have sat in meditation. It is an enormous rock with rounded edges and a flat surface. The top of the boulder is accessible with a hop from the riverbank and a short scramble up the side. At one time, there were four of us (part of the following I seemed to attract wherever I went) atop the rock, with room for several more.

The rock's top surface is marked by two holes, each about half an inch (1.5 centimeters) in diameter and three-quarters of an inch (2 centimeters) in depth, and bored about 4 inches (10 centimeters) apart. The holes are obviously artificial, but made when, how, and by whom, no one could say. Local lore has it that Koribaba carried, as a walking stick, something described to me as a chest-high pair of tongs, similar to fireplace tongs but longer. Or was it, perhaps, more like a two-pronged spear or pitchfork? The description lost something in its translation. In any event, the ends of this implement conveniently matched the holes drilled into the rock, and he would use the holes to stand the instrument while he sat.

Did Koribaba drill the holes? Did someone drill them for him? Or were they already there when he arrived and just happen to match the prongs of his walking implement? The villagers were not even willing to speculate.

The river was little more than a rocky riverbed with a stream running through it. This was disappointing, as it was supposed to have been the river in which Tempū sat each morning in water up to his chest; none of the pools appeared large enough or deep enough to accommodate ten or more sitting yogis. Not to worry, the villagers assured me; the shortage of water is a recent phenomenon, and people over thirty remember an abundance of swimming holes in the river of their childhood. The depletion of water is due to agriculture: proliferation of terraces and fields upstream from Gorkhey and diversion of water into these fields has caused the river to wither.

The river is called Mayung Kara (pronounced *moyung kora*) by the villagers. Formerly, though, it was known as Jogi Kara, where *jogi* is an alternate spelling of yogi. Koribaba, evidently, had sufficient charisma to cause the villagers to name their river "the yogi's river."

On the riverbank to the side of the boulder is a strip of flat land that the local children use as a soccer pitch; it is only about sixty-five feet (twenty meters) in width and 200 feet (sixty meters) in length, and many a soccer ball must have escaped the pitch and landed in the river. When the Tempūkai visits, I was told, they pitch their tents on this narrow green. Photographs of these tents, as well as of the villagers and Japanese visitors dancing together around a campfire after dark, appear together with the account of the first Tempūkai visit in the July 1993 issue of *Shirube,* and I noted the charred remains of a fire, far more recent than 1993, in the middle of the field.

Tempū speaks of a small community of yogis studying under Kariappa, and the green, while smaller than I had imagined, is just large enough to host hut-like accommodations for several yogis, as well as that of their master. The problem is that the people of Gorkhey today have no knowledge or recollection of such a settlement. The description of Koribaba, as it has been handed down to them, is not that of a teacher with an ashram but that of a hermit.

In his 1993 account, Shimizu describes being told by a ninety-two-year-old man that he distinctly remembers having seen, when he was nine or ten years old, an East Asian man living on the green together with Koribaba. This report is, so far, the only eyewitness testimony on record to support Nakamura's story of his sojourn in Gorkhey.

Upon inquiring, I discovered that the man in question was named Bishnu Prasad Lamichhane; Lamichhane is an indication of both his tribe and his caste. Bishnu Prasad died in 2002 at the ripe old age of 102, but quite by chance, when walking up to the Mangaldas temple, I met his first and second sons. The Mangaldas temple overlooks Gorkhey from the ridge on the far side of the river, and we sat together on a bench by the side of the road, admiring the view and conversing by way of the young man accompanying me, a schoolteacher with a university degree and good command of English. The house—their father's house, now in the hands of the eldest son—was located just up the road on the ridge, a fifteen-minute walk from the village. The eldest son and I compared ages; at sixty, he was four years younger than me. As a boy, their father, the men told me, used to tend cattle every day on the far riverbank across from Koribaba's rock; thus, he was privy to the fakir's comings and goings and could not help but notice when a foreigner with East Asian features came to stay.

It was also Bishnu Prasad who directed Shimizu and his party to a water-fall on the other side of the ridge, asserting it to be the waterfall visited daily by Nakamura Tempū. As this waterfall is on the road we were to take when leaving Gorkhey, a slightly different route than the one we had come in on, we visited it the following day. It is located about three miles (five kilometers) from Gorkhey, and getting there involves a couple of reasonably steep uphill climbs—easily a forty-minute walk (Shimizu reports having walked for almost an hour). The waterfall is currently

The waterfall?

little more than a trickle running over a high rock ledge, a far cry from the roaring torrent that Tempū describes. But this also, apparently, was not always so. In bygone years, I was told, a substantial volume of water flowed over the falls. In this case, the upstream diversion of water was due not to agriculture but to landslides; as immovable as they appeared, these mountains and their rivers, I was being given to understand, were subject to constant change. Shimizu also reports finding a ledge that provided a comfortable place to sit and meditate; the same ledge was not obvious to me.

Shimizu and his party came away from their visit duly convinced they had found Tempū's waterfall; however, a second possible candidate for that distinction came to light about ten years ago. Following our visit to Koribaba's boulder, I was led up the road above the village and then onto a path that climbed along the side of agricultural terraces. Word of my presence had spread, and the trail of people behind me on this path soon grew to about twenty strong.

We veered away from the fields, off into a shallow, forested ravine. Here I was shown a giant sloping slab of rock and then directed toward what appeared to be a somewhat crude inscription near its top; several letters had been carved into the stone. The carving was sufficiently weathered to give the impression that it had been there for many years.

The rock inscribed
with Kirati characters

The characters were identified to me as Kirati, the first indigenous Nepali script. The Kirats were responsible for uniting, through conquest, most of the territory that makes up the modern state of Nepal, and the script they devised is still used by Kirat descendants, the Limbu and the Rai. Nothing in recent village history, however, suggests that Gorkhey was ever inhabited by either Limbu or Rai.

One man in the group gathered leaves from a plant, which, when squeezed, released a dark green juice; this he dripped into the indentations in the rock, thereby highlighting the letters in green against the gray of the stone. There were four characters in all. The first of these, the villagers could not read; the remaining three, however, represented, I was told, the phonetic syllables *ku, ruu,* and *paa—karaapaa.* The similarity of these syllables to the name Kariappa was not lost on the villagers.

The story they told was as follows. After the 1993 visit of the Japanese, a concerted search was undertaken by the villagers to find some kind of writing in stone. Why they should have expected to find such writing was not exactly clear, but from what I could understand, it was attributable either to something that the Japanese said or to something that the villagers thought they had said. The expectation also seems to have been that the writing they would find would be in Japanese characters. Given that the Japanese and the villagers were communicating by way of a Nepali-English

Kirati inscription, presumably reading "karaapaa"

interpreter, one can only surmise that what was said by one party may not always have been what was heard by the other. Be that as it may, when the search, which continued for several years, and which focused on the rock cliffs around the waterfall and the rocks along the river, produced no results, it was abandoned. The Kirati characters came to light much later, by accident, when someone searching for herbs and wild vegetables in the forest just happened to sweep away collected leaves from the top of the stone.

Later in my journey, when I told this story to a man from Manebhanjang, he cautioned me to obtain an academically qualified opinion regarding these characters and their readings. His point is well taken, but so far, I have been unable to locate a person with the appropriate qualifications. What I can say is, comparison of the characters in my photographs to the Kirati alphabet, available on several websites, does suggest, at least to this layman's eye, that the villagers are correct in their assessment.

Upon completing my examination of this rock and the letters inscribed, I was asked to look behind me. Just above the rock was a small ledge, less than six feet (two meters) high and partially covered by ferns. Over the top of this ledge flowed a trickle of water: not much of a waterfall today, but given the way these mountains and their streams change, it could have once been quite a spectacular little cataract. Could it not have been, the villagers were suggesting, Kariappa and Tempū's waterfall?

The waterfall?

I was skeptical. Neither the waterfall nor its location matched Tempū's description—too small in height and too close to the village. The next morning, however, in the twilight hours before the village awoke (I was still functioning on Beijing time), I returned to the spot alone. This was unpremeditated; my feet, having walked the path the day before, just carried me there. The rock with the engraved letters has no flat surface, but one corner, I noticed, had a small area with a step-like riser just about the height of a sitting cushion. I settled onto this corner of the rock and confirmed what I suspected; it was comfortable and almost perfectly suited for sitting. I crossed my legs, closed my eyes, and fell, almost immediately, into meditation.

Spontaneously, out of the bottom of internal stillness, came the words, "This is it. This is the place." The vibration of these words occurred more as a physical sensation than as an auditory one, and my body was tingling with a kind of excitement.

Does this mean that I had found Kariappa and Nakamura's waterfall? Of course not. I am sufficiently seasoned to be skeptical of internal voices, and as I write this now, in retrospect, the likelihood of that ledge being the waterfall in question seems even less than it did then. Furthermore—and this occurred to me at the time—the words "This is the place" may be heard as a declaration not of physical location but of the meditative space

I was occupying at that moment, the quietude that Kariappa called the voice of heaven.

What I will say, however, is that, first, had there been a strong stream of water flowing over the ledge, that stream would have landed just above where I was sitting, and the sound it generated would have been more than enough to mask any other sounds from the surrounding forest. And second, while the distance to this location from Koribaba's green beside the river is not more than half a mile (one kilometer)—a poor match for the long climb described by Nakamura—all of that half mile is uphill, and some of it quite steeply so; considering the dilapidated state of Nakamura's condition and the fact that Kariappa had him carrying a stone on his back, it would probably have been, at least during the early months of his stay, enough of a hill to challenge him.

My visit to Gorkhey raised more new questions than it did answer old ones. But I also came away touched by the honesty and good-natured hospitality of the people I met during my stay. One day, I hope to return.

One more impression bears mentioning, and that is as concerns the spiritual milieu of the surrounding region. In the course of my search for leads with regard to Kariappa's identity, I came across stories of several other spiritual personages connected either directly with Gorkhey or with its proximate local. One of these was the guru Mangaldas, celebrated by a colorfully ornate temple overlooking the town. Mangaldas was a revered leader of the Pranami faith, a Hindu order devoted to the worship of Krishna. His principal congregation or following was in Kalimpong, a hill town on the other side of Darjeeling; however, the temple above Gorkhey marks his birthplace. Mangaldas was born in 1896, and he renounced worldly aspirations to become a Pranami initiate at the age of twelve. That conversion and his subsequent training occurred far away from Gorkhey, and it is safe to assume that Nakamura and he never crossed paths; however, he may very well have had an association with Kariappa. Like Kariappa, he was a strict vegetarian and advocated a vegetarian diet. He was also a renowned healer.

Just above Gorkhey at the time of Nakamura's sojourn resided the holy man Nagthang Tsampa. Nagthang Tsampa was an ordained Lama of Tibetan Buddhism. He was born in Ladakh but underwent his principal Buddhist training in Sikkim. He also traveled to Burma and is said to have cured the Burmese king of a chronic disease. In 1910, the year of Nakamura's arrival in Gorkhey, he established a monastery at Chitrey, on the India-Nepal border just above Manebhanjang. Chitrey is within walking distance of Gorkhey, and the roofs of Gorkhey are plainly visible from points on the ridge just beyond the monastery. This I know because I looked down on them after spending a night in a Chitrey guesthouse at the beginning of my Sandakphu trek. Was there contact between Nagthang Tsampa and Kariappa? At the very least, they must have been aware of each other's existence. Conceivably, Kariappa and Nakamura even visited Chitrey on their inbound journey to Gorkhey, for such a visit would have taken them only slightly out of their way.

While on the Sandakphu trek, at the next stop beyond Chitrey in the town of Tumling, I had one of the more interesting conversations of my entire trip with a man from Manebhanjang (the same conversation in which I was advised to get a qualified opinion regarding the letters carved into the rock above Gorkhey). The proprietor of an earthmoving concern commissioned to do road repair in the vicinity, he had stopped for lunch at the guesthouse where my guide and I were staying and ended up remaining through most of the afternoon while torrential rains fell outside.

Tumling is at almost 10,000 feet (3,000 meters) elevation, and the storm brought with it a penetrating chill. Eight or nine people in all, we huddled around the wood stove in the kitchen, with the conversation oscillating between a Nepali dialect and English. The man knew Gorkhey well and was intrigued by the story of my visit. He also listened with great interest while I summarized for him the story of Nakamura Tempū.

From there, our conversation escalated to the more arcane, including even a discussion of the case for ancient aliens. The man had been watching a History Channel series about the ancient aliens thesis—the thesis that visitations from extraterrestrials in the ancient past were influential, if not causal, to the rise of human civilization. His open-mindedness was refreshing; he was intrigued, but not so intrigued as to relinquish his skepticism.

Almost as if the ancient aliens discussion was meant to test the waters, he launched into a story told to him by his mother. The story originated with his mother's brother, his uncle; both mother and uncle are now deceased, but as a young man, the uncle had taken pity on a fakir he noticed spending his nights outside in the winter snow while wearing only a single layer of cloth. When the uncle brought the fakir food, however, the fakir refused it. All the more adamant, the youth persisted with his offerings over a period of ten days, until finally the fakir relented. Not only did he accept the food offered, but he began to instruct the young man in the ways of yoga.

The young man eventually renounced the world and set off on a pilgrimage together with this guru and a band of some twenty other followers. Their journey took them through towns and villages in this northern corner of India and neighboring Sikkim, and they endured all manner of weather and privation, relying solely on their faith in their master; the master, moreover, never failed to provide the spiritual sustenance necessary to pull them through. At last, they arrived at a sacred lake located high above tree line at the base of Kanchenjunga. The guru gathered his following and delivered a final sermon. They had graduated, he told them, from his tutelage, and each was now free to pursue his own spiritual path. He would leave them, only to return in another age. With this, he raised his right hand and pointed at the sky. Then, in full view of his following, he proceeded to dematerialize; first to go were his feet, then his legs, then his torso, and so on. Last to go was the arm and hand, still pointing toward the sky.

The master was known to his students as Baraguru, and legend has him appearing and disappearing in different ages and at different locations throughout the mountains of West Bengal, a profile provocatively similar to that of the avatar Babaji described by Yogananda in *Autobiography of a Yogi*. The man telling me this story guessed the timing of its occurrence to have been the late 1920s or early 1930s—later than Nakamura's sojourn but well within the span of Kariappa-Koribaba's residence in Gorkhey. Was there any contact between these two holy men? Were they perhaps even of the same spiritual lineage? Without more to go on, it is impossible to say.

Like many a visitor before me, I came away from India in awe of the richness and depth of its spiritual tradition. The Indian subcontinent, if plagued by immense social, political, economic, and environmental problems, also has a long-established reputation as a repository of wisdom and an incubator of men of extraordinary insight, and the corner of that subcontinent in which Gorkhey is located is evidently no exception. Tempū's stories are no more fantastic than those told by either Yogananda or my acquaintance, and I harbor no doubts regarding their authenticity. One of my hopes for this book is that someone, somewhere, will read it, connect the dots to information not yet at my disposal, and bring the identity of Kariappa to light.

7.
THE VOICE
OF HEAVEN

The sun at this latitude varied little in its arc throughout the year. Rising hastily off the moisture-laden eastern line of hills, it traversed the sky almost directly overhead at noon and disappeared again in the west at almost the same time each day, punctuating vibrantly bright days with dark nights of almost equal length. And with little to distinguish the cyclical progression of days, Nakamura soon lost track of just how long it had been since he had arrived in the valley.

One evening, early in his stay, when the moon is full, Nakamura wanders out of his stable to the green on the riverbank and is startled to find he is not alone; the soft light of the moon reveals an eerie montage of human forms. The yogis, he quickly assimilates, are engaged in practice. Each is fixed in some odd contortion. One stands on one leg, his other leg bent so that the raised foot rested on his straight leg's thigh, and his arms stretched overhead, palms together and fingers pointing straight to heaven. Another has arched himself over backward, hands and feet planted firmly on the ground and a branch spiked with thorns placed directly underneath. Yet another hangs by his knees from a high limb of the linden tree.

As the months go by, Nakamura observes that this nighttime practice is recurrent with each rising of the full moon, and one night, Kariappa invites Nakamura to join. "Assume a position in which you think you will be comfortable," Kariappa instructs. "Any position is fine, but you must face the moon."

Nakamura seats himself with his back against a tree. In addition to observing the moon, he is not to move so much as a muscle until Kariappa returns. Which will be, Kariappa says, in about an hour.

Nakamura looks up at the moon. It is like the face of an old friend; a face he had gazed upon since he was a child. It is also a faithful companion. Everywhere he has been—China, America, Europe, and now India—the same moon has followed.

Within minutes, he begins to feel discomfort. The bark of the tree bites into his back. The unevenness of the ground makes sitting upright a chore and puts strain on his spine to retain its balance. With each passing minute, the discomfort increases, so that, by the time Kariappa returns, he is sweating profusely. Asked if he has observed the moon, Nakamura assures Kariappa that he has seen more than enough of the moon for one evening.

"Then show me what you saw," Kariappa says. "Draw me a picture."

Puzzled, Nakamura takes a stick and etches a circle in the dirt.

"You fool! Is that all?"

The old man's response has the report of a cracking whip, and Nakamura smarts from the sting. He hangs his head. So consumed had he been by his own discomfort that he failed the assignment. The only moon he had observed was the moon in his memory, the moon that reminded him of his past; the moon hanging overhead had escaped him.

The yoga practice of maintaining a stance, or asana, for long periods of time, he comes to appreciate, is not so much a physical discipline as a mental one. It demands intense concentration. Regardless of physical discomfort, the yogi's attention is not to waver, and how long a yogi can remain in an asana is less important than how long he can retain a state of focused attention.

The following day, Kariappa reprimands him again, this time in a quieter voice. "You act like time is on your side," he says. "You have been here for half a year, yet you continue to act as though your training has yet to begin. How can I teach you if you don't put your heart into what I ask you to do?"

Kariappa's methods are an enigma to Nakamura. Seldom is he told the purpose of the practice he is instructed to pursue, much less its goal or the marker of its success. Nor has Kariappa said anything further with regard to that important thing he is to learn. But then, Nakamura knows not to ask, for whatever the important thing is, he is almost certainly expected to figure it out on his own.

To his way of thinking, Nakamura is making the noblest of efforts. Battling a physical affliction, he is, nevertheless, immersing himself in the ice-cold river every morning; he is climbing the path to the waterfall and sitting there at his perch by day. These are the only specific instructions that he has been given. What is he missing? What more can he do? Tempū would later say:

> People say that my study of yoga is what brought me to the realizations that are the basis of my philosophy. Of course, my exposure to the ways of yoga was a major influence. But my study of the ways of yoga in India was not like the pursuit of an academic discipline. It was not like an arranged curriculum where you read a book or attend a long and detailed lecture and are then expected to think hard about what you have read or been told. It was a case of exposure, day and night, to a teacher who sometimes joked, sometimes spoke seriously, and sometimes scolded, but who never, ever explained. What I took away from my time in India, I figured out on my own.
>
> So when people say that my philosophy is based upon the philosophy of yoga, they couldn't be more wrong. I was never taught what I am teaching, and I was never shown the practices that make up my method in the way that I am showing them to you.[1]

Then there was the matter of the waterfall. If he was not making sufficient progress, was not the waterfall the problem? Its din was nothing but an annoyance; what possible purpose could it serve to sit in the echo of that painful roar day after day?

Mustering his courage, he tactfully raises the issue one afternoon during their descent while trailing behind his master's donkey.

"The first condition of *dhyana* is the settling and quieting of the mind, isn't it?" Dhyana is what his master calls the practice of sitting meditation.

"Of course," Kariappa answers.

"If so, then wouldn't I be better off sitting somewhere quiet?"

"You can't settle your mind because of the falls?"

"How can I? My ears are still ringing from that sound even now when talking to you."

"If you can't quiet your mind in the presence of the sound of water running over the falls, you won't be able to do so anywhere else."

"But the noise is so loud. How can you expect me to practice dhyana in the presence of that kind of distraction?"

"The waterfall is the best place for you to practice dhyana. That's why I chose it for you, so that you can develop your abilities and make faster progress."

"But why?" Nakamura asks. Surely he would find it easier to focus his mind in a quieter environment.

"To the contrary," Kariappa insists, "this place is the ideal training ground for you. You need to learn to be able to hear the voice of heaven," he says. "And you need to learn to be able to hear it as soon as possible."

"The voice of heaven? What is that?"

"Just what I said. The voice of heaven."

Nakamura looks skeptically at his master. How can heaven have a voice? Is he being exposed to some primitive, animistic belief?

"So," he asks, "Have you actually heard this voice of heaven?"

"I hear it all of the time." Kariappa does not rise to the sarcasm in Nakamura's voice. "I hear it now as we are talking. I even hear it while I am asleep."

Nakamura is all the more incredulous. "What language does this voice of heaven speak?" he asks.

"It doesn't speak a language. It's a voice, a sound. But since you are bothered by the simple sound of falling water, you can hardly expect

142

to hear the voice of heaven. You probably don't even hear the voices of earth."

The conversation has taken another turn.

"The voices of earth?"

"The sound of the wind in the trees. The songs of the birds. The chirping of insects. All these are voices of the earth."

"Of course I can hear those things," Nakamura responds indignantly.

"Not now," Kariappa says, "but when you are sitting at the falls."

Nakamura is speechless. The sound of the falls is loud enough to muffle the song of any bird or the chirping of any insect; this he knows better than anyone. What does Kariappa mean by suggesting otherwise?

"As long as you believe that it is impossible, as long as you refuse to try, then there is no way that it can be otherwise. But how can you be so sure that it is impossible?" Kariappa responds, despite the fact that Nakamura has yet to verbalized his question.

Not one to back away from a challenge, Nakamura agrees to give it a try the following day.

"If you don't get it the first day, then try again the next. At the longest, you should catch on within two or three days," Kariappa advises. The advice comes, however, with no instruction on what to do or how to listen; such details, Nakamura understands, he will need to figure out on his own.

At the falls, he settles in with determination. If Kariappa can hear, as he insists he can, the sound of the birds over the sound of the falls, then surely Nakamura can as well.

Closing his eyes, he focuses his attention on the auditory aspect of his experience. But focus as he might, he hears nothing but the roar of the water going over the falls. As the morning wears into afternoon, Nakamura's frustration grows. And as his frustration grows, his attention begins to wander.

"This isn't working," he thinks. "It is useless. No one, not even Kariappa, can possibly hear anything over this noise."

Dejected, he looks out at the falls. In the afternoon light, a sparrow is flying in and out of the spray. Presently, it lands on an outcrop of ledge protruding from behind the wall of water.

Just at that moment, it happens. A tiny tear occurs in the curtain of sound. And through that tear, loud and clear, comes the chirp of a sparrow.

Nakamura reacts with startled surprise. "Impossible," he thinks. The tear has closed as quickly as it appeared. But by patient back-engineering, by taking his mind back to the same place it had been when the tear first appeared, he is able to find it again. Just for an instant, the curtain of sound parts, and through the opening, he hears the bird's chirp.

Against the roar of the falls, he has successfully distinguished a voice of the earth. Furthermore, his listening has penetrated that roar, he realizes, not when he is trying hardest to hear, but when he is trying least. As long as he fixes his attention on hearing something other than the sound of the falls, the sound of the falls is in the way. But the moment his attention shifts away from his own listening—in this case, his attention had shifted to his field of vision and the flight of the bird—what had been foreground noise shifts to the background.

Retracing the same steps, Nakamura succeeds, if again for only an instant, to recreate the same results a third time, then a fourth, and then a fifth. Each time the task becomes a little easier. And each time, it lasts a little longer; he is able, ever so slightly, to prolong its duration, so that what at first had been momentary now occurs over an interval of a second, then a couple of seconds, then longer.

After three days of practice, Nakamura's proficiency becomes such that he is listening at will for the sounds of not only birds but of insects and even the wind in the trees.

"It appears that you have gotten it," Kariappa remarks before Nakamura says a word. "With practice, you will soon be able to hear far more than the chirping of insects. When the mind is still, it can hear even the sound of ants walking and earthworms burrowing."

Nakamura listens to this statement with acute interest. Such powers, should they be attainable, lie well beyond his current capacities, but he is, nevertheless, more inclined now than before to take his master at his word.

"However, in order to be able to do that," Kariappa continues, "you must first learn to hear the voice of heaven. When you can hear the voice of heaven, you will be able, with training, to pick any one sound out from among all of the sounds that surround you and to hear it clearly."

This may be so. But in order to get there, he needs more guidance: Where to look for this voice of heaven? How will he know it when he hears it? What will it sound like?

"These things you will need to discover," Kariappa answers with finality.

Bolstered by his one small success, Nakamura takes up this new challenge with body and soul. The voices of earth, after all, had revealed themselves to him when he stopped trying to listen for them; perhaps he can discover the voice of heaven through application of the same principle. From his seat beside the waterfall, he now listens at will not only to birds and insects but to all the sounds of the surrounding forest. What he needs to do, he reasons, is to put these sounds aside, just as he has the sound of the falls. Maybe then this mysterious voice of heaven will speak to him.

But however reasonable this sounds in theory, it proves difficult in practice. Day after day, Nakamura returns to the falls and sits, legs crossed and eyes closed, listening intently for any hint of heaven's voice. Evening after evening, with nothing to report to his master, he returns to the village in silence.

At the end of two weeks, his frustration comes to a head. "The sounds of birds, animals, and insects—these I can pick out from behind the sound of the falls at will. But I still can't hear anything that sounds like it might be what you call the voice of heaven," he says.

"You still don't hear it?" Kariappa asks with amusement.

"No."

"Maybe it's because you are not trying. If you can hear the voices of earth, you should be able to hear the voice of heaven too."

Nakamura protests. The one thing he cannot be accused of is not devoting enough effort: he is giving it his all.

"Then let me ask. When you are trying your hardest to hear the voice of heaven, are you also listening to other sounds? Are you listening to the sounds of the birds and the forest as well as the sound of the falls? If so, then you will not be able to hear the voice of heaven. To catch the voice of heaven, you must learn to listen past these sounds. You must listen through them."

Nakamura thinks he understands what his teacher is saying. The next day, he resumes his meditations with renewed concentration. He is unable, however, to put into practice what he had grasped conceptually. The harder he tries to ignore the sounds that reach his ears, the more present and more distracting they become.

Three months go by. Nakamura's isolation in this valley and its surrounding mountains is complete; news of the outside world does not permeate it, the village offers no distractions, and except for the occasional word of advice he receives from Kariappa as they travel to and from the falls, he interacts with almost no one. He continues to suffer the symptoms of his disease, but otherwise, his life has been relieved of almost all practical concerns; he is able to devote himself entirely to solitary meditation. His attention turned, for long hours on end, away from his surroundings and toward the state of his own interior, he gives himself up to the singular pursuit of this one assignment, the discovery of the voice of heaven. Still, he has nothing to show for his dedication and effort. The task is driving him close to madness, and on more than one occasion, he is reduced to tears.

He swallows his pride and seeks direction again from his master. "This business of separating the listening of the mind from the listening of the ears is not easy," he admits.

"It may seem difficult," Kariappa responds. "But actually, it is only difficult because you say it is difficult. The problem is, you are trying too hard." His teacher is now telling him the inverse of what he had said three months ago. "Why don't you stop trying and see what happens?"

"Try less? What do you mean?"

"Right now, you and I are talking. But you still hear sounds other than the sound of my voice, right?"

"Yes, of course."

146

"But you don't pay them any attention, do you? Your attention is focused on what I am saying, right?"

"That is right."

"So, don't you see? Right now, the listening of your mind and the listening of your ears are separated. But you are not trying to separate them, are you?"

Yes, this does make sense. Tomorrow, he would try again—only this time, he would try less.

Try again he does. He tries this and he tries that. He tries not trying. But everything he tries—even trying not to try—is more of the same: he is trying more, not less.

Nakamura sits, as he always does, on the ledge at the base of the falls. "I am wasting my time," he thinks. "Clearly, this is not working."

The absurdity of it all. What is he doing, and why is he doing it? These might well be his last days on earth; yet here he is, spending that precious time in pursuit of a sound he is not sure he would recognize were he to hear it. A sound he cannot be sure even exists. After all, all he has to go on is the word of one old man; how can he be sure that the alleged sound is nothing but a trick of the old man's imagination?

Furthermore, why is hearing this voice of heaven so important anyway?

"Enough is enough," he declares. Not to disrespect his master, but continuation of this nonsense is pointless. He does not go so far as to preclude the option of picking up again later; perhaps after a night of sleep. But for today, he is done.

Nakamura stands and takes leave of his ledge. The riverbank just downstream is lushly carpeted with grass, and he throws himself into it. He rolls over on his back and spreads his arms and feet wide. Overhead, fluffy clouds are suspended in a blue sky. From this position, sky and clouds fill his field of vision. As he lets go of the tension in his body and sinks into the grass, he has the odd sensation that he is being sucked into the sky's emptiness.

Absentmindedly, he admires the artful sculpturing of the clouds. His thoughts and cares absorbed into the sky, the mind he has been straining so hard for so long goes on strike. Then he sees. The background to this scene is filled with sounds, the sounds of birds, animals, insects, wind in the trees, as well as that of the river, but he is paying them no attention. His attention is up among the clouds. Mental activity is subsumed by an absolute passivity, and the seeing and hearing head on his shoulders is replaced by a spaciousness, inside of which seeing and hearing occur. Emptiness has fallen out of the sky and rests on his neck in the place where his head once was. Even the notion of a self, of a Nakamura Saburō separate from the sky above and the earth below, drops away.

Nakamura sits up. What has just happened? For a fleeting moment, a moment that felt like an eternity, he has witnessed a background of absolute silence in which all the sounds of the world appeared to be framed. And in that moment, that background, the instant it was acknowledged, had become foreground.

He looks around. Nothing has changed—the same river, the same forest, the same sky—yet everything has changed. The river is dancing with light, the forest is dancing with joy, the sky is a visible link to the farthest reaches of the universe. Warm tears run down his face. The world is whole, perfect, complete. Furthermore, he is inseparable from that world; he, too, is whole, perfect, complete.

When he reports this experience to Kariappa, the master smiles. "Congratulations," he says. "That is the voice of heaven. The voice of heaven is the voice of no voice, the voice of absolute stillness. It is the voice of the stillness that is the wellspring of all the sounds of the world."

"You are an educated man," Kariappa continues, "so you know that, even while we are sitting here, the earth is revolving around the sun at a speed of about twenty miles per second. You know that there are sounds and forms of light that operate at wavelengths too long and too short to be detected by human perception. You can't see them, but they are there. So you see, silence always contains sound. Silence is what gives rise to the sounds you can hear and the sounds that you can't hear. This is the voice of heaven."

Nakamura is dumbfounded. He has never heard the ancient sage speak in this way before. He has never questioned his master's versatility in the ways of traditional wisdom, but he has also always assumed that the man and his wisdom are exclusively of humble and primitive origin. With a mixture of wonder and chagrin, he now realizes that his master is also versed in the language and logic of modern science.

"I see," says Nakamura. "So when the mind hears that silence, it is listening to the voice of heaven."

"Yes, yes. That's right."

"But then, I have another question."

"What is it?"

"So now what? Now that I have discovered the voice of heaven, what am I supposed to do with it?"

Kariappa looks at him, long and hard. "I misjudged you. I never thought that you were so stupid that you would need to ask," he says finally.

"But I don't know; that's why I'm asking," says Nakamura.

"All right, then, I shall explain. In the moment that you are listening for the voice of heaven, you are also calling forth your inherent vital force. Anyway, you don't need to worry about that now. You will see for yourself in due course."

And in due course, he does see. The days that follow are filled with delight. As his proficiency in listening for the voice of heaven grows, thoughts of his sickness recede; the symptoms are still there, but they concern him less. Moreover, the simplest activities become the stuff of adventure, and each new dawn a cause for celebration. At times, he is overwhelmed by a sense of profound grace; for what, if not divine providence, could account for the creation of this idyllic playground and the fact of his existence in it? What else could possibly account for the circumstances that brought him to be in this place?

While medical science recognized the natural ability of the body to rejuvenate and regenerate itself, it had no answer for, nor did it really ask, where that regenerative power came from. But if all the sounds and vibrations of the natural world were carried into being by a primordial stillness, then it made perfect sense that that stillness should also be the source of human vitality. And indeed, the discovery of the voice of heaven marks the turning point in Nakamura's path to recovery; for in direct proportion to the decrease in attention he gives to his disease, his health improves. The symptoms he is so used to, he notes, are abating. The fever is weakening its hold, and he is sleeping better and coughing less.

Effortless, instant access to a state of quietude and stillness is available to everyone, but it must be cultivated, Nakamura Tempū insists. That cultivation, he goes on to say, is also essential to the work of uniting functions of mind and body into a single whole.

Furthermore, his teachings are replete with a simple and practical methodology for that cultivation. Tempū recognized, when he first began teaching the principles of mind-body unification, that the type of training he had undergone in order to discover the voice of heaven was incompatible with the demands of modern life, and that a more congenial and practicable solution was called for. He succinctly but comprehensively describes his method in a lecture delivered in August 1956 and published in *Seidai-na Jinsei* (A Prosperous Life), an excerpt from which I include below.

Tempū mentions in this passage that the discovery of his method is based on a "hint" he received while in India; the story of that hint, elaborated elsewhere in his talks, goes roughly as follows. One day, soon after recognizing the voice of heaven, he was listening to the sounds of the cicada. The cicada chorus is an omnipresent feature of the hotter months in Nepal, just as it is in Nakamura's native Japan, and once he had honed his powers of concentration and his abilities to distinguish the sounds of earth, he would sometimes amuse himself by singling out the drone of an individual insect from the background of the greater body of sound; each insect was recognizable and distinguishable from others through differences in pitch, sound quality, and intensity. On this day, he singled out the sound of one insect and focused on it with total and undivided attention. He focused on it until the sound and the act of listening seemed to converge. Soon, his thoughts, his awareness, and his attention all merged with this sound.

Just at that moment, the cicada brought its droning to an abrupt halt. Nakamura's mind, suddenly released from the sound to which it had attached itself, was left dangling in external space. Just as it had that day on the riverbank, his awareness was propelled again into boundless and timeless emptiness, and he was liberated from his small and separate sense of self.

The core meditative practice within Tempū's mind-body system is one he calls *anjō-daza*: *anjō* means "rest" or "stillness," with the additional connotation of "stability"; *daza* means "sitting meditation." In anjō-daza, the drone of the cicada is replaced with an electric buzzer, the sound of which is abrasive and impossible to ignore; by directing one's total attention toward this unpleasant sound, one is momentarily left in a state of emptiness when the buzzer is abruptly switched off, a state described in Zen as "body-mind dropped."

I shall also note that the method as presented supposes a gathering of practitioners and an administrator—someone to operate the buzzer (and to ring the bell, as is also explained); however, with a bit of innovation, such as the use of a recording device or the substitution of another naturally occurring sound, the principle behind the method is easily applied to solo practice.

I discovered the principle of this method while sitting beside a waterfall in the mountains of India. As I have already mentioned, I was becoming more adept at listening to the voice of no voice, and as I did so, random and distracting thoughts fell away: I became better able to focus and concentrate my attention. Later, acting on a hint that I had received during that time, I developed the method I call anjō-daza.

*By concentrated attention, I mean a state of heightened spiritual aware-
ness where the mind is quiet but alert—so alert that it notices even
the smallest details of experience. In order for me to attain this state,
I spent months of training amid those special surroundings where I
was completely removed from the distractions of the world and could
devote myself entirely to that one purpose. Practically speaking, for most
people, devotion to the discovery of this spiritual realm while at the same
time answering to the demands of daily life would be difficult, if not
impossible. But using the method that I am about to show you, virtually
anyone can taste the serenity of this realm in just a short period of time.*

*First, however, I will say a little more about why it is important to
be able to access the realm of spirit. With access to a state of spiritual
awakening, you will discover that the energy of life that moves through
you, your vitality, is linked to the primordial energy that moves the
universe. And when you discover that, your vitality and this energy
will become fused together, will become one. When the mind enters this
spiritual state of awareness, it ceases to operate from the basis of its own
small thoughts but instead hands over responsibility for its operation to
the universe's infinite wisdom. And when its thoughts are replaced by
universal wisdom, the mind sees without blinders: universal truth is
revealed to it directly, without any need to depend on external guideposts
or instructions.*

*The actualization of this state of awareness is the goal of not only anjō-
daza but also the notoriously difficult practice of Zen. The reorientation
of the mind; the loosening of the pulls on it from feelings and rational
thoughts; the cultivation of free will—that is to say, the cultivation of
right-mindedness—these are the true purposes of religion. Spiritual
liberation is the ultimate secret to the cultivation of true humanity.*

*In actuality, whether we wish it so or not, we are always tethered to the
universe; whether we realize it or not, the source of human vitality is*

always none other than the universal order. So we are already, inherently, connected to the body of universal wisdom, just the way that a lightbulb is connected to the local power station. But by the same analogy, just as the lightbulb only goes on when you throw a switch, it takes the throwing of a switch to infuse ourselves with the light of universal wisdom. And that switch is the mind. When the mind enters a particular state of awareness, we automatically connect with the source of human vitality and infinite wisdom.

The particular state in question is the state of no thought, the mental state of emptiness. Now, I know what you are thinking, because as soon as I mention the state of no thought or emptiness, almost everyone— especially those of you who have had some experience with Zen meditation—answers, "Easier said than done." But if this is what you are thinking, then it is probably because you are confused about what it means to have no thoughts or to be mentally empty. Most people's concept of emptiness is unrealistic. Some imagine it to mean that your head is transported to a place in the clouds, that you are suddenly removed from ordinary reality to some dreamlike plane of existence.

So let me say it this way. When the mind places none of its attention on the business of living, it is free of distractions. How is that?

When our minds are filled with desires and attached to goals and ideas, we mistake life for the activity of the mind. But when the mind is not concerned with the business of living—or perhaps a better way of saying it is, when the mind is not concerned with the body, and when the mind is not concerned with the mind, it is free of distractions. It is empty of thoughts. Is that better?

Most people devote an inordinate amount of attention to their physical condition and their circumstances, or to how they feel as a result of their condition and their circumstances. Wouldn't you agree this is so? In fact, some of you may be thinking, "Of course I think about my physical condition. After all, I am human. When things go wrong with my health, of course I think about it. And when things are not going my way, when I am upset or angry or otherwise ill at ease, of course I think about it. That is only natural." But by thinking it natural to think such unnatural thoughts, you are throwing off the switch that connects you with the source of your vitality without even realizing it. You become a magnet for illness and misfortune.

Return the mind as often as possible to a state of no thought and emptiness and you will find that, automatically and effortlessly, you will reconnect with the source of your vitality. This is the way you are designed to work, just the way that the lightbulb automatically connects to the power station when the switch is thrown. Usually, however, the times when we need access to the infinite power station the most, when we are overcome by illness or are suffering misfortune, are the very times we react in such a way as to inhibit that access. This is important, so please listen up. When the mind is not concerned with the body, and when the mind is paying no attention to its thoughts and feelings, it slips naturally and effortlessly into a state of heightened spiritual awareness.

The fundamental essence of the universe is energy—call it vril, or prana, or ki—and this vril is also the spiritual essence of what religion calls God or Buddha. God and Buddha do not inhabit just shrines and temples; they are everywhere. They permeate every corner of the infinite universe. They are right here, where you are right now. But unless you are open to that presence, unless you allow yourself into the atmosphere that is spirit and spiritual awareness, you cannot expect to receive its guidance.

When the mind is not concerned with the body and not concerned with its thoughts and feelings, and when it falls into that spiritual dimension, the universal fabric of vril and one's vital energy become not just in sync but unified. And because they are unified, because they are one and the same, we are naturally infused with more and more vitality. Like a sponge in water: the cellular structure of the sponge becomes infused with water when put in contact with it.

In "Awakening to the True Nature of Self" [chapter 1 of Kenshin Shō *(Abstract of the Polishing of Mind)], I write, "The substance of self is spirit. This spirit is neither of the body, which can be seen, nor of the mind, which cannot be seen but which we nevertheless know to be real. It is a kind of energy that inhabits the universe like a gaseous cloud. Both sensually and rationally inapprehensible, it is knowable only directly, through insight. Furthermore, the body and the mind are tools of spirit; they are operatives of this energetic cloud. Or, more accurately, the mind is a tool for the movement of the energetic cloud of spirit, and the body, a tool for the expression of the movement of mind."*

So when the mind is not serving the body, and when it is not serving the mind, it naturally serves the purposes of spirit. And when the mind serves the purposes of the energy that is spirit, then the full power of the universe, the fundamental source of creation, is reflected directly in our lives.

I didn't know any of this when I first arrived in India. At the time, I was miserable. I was almost constantly running a fever of about thirty-eight degrees [100°F], I wobbled when I stood up, and when I over-exerted myself, I coughed up blood. Sometimes even my saliva would taste like blood. Furthermore, I was surrounded by people of another skin color and hair color with whom I couldn't communicate because I didn't speak their language. I had no one I could turn to or call upon for help. My only lifeline was the man who had led me to this place from Cairo, that holy man, Kariappa.

Then too, I was used to loneliness. For most of the eight years prior to my arrival in India, ever since the beginning of my assignment to

Manchuria as a spy, I had been on my own. Were it not for that—had I, say, been suddenly abducted from friends and family and landed amid these strange surroundings—I would have almost certainly succumbed to neurosis and serious homesickness. But after having spent over three years carrying out a mission in the hinterlands of Manchuria that included hiding in fields, sleeping in forests, and looking constantly over my shoulder for the enemy, loneliness didn't bother me.

Furthermore, I was no stranger to the specter of death. I had been in tight places—places where the odds on survival were exceptionally grim—so many times that I was not easily rattled by danger. You could say that, while I was in Manchuria, I didn't look at death with the same fear that most people do. Not that I wished for death; I had no more desire to die than anyone does. But I wasn't plagued by the fear of death. I knew that, unless I was fully resigned to the prospect of death, I couldn't fulfill my duties.

Even so, now sick and alone in this faraway place, and especially when the symptoms of my illness became particularly severe, I felt the need to tell someone. Not that telling anyone would do any good; that I understood. But when you have only one person in the world to talk to, you want to tell that person your troubles. In my case, it so happened that the one person I could talk to was my teacher. So I would remark, casually and without really thinking about it, how depressed I was, how terrible I felt. The words just slipped by my lips.

To which he would invariably answer, "If you have nothing better to do than worry, then go up the mountain and listen to the waterfall." At first, I had no idea what he meant by this; he certainly didn't explain. It only seemed to me to be a heartless thing to say.

Were he to have said something like, "I'm sorry to hear that. Is there anything I can do for you? I know it's hard, feeling terrible the way that you do all the time," I would have accepted it as an offer of sympathy. Even if that sympathy did nothing to alleviate my pain. Ordinarily, most people would give an answer like that. Not that social convention is necessarily a good thing, just because everyone subscribes to it.

But no. Instead, he would just say, "Go sit by the waterfall if you have so much free time." As cold and insensitive as I thought this answer was in the beginning, it proved, in the long run, to be a major contribution—or rather, I should say, it was pivotal—to my recovery.

The waterfall was deep in mountains covered with virgin forests, and even during the daytime, it was dark. Once my eyes got used to the darkness, it was no problem, but at first I couldn't tell whether what I was looking at was rocks or pines; it was like being thrown into a dark cellar without a flashlight. I would sit beside the basin of this waterfall, where water had been running for maybe tens of thousands of years, with no clue as to why he wanted me there.

In the beginning, I was inundated with thoughts and feelings: "What is to become of me? What if I were to drop dead, right here right now, in this God-forsaken place without another living person around? Just what am I doing here? What possible good could come of sitting by a waterfall in this dark and secluded wilderness?" Doubts and fears came up, one after the other, and there was nothing I could do to shut them off. My mind was bucking like a wild stallion. It threw up every concern it could come up with—the flimsy state of my health, the uncertainty of my future—and it imagined all the things, possible or impossible, that could go wrong.

In due course, however, these thoughts were drowned out by the roar of the falls. That roar was impossible to ignore; it was a noise so loud that I wondered whether it was enough to leave me deaf. Soon, in the presence of that sound, it became difficult to think, even when I tried; my consciousness was completely occupied by that incessant roar.

Before becoming empty of self and free of thoughts (muga-munen; "no self, no thought"), the mind first becomes fully alert and aware (yuga-ichinen; "all self, one thought"). I was lucidly cognizant of a person I identified as "me" sitting at the base of a waterfall. But even so, I didn't think about this cognizance. My attention was so fully occupied by the roar of water flowing over the falls that all thoughts and unmanageable worries about my physical condition fell away. Not as the result of any action upon my part but as the natural consequence of exposure to that sound; my thoughts and worries were consumed by the sound of water. The mind naturally becomes caught up in and consumed by that which is foremost in its attention.

Sometimes, I then began to notice, I would be so caught up in the sound of the falls that the sound would disappear. The lapse was only momentary, and I would only become aware of it after the fact. I would think to myself, "Did I fall asleep? For a moment there, I heard nothing. For a moment I was engulfed in complete silence."

This was the training that I underwent during my first six months in India; how long it went on for, I can't say, because I didn't count the days and weeks. But during that first month after discovering silence in the presence of sound, my mind began moving of its own accord from a place of self-awareness (yuga-ichinen) to a place of no self and no thought (muga-munen), and finally to a place of emptiness, completely devoid of thoughts or feelings (munen-musō; "no thought, no concept"). From there, naturally, and effortlessly, my mind would enter a state of liberation. I felt that I was inhabited by spirit, and I felt that the boundless energy of universal creation was flowing into my being and circulating throughout my body.

And once this began to happen, the fever that had plagued me for eight long years subsided. I stopped coughing up blood. Above all, the palpitations of the heart that appeared whenever I exerted myself went away, and I became able to practically run up the mountain. I had more energy and stamina than I had had in years.

Even so, I didn't understand what was happening to me or why. So one day, after about two months had passed, I asked my teacher about it. But to my question, Kariappa answered with a question of his own.

"You haven't said much to me about your health lately, have you?" he said.

"No. My condition seems to be improving, so I have had less to complain about."

"If only you had responded that way in the beginning, you could have saved yourself from a lot of suffering. But all you could do was tell me about how badly you felt, and so you wasted a lot of time."

I was astonished to hear these words.

"No matter how bad someone feels, even if they are on their deathbed, they forget all about it when they fall asleep," he said. "And then, when they wake up, they feel better. They feel rejuvenated. It's the same with you. You are feeling better because you are paying less attention to your ailments, and consequently, the universe is giving back to you in the form of vitality.

"Your body is not of your own creation," he continued. "Yet, when you feel the slightest discomfort, you act as though it is your job to worry. You act as though worrying will set things right. If worrying served any useful purpose, then I would tell you to continue worrying from morning until night. But it doesn't. And unless you give up this useless habit of worrying when it only makes things worse, then you cannot expect to ever regain your health or your strength.

"In the beginning, every time you complained to me about how you felt, I told you to go listen to the sound of the waterfall. Do you remember? So now, do you understand why?"

"Yes, I do. I understand," I answered.

Of course, he didn't explain this to me in the same way that I have just explained it to you. He didn't go into as much detail. But this is what he meant.

Work is made all the more difficult and all the more tiring when you try to avoid it. The load you are actually carrying is always lighter than the load you are thinking about carrying, and with enough self-conviction, you can make even a sheet of paper feel heavy. That is the meaning of the saying, "When you are given a load to carry, don't become a slave to the burden."

So now I will give you some simple instructions, which, if you follow them, will lead you to discover the realm of spirit. You don't need to go to the Himalayas or to look for a waterfall to sit under either. This method works on the principle that when the mind is correctly focused, it moves of its own accord into a place of no thought. It was one of the first practices that I invented after returning from India, and since then I have taught it to hundreds and thousands of my students. And almost all of them report good results. So now I will teach it to you.

Sit comfortably and close your eyes. Find a position that is comfortable and that you can hold for a reasonable length of time. You can cross your legs or not, whichever is easiest. But don't lie down: sit upright.

And close your eyes. Don't have your eyes open. Later, once you have mastered this method, your eyes can be open or closed and it won't make any difference. But when you are first learning, it's best to keep them closed; the mind has a way of being easily distracted by what it sees.

Also, don't shift or readjust your posture. To the extent that you are able, hold the position that you first settle into for the duration of the exercise. Of course, if your legs are going to sleep, or if you are experiencing extreme pain, then you can readjust your position. If we were engaging in an ascetic form of meditation, then I would tell you that, even in those circumstances, you should not move. But you are beginners, so for now, it doesn't matter.

Now I am going to sound a buzzer. You will find that, even though it is unpleasant and annoying, this sound will pull on you. Just allow it to pull; in fact, give it your complete attention. When you are totally focused on the sound, and when the sound fully occupies your attention, no other thoughts will arise. This is the state we call single-mindedness or unity of self and thought (yuga-ichinen). Then, when you are in that state—the state wherein the mind, through the mechanism of the ears and the sense of hearing, is fully absorbed in the sound of the buzzer—I am going to switch the buzzer off. And in that moment, you will find yourself briefly suspended in a state of soundlessness, a state of total silence.

This is the domain of total silence, the sound of no sound. This is the point of entry to the realm of spirit. What in Zen is called sanmai *[from the Sanskrit* samadhi; *the state of conscious and focused concentration that produces quietude of mind]. Silence is the ultimate reality; it is the face of the all-pervasive energetic substrata that makes up the universe. It is unknowable through either sensory perception or the faculties of the mind. But with practice, you can develop the ability to go beyond your mind and slip effortlessly into this quiet place, regardless of how chaotic or distracting your surroundings. Should you become physically ill or mentally distraught, you will be able to access this core state of wellness and stability. Not right away—not necessarily from today, you understand—but with practice.*

So listen to the buzzer and allow yourself to be drawn in.

[The buzzer sounds: ....]

When you are totally absorbed in the sound of the buzzer, you are in a state of single-minded concentration (yuga-ichinen). So, next, I will turn the buzzer off. Watch what happens. When the sound of the buzzer is cut off, you are suspended in silence.

Just for a moment. In the beginning, this moment may only last for one or two seconds. But with practice, you will be able to remain in this state for longer. The physical act of cutting off the source of the sound will be enough to put you into the place of no thought (munen-musō), even if, another moment later, you become aware of the outside sounds of the traffic. Or, if there are no outside sounds, even if you suddenly develop an itch or feel a bead of sweat running down your arm. These little distractions will be enough to return you to your normal state of consciousness. In the beginning, almost everyone is easily distracted and falls back quickly into their old patterns of thinking and feeling. But, with practice, you will develop the ability to effortlessly and instantaneously reenter that state of listening for the voice of no voice.

Until you develop that ability, however, it's better that I help you along. That is the purpose of the buzzer and the bell. It's the same with the bell.

[The bell is a small gong, of the type used in Buddhist meditation. Tempū strikes the bell: ....]

Your mind will be drawn into the clear tone of the bell's vibration. This vibration will gradually subside; it will become weaker and weaker until you can no longer hear it. But if you continue to focus your mind on the sound of that vibration, and to listen for it even as it subsides, then, when it can no longer be heard, you will find yourself listening to the sound of silence.

Silence, or emptiness, is the true face of reality. The world of sound, the world of colors and vibrations that we perceive with our senses, is only that reality's temporary and phenomenal outer shell. So you want to pin your identity to emptiness, and this you do through the vehicle of mind. You want to do this because, in actuality, emptiness is overflowing with life-giving energy. When you identify yourself with emptiness, it is as though you are plugging yourself into the infinite and universal source of vitality. This connection is automatic, the consequence of universal principle.

Whether or not you intellectually understand what I am telling you isn't important; intellectual understanding will come with time. What is important is that you develop the ability to put yourself in contact with the realm of no thought instantaneously and at any time and place. When you develop that ability, mountains may crumble but your presence of mind will not waver. The difference between a completely matured person and a person who is not yet formed is just that: the person who is not yet formed is easily upset by even the smallest of things. Conversely, the person not easily agitated knows almost no fear. This is because, ninety-nine times out of a hundred, fear is simply a state of mental agitation, resulting from over-concern for physical safety and physical well-being. People not subject to such agitation have been known to sleep through earthquakes strong enough to rattle heaven and earth, only to ask, "Really?" when told about it afterward.

Nothing is so unpredictable as life. As long as we have a body, as long as there is blood flowing through our veins, we can rest assured that we will face one calamity after another. Sickness, injury, and misfortune will come our way, no matter how hard we try to avoid them. So what is the point of spending your life worrying about what might go wrong? If you spend your life worrying about what might go wrong, you will lose your purpose for living. Not only that, you will also lose your resilience and your vitality.

So make it your habit to practice often this method that I have just shown you—as often as you are able. Practice anjō-daza. If you are religious, this is the practice of uniting yourself with God or Buddha. If you prefer philosophical terms, it is the practice of uniting yourself with the primordial energy of universal creation. Either way, if you engage in this practice, you will find yourself soon becoming made over. You will find yourself able to call forth more vitality than you had ever thought possible.[2]

8.
KUMBHAKA

During the following months, Nakamura's physical condition improved at a remarkable pace. For the first time in years he was sleeping soundly through the night and waking up fully rested. His fever, for so long a constant companion, subsided and did not return. His complexion went from pale to healthy pink.

He also began to gain weight. In his prime, Nakamura had weighed 140 pounds (sixty-four kilograms). Prior to his departure from Marseilles, when last he had access to a set of scales, he had weighed in at eighty-four pounds (thirty-eight kilograms), and even that weight, he knew, had been further diminished by the time he reached India. Now, however, his body was reclaiming its former mass. At first, he mistook the change for some kind of swelling. But no, it was his body filling out to its former proportions. Kariappa said to him:

Think about it. The moment a person separates himself from sickness and misfortune, he ceases to be a sick person or an unfortunate person. It is possible to endure misfortune without becoming misfortunate. It is possible to endure sickness without becoming sick.

Conversely, even if you are well but think you are sick, you will be just as someone who is sick. Even if you suffer no misfortune but think you are misfortunate, you will be just as someone who is misfortunate.

So it's up to you. You may not have chosen to contract the sickness that you now carry, but you can choose whether or not you want to be a sick person. If not, leave matters of physical infirmity to the body—no reason to allow them to carry over to the mind.

And the way to ensure that the mind remains free of the body's infirmities is to return it from time to time—the more frequently the better—to the state of listening in which you can hear the voice of heaven, the voice of stillness. The mind, when it listens to the voice of stillness, is completely at rest. It is free from worry, care, and concern. You can afford to allow your mind to rest from time to time. At rest, the mind is in a perfect state of health. It is perfectly aligned with the impulsive creativity of the universe. And it calls forth the vital force within you that will make you whole, both physically and spiritually.

Very soon now, you will be completely well.

Kariappa looked at his student approvingly. "Do you see now? Your body has access to all of the wisdom that it needs in order to heal itself. That wisdom is inherent to the energy, or prana, that is the wellspring of life."[1]

Nakamura reflected again on the path that he had walked: all of the years that he had spent wrestling with demons and wallowing in self-pity and despair, all that time he had been standing in his own way.

But then, only because of sickness had he come to a realization that was ever so more important than the restoration of physical health. Tuberculosis, his dark companion, had been a teacher in disguise.

At the same time, he could also see that his return to health was not solely due to spiritual transformation. The vegetarian diet to which he had so vigorously objected in the beginning had been essential to his reconstitution, as had the clean mountain air and the yogic practices of controlling the breath—*pranayama*—he had been taught. Likewise, his morning submersions in cold water had invigorated his immune system, while the physical exercise of climbing to the waterfall every day had rebuilt his stamina. All of these factors would be taken into account when Tempū came to formalize his system of mind-body unification.

Above all, however, he had to attribute his return to health to the simple realization that the mind leads the body: this because health must be possible before it can be real. Only when Nakamura had opened himself to physical restoration as a possibility had latent forces come to the fore and reestablished his balance and equilibrium. The changes in his mental disposition, he felt, had affected his physiology all the way down to the cellular, perhaps even molecular, level of its composition.

With spiritual equanimity comes clarity of mind. With clarity of mind comes physical health. With physical health comes greater clarity of mind. And with greater clarity of mind comes reinforcement of faith and greater equanimity. Health and deliverance, especially deliverance from fear, were not, as Nakamura had once held them out to be, goals of living but byproducts of the equanimity that comes with spiritual realization. As fodder for meditation, Kariappa continued to assign him riddles, and now he began to see directly into their meaning.

The first of these was the one given to him early on: Why was he born and what was the purpose of living? Earlier, he had thought long and hard on this, to no avail. Interrupted by his search for the voice of heaven, he now returns to that riddle. But he also sees it in a new light.

"I think I know," he says to Kariappa one afternoon. The answer had come to him not through rational inquiry but almost as a vision. He saw himself as a tiny speck in a grand universe that was alive and growing. His life had no purpose or meaning outside the purpose and meaning of this grand design—a design that, as a finite being, he could only hope to grasp in parts, never in aggregate. The reason he had been born was almost ineffable, for the saying of it detracted from the majesty and the wonder of it all. He owed his birth to universal causality, and the purpose of living was to serve the unfolding of universal purpose, to further the universal evolutionary imperative.

"That's good," replies Kariappa. No word need be spoken; the glow on Nakamura's face says everything there is to say.

Months go by. Nakamura is now in his second year on the Indian subcontinent. One evening, Kariappa and Nakamura return to the village to find it astir with excitement. A yogi has just returned from a ten-year retreat in the wilderness.

The valley in which Gorkhey sits is but one of several in succession along the approach to the Kanchenjunga massif. The more remote of these valleys, as yet uninhabited, are carpeted with virgin rain forests hostile to human penetration: home to tigers, panthers, bears, and poisonous snakes, they also provided a natural breeding ground for all manner of tropical diseases. The more advanced yogis venture into these forests and the high Himalayan wilderness beyond to sequester themselves from all human contact and to devote themselves to spiritual practice. Retreats of one to two years are not unusual, but rarely do they extend beyond three. The yogi in question had been gone so long that most of the villagers had given him up for lost to the wilderness.

He is, however, very much alive and looking radiant. Kariappa's eyes twinkle with pride.

The next day, while he and Nakamura pause on their journey up the mountain path, he explains to Nakamura how extraordinary is this man's accomplishment. Nakamura listens to his descriptions of the wilderness.

"I would like to go there," he says.

Kariappa laughs.

"Not in your current condition," he says. "You wouldn't last a day. Before going into the forest, you must first master kumbhaka."[2]

Nakamura is hearing the word for the first time. "What is this kumbhaka?" he asks.

"It is the most sacred of states, when mind and body are fully awake yet fully at rest. In this state, even the tigers will leave you alone."

Kariappa has Nakamura's full attention. "How does one learn this kumbhaka?" he asks. "How is it done?"

"This," Kariappa answers, "you must discover. It cannot be taught. Kumbhaka is the essence of yoga. It cannot be explained. But in the yoga literature, it is described as the state wherein the body is maintained like an urn filled with water."

The description makes no sense. But then, by now he is used to his master's cryptic explanations and understands that his questions will need to wait.

"Time to go," Kariappa says. They continue on up the path.

Upon coming to retrieve Nakamura from his perch by the waterfall one late afternoon some ten days later, Kariappa looks down from his donkey and smiles.

"Today you are very lucky," he says. "I am going to allow you to witness something special, something you will need to see to believe. This evening, you must come to the meeting hall."

The meeting hall is a communal structure located on the outskirts of the village used by Kariappa from time to time for closed sessions with his closest students. Following the evening meal, Nakamura falls in behind a file of yogis making their way to the hall and takes a place inside among a gathering of some forty men. The men are seated in a wide circle around a single sheet of white cloth spread out on the dirt floor.

Presently, Kariappa enters, followed by the yogi who, ten days earlier, had returned from the wilderness. Kariappa walks to the round cushion put out for him at the head of the room and sits. The yogi goes to the center of the circle and seats himself in the middle of the white cloth.

A flute and a bell played by men seated on either side of Kariappa strike up a slow and hauntingly ethereal tune. Not unlike the music played in Shinto shrines, Nakamura reflects.

Then, as this music continues, the men in the circle rise, one by one, and walk slowly but deliberately around the white cloth and the seated yogi at its center.

The yogi has his eyes closed, and judging from his demeanor and deep, slow breathing, he has already entered a meditative state. Now, however, he raises both hands to his neck. His breathing stops, and his hands close tightly, his thumbs applied to either side of his esophagus just under his jaw. His face turns purple. Then both his hands and his neck go limp.

Nakamura watches this surreal spectacle with detachment, as if in a dream. The white cloth, the somber mood, the publicly witnessed self-execution—all bear similarities to the practice of *seppuku*, ritual suicide in atonement for failure, once an accepted part of the Japanese samurai code.

The flute and the bell cease. One of the yogis steps forward. He uncrosses the legs of the still seated corpse and stretches it out to its full length. Then the body is neatly wrapped in the white cloth.

The doors to the hall open. A small army of men, straining under the weight of their load, carry a marble coffin and deposit it beside the wrapped body. The lid, requiring eight men to lift, is removed, and the white bundle gingerly laid inside. Then the lid is lifted back on and hermetically sealed with a generous coating of pine tar.

Transported back outside, the coffin is lowered into a hole that has been prepared in advance. The excavated earth is shoveled in, around, and over it, so that when all is done, only a low mound remains. The yogis quietly dispersed and return to their huts.

Nakamura is mystified. The parties to this ritual show no emotional expression of any kind, and Kariappa makes no mention of the event, either the next day or during the days following, nor can Nakamura, still stunned, bring himself to ask.

Seven days and seven nights pass. On the morning of the eighth day, Nakamura is called once again to the meeting hall and arrives to find the same group of yogis gathered. When the doors are thrown open, the same stone coffin, he is surprised to see, is carried back into the room. The hardened pine tar is chiseled away and the lid removed. The shrouded corpse is lifted out and laid on the floor. Once again, the flute and bell begin to play.

The skin color of the body that appears from the cloth is ashen gray; Nakamura has seen enough corpses to know a dead man when he sees one. Yogis on either side of the corpse, however, begin rubbing it with *gheeta*, a kind of butter made from goat's milk. Over the butter they apply a white powder. This they massage into the body, beginning at its extremities—hands and feet—and moving up its arms and legs. The other yogis in the circle, in time to the flute and bell, chant something from Vedic scripture.

Some thirty minutes into this process, Nakamura notices a change in the condition of the corpse. Its flesh is responding to the pressure applied by its masseurs, and a faint glow of pinkness is returning to its skin. The yogis increase the intensity of their massaging of the muscles, their thumbs and fingers deftly seeking out the same vital spots manipulated by *shiatsu* masseurs in Japan. Presently, the man's chest quivers. Nakamura questions his eyes; he blinks hard and looks again. Unmistakably, it rises and falls. The dead man is beginning to breathe.

On a cue from Kariappa, the flute, bell, and chanting cease. The room becomes still. The man on the cloth opens his eyes and as easily as someone waking from a deep sleep, sits up and folds his legs.

The room erupts with shouts of celebration. Looking over at Kariappa, Nakamura sees his eyes gleam. His face opens into a broad smile.[3]

The next day, Kariappa asks Nakamura what he thought. Nakamura is still dumbfounded; nothing of what he has witnessed makes sense, and certainly everything that he has learned, in medical school and elsewhere, tells him that what he saw is not possible.

Kariappa laughs.

"To you," he says, "what you saw appears to have been a miracle. But to the yogi himself, the experience was no different than going to sleep at night and waking up again in the morning."

Kariappa is speaking from experience. He has, Nakamura learns later, performed the same rite of passage on two separate occasions. For the yogi, as it had been for Kariappa, this rite constitutes the equivalent of a final examination: forthwith, and with Kariappa's blessing, he will move away and begin to take on students of his own.

"But," Kariappa continues, "understand there was no guarantee that he would return to us. Out of every three people who attempt this test, only one succeeds. For the other two, the sleep into which they enter is one to which the morning never comes.

"The point, however, is that these yogis—both the ones who return and those who don't—have no fear of death. They are different from you. As yet, you do not recognize the full extent of your own power. But perhaps you now begin to see that the vital force, prana, has far more strength and resilience than you imagine."

Nakamura Saburō has to admit that this is so.

Another year passes. Nakamura is now in his third winter in Gorkhey, and winter in these parts, especially after the oppressive heat of summer, is almost blissfully mild. No longer the troubled and lonely figure he had been when he first arrived, he has developed an affinity for this village. He is comfortable here, isolated from the cares of the world. With but little persuasion, he could easily accept it as his permanent home.

Each morning, he rises early to greet the new day. As always, these days begin with the mandatory immersion in the river. Nakamura settles into his habitual spot and sits, submerged to his chest, with his legs crossed in a half-lotus, hands cupped in front of him with interlocking fingers. The practice that had been pure torture two years ago Nakamura now finds refreshing. Breathing slowly but freely and without excess force, he is able to generate as much internal heat as he needs to keep warm.

Kariappa passes among the seated yogis, observing their posture and breathing. "That's it. That's good," he says softly as he passes Nakamura. Nakamura is puzzled but pleased. Kariappa has never said anything in the past. What is it, he wonders, that has elicited his approval?

The next day, the same thing happens. "That's good," Kariappa says as he passes.

On the third day, Kariappa again commends Nakamura as he passes. The session ends and Nakamura, as usual, rises to his feet to walk to the shore.

From the riverbank, Kariappa's voice rings out like a rifle shot. "No good, no good. That isn't it."

Now Nakamura is genuinely mystified. What is so right about the way he sits in the river and so wrong about the way he stands and walks to the shore?

The next day, the same scene is repeated. Just what is it that his master is looking for?

Whatever it is, Nakamura clearly has it while he sits in the river. "All I need to do," he reasons, "is to maintain the same attitude when I stand."

Easier said than done, he soon realizes. Kariappa watches his efforts in silence.

In the river, Nakamura is relaxed and centered. Once he rises from that position, however, it is a different story: he awkwardly searches for firm footing on the slippery rocks while the river's currents pull at his legs and feet.

Gradually, however, he gets what he thinks is the knack of it. He is able to maneuver the river without giving up his balance or poise.

A full two weeks have gone by since Kariappa had first commended him on his posture while seated. "Congratulations," the master says with a broad smile. "You have learned it. That is kumbhaka, the state of holding the body like a jug filled with water."

Nakamura ponders these words. A jug holds water because it is closed; the water inside the jug always seeks a state of rest and distributes itself equally, thereby exerting pressure evenly against the walls that contain it. The water, he realizes, is a metaphor for prana, the universal vital energy. The body can be described as a vessel intended to be filled with and to hold this fluid prana. But in a body that is porous and not properly conditioned, this vital energy leaks away. Kumbhaka is the practice of maintaining a state of ever-ready fullness and equilibrium. It is a state of subtle relaxation but equally subtle tension, of calmness but full alertness, and of immovable solidity combined with vibrant vitality.

Yoga is a broad term encompassing a variety of disciplines, and the yoga with which Nakamura Saburō came into contact had little in common with the exercise-based yoga systems widely taught and practiced today.

Those systems, purportedly of the hatha yoga tradition, trace back largely to the teachings of Tirumalai Krishnamacharya, beginning in the 1920s, as well as those of his principal student, B. K. S. Iyengar, and they are heavily influenced by Western calisthenics, gymnastics, and military drills; Nakamura's training, as he describes it to us, appears to have been primarily grounded in contemplation.

The word *yoga* comes from the Sanskrit root *yuj*, variously interpreted to mean "to join" or "to unite" (through the Indo-European connection, the English word *yoke* shares the same root) and "to focus attention" or "to concentrate." The two interpretations are not mutually exclusive, since concentration is the activity through which subject and object are joined. As a discipline, yoga appears to date back at least several millennia, but its first comprehensive codification as a complete system occurs in the *Yoga Sutras of Patanjali*, written in about 400 CE.

The *Yoga Sutras*, however, describe only the barest bones of that system. A collection of single-sentence aphorisms that, in their concision, are at once both profound and profoundly obscure, the entire text of the *Yoga Sutras* consists of just 194 entries and, in any one of its many modern English translations, can easily be read by the average reader in thirty minutes. On the other hand, the commentaries that have been written by scholars and yoga lineage holders over the centuries, various in their interpretations and legion in number, could easily fill a small library.

The entire teaching as pertains to pranayama, the extension of vital energy through control of the breath, is addressed in the *Yoga Sutras* in just five verses:

2.49. *When this is gained, there follows the right guidance of the life-currents, the control of the incoming and outgoing breath.*

2.50. *The life-current is either outward, or inward, or balanced; it is regulated according to place, time, number; it is prolonged and subtle.*

2.51. *The fourth degree transcends external and internal objects.*

2.52. *Thereby is worn away the veil which covers up the light.*

2.53. *Thence comes the mind's power to hold itself in the light.*[4]

Of the above, 2.50 and 2.51, specifically, are elucidations of the practice of kumbhaka, itself elemental to pranayama. As intimated to Nakamura by Kariappa, the derivation of the name comes from the filling up of a pot or earthenware vessel *(kumbha)*. One of the most thorough and illuminating explanations of pranayama and kumbhaka in existence in English occurs as part of a series of lectures on the *Yoga Sutras* delivered by the venerable Hindu scholar and teacher Swami Krishnananda between March and August 1976 at the Divine Life Society's ashram in Rishikesh. Both the sound recordings and the transcripts of these lectures are publicly available on the website Swami-Krishnanada.org. Several excerpts from Krishnanada's discourse follow; readers interested in delving deeper should read it in its entirety.

Regarding prana and pranayama, Krishnanada says:

The prana is different from the breath. This is also a feature that has to be observed. The prana is a very subtle tendency within us. We may say the characteristic of the total energy of the system is the prana. It is not located in any part of the body particularly. Though it has special emphasis laid in different parts of the body, it is equally distributed everywhere. Prana is nothing but the sum total of the energy of the system. Whatever our total capacity is, that is our prana-shakti. *But this capacity is outwardly directed. This is the difficulty. It is not introverted, and it is impossible to draw the prana within.... Concentration is impossible for most people because they are completely "sold out" to the outside world. We become slaves of conditions and circumstances, and puppets in the hands of these extrovert forces.*

This is precisely the thing to be noted in the practice of yoga. This tendency has to be brought back to its original causative condition.... The practice consists of a gradual retention of the breath, of the flow of this outward tendency in us, the prana, by the technique called pranayama.[5]

With regard to kumbhaka, Krishnananda explains that there are three variations of kumbhaka, described as "outward, or inward, or balanced" in sutra 2.50, quoted above.

The pranayama technique intends to shorten the period of... inhalation and exhalation processes in order that the force with which this process goes on, or continues, is brought to the minimum so that there is no strength in this flow, though the flow is tending to go outward and inward as it has been doing ever since the birth of the individual....

If we are cautious and contemplative, we can feel how the prana moves when we deeply breathe in. The purpose is to stop this lengthening of the breath, outwardly as well as inwardly—to shorten it as far as possible, until it becomes so short that there is practically no movement at all. That cessation of movement is called kumbhaka.

This cessation of the breath can be brought about in many ways. Though the yoga shastras *speak of several types of pranayama or kumbhaka, Patanjali concerns himself with only four types—which are actually not four, really speaking. They are only one, mentioned in four different ways. Bāhya ābhyantara stambha vṛttiḥ (2.50) are the terms used in the sutra.* Bahya *is external;* abhyantara *is internal;* stambha *is sudden retention;* vritti *is the process. The external retention is what is known as* bahya vritti, *the internal retention is what is known as* abhyantara vritti, *and the sudden retention is what is known as* stambha vritti....

The prana can be stopped by way of retention after exhalation.... We breathe out, gradually and intensely, in a very spontaneous, flowing manner, and then do not breathe in; this is one pranayama.... This sort of retention of the breath, which means to say the cessation of breathing in after the breathing out, is called bahya vritti—the pranayama, or the kumbhaka, which follows expulsion.

Or there can be abhyantara vritti, which is retention of the breath after inhalation. We breathe in, in the same way as we exhale—calmly, forcefully, deeply—and then do not breathe out. That retention of the breath after deep inhalation is a pranayama by itself. The way in which we retain the breath is called kumbhaka. Kumbha means a kind of pot which can be filled with things. We fill our system with the whole prana in pranayama. You may ask me, "Is not the body filled with prana at other times? Is it filled with prana only during kumbhaka?"

The idea behind this filling is very peculiar. Though the prana is moving everywhere in the system even at other times than during the time of kumbhaka, something very peculiar takes place during kumbhaka which does not happen at other times. During kumbhaka the prana in the system is filled to the brim, and it remains unmoving and unshaken, just as a pot may be filled to the brim and the content or liquid inside does not shake due to its being filled up to the brim, to the utmost possible extent. There is no movement of the prana in kumbhaka; it is not trying to escape from one place to another place....

There is a third type called stambha vritti, which is not followed either by inhalation or exhalation. Suddenly a cobra drops on our head, just now. What will happen? Our breath will stop at that time; we will not breathe in or breathe out. From the ceiling some snake drops, and we see it on our lap. What happens at that time? The breath is not there—it has stopped. Did we breathe in or breathe out? Neither did we breathe in, nor did we breathe out; nothing has happened. We do not know whether the prana exists at all. It has immediately stopped activity due to the shock it received. Any kind of sudden stopping of the breath is called stambha vritti.

Of course, it does not mean that this stambha is to be introduced into pranayama by shock or fear; that is not the idea. What is intended is that the absorption of the mind in the object or ideal of yoga should be so comprehensive—so deep and absorbing, and intense—that there will be no time for the mind to supply the motive force to the prana to move at all. When we are deeply absorbed in a particular thought, very deeply absorbed, and we are not able to think anything other than that one particular thought due to intense affection or intense hatred, or for any reason whatsoever, the prana stops; there will be no breathing at that time. When we are overpowered with the emotion of love, or fear, or hatred, there will be a stoppage of prana....

Yoga is nothing but practice, a hundred-percent practice—only that and nothing but that. We are not going to tell a story or listen to any kind of narration. It is a very serious matter that we are discussing, which is life and death for us—namely, how we can become better inwardly as well as outwardly so that we take one step, at least, toward the superhuman condition which is waiting for us.

When this is acquired, this mastery is gained, some sort of a control is maintained over the pranic movements. Great consequences—unexpected and unforeseen—will follow. We will see strange phenomena appear within us as well as outside us if we gain mastery over the prana, because this kumbhaka that we are speaking of is nothing but another form of concentration of mind, as the mind is associated with the prana always. The object, or the ideal before oneself, is united with the meditating consciousness in a fast embrace, as it were, when the prana is withheld, and it is made to stick to one's consciousness inseparably. It becomes one with one's own self, and there is a sudden impact felt upon the object on account of the kumbhaka that we practice. The kumbhaka, the retention of the breath that we practice, coupled with concentration of mind on the object that is before us, will tell upon the nature of that object which we are thinking of, whatever be the distance of that object. It may be millions of miles away—it makes no difference. This is because prana is omnipresent. It is like ether, and so it will produce an impact upon the object that we are thinking of in our meditation. It will stir it up into an activity of a desired manner, according to what we are contemplating in the mind. This effect cannot be produced if the prana is allowed to move hither and thither, distractedly. If we want quick success in meditation, the retention of the breath is absolutely necessary because it is this that impresses upon the object of meditation the necessity to commingle itself with the subject. Therefore, a combination of pranayama and dharana, *concentration, is the most effective method of bringing about a union of oneself with the ideal of meditation.*[6]

Kariappa was most probably capable of reciting *The Yoga Sutras of Patanjali* from memory. Nakamura, on the other hand, knew nothing of their existence, nor was he privy to the sort of detailed explanations of pranayama and kumbhaka quoted above. Pranayama is mentioned often by Nakamura in the exposition of his philosophy and mind-body practices: in particular, he developed a sequence of breath exercises (discussed in chapter 13) based on the principles of pranayama as learned from Kariappa. His understanding of pranayama, both theoretical and practical, is, however, experientially derived: it was absorbed through practice and then deciphered through reflection.

The practice of kumbhaka is also core to Nakamura Tempū's mind-body system. Tempū would distill what he learned in India into a practical and teachable method, the basic instructions for which are to relax the shoulders, to allow the body to center itself in the *seika-tanden*, its "one-point" or center of gravity located approximately three finger-widths below the navel, and to tightly close the anal sphincter. The third of these instructions, the closing of the anal sphincter, is particularly novel. Japanese culture has stressed the importance of *hara,* or seika-tanden, training for centuries, whereas the importance of also tightening the anal sphincter is mentioned only among the most secret teachings of some of the older martial disciplines.[7] Furthermore, tightening of the anal sphincter is almost impossible unless the shoulders are relaxed and the body is centered, and conversely, the act of tightening the anal sphincter automatically brings the body into relaxed alignment and its center of gravity down; thus, the other two elements of the instructions can be collapsed into this one.

In 1947, during the American occupation of Japan following World War II, Nakamura Tempū was invited to speak to members of the foreign community, including Allied General Headquarters staff. He lectured in English over the course of three days to about 250 participants assembled in the basement of the Mainichi Newspaper building in Yūrakuchō. On one of these days, following his explanation of kumbhaka, an American woman, in her thirties, rushed to the front of the room. Unable to contain her enthusiasm, she bent forward and kissed Nakamura Tempū on the cheek. Introduced to yoga in New York, she had been practicing for more than ten years, she told him. "But the one thing I have never been able to understand is the meaning of kumbhaka. What ten years of yoga failed to make clear, you were able to explain in fifteen minutes."

No transcript remains of that particular talk. Following, however, is an excerpt from a lecture delivered on January 19, 1967.

The last thing I wish to talk about today is how to gain control over the reaction mechanism of the nervous system. This is important, especially in the face of dangerous or stressful circumstances. During the war, I taught this method to many of the young men going into the Imperial Army and Navy, and they later told me it made all the difference—that because of it they survived situations where many of their friends and comrades perished. The science behind the method I will leave for another day; today we'll just focus on the method itself.

So how do you normally react to sudden, jarring occurrences or other unexpected stimuli? You react with surprise. Or with anger. Or with distress. Don't you? Today I'm going to show you how to receive the shock from such occurrences or sudden, unprovoked stimuli with your belly.

From the look on your faces, it's obvious you don't know what I'm talking about. So I'll say more. Let's suppose that you have exper-

ienced something disturbing—some kind of sensory stimulus or emotional shock. The first thing you need to do is bring power into your belly. But at the same time, you also must tighten your anal sphincter and relax your shoulders. One, two, three. But all at the same time. Understand?

In other words, shoulders, anal sphincter, and belly function as a triune whole. In yoga, this is called "kumbhaka." It is considered to be the most sacred of mind-body states.

When you put power in your belly, tighten your anal sphincter, and relax your shoulders, nothing can upset you. No matter how great the stimulus or shock, you will remain unperturbed. Not only mentally: physically, you will also remain calm and composed. As it is now, when you are subjected to a sudden stimulus or shock, you are easily thrown off-kilter or become riled up. One loud noise and you are startled.

In the old days, bushi [warriors] used to talk about the importance of conditioning the hara [belly]. It was understood that conditioning the hara was the golden key to success and survival in battle. This is because the abdominal nerves that come together in the area around the navel connect directly to the central nervous system and have everything to do with maintaining nervous equilibrium. The thing is, people today pay no mind to the importance of conditioning the hara: the only mind they pay the belly is to feed it when it is hungry.

So I repeat: the way to respond when something sudden occurs is to receive it with your belly and to make shoulders, belly, and anus one. Put power into the tanden [the point located approximately three finger widths below the navel], close the anal sphincter, and relax the shoulders. Why is it important to relax the shoulders? Because raising the shoulders raises the diaphragm, and when that happens, you feel like your insides have been hollowed out. Your balance becomes disrupted, and physical *instability, in turn, disrupts the nervous system and its ability to respond effectively and in an unencumbered way.*

Most of you know the old saying that, if his anus is still closed, the drowned man can be resuscitated. Or that, if his anus is still closed, the man unconscious, after falling out of a tree, can be saved.

The most vulnerable of areas in the abdomen is the solar plexus. But even if you receive a strong blow to the solar plexus, as long as you maintain the state I am describing—power in the belly, relaxed shoulders, and closed anus—you will not be affected. No crumpling over in pain; no loss of your equilibrium. Physically, that is how big a difference this practice can make.

So please practice what I have just taught you. Practice it many times a day—the more often, the better. That way, in a pinch, not only will you be able to regulate and control your nervous response mechanism, but you will also cultivate unshakable calm, equilibrium, and self-sufficiency. You will no longer be at the mercy of your feelings and emotions. You will no longer fall victim to states of panic. It is said that practice is the second source of intuition: with practice, you will learn to respond this way naturally and intuitively....

Many of you are probably thinking, "Is that all there is to it?" But I only teach practices anyone can do.... Furthermore, why should a method for becoming human be difficult? If I were attempting to show you how to become a monkey, or a horse, or an elephant, that would be difficult. But there is nothing difficult about humans becoming human. It's only natural.

So attempt it.... But when you do, you must do so whole-heartedly. That means practicing it daily and without negativity in your thinking. Don't allow negative constructs to creep in and color your thinking. Or if they do, be aware of them and don't allow them to take up residence. Cultivate a mental attitude that is bright, cheerful, vivacious, and courageous.

And anytime you are impacted by a sudden event, go immediately to a state of kumbhaka by making the function of your belly, your anus, and your shoulders one.

That's all that is required. Just try it.... But again, you can't do it half-heartedly; you have to invest yourself in your trial. It's not enough to assume, "Oh, so this is the way that it's done," and then to just mechanically follow the directions. The same way it's not enough to just pound on steel; when a sword-maker pounds on the same piece of steel, he invests himself totally in the enterprise. Whether you produce a blade like the ones produced by Masamune [famous late-thirteenth- to early-fourteenth-century sword smith] or a kitchen knife too dull to chop vegetables all depends upon what you put into it....

Often people come to me and say, "Sensei, this kumbhaka business is difficult, isn't it? It sounded easy enough until I tried it. Especially the part about closing the anus; seems like, whatever I do, the hole in my anus remains open."

To which, my answer is always the same, regardless of to whom I am talking. "Asking yourself whether or not the hole in your anus is properly closed is something that an ordinary person does. If you are serious about learning what I am presenting to you, you need to think at a level one step higher."

"You mean there is a way of thinking that is a step higher?"

"There is."

"So how should I think, then?"

"When you notice that your anus is not tightly closed, all you need to do is close it. No need to beat yourself up over the fact that it isn't closed. Just close it. That's all there is to it."

"Oh. I see."

It's an obvious answer, but until you tell people, they don't seem to see. It's the way the mind works. When you approach something with less-than-complete confidence, you think right away, "There I go again. I can't seem to do anything right. Why do I even bother to try? Why am I wasting my time listening to Tempū-sensei?" But don't think that way....

Instead of telling yourself you have failed and then feeling guilty about it, don't dwell on it. Clear out all thoughts and return yourself to a positive state of mind.

You will always have negative thoughts. The trick is to pay them no mind. The worst thing you can do is to be upset or feel sorry or remorseful or guilty for having negative thoughts. When you are in the dark, all you need to do is turn on the light to make the darkness go away. It's the same; all it takes is a return to a positive state of mind to displace negativity.

So the first step is not to agonize over negative thoughts when they occur. In other words, when negative thoughts occur, don't allow them to capture your attention; just let them go. Instead, relax your shoulders, concentrate energy in your belly, tighten your anus, and focus your attention on retaining a positive state of mind.

...The opposite of negativity is positivity, so all it takes to dispel negativity is to practice kumbhaka and to think positive thoughts. Just by thinking positive thoughts, your mind will light up with an inner radiance. That is the light that dispels darkness.[8]

The "one important thing" that Nakamura was to learn from Kariappa goes unnamed right up until the end of his sojourn on the Indian subcontinent. This is because it had become so self-evident that, in the context of his relationship with the ancient sage, to name it or to put it into words would have been an injustice. Later in life, however, Nakamura will devote himself to teaching that one important thing to thousands and tens of thousands of followers, and he will say it in many different ways. The one important thing is what it means to be human and alive; it has to do with the human constitution. We humans are each singular and unique because we each have a singular and unique mind and a singular and unique body. But the essence of being, and consequently the essence of our humanity, is not the mind or the body but the one universally pervasive life force that animates everything from the heavenly bodies to the earth's biosphere. The unification of mind and body is not something to be achieved through activation of mental and physical capacities. It is to be achieved through identification with that which is neither mind nor body but which animates both mind and body.

That said, there is a particular order to this triune human constitution. Just as water flows from higher to lower, energy flows from states of higher frequency to states of lower. In the cosmology according to yoga, spirit flows from source to mind and from mind to body: the mind is the mirror of spirit, and the body is the mirror of mind. In that sense, the unification of mind and body is most fully realized in the state that Nakamura calls kumbhaka (to what extent his description of that state and his method for achieving it is consistent with the teachings of yoga is an entirely different discussion and one best taken up by someone better versed than me in the ways of yoga). And it appears that Nakamura's successful embodiment of the practice of kumbhaka was the final milestone in his yoga journey. It was the final transmission that Kariappa had been patiently waiting for him to master.

One evening, about a month after being commended by Kariappa for his success in acquiring the teaching of kumbhaka, Nakamura is called into Kariappa's cottage. "You have pleased me greatly," the master says.

"You have mastered the art of listening for the voice of heaven, and you have cured yourself entirely of a dreaded disease. Moreover, you have acquired the teaching of kumbhaka in record time; not one of my students has ever learned this so quickly.

"You are now capable of many things," he continues. "You could go into the wilderness to deepen your understanding. I do not doubt your readiness or ability to pursue the ascetic path of a yogi. But you are not from here. Your future is back in your home country with your family and your countrymen. That is a life about which I have nothing to teach you; so from here on, you are on your own. I can only wish you a long, happy, and prosperous life."

As Nakamura listens to these words, tears flow uncontrollably down his cheeks. The man who rescued him in Cairo, led him into these secluded surroundings, and showed him the way back to health is now returning him to the world; he is giving him back his life. Nakamura is at a loss for words; nothing he can say or do is adequate to express the indebtedness he feels toward Kariappa: it is what is called *on* in Japanese, the incurrence of a debt that can never be repaid. The two sit together in silence while Nakamura's tears subside.

Two days later, Nakamura dons the clothes he had shed two-and-a-half years earlier and takes his leave of Gorkhey. Kariappa goes with him, taking him first to the holy city of Benares (Varanasi) on the Ganges, where he bestows upon him the spiritual name Aurabinda, signifying his attainment of self-realization.

"From now on, you never walk alone," he says. "Any time you encounter difficulties, know that, in my stead, your higher self is looking over you. Rest assured that your higher self will always provide a solution."

In Calcutta, Nakamura boards a steamship bound for Shanghai, never to set foot in India again.

II.

EVER MOUNT FUJI

Fair weather, all's well
Hidden under clouds, all's well
Ever Mount Fuji
—Yamaoka Tesshū

This five-seven-five-syllable haiku was a favorite of Nakamura Tempū's; he quoted it often and reproduced it for his students with ink and brush. Yamaoka Tesshū, a famous swordsman and statesman of the Meiji Restoration, was also a masterful calligrapher, and he is said to have composed this haiku directly following a spiritual awakening that transformed his work with both the sword and the brush. Tempū delighted in telling vignettes from Yamaoka's colorful history, and he can be viewed, in many respects, to have been Yamaoka's spiritual successor.

9.
CHINA

While Nakamura Saburō was in reclusion, engaging in the contemplation of big questions—Who am I? Why am I here? Where am I going?—the world, he is not surprised to learn, has continued to turn, and the march of history to unfold. As he steps ashore in Shanghai, after a hiatus of five years, he is thrust rudely back onto the stage of human events.

Since Nakamura's departure from Europe, the long but encumbered equilibrium in place since Napoleon's final exile had been shattered by the outbreak of the First Balkan War, the domino effect of which was soon to unleash a fury of aggression such as the world had never seen. Meanwhile, in China, the winds of change had finally caught up with the Qing dynasty, ending its three-hundred-year-long mandate from heaven, and a new republic had been formed. Now, only a year and half later, that republic was quickly disintegrating.

The standard-bearer in the republican cause was Sun Yat-sen, one of the few figures in later twentieth century China to be claimed by both nationalists and communists as one of their own. A son of Pearl River Delta peasants, Sun lived most of his life outside China, and most of that time, in exile. He was educated in Hawaii and Hong Kong and had only just begun a career as a physician when, in his late twenties, he set aside all other professional ambitions to pursue revolutionary politics.

Acting from Hong Kong in the wake of the Qing's 1895 defeat by the Japanese, Sun's first revolutionary organization, the Revive China Society, precipitated what would be the first of many failed uprisings of his instigation. On this occasion, Sun narrowly escaped from Chinese territory with his life; and for the next sixteen years, the Chinese authorities in pursuit, he traveled the globe, cultivating as he went an international network of influential patrons and friends. His first stop was Japan.

As the first Asian nation to have successfully engineered, on its own terms and without colonial oversight, the transition from agrarian to industrial economic base, and from feudal autocracy to populist constitutional monarchy, Japan opened Sun's eyes to what might be possible for China. His first visit was brief; but after surviving a kidnapping at the hands of the Chinese embassy in London, he returned two years later and this time stayed for three years.

Sun earned the respect of a number of progressive Japanese intellectuals and flourished under their benefaction. He became an earnest student of Japanese culture, learning the language, adopting its manners and habits, and even adopting the Japanese name Nakayama, a name by which he is sometimes still called in Japan today. Among Japanese company, Sun was known to refer to Japan as his "second home."

The intellectual current most sympathetic to Sun and his ambitions was, in subsequent years, named "pan-Asianism." Later, during the 1920s and 1930s, this term would be appropriated within official circles to describe Japan's Asian policy, and consequently, would degenerate into a euphemism for imperialist ambitions; but late-nineteenth- and early-twentieth-century pan-Asianism was a doctrine born of purer motives. Its vision was to free Asia of Western colonialism, and its proponents supported and openly endorsed a number of causes advocating self-determination and indigenous rule. The Japanese response to the English-American "open door" doctrine in China, one that suggested to them intentions of partition and Western encroachment, was to advance a "preserve China" policy favoring reform and modernization.

The pan-Asian idealist and romantic Miyazaki Torazō, also known as Tōten, was the first to discover Sun and to take him under his wing. Miyazaki was five years Sun's junior, but he shared Sun's passion for the dream of a modern and independent China, and he worked tirelessly behind the lines to secure funding and arms for Sun's long succession of attempted coups.

Miyazaki introduced Sun to both the distinguished statesman Inukai Tsuyoshi and Genyōsha leader Tōyama Mitsuru. Like Miyazaki, Tōyama became one of Sun's most ardent supporters, their friendship continuing until Sun's death in 1925 and long past the expiration of Sun's political shelf life. Unlike Miyazaki, Tōyama was senior to Sun by eleven years, and Sun looked up to Tōyama for his political acumen, valuing his guidance and advice. Soon after Miyazaki's introduction, Tōyama secured for Sun, at Genyōsha expense, a house in Tokyo and provided, in light of the Chinese regime's repeated efforts to have him assassinated, constant bodyguard protection—among those assigned to which detail, as mentioned in chapter 2, was the young Nakamura Saburō.

That was fifteen years earlier. By the time Nakamura Saburō's narrative places him back in Shanghai, Sun's career has passed its zenith and is in meteoric decline. On the coattails of a successful 1911 insurrection in which he did not directly participate, Sun had been elected in absentia to lead the new republic by an alliance of revolutionary forces made up of highly competitive northern and southern factions. The qualities that most recommended him for this role appear to have been his charisma and his political impotence: the vying parties mutually viewed him as unthreatening and as someone over whom they could exercise control.

After returning to China from abroad, Sun was inaugurated to the office of provisional president in Nanjing on January 1, 1912. By mid-February, his presidency was over. Sun had always excelled as a catalyst for revolution and as a fund-raiser, but never as a visionary (few of the ideas to which he gave voice in his speeches and writings were original) or as an administrator.[1] On February 15, after heeding the advice of his confidants, he abdicated to the far more politically astute Yuan Shikai.

Yuan, on the other hand, was no revolutionary. He had been brought up as a mandarin and served as both a general and a high-ranking administrator under the Manchu regime. A favorite of the Empress Dowager Cixi, he had found himself suddenly on the wrong side of power after her death in 1908. Then, during the Revolution of 1911, he recognized an opportunity to reverse the tides of his personal fortunes. First, he recommended himself to the imperial court as the man best suited to represent their interests at the meeting of the Revolutionary Alliance, and then, upon appointment, he ruthlessly consolidated his own power at the regime's expense; it was, in fact, Yuan who secured the peaceful abdication of young Pu Yi, China's last emperor.

Sun's act of handing over the seat of power to the wily Yuan is eulogized in China's official histories as selfless and well-intentioned, even if misguided, suggesting that he recognized in Yuan someone more capable than himself of uniting north and south and of thereby furthering the republican agenda. The more likely explanation, however, is that Sun had little choice. He understood only too clearly that in Yuan, he had met his match and that to remain in power would be to invite bloodshed, including his own. His abdication, more accurately described, was a last-ditch effort to prevent the premature fracture and demise of the young and all too fragile republican enterprise.

But if he thought he was acting to preserve the republic, he grossly underestimated his successor's intentions. Fifteen months after Sun's abdication, the republican reform agenda had fallen by the wayside and Yuan was well on his way to consolidating his rule under military control.

Both Inukai Tsuyoshi and Tōyama Mitsuru had been adamant in their warnings to Sun that Yuan was not to be trusted. The Meiji government, on the other hand, had no investment in Sun; exercising characteristic diplomatic caution and naively calculating that the promise of stability was more in Japan's interest than that of reform, it sided with the regime. Then, when several of the southern provinces attempted to break away from the republic in protest of Yuan's actions, raising the specter of chaos, Tokyo belatedly realized that it lacked a China policy.

Their solution was to appoint none other than Yamaza Enjirō, last seen by Nakamura in London, as their special envoy to Beijing. Yamaza, age forty-seven, was a veteran of the negotiations at Portsmouth, New Hampshire, that sealed the Russo-Japanese War—negotiations for which he and the other negotiators received nothing but criticism but that, realistically, resulted in the best deal that Japan could have expected. He had a reputation for engineering solutions to difficult situations, and in that sense, he was well suited for the task in China. But in the context of China-Japan relations, the choice was volatile; Yamaza, known for his Genyōsha and pro-republican allegiances, was subject to suspicion by the Yuan regime. Moreover, Yamaza made little effort to mitigate those suspicions: upon his recall from London, and in preparation for his China assignment, he consulted extensively with Tōyama Mitsuru and those of Toyama's Genyōsha strongmen who had participated in the revolution that brought Sun to power.

The exact sequence of events as they relate to Nakamura's story is obscure. Presumably he arrived in Shanghai in late May or early June of 1913, whereupon he sought out the Genyōsha's Shanghai cadre; and presumably, through this cadre, he was placed in touch with Sun Yat-sen. Sun was only recently returned from yet another Japan visit, one that had included a weeklong stay in Fukuoka, surrounded by Genyōsha comrades-in-arms. His trip had been cut short by news of the assassination, by Yuan's minions, of fellow patriot and longtime friend Song Jiaoren. Now he was once again engaged in the business he knew best, that of insurrection.

Yamaza's precise role with regard to Sun's second revolution is not on record for obvious reasons: as a representative of the Japanese government, he would have been sure to have swept away any trail of evidence linking him to a revolutionary faction. What we know is that his commission in Beijing began in July (although one source says June), but that Genyōsha records place him in Fukuoka on July 20, just as Sun's attempted come-back was underway. Could he have visited China in June to assess the situation—and perhaps even to meet with Sun Yat-sen and the Genyōsha's China cadre prior to the beginning of his commission?

This, I suspect, was the case. Nakamura anecdotally claims to have run into Yamaza on the street one day in Shanghai. If so, the most probable, if not only possible, timing for such an event would have been early June. Nakamura was not in Shanghai from sometime in early June through mid-July, and Yamaza, whose commission placed him in Beijing, would have been hard-pressed to come up with a viable excuse for visiting Shanghai after his commission began. Also, the meeting could hardly have been as coincidental as Nakamura's story would have us believe—what brought them to the same street at the same time almost certainly involved a Genyōsha address, or perhaps even a prearranged meeting.

Whatever the circumstances, the convergence of Nakamura, Sun Yat-sen, and Yamaza Enjirō at this volatile moment in China's history is the stuff of which high drama is made, and in this, we are not to be disappointed. That drama, as we know from Nakamura Tempū's accounts, involves intrigue, armed conflict, and daring escapes, but the order and context of these events is not entirely clear. Nakamura tells us Sun first sends him to Beijing, and the mission, the exact nature of which goes unstated, has him lodged inside the Forbidden City and attended by the remnants of the imperial dynasty's courtesans, still legion in number. He lives there, he says, in regal splendor and surrounded by beautiful women, for almost two months.[2] His asceticism as a yogi is already a thing of the past.

When signs from Nanjing indicate that revolt is imminent, Yamaza tells him to return to Sun's side, where he reassumes his role of bodyguard. The assignment involves round-the-clock vigilance, and attempts on Sun's life occur almost daily.

Fundamentally altered by his experiences in India, Nakamura is no longer the impetuous firebrand he had been in Manchuria but has cultivated a capacity for tranquility in the face of danger. Tempū, in describing his experiences during this period, invokes the seventeenth-century swordsman Miyamoto Musashi, said to have been undefeated in over sixty duels. In the book that is his legacy, The Book of Five Rings, Musashi wrote, "The way of the warrior is the way of illumination and the elimination of all confusion. Day after day, moment after moment, he must be attentive and aware. He must polish away blemishes from both mind and spirit, and he must hone the judgment of both his eyes and his intuitive vision to a fine edge. In the cloudless state, the state of clarity after confusion is banished, he must discover and realize true emptiness."[3]

Nakamura did not, however, come away entirely unscathed. When defending against the sword of a would-be assassin on a dark Shanghai street, he severed the nerves to his right middle finger. The cut was sewn together with silver wire by an English surgeon and eventually healed, but the nerves in this finger were permanently damaged; a photograph, taken late in life, shows him holding a teacup in his right hand with this stubbornly uncooperative finger extended.[4]

After consolidating resources and political will in the south, Sun took his insurrection live on July 12. It lasted for all of seventeen days. Sun's revolt, if heroic, was poorly conceived, insufficiently funded, and militarily no match for Yuan's machine; the provisional Kuomintang government abandoned Nanjing on July 29. Revolutionary forces continued to conduct guerrilla-like raids for another month but were effectively laid to rest by early September. Then, on the October 10 two-year anniversary of the 1911 Revolution, and with pompous ceremony, Yuan had himself inaugurated to an uncontested five-year presidential term.

Once again, Sun Yat-sen was on the run. After the fall of Nanjing, together with Nakamura and a small cadre of close associates, including Shanghai governor Chen Qimei and a young lieutenant named Chiang Kai-shek, he boarded a steamship in Shanghai bound for Canton. En route, however, the party received word that their movements had been apprehended and that the regime was waiting for them on the other end; from Fuzhou, they caught a boat to Taiwan, and there they boarded a Japanese steamship bound for Japan.[5]

Yamaza Enjirō continued as special envoy to Beijing for another ten months. Amid postrevolutionary chaos in the provinces, he frenetically negotiated options and then lobbied the Japanese government to purchase coal rights in Shanxi and oil rights in Szechuan, becoming all the while more frustrated both with Yuan's duplicity and with Tokyo's stubbornness and unwillingness to act. He died suddenly in Beijing on May 28, 1914. He was forty-eight years old.

Even in death, Yamaza was the source of controversy, for while his demise was officially attributed to natural causes, and while no evidence to the contrary was ever found, it was popularly speculated, both then and later, that he had been poisoned; indeed, cries within the Japanese parliament and the Japanese popular press to have Yuan held accountable were loud enough to become one more bone of contention between China and Japan.

Yuan, however, even if known for the alacrity with which he dispensed of his enemies, was a ruthlessly political animal, and to inflict vengeance on a foreign diplomat would have served little political purpose. In the opinion of Hasegawa Shun, Yamaza's principle biographer, the more probable explanation for Yamaza's untimely demise was overwork in lethal combination with his penchant for alcohol. Yamaza consumed inordinate amounts of alcohol and was known to have written some of his most lucid correspondence while under the influence, including a long letter in November to Tōyama Mitsuru in which he vented his frustration with the Foreign Service and declared his intention to resign.[6]

Nakamura was among the many to be saddened by the news of Yamaza's passing. He had lost a mentor and a friend, and he had departed from China without the opportunity to say good-bye.

10.
THE PRODIGAL'S RETURN

The boat carrying Sun Yat-sen and Nakamura Saburō docked in Kobe on August 9. Before the refugees could land, however, it was beset by police and newspaper reporters; back in China, Sun's name had been posted on Yuan Shikai's "most wanted" list, and consequently, he was now persona non grata in Japan. From the hold of the ship, Sun got off a telegram to one of his Genyōsha supporters, who in turn took it immediately to Inukai Tsuyoshi and Tōyama Mitsuru. Tōyama was unequivocal. "Now more than ever is the time to welcome Sun as a guest," he declared. A contingent of Genyōsha operatives dispatched to Kobe smuggled the fugitives into a rowboat and then onto a steamship bound for Yokohama, while Inukai prevailed upon Prime Minister Yamamoto Gonnohyoe (Gonbei) to exercise clemency. The men were allowed ashore in Yokohama as political refugees.

As their ship approaches the Izu Peninsula, Mount Fuji looms large on the horizon, silhouetted by the afternoon sun. Nakamura is brought to tears. The sight of Fuji's conical summit has long been a subject of his daydreams, a fantasy too remote, he had supposed, to ever be fulfilled.

They dock in Yokohama and spend the night in the port's Chinatown. In the early hours of the following morning, Nakamura takes the train to Shinbashi Station in Tokyo and walks the mile or so (two kilometers) to Tōyama's residence in Akasaka.

The time is just past six. His feet know where they are going, for they have walked the same path countless times in years past. But as he steps through the gate and approaches the house entrance, the morning light casts him momentarily into a separate but parallel dimension of existence.

He tingles with a sense of presence to the moment and the mystery of life. The light is nothing new, for it was always his habit to catch Tōyama at home early; once this man of many concerns set off for the day, there was no telling what time he might return. But almost six years has passed since the last time Nakamura stood in front of this door.

Just as always, he slides the door open, steps into the foyer, and announces his presence in a loud voice.

"Yes?" The voice is that of Tōyama's wife, who comes scuttling out of the kitchen. Seeing Nakamura standing in the doorway, she lights up in a combination of surprise and disbelief.

In the past, upon sight of Nakamura, and after exchanging "good mornings," the woman of the household has always scurried off to alert her husband, who, moments later, has appeared and addressed the still standing Nakamura from his seat on the raised floor within. Their business finished, Tōyama having delivered whatever he had in the way of instructions and Nakamura having delivered whatever he had in the way of news or information, Nakamura has always quickly exited and continued on his way. The number of times he has been asked to remove his shoes and to enter beyond this vestibule, he can count on the fingers of one hand.

This morning, however, the well-worn scenario veers sharply off script. After getting over her surprise—more like the shock of seeing a man returned from the grave—and exchanging mutual acknowledgments of how long it has been, she asks Nakamura to please wait.

He waits for what seems like an inordinate length of time. He even begins to worry. Is the old man perhaps not well?

Momentarily, however, not Mrs. Tōyama but one of Tōyama's live-in students appears to invite him inside. Perplexed, he removes his shoes, steps up into the house, and follows the young man down a short corridor. The student leaves him in front of two closed sliding screens, the entrance to the Tōyamas' sitting room.

From inside, Mrs. Tōyama bids him to enter.

Nakamura's manners, instilled in him since early childhood, have not suffered from five years of living abroad. Seated on the wooden floor, he bows his head in front of the closed screens, announces himself by name, and waits for a second invitation. The invitation granted, he slides open the left-hand screen and bows toward the front of the room. Head still lowered, he apologizes for his rude intrusion and long absence.

Propriety, however, is interrupted by the small but audible gasp he emits when he raises his head. The far corner of the sitting room accommodates a shallow alcove, a traditional feature of Japanese houses called a *tokonoma*, adorned with a scroll—in this case, a piece of calligraphy in Tōyama's hand—and a vase of arranged flowers. The seat of honor, the space in front of this alcove, is occupied by an empty cushion. And on the hosts' side of the room, facing the small alcove, Tōyama Mitsuru and his wife sit dressed in their finest formal attire, kimonos adorned with the Tōyama family crest. Bewildered, Nakamura wonders if he has caught them at a bad time; perhaps they are just about to leave for an important engagement. But no, this time it is Tōyama who beckons him to enter and invites him to sit on the empty cushion.

It is an invitation without precedent. In years past, Tōyama has most often addressed Nakamura with the Japanese equivalent of "hey, you," and when he did address him by name, it was "Nakamura," bereft of the honorifics "kun" or "san." The nature of their relationship was forged during the days when Nakamura lived with the Tōyamas in Fukuoka, where he was treated like a son and reciprocated with filial deference, attending to many of his surrogate father's most mundane requests and learning to anticipate his every move absent verbal cues. Should Tōyama, for example, show signs of leaving the house, Nakamura would run to put his wooden clogs out for him and then take even the smallest bundles or satchels away from him to carry on his behalf.

"Please. Have seat." Tōyama repeats the invitation a second time.

"I am fine where I am." The deference is more than formality; Nakamura cannot bring himself to occupy the position of honor in the Tōyama household. But when Tōyama insists a third time, he reluctantly acquiesces. Even so, he hedges by keeping his knees on the floor while perching his buttocks just barely on the cushion's edge.

Now it is Mrs. Toyama's turn. Nakamura's awkwardness elicits a giggle. "My husband has something to say," she says. "Please seat yourself on top of the cushion. After he is done, you can go back to sitting on the floor."

Nakamura has no choice. He centers himself on the cushion and, back erect, faces his teacher.

"This is a most fortunate surprise," Tōyama begins. "You've been gone for how many years? We'd pretty much given up on you.

"You are chosen," he continues.

Nakamura questions his ears. What could the man be saying?

"You are chosen," Tōyama repeats. "All the great prophets—the Buddha, Christ, Mohammed—went off somewhere before they embarked on their respective missions. They disappeared for several years. But after that, when they returned to the world, they returned as different men. They returned as leaders.

"As I just said, we'd pretty much given up on you for dead. Yet here you are, more alive than ever. Even before you entered this room, as soon as my wife told me that you were waiting outside, I knew that you'd returned a different man. You're now a man who has found himself.

"In the words of Mencius, 'Heaven only anoints the man it has tested. Only he, who, through force of will, has withstood and overcome suffering, is empowered to do great works.' We must assume that heaven has intervened and that you've been chosen.

"What this mean is that, from now on, your life is no longer yours. You've been allowed to return to the world on the one condition that, from now on, you live your life in the service of humanity. Do you understand what I'm saying?"

"Yes, sir." The response is automatic; Nakamura is too dazed to acknowledge the full meaning of what has been said. The entire event still smacks of the surreal.

"Good. In that case you can get down off that cushion."

Nakamura slides off of the cushion and onto the tatami floor with relief.

"What a long time it's been. Come into the room next door and let's have breakfast. I want to hear about your travels." Without intermission,

Nakamura Tempū (right)
with Tōyama Mitsuru (left),
probably in the 1920s

*(with permission from the
Tempu Society, a nonprofit
public interest foundation)*

Tōyama has dropped all formality and is just the man of the household. But the words of his short speech remain lodged in Nakamura's psyche.[1]

Whether or not he was, as Tōyama had said, "chosen," Nakamura could not deny that he was now sailing with the winds of fate squarely behind him. Not only was he returning with his health fully restored, but he was also returning wealthy. Nakamura had come into money in China and was carrying on his person a small financial fortune. The amount of this wealth, as Tempū tells the story, is almost 2 million yen, this at a time when one yen was of sufficient value to feed the average urban household for a year. (As with the sums Tempū claims to have been paid in New York, this figure is deserving of skepticism. Two million may be accurate, or it may be exaggerated. Or his memory may have failed him. Or he has adjusted the original figure to reflect 1950s values. The actual amount, however, is of no consequence to his story; all we need know is that it was an extraordinary sum.) Exactly how did he come into this wealth? By Nakamura's account, it was bequeathed to him by Sun Yat-sen, who was carrying away from China the remainder of the revolutionary funds. This explanation saves Tempū and his narrative from having to deal with inconvenient details, but it is nevertheless difficult to swallow whole; the actual explanation can hardly have been so simple.

True, Sun did have Nakamura to thank for his life, and this on more than one occasion. He would naturally have felt indebted. But then, the funds in question would have belonged not to Sun, personally but to the republican movement. Sun's reputation with regard to the handling of money remained clean throughout his career, and the whimsical bestowal of funds meant for his revolutionary cause on an individual associate as an expression of personal gratitude is decidedly out of character. Moreover, his obligations and sense of indebtedness extended to others as well; why was Nakamura chosen above others in his company?

One possible explanation is that the money was somehow tainted. Sun may have purposefully divested himself of it because it constituted a political liability. He may even have been unable either to bank it or to exchange it for Japanese or other foreign tender. Sun's traveling companion and fellow refugee Chen Qimei was notorious for his access to some very deep pockets in the Chinese underworld. Were Chen and his connections perhaps the source of these funds? These are questions for which there are no immediate answers.

The other element of Nakamura's story lacking an explanation is why, also by his own account, he chose to pose as one of the refugees seeking asylum and to enter Japan under his Chinese passport and assumed name—that is, as Sun Yat-sen's half-brother. Was this because he was still responsible for Sun's safekeeping and wished to maintain a low profile? We know that Yuan's agents were hot on Sun's trail, for Sun sustained three more attempts on his life while in Japan under Nakamura's protection; one of these is the incident, related in chapter 1, where the attacker was overcome by Tōyama Mitsuru's unflinchingly steadfast demeanor.

Or was the reason to do with his legal status? Presumably, the legal liabilities incurred as a result of his illicit departure five years earlier had expired under the statute of limitations, but perhaps he needed to sit out some additional waiting period for those charges to disappear from the books. If so, then almost certainly he could have counted on help from the same friends in the Foreign Service who had assisted him in New York and London. Nakamura spares us these details but does note that he resides, for most of this period, within a "teahouse," the euphemistic term for a geisha establishment, called Hakkakudō, and that he passes

much of his time spending his money liberally in the Shinbashi entertainment district.

He did, of course, show his face at home, where his mother and his
wife both shed rivers of tears. Neither, it seems, had ever wavered in her
respective conviction that he would eventually return. Their welcome is
dampened only by the news that his father was no longer of this world,
having died of a stroke in October 1909.

As well as Nakamura's father, the Meiji Emperor was also deceased, having died while Nakamura was in India. And on the day of the emperor's
funeral, in one of the last and most notorious displays of imperial loy-
alty, Count Nogi Maresuke, the revered hero of the Russo-Japanese War,
together with his wife, committed ritual suicide.

Just as Nogi's death symbolized to many the end of Japan's romantic
warrior tradition, Meiji's death was felt for the vacancy in leadership that
it left behind; the ascending Taishō Emperor lacked both Meiji's charisma
and his statesmanship. Where Meiji's forty-six-year reign was generally
thought of as a great leap forward into modernity, Taishō's fifteen-year
reign would be characterized by a lack of direction and domestic unrest.

Concurrent with Nakamura Saburō's return, a tentative peace was bro-
kered in the Balkans, but greater Europe was a tinderbox threatening to
explode. When the dogs of war were released one year later, they attacked
with vehemence and consumed much of the civilized world. Japan, by virtue of its distance from the main theaters of conflict, was only marginally
engaged; but it did, at British bidding, expel the Germans from Tsingtao
in China, thereby acquiring Germany's lease-holdings in Shandong Province. It also used the momentum of the war to negotiate a second treaty
with the Russians, enhancing that of Portsmouth and further securing
hegemony in Manchuria.

Financially secure, Nakamura is content to savor home and his reentry
into Japanese society. Soon bored with leisure, however, he takes up financial speculation in the securities markets as a hobby. Not until the summer

of the following year does he seek out gainful employment, and then, the position he lands with the Jiji News Service, the publisher of a Japanese equivalent to the *Financial Times,* appears to be more of an extension of his newfound hobby than the choice of a career.

As well as financial speculation, however, Nakamura's wealth allows him to pursue another hobby with even greater passion. That hobby is the women of the entertainment districts.

Nakamura owed his introduction at an early age to the world of tea-houses to Tōyama Mitsuru. Tōyama, simple in his day-to-day habits, was also, in his own right, a playboy of no small reputation; in the course of his early days as a political activist, he was known to have left a trail of conquests from one end of Japan to the other. But in this one calling, he is eclipsed by his protégé Nakamura Saburō.

One of the more extraordinary aspects of Nakamura's investment in this hobby is the fact that he does not drink. No stranger to vice, Naka-mura is nevertheless totally abstinent when it comes to the consumption of alcohol. Drinking is and has long been an accepted part of the Japanese social fabric, especially among the political, military, and entrepreneurial elite, the circles within which Nakamura mingles, and his ability to thrive in such society while eschewing one of its most sacrosanct conventions bespeaks a remarkable nimbleness and social dexterity.

His aversion to alcohol is not innate; during his younger days, he was known to have carried on with the best of them. The change occurred in 1903, when he and his associates, Kondō and Hashitsune, were briefed at the Japanese legation in Beijing prior to entering Manchuria. On the eve-ning of their last night in Beijing, the night before they were to embark on the journey that would take them behind enemy lines, young Nakamura brazenly proposed that the occasion was deserving of a proper send-off celebration.

Aoki Nobuzumi, the legation attaché, was merciless in his condem-nation. "If you think drinking will do anything to further this assignment, then you had better think again," he said with pique. "This is no time for celebration. This mission is going to require mental clarity and attention to detail, and the nation is depending on you. I advise you get a good night's rest."

Nakamura's ears burned. The reprimand and the humiliation he suffered from it made such an impression on him that he never partook of alcohol again.

Thus, his participation in the after-dark world of Tokyo's entertainment districts revolves around the women and their art. The word *geisha*, also *geiko*, means literally "performing artisan." It is a professional title, earned with hard work and born with pride. Aspiring women live austerely and undergo years of rigorous training before reaching formal recognition within their guilds. Ostensibly, the arts in question revolve around music and dance, and geisha are, by definition, accomplished musicians and dancers. But musical and dancing skills alone do not a geisha make; more important is her ability to stimulate conversation and to put her patrons— men from the upper echelons of society whom, she must assume, are also shrewd and astute judges of human character—at ease.

Moreover, this art of entertainment places almost equal responsibilities on the guest. The first of these responsibilities is, of course, financial. Off-limits to all but those who can afford the price of admission, teahouse entertainment is decidedly a wealthy man's game. But while money will always go a long way toward winning a geisha's heart, seldom is it the deciding factor. Teahouse indulgence calls on the sophistication and skill of the patron. And one of the allures of the sport is that skill improves with practice.

On top of providing for his family, the money that Nakamura Saburō received in China is sufficient to support his penchant for teahouses and the pursuit of their principal assets. And in the course of this wanton behavior, he inadvertently comes into contact with prominent figures in the business and political world. Good company makes for good entertainment, and Nakamura soon becomes sought after as an addition to guest lists of some of the teahouses' most prominent patrons. He is also regarded highly by the establishments themselves for the business he attracts.

Among the acquaintances he makes in the course of such gatherings is a man named Hiraga Satoshi. Hiraga lives in Tokyo but plays a major role in the economic development of Osaka and the Kansai region. By the time Nakamura meets him, he has completed a long banking career and has helped to found both the Hankyu Railway Company and Daiwa Securities. Several years later, he will also found the Fuji Fire and Marine Insurance Company.

Hiraga is quick to recognize in Nakamura the qualities of a leader and introduces him to one of his protégés, Ikeda Kenzō, president of the Daihyaku Bank. Ikeda, likewise, recognizes Nakamura's talents and recruits him to a Daihyaku affiliate, the Tokyo Industrial Depository Bank. And soon thereafter, as bank president, Nakamura is elected to the boards of some of the bank's most prominent corporate clients, including Izu Electric Lighting and Nippon Milling.

Predictably, Nakamura proves Hiraga and Ikeda correct in their assessments of his talent. He has an uncanny ability to see to the heart of problems and to make the right decisions at the right time—with the consequence that the businesses he touches almost invariably flower and thrive. And with every success, his reputation, along with his personal wealth, grows.

His heart, however, is not in his work. If anything, he finds the world of business too easy, and he soon becomes bored. His typical day begins at the bank and unfolds with visits by carriage to each of the corporations with which he is involved. By three in the afternoon he has finished his workday and is already weighing his options for the evening ahead.

"Will it be Shinbashi, Yanagibashi, or Kagurazaka tonight, sir?" his driver asks.

Frivolity ends, however, where his mentor, Tōyama, is concerned. Tōyama, now in his early sixties, is at the peak of his career. When he travels to address different groups and gatherings around the country, Nakamura often accompanies him.

At some point during this period, Tōyama begins to introduce Naka-mura by the name Tempū. While less the practice today, in Tempū's day, Japanese given names were subject to change; not uncommonly, people would assume different given names at different periods in their lives, especially as they rose in social position. Sometimes these names were self-selected, but at other times, as in this instance, they were bequeathed by a mentor.

Tōyama had often remarked during Nakamura Saburō's younger, more tempestuous years that this sorry fellow suffered from the afflic-tion of having been born too late in history—that if only he had been born amid the mayhem of the sixteenth century, a period commonly referred to as the Age of Warring States, he would have been in his own element. As previously noted, Tempū is written with the characters 天, "heaven," and 風, "wind," "heaven's wind," taken from the name for one of the sword *kata*, or forms, of the zuihenryū-battōjutsu sword discipline passed down within the Yanagawa clan of Tōyama's native Fukuoka. But then, as posterity would have it, to the many thousands of people touched by Nakamura and his teachings, the name came to stand for the seemingly heaven-sent breath of inspiration that his teachings imparted. While Nakamura began answering to Tōyama by that name, he did not begin to use it himself until after that next of turn of the wheel—that is, not until he began teaching.

11.
TIGERS AND MINERS

There's a fellow in Osaka I call "Tiger Man." His real name is Kaneko, and he joined the Tempūkai in 1955. I would guess he's about sixty years old; he's now the president of a real estate company. The day I met him, Kaneko told me he had been searching for me for over twenty-five years.

The way he tells it, years ago, he was visiting a friend in Ashiya, and the friend had a framed photograph in his sitting room of a man, neatly dressed in haori and hakama, standing in a cage with three tigers. The man in the photo has a big smile on his face.

"Who's this?" Kaneko asked him. "From the way he is dressed, he's obviously no animal trainer."

"I know," the friend answered. "That's why I put it up, because it's so unusual. I don't know anything about the man in the photograph, but a relative of mine is a photographer at Jiji News, and he took the picture. He sent me a copy because he thought I'd find it entertaining."

"Is the man in the photo still alive?"

"As far as I know."

"What's his name?"

"Nakamura Tempū."

"What's he doing inside the cage?"

"That, I can't tell you. All I know is that, according to the article, the tigers are part of an Italian animal trainer's traveling show, and they are untamed, but that this man went into the cage anyway."

"What an amazing story! And there's even a photograph to back it up. From all I can see, it looks real. I have to meet this Nakamura Tempū."

That's how it began. Kaneko says he kept his eyes and ears open for any mention of a Nakamura Tempū for the next twenty-five years. If he'd asked at the Home Ministry, they would have told him where to find me right away. But he didn't. And he says he was a policeman before he went into real estate! But no, he just watched the newspaper. And since I don't advertise, he never saw anything about me or the Tempūkai.

Twenty-five years. How about it, ladies? Would you spend twenty-five years looking for a guy, just because you saw his picture in the newspaper and thought he was handsome? Say you were twenty-five at the time: that would make you fifty! And if you age, the guy in the photograph is going to have aged too; he's not going to be the same handsome boy he was twenty-five years ago. Today's women don't have that kind of tenacity. Give a woman three to five days at most; after that she'll be shopping for someone new. Just as if shopping for a new house.

But Kaneko obviously wasn't interested in me for my looks. He was curious about the photograph. He wanted to know, was it for real, or was it a fake? What was the story behind it? What induced the man in the photo to go into a cage with tigers?

So when he finally meets me, he says, "Sensei, I have been looking for you for twenty-five years."

"That's a long time! Sorry to put you to so much trouble." Even though
I'd never asked to be looked for by anyone.

*"You see," he says, "this friend of mine in Ashiya had a photograph in his
living room of a man, dressed in formal haori and hakama, standing in
a tiger cage. It was such an extraordinary picture. And it was you! You
were much younger, of course, but it was obviously you."*

*"I'd almost forgotten about that," I told him. That's why I call him "Tiger
Man," because he reminded me of the tigers. I really had forgotten. It
wasn't any great feat; it's just that I knew I could do it. I had complete
confidence in myself. You could do it too, if you had the same kind of
confidence. But from the looks on your faces, I don't recommend it. Not
unless you want to be eaten alive.*[1]

The year was 1918; the month, February. An Italian animal trainer[2] has
brought his show to Tokyo and is to perform in Yūrakuchō. From someone,
the animal trainer has heard about a true samurai, the only one left in all
Japan, named Tōyama Mitsuru, and he asks to be introduced. The Italian
Embassy contacts the Japanese Ministry of Foreign Affairs, the Ministry
contacts Tōyama, and a time and place for the meeting is arranged.

Nakamura accompanies Tōyama to this venue, together with Uchida
Ryōhei and Tōyama's nephew, a man named Matsushita.

Uchida Ryōhei is Nakamura's Meidōkan sempai introduced in chapter 1. Like Nakamura, he is also a seasoned veteran of espionage and
war. Prior to the Russo-Japanese War, and in accordance with the martial
precept "know thine enemy," Uchida learned Russian and assumed clandestine residencies in Vladivostok and St. Petersburg. Then, in 1901, he
founded a political and paramilitary organization called the Kokuryūkai,
known in English as the Black Dragon Society. Despite its sinister connotations, the name has nothing to do with either blackness or dragons
but is derived from the characters used to write Heilongjiang, the Chinese name for the Amur River that separates Manchuria from Siberia

and the Russian Far East; Uchida and his organization, in the interest of national security, are advocates of Japanese intervention in Manchuria. The Kokuryūkai masterminded and successfully carried out a number of espionage and sabotage activities in Manchuria during the Russo-Japanese War, and they were instrumental in the creation of the Manshū Gigun, introduced in chapter 4.

Western analyses of twentieth-century Japanese history have been quick to malign Uchida for his militancy. But while, yes, Uchida was unapologetically militant in both his ideals and his methods, that militancy was not the unmitigated Japanese militarism of the 1920s and 1930s but a patriotic response to existential threats on his fledgling nation's borders. Japan's 1932 virtual annexation of Manchuria through the creation of Manchukuo, for example, was a perversion of the Kokuryūkai agenda and occurred without its support. Likewise, Uchida was neither a proponent of the Japanese invasion of China nor of the Pacific War (he died four years before the attack on Pearl Harbor), and his other affiliations included the Ōmoto-kyō and the Red Swastika Society: Ōmoto-kyō was the charismatic Deguchi Onisaburō's Shinto-based religious sect of decidedly pacifist persuasion. Tōyama Mitsuru was also a Deguchi admirer, and while neither Tōyama nor Uchida ever became Ōmoto-kyō members, they openly supported many of Deguchi's initiatives. Deguchi was later jailed, and his religion all but eradicated because his universalist message was thought to threaten the imperial regime. The Red Swastika Society was the philanthropic arm of a Chinese Daoist organization that, among other noble public works, took on the thankless task of burying bodies after the infamous 1937 Nanjing Massacre perpetrated by Japanese soldiers.

Uchida and Tōyama were aligned in political objective, if not always in method, and Uchida looked upon Tōyama with much the same respect as did Nakamura; he and Tōyama appear together often in period photographs. Nakamura, on the other hand, is sparing in his remarks regarding Uchida, and I surmise that, while mutually respectful, he and Uchida did not see entirely eye to eye.

This, then, is the lineup of characters when the animal trainer with his Japanese interpreter enters the hotel sitting room where the meeting is to take place. The Jiji News Service, the same paper for which Nakamura had worked for a short time after his return from abroad, has gotten wind of the development and has a reporter-photographer—the cousin to the friend of Kaneko described in Tempū's remarks above—on hand.

The trainer quickly acknowledges each of the men in the room, and they all take seats; whereupon he turns toward Tōyama. "Just as I thought," he says through his interpreter. "This fellow would be safe inside the cage. The cats wouldn't bother him."

The ability to determine who is fit and who is unfit to go into a cage with wild animals comes with the territory of the man's profession. "I can tell by looking at his eyes," he explains.

Nakamura, who had been massaging his mentor's shoulders up until the trainer had entered the room, is sitting just behind Tōyama. The man notices him. "Ah! This fellow too," he adds.

Not to be outdone, Uchida asks, "What about me?"

"Not you. They would tear you to pieces."

"And me?" Matsushita chimes in.

"No. You don't have it either."

Tōyama is delighted. "This man knows what it's like to walk the line between life and death," he says. "That's why he can see what he sees in others."

After belated introductions and light conversation, the man, whose actual performances are not to begin until three days later, offers to show the men his lions, tigers, leopards, and elephants, and the party walks the several blocks separating them from the hall in Yūrakuchō.

"I must first warn you," the trainer says before they enter by the backstage door. "I have three Bengal tigers, a mother and her grown cubs, that aren't broken in yet. They're likely to make a lot of noise when we approach. But you needn't worry; they're safely behind bars."

Sure enough, as they enter the dimly lit room, they are greeted with a ferocious snarl from the mother tiger.

"That's her," he says. "It'll be another six months before she settles down and I can use her in my shows, but I bring her on the road with me to get her used to it."

"She is indeed a feisty one," Tōyama comments as they stop in front of the cage. The mother cat, her two cubs by her side, has all fangs bared and glares at them between snarls.

"What about it, Nakamura?" Tōyama asks. "Will you go in?"

Nakamura can tell that his mentor's words are only half in jest. He is also secretively flattered, for he understands that Tōyama would no more put him at undue risk than he would his own son: he makes the suggestion only because he has absolute confidence in Nakamura's ability to win over the cats. "If you say so," Nakamura answers.

The two of them look at the Italian trainer, who, in turn, does not so much as bat an eye. "Come this way," he says. The man who knows these cats best, Nakamura reflects, is likewise urging him on; the trainer, as a visiting foreigner, could hardly expect to receive sympathy from the Japanese courts should one of his guests be eaten alive.

Then too, Nakamura is no stranger to wild cats. During his long hours of sitting beside the waterfall in the Himalayan foothills, he became an object of curiosity to an itinerant leopard. The cat gradually took to him, venturing ever nearer, until, on one occasion, it came right up to him. Nakamura, with no cause to feel threatened, exhibited not the slightest reaction of fear; extending a hand, he patted the cat lightly on its face.

Laden with pigeons, 1960

(with permission from the Tempu Society, a nonprofit public interest foundation)

"Wild animals," Tempū explains as part of his story, "prey on fear. They sense fear immediately, and they react instinctively to a threat. But animals are also predictable. As long as you neither project fear nor threaten them, they will cause you no harm."

Nakamura Tempū is widely reported to have had a magnetic effect on animals of all kinds. He was a great dog lover, and violently tempered strays were quickly domesticated under his care. Birds also took to him, and a remarkable photograph from about 1960 shows him seated in a park in Kyoto reading a newspaper, his arms and shoulders laden with pigeons.

That magnetism manifested itself in other ways as well. Sasaki Masando-sensei once told me that, when a bird found its way into a lecture hall where Tempū was speaking, causing a commotion as it flew around looking for a way out, Tempū simply raised his hand and pointed at it with his finger. The bird fell out of the air like a stone and lay still on the floor. Tempū gently picked it up, carried it to a window, opened the window, and released it; the bird flew away. This event was witnessed by somewhere between sixty and one hundred people, and others besides Sasaki have also talked or written about it.

Then there were the geese that his wife and her maid brought home from the market one day. This was when vendors still brought their geese to the marketplace alive and wrung their necks upon demand from their customers. Nakamura, who was sitting under the eaves in the sunlight when the ladies returned home, asked to see the geese before they plucked them.

"This one is too far gone," he said, putting one of the two geese aside. The other, however, he held on to and began stoking its neck. The women, used to his eccentricities, continued into the house and went about their chores. But when they checked about twenty minutes later, they could see that the goose was showing signs of life. And after ten more minutes, the goose was on its feet and squawking as if nothing had happened. The goose had also apparently bonded with Nakamura, for it proceeded to follow him in and around the house, squawking all the while, until the women had had enough and banished both him and his goose to the yard.

215

The cage consists of a double barrier. This allows the caretakers to bring food through the outer barrier and to throw it to the cats through the second, inner door without risk of the cats' escape. It also prevents the cats from reaching passersby with their paws. The trainer opens the door to the outer cage for Nakamura and hands him a key; Nakamura opens the inner door on his own and slips inside.

The tigers are quiet. They look him over with curiosity, and one of the cubs brushes his leg. Nakamura is sporting a broad smile as all three cats then sidle up to him, the two younger ones curling up at his feet, the mother tiger calmly standing guard behind him.

At that moment, the flashbulb on the reporter's camera goes off with a pop. The mother leaps forward at the cage bars with a ferocious growl, fangs bared.

Tōyama laughs. "Yes indeed! She has plenty of spunk," he remarks.

Nakamura, still smiling broadly, nods in agreement. He strokes the mother tiger lightly on the head until she comes away from the bars and takes a seat on the floor. Then, when he has had enough of tigers, he quietly lets himself out of the cage and returns to the party on the other side of the bars. The reporter's photograph—the same photograph Kaneko is to see in the reporter's cousin's living room—appears in the Jiji News the following day.

Many years later,[3] Kaneko spots a paragraph-long editorial in the Mainichi newspapers mentioning the Tempūkai; a member of the Mainichi reporting staff who is also a Tempūkai participant is responsible for the editorial's placement. To Kaneko, the name Tempū means only one thing, the man in the tiger cage. He contacts the newspaper and learns that the Tempūkai is meeting in Tennōji. Kaneko drops all other obligations and joins the Osaka Tempūkai summer training session then underway.

* * *

The new economic order was not to the equal benefit of all. Wealth was being consolidated into the industrial metropolises along Japan's eastern seaboard, while vast segments of the rural population, especially in the north and the west, languished in abject poverty, and as effects of the Great War, still raging in Europe, reached the nation, starvation in these areas became rampant. Inevitably, as the gap between rich and poor widened, civil unrest erupted.

Nakamura, upon arriving one afternoon in the coastal town of Odawara, just south of Tokyo, is handed a telegram. From Tōyama Mitsuru, it reads, "Your help needed; return immediately." No more need be said. He has come to Odawara for a meeting of financiers at which he is scheduled to speak; instead, after hastily enlisting a substitute, he returns to Tokyo.

This is early March 1918, less than one month after the appearance of the tiger cage photograph in the Jiji News. Disembarking at Shinbashi, Nakamura takes a carriage directly to Tōyama's residence. Tōyama's instructions are typically sparse. "I want you to go up to Taira. Trouble's broken out at Nezu's coal mine and I need you to sort it out."

As he is leaving, Nakamura is handed an envelope by Tōyama's wife. He peeks inside: 1,500 yen in cash. Whatever the problem, money, it seems, is going to be part of the solution, for 1,500 yen is a sizeable sum: twice that amount will build a decent-size house. As events are to turn out, however, he is to return the envelope with contents intact.

Taira is part of the modern-day city of Iwaki in Fukushima Prefecture. Today, the travel time from Tokyo by high-speed electric rail is about two hours, but in 1918, it was an eight-hour journey behind a steam engine. Taira's Jōban coalfields, ranked third in Japanese coal production after coalfields in northern Kyushu and Hokkaido, were especially lucrative because of their proximity to Tokyo.

The man Nezu, to whom Tōyama had referred, was the illustrious entrepreneur Nezu Kaichirō. Nezu had made his initial fortune in investments, gone on to become a railroad magnate and financier, and then diversified into everything from electricity to beer. He was also a prominent political figure, having served four terms in Japan's upper house, during which time he could not help but become acquainted with Tōyama Mitsuru.

The mine in question, one of many dotting the Jōban coalfields, was known as the Iwaki Mine. As it turned out, it belonged not to Nezu but to Asano Sōichirō, another industrialist and financier who controlled a major share of nationwide coal distribution, as well as the manufacture and distribution of cement. Nezu, however, had a minority stake and substantial capital at risk in Asano's Jōban mining venture, and his nerves were wearing thinner with each day that the strike continued.

This was just one of more than one hundred similar strikes to occur around this time at mines throughout the country. If the war underway in Europe never reached Japanese shores, the effects of depressed foreign economies did, and when the pinch was felt in financial circles, it was passed on to workers. On top of this, rice speculators, acting on rumors of possible Japanese troop deployments to Siberia, were jacking up the price of rice. Rice prices had almost doubled by the time of the strike and would triple by late summer, sparking riots nationwide.

Despite these circumstances, Iwaki's owners' concern was only for their investments; they remained impervious to the suggestion that the miners might have legitimate grievances. Nothing, however, would entice the miners to return to work for sub-subsistence wages. Destitution had pushed them past a threshold from which there was no turning back, and collectively, they had resolved to go down fighting. The resulting standoff was now into its second month.

The striking miners were 1,500 strong. Armed with hunting rifles, pickaxes, and knives, they were ensconced behind a barricade at the mouth of the mine, rendering it inaccessible.

The first cry for help from the owners went out to an ordained Buddhist scholar and teacher of the Nichiren sect named Tanaka Chigaku. Tanaka was the founder of a politically motivated Buddhist organization called the Kokuchūkai, or National Pillar Society, a progenitor of today's Sōka Gakkai. A skillful orator, he was also renowned for his powers of persuasion, and it was upon these powers that Asano had set his hopes.

The ungodly miners, however, were not to be persuaded by talk of Amida and salvation unless that salvation was backed by hard cash.

Tanaka's entourage was met at gunpoint and categorically refused a meeting with the strike leader.

Next up was General Ōsako Naomichi. Ōsako was a frontline veteran of both the Sino-Japanese and the Russo-Japanese wars, and many of these same miners had served under his command. But if Ōsako assumed the respect shown him in battle gave him leverage now, he was badly mistaken. The miners had no more patience for generals than they had for priests, and Ōsako, too, was turned away at gunpoint.

Sensing Asano's desperation, Nezu finally turned to Tōyama. Nezu had contributed liberally to a number of Tōyama's political causes, including Sun Yat-sen's revolutionary activities, and he was also well aware of Tōyama's affiliations with the mining industry: a substantial part of Tōyama's political and financial capital was beholden to the coal mines next door to his native Fukuoka in Kitakyushu. Nezu also understood, having often been at odds with Tōyama over items on the industrial agenda as they related to workers' rights, that Tōyama's political allegiances were not for sale. But then, in this instance, Nezu reasoned, only a workers' champion could hope to get close to the mine owners' unsavory opposition.

The sun has already disappeared behind the hills when Nakamura arrives at the scene of the strike. The directions he had been given are vague, but after following the telltale track of a cog railroad through the forest for about an hour, he emerges into a meadow with a panoramic view of the standoff. In the middle of the meadow stands an open tent under which some thirty uniformed policemen sprawl nonchalantly in folding chairs. A short distance from the tent, the meadow is cut by the Yumoto River, and spanning the river is a wooden bridge, solidly constructed but showing wear from years of coal-cart traffic. On the far side of the bridge, backed by low hills, stands a roughly thrown-together bulwark. A primitive flag flutters atop the bulwark, marking it as the miners' line of defense.

In the fading light, a policeman catches sight of Nakamura as he approaches.

"Who goes there?"

Nakamura holds his answer until he is within normal voice range. "My name is Nakamura. I have come from Tokyo to speak with the miners. I'm here to mediate."

The policeman calls for his superior, a sergeant, who emerges from the tent and eyes Nakamura from head to toe, not knowing what to make of their dapperly dressed visitor; haori and hakama are unusual attire at a coalfield.

"You have come from Tokyo, you say. Who have you brought with you?"

Both Tanaka and Ōsako had descended upon the meadow decorated in regalia appropriate to their respective stations and accompanied by a small army of support staff, some armed. So when Nakamura assures the sergeant that he is the current mission in its entirety, the sergeant understands only that he has a probable nutcase on his hands.

"I see, I see," he says. "Now please turn around and go on home."

"You misunderstand," Nakamura replies. "I'm here on behalf of Tōyama Mitsuru."

Mention of Tōyama has an immediate effect. This is, after all, mining country; Tōyama Mitsuru is revered by the miners of Kitakyushu, many of whom, a vagrant lot, have migrated here to Iwaki. Furthermore, almost forty years ago, Tōyama, traveling barefoot and with his few belongings wrapped in a satchel slung over his back, made a Freedom and Peoples Rights Movement campaign stop in Iwaki that lasted for several days and won the hearts and minds of local leaders; the Genyōsha and its causes have been favorably received here ever since.

The police sergeant apologizes for his rudeness and invites Nakamura into the tent. But Nakamura's interests lie on the other side of the bridge. The time is getting late and he needs to be on his way.

That, the policeman insists, is madness. "Those men will open fire on you if you so much as set foot on that bridge."

"Maybe so," Nakamura says, "but unless I cross the bridge, I can't get to the other side."

Overhearing this conversation, policemen come swarming out of the tent. The police have no side in the labor dispute; their sole mandate is to prevent bloodshed, and this sudden visitor is about to put that mandate at risk. The sergeant is now certain he is dealing with a madman.

He stops short of physical restraint, however, and Nakamura, politely but firmly turning a deaf ear to his objections, walks toward the bridge. Sure enough, as soon as he steps onto its timber surface, a rifle shot rings out.

Nakamura does not break stride. More shots ensue. Hardly the first time he has been under fire, he judges the proximity of the bullets as they pass: given how easy a target he is at this range, the shots are evidently intended to maim but not to kill. Later, he counts a total of five bullet holes in the sleeves of his kimono.

"It never occurred to me to be afraid," Tempū would explain. "What is danger? The only danger was to my physical body. Now, I have a body, just as I have a mind. But the difference is that I know I am neither that body nor that mind, so there is nothing to fear.

"Furthermore, I was clear in my purpose. The people on the other side of the bridge were in distress. They and their families were victims in need of help. If anyone was in danger, it was them; their lives were at stake. Knowing that, how could I be concerned about the safety of my own skin?"

When Nakamura reaches the bridge's halfway point, a figure appears from behind the bulwark. "Are you deaf?" he yells. "Can't you hear shots being fired? They're meant for you."

Nakamura does not stop. "I thought they might be," he yells back. "But whoever fired them is not very good with a rifle. As you can see, he missed, and I'm still in one piece. I've come to talk to your leader."

The man on the other side of the bridge is now palpably incensed. Who does this intruder think he is? What gall, to issue provocations when so outnumbered. He unleashes a torrent of insults and profanities that Nakamura, continuing to march forward, ignores. In desperation, the man brandishes a short sword from inside his jacket.

"Nobody is allowed across this bridge. If you come one step closer, I'll make tofu out of you."

"Is that the way you treat visitors? To make tofu out of them?"

"Yes! And I would be delighted to serve you up in the usual way."

By this time, Nakamura is standing within three feet (one meter) of the miner. He looks him squarely in the eye. "You can serve me up any way you like," he says. "But first, let me talk to your leader."

The miner, realizing he is up against no ordinary adversary, backs down. Nakamura is led behind the barrier to a shack, where he is introduced to a gray-haired man with piercing eyes and a square jaw. This is the miners' leader—in better times, their foreman.

Nakamura comes directly to the point. "Your men have been out of work for a month," he says. "They and their families are going hungry. We need to do something for them."

"How much money did you bring with you?" the leader asks.

"None," is the reply. "But I do have a proposal." Nakamura points to the small mountain of coal piled outside the mine. "Your men can fetch a fair price for that in the village. Give them each a sack. Each man can take away as much as he can carry, and he can keep the receipts from what he sells."

The leader looks back at him incredulously. "That'd be larceny," he says. "The owners will have us arrested."

"Leave that to me," Nakamura replies. "I'll assume full responsibility. I give you my word. But there's one condition. After selling the coal, your men need to return to work."

When news of this arrangement passes down the line, the camp breaks out in excitement. After a round of backslapping, the miners attack the mountain of coal. Nakamura hastily retreats across the bridge to inform the police of what has transpired and to order them to allow the coal-bearing miners to pass.

When word reaches him of this outcome, Nezu is outraged: his mediator has given away the store. Ten days later, Nakamura, charged with misrepresentation of authority and misappropriation of private property, is served with a summons to the Taira regional court. The news is enough to spark a second revolt among the miners.

All charges are dropped, however, soon after Tōyama appears on Nezu's doorstep. Tōyama is bristling. "Didn't you come to me?" he asks. "Didn't you tell me I had your permission to do whatever I needed to do in order to solve the problem? Well, I sent Nakamura. So what right have you, now, to question his authority?"

Cowered by this scolding, Nezu is returned to his senses. Nakamura is not only pardoned but told he is to be rewarded 10,000 yen.

"I'll accept the reward on two conditions," Nakamura responds. "One is that you give it to me in one-yen notes. And the other is that you do so in person in front of the miners."

Nezu is miffed by these unusual demands but has no choice but to consent. Several days later they meet again at the mouth of the mine. When the sizeable bundle of one-yen notes is exchanged, Nakamura hands it immediately to the foreman.

"Distribute this to your men," he says.

The foreman is taken aback. "Keep at least part of it," he says. "You more than deserve to be compensated for what you have done."

But Nakamura is adamant. This money belongs to the miners; they are the ones deserving of it.

What effect this action has on Nezu, we can only speculate. But what we do know is that, in addition to the mark he made on Japanese industry, Nezu would leave behind, upon his death in 1940, an impressive philanthropic legacy. His private residence was posthumously converted into an art museum that continues to the present day.

Nakamura came away from these two incidents, the one involving fierce tigers and the one involving desperate miners, subtly but profoundly changed. The change was twofold. First, his experiences during these incidents were catalysts in his ideas concerning faith—not religious faith or faith in the sense of belief but the kind of unshakable, rock-solid confidence and certainty that had allowed him to befriend both wild animals and desperate men. That faith, or power of conviction, is what is meant by the Japanese word *shinnen*. Second, his encounter with the miners reminded him that not all the world was as fortunate or as well fed as he. It caused him to question his ways.

Of shinnen, Tempū would later say, "For many years I thought of myself as a man of no talents. I wasn't good at anything. Unless, of course, you put a sword in my hands."

My teacher, Tōyama Mitsuru said, "You were born too late. If only you had been born in the sixteenth century, you would have probably vanquished all adversaries with your sword and become supreme ruler of the land. But it's not the age for that anymore; you came along at the wrong time." Of course, I didn't choose when to be born, but I really thought he was right. The only time I felt that I was good for something was when I was holding a sword. Aside from using a sword, I couldn't do anything.

Until the age of about forty, I couldn't read my own handwriting. I'd look at something I'd written and ask, "What does it say?" The characters were illegible. As for drawing, forget it. I couldn't have drawn a picture of three dumplings on a stick if you'd asked me to. Not even three circles in a row connected by a line through the middle. [At the time he is speaking, Tempū is known by his audience to be a masterful calligrapher; he produces bold works for his students upon request and can do so in a number of different classical styles. He also produces simple but highly artistic sumie, *ink and brush paintings.]*

But then, if you put a sword in my hands, I could do things that surprised even me. You've seen me demonstrate [he is speaking at one of the Tempūkai summer retreats], so you know.

224

Otherwise, I was hopeless. When I was asked once to fix a wooden box, I couldn't even drive a nail. That's how clumsy I was. Now my fingers are as nimble as a hairdresser's. But not back then.

The discovery of the power of faith (shinnen) *is what made the difference. Now when I see someone doing something, I say to myself, "I can do that too." And I can. Usually on the first try; usually without practice. Furthermore, it didn't take long for this change to occur. Once I began believing in myself, it happened very quickly.*

Sometimes I would find myself wondering, "This newly acquired ability to learn, is it permanent? Or is it some temporary, transitory phase?" And at first, when I had just successfully completed some undertaking, I would ask myself, "Which is it? Is the real me the clumsy and incapable person I used to be, or is it the unencumbered, happy person I am now?" The change was so rapid that I had difficulty believing that it was for real and that it was lasting.

But as time went on, that old self with all of its doubts never returned. Furthermore, when I began to seriously study this phenomenon from the standpoint of the biological and mental sciences, I discovered that the mind's ability to think is a truly mysterious, underappreciated, and underutilized power. I also discovered the relationship between the conscious and the unconscious parts of the mind. And as I came to understood more about the mind and its capacities, my faith and conviction—and my ability to call forth that faith and conviction— became stronger and stronger, until it was as solid and immovable as concrete. Until it became as it is today, indescribably strong. It really is indescribable. No matter what I say, words can't do it justice.[4]

But then, in inverse proportion to this newfound ability to cultivate faith and conviction, his doubts as to what purpose he was serving grew. The miners' eyes had spoken; they had shown him the same fear and despair that he had battled while suffering tuberculosis—only, in the case of the miners, that fear was not just for themselves but also for their dependents, their families. Nakamura had said good-bye to a life of fear and despair years ago, but what had he replaced it with? Of late, his greatest challenge was the choice to be made between geishas each afternoon.

Furthermore, here he was, someone who had been to the underworld and back. He had journeyed into territory from which most men never return. Why was it that he, of all men, should had been granted a reprieve? Why should he have been returned to the world of the living? The face of the venerable Indian sage Kariappa, through whose graces his second lease on life had been granted, flashed before him. The words Tōyama had spoken upon his return resounded in his ears: "Your life is no longer your own. From now on, your life belongs to the world." Fortune had blessed him with two extraordinary teachers, but could he say that he was living up to the expectations they held for him? The answer was obvious and the shame of that answer excruciating.

But then, what was he to do? What could he do? What of value could he contribute to humanity? No answer was immediately forthcoming.

12.
THE TURNING POINT

Not until a full year after the Iwaki Mine incident does the first hint of an answer suggests itself, and from a most unexpected quarter. Nakamura's wife, Yoshi, upon the rare occasion of finding her husband seated at the family dining table, asks, "You know those stories that you sometimes tell us about your experiences in India? Would you be willing to tell them to a few of my friends?"

Yoshi was nineteen when wed to Nakamura Saburō. Transplanted from rural Fukuoka to metropolitan Tokyo, she entered the Nakamura household practically on the eve of her new husband's dispatch to parts from which, she was duly informed, he was not likely to return. Their first and only child by birth (they would adopt a second daughter years later) was conceived during his summer 1904 leave and born in April 1905 while he was back in the field. Then, when he was returned to her alive a second time, she welcomed home but a ghost of the man she had married. And after months of nursing him during his sequester, she saw him off yet again—this time, against the counsel of doctors and friends, to the other side of the world.

If, after a hiatus of five years, Nakamura's return from that underworld was testament to his perseverance, and if it singled him out, in Tōyama Mitsuru's words, as one who was chosen, then his perseverance and good fortune were matched by Yoshi's tenacity and stoicism. Characterized as quiet, easygoing, and even-keeled, Yoshi, like Nakamura, was of bushi lineage, and she brought with her to the institution of marriage the resolve of a samurai daughter. Her devotion to her husband, as it was based not upon personal choice but upon the destiny chosen for her by her parents and the sanctity of a pact made between families, was absolute. Even during Nakamura's lowest ebb, while he remained secluded in his room, it was Yoshi—not he—who kept alive the flame of conviction in his ability to beat the odds.

Nakamura provided financially for his family during both his absences, and now, with his success as an entrepreneur, they enjoyed relative affluence. In that sense, Yoshi was fortunate; she had stature within the community and a wide circle of friends. Whatever pain her husband's infidelities caused her, she did not allow it to show. Fidelity, after all, while certainly desirable, had never been part of the bargain.

For all of his sordid behavior, she was also secretly certain—call it woman's intuition—that her husband had yet to become all he was meant to be. Never one to press or restrain, she simply waited and endured. But for Yoshi's subtle influence, however, the transformation of Nakamura Saburō, the playboy, into Nakamura Tempū, the teacher, would almost certainly never have occurred.

Nakamura is less than enthralled with the proposition of sacrificing a whole afternoon to a group of neighborhood women; but then again, given his record of late, he is also in no position to refuse. "But a small price to pay," he reflects, if it will keep him in his wife's good graces; Yoshi has every right to exact of him more.

Only later does he discover that she also has a second agenda. Yes, indeed, she has spoken of her husband's stories to some of her friends, and these friends have expressed an interest in hearing them from the horse's mouth. But her more pressing priority is the welfare of a first cousin. The cousin has recently arrived in Tokyo from Fukuoka and is overwhelmed by the pace and demands of big-city life. He has suffered a series of setbacks and is becoming more and more desperate. If anyone can help him break out of his downward spiral, she feels certain, it is her husband.

The familial dimension, however, makes this a difficult favor to ask: neither is she sure the cousin will be open to her husband's counsel, nor does she wish to burden Nakamura with any untoward sense of obligation or responsibility. On the other hand, the gesture of inviting her cousin to an already planned gathering at the Nakamura household need not be explained to either cousin or husband, and when the unsuspecting cousin appears on a Sunday afternoon several days later, he finds himself awkwardly seated among a group of matrons.

Nakamura has made no preparations and wonders what to say. What could these women possibly want to hear? No sooner does he open his mouth, however, than words come out in sentences, and sentences follow seamlessly, one to the next. The experience is both uncanny and exhilarating; his stories seem to tell themselves, and someone other than he seems to do the talking. The allotted two hours go by before either he or his audience notices. But when at last the advancing hour can no longer be ignored, the group, to a person, asks to hear the sequel on another occasion. Yoshi glances apprehensively at her husband. To her surprise and relief, he agrees without a trace of hesitation.

After the guests have left, and after barely acknowledging Yoshi's thanks, Nakamura reflects out loud on what has just happened. Sights, sounds, and sensations he has not thought about in years—some not since the moments of the events in which they occurred—had percolated into his consciousness, seemingly, out of nowhere. It was, he observes again, as if the stories themselves had wanted to be told.

With this beginning, gatherings at the Nakamura household became a monthly occurrence. Word circulated among the women of the neighborhood, and some of the women even succeeded in enticing their husbands to join. In due course, Nakamura's stories, of which his supply seemed limitless, began to congeal around a basic premise: "Life is a succession of challenges, but how you respond to those challenges need not be dictated by circumstances. The determination and strength of conviction that you bring to bear on these challenges are what most affect their outcome. Act mindfully and with clarity of purpose and the path ahead will inevitably open."

Moreover, not only was Yoshi's cousin now finding his way so reliably that Yoshi had ceased to worry, but the faces of the other attendees also were beginning to glow in a way they had not before. On these afternoons, an auspicious aura seemed to descend over the otherwise ordinary Nakamura residence, impregnating all within with a sense of hope and renewal.

Otherwise, however, Nakamura's way of life was little changed. He continued to spend much of his time away from home, ostensibly on business but more often than not in the company of geishas. But then, all was not right. Although he had mentioned it to no one, not even Yoshi, he was having trouble sleeping. Many a night, after awakening in the dark to a plague of doubts and finding it impossible to go back to sleep, he would pass the hours until sunrise sipping tea and smoking his beloved Cuban cigars.

Furthermore, his old companion, the disease, was rearing its head again. Under Kariappa's tutelage, Nakamura had successfully pushed that disease into remission. But remission is not the same as cure, and tuberculosis, once it takes up residence, stays with its host for life. Whatever measure of control Nakamura exercised over it, he had gained through austerity and dedicated practice; that austerity and practice removed, the effects of his decadent behavior were now catching up with him. The telltale cough and fever had reappeared.

Following the second of Yoshi's Sunday afternoon gatherings, Nakamura remarked with astonishment that the event had had as much or more effect on his own well-being as it had had on that of their guests. Although he had spoken continuously for over two hours, he felt no fatigue; to the contrary, he felt energized in a way that he had not in years. Moreover, satiation and fulfillment such as he was now feeling was not to be derived from the most lavish of soirees or the company of the most talented and sought-after of geishas. That evening, for the first time in many months, he slept soundly until morning.

"I have been thinking," he confesses to Yoshi several months later. "You know the gatherings that you have been putting together? What if I were to make them my vocation?"

230

Yoshi looks at him in disbelief. "Are you serious?"

Nakamura nodded. "Yes," he assures her.

Yoshi is unconvinced. "Nothing would please me more," she responds. "But only if you are sure. If you are less than absolutely sure, then it's probably not such a good idea."

A prudent observation, Nakamura has to agree. But how could he be sure? All he knows is that these simple gatherings provide him with a sense of purpose absent from the rest of his life. Even at the risk of failure, would he not be better off pursuing that which made him happy, as well as contributing to others, rather than continuing to serve, successful as that service might be, the business interests of the powerful and wealthy?

But then, what of his responsibilities to his family? Could he rightly subject them to uncertainty and undue risk, just because he is experiencing a personal crisis and having second thoughts about his self-worth?

Two days later, Nakamura is sitting again beside Tōyama Mitsuru. The occasion is the formal opening of a Nichiren sectarian organization called the Dai-Nippon Kyūseidan, the Greater Japan Association for World Salvation. Nichiren Buddhism has a proclivity for political activism, and this organization is a case in point: in advancing its moral ideals, it seeks to fulfill a somewhat sinister nationalistic agenda. The association is founded by General Ōsako Naomichi with the support of Buddhist scholar Tanaka Chigaku, the same two personages sent to mediate the Iwaki Mine dispute ahead of Nakamura. Invited by Ōsako and Tanaka to speak at their opening, Tōyama has called on Nakamura to accompany him, prefacing his request with the remark, "I'm not much of a public speaker."

The billing of Tōyama Mitsuru as the ceremony's guest of honor has had its desired effect. When Ōsako introduces him from the podium, all seats are taken and people are standing at the back of the room. "It is my great honor and privilege to introduce to you one of the great prodigies of all ages, Tōyama Ō-sensei,"[1] he says.

Tōyama-sensei nods toward the crowd as he ascends the podium. He then proceeds to stand there, facing his audience, without saying a word.

"This goes on," Tempū says, "by my watch, for three minutes. Someone in the back of the audience yells, 'We can't hear you.' To which someone in the front responds, 'Shut up and admire his face.' Tōyama, in the meantime, pays neither of these comments any attention. He continues to look out at the audience."

Tempū continues. "It takes more than guts to pull off a stunt like this. It takes balls. Here, he has just been hailed by a general in uniform, to thunderous applause, as one of the great prodigies of all ages. To which he responds by getting up, nodding, and facing his audience for three minutes in complete silence. Now, I've been speaking in front of large audiences for forty years, but I don't think I could last for more than a minute...

"Later, I asked him, 'Sensei, what were you thinking? What was going through your mind while you stood there like that?' To which he responded, 'I wasn't thinking about anything. I was just waiting for the audience to calm down so that I could introduce you.'"[2]

Which is what he does. At the end of his seemingly interminable silence, Tōyama flashes his signature smile and opens his mouth to speak. "I'm hopeless as a public speaker. But Tempū here knows everything I want to say, so I'm going to ask him to speak on my behalf."

This is news to Nakamura. "So that's why he asked me to come along," he reflects. But then, he does know exactly what Tōyama wants to say. Nakamura takes the stage and addresses the audience, effectively channeling his mentor's thoughts and sentiments, for a full hour.

The year is the eighth of Emperor Taishō's reign. Six months ago, in Europe, an armistice had been reached and the tides of economic fortune are beginning to turn. Meanwhile, at home, liberal currents in education coupled with divisive gaps in the economic spectrum are spawning a pluralistic polity, wherein disparate foreign ideas like democracy, communism, socialism, and even anarchy are taking hold. In sharp contrast with the unbridled public optimism and energy of the Meiji era, the age of Taishō has given rise to widespread cynicism and apathy, and Nakamura, as he stands at the podium, can feel these same currents in the room.

"Not an easy crowd to please," Tōyama notes when Nakamura returns to his seat.

During a pause in the proceedings, Nakamura turns toward Tōyama. "Sensei," he says, "I have been thinking. I am considering leaving business to teach. It seems to me that perhaps I could be of some service to the nation by contributing to our spiritual culture. So many people are confused about their priorities. They lack direction. I may be able to give them some advice. What do you think?"

Tanaka Chigaku, sitting on the far side of Tōyama Mitsuru and having overheard, is first to speak. "Nakamura," he says, "Don't be foolish. Stick to what you're good at." Nakamura has touched a nerve. Japan's spiritual culture, Tanaka means to say, is his turf, and the suggestion by a young nobody that he should have something to contribute to its cultivation is an impertinence.

"You're still young," he continues. "Take it from one who knows. First of all, spiritual work requires money."

"That, I have," Nakamura answers.

"You may have money now. But no matter how much you have, it won't last long. And it's not just a question of money. It's also a question of reputation. You may be well known in the business world, but your name carries no weight with the man on the street. Better that you bide your time until you have ripened a little more."

Between the two of them, Tōyama sits quietly, stroking his long white beard. Nakamura addresses him again.

"Sensei, what do you say?"

Tōyama strokes his beard one more time. "It's worth a try," he says at last. "Have at it."

Nakamura returns home. He sits Yoshi down and says to her, "I'm thinking of going forward with the idea I spoke to you about the other day."

Yoshi says nothing but looks him squarely in the eye. A full minute goes by, while she searches his face for any hint of uncertainty.

"You're serious," she says at last. "What did Tōyama-sensei say?"

"He said, 'Have at it.'"

Nakamura restates the risks. They will face probable ridicule and possible financial ruin. They may even end up living on the street. All this Yoshi understands, but she is unmoved. Financial security has never taken priority in their marriage—she had, after all, married Nakamura just as he was going off to war—and she understands, in her own way, that a life worth living involves risk. Living in the shadow of a man attempting to make a difference in the world appeals infinitely more to her than the continuation of her current role, one that, despite its material benefits, means turning a blind eye to her husband's conduct.

His remark to Tanaka with regard to his financial resources notwithstanding, Nakamura quickly realizes that, in order for his plan to work, he cannot serve two masters; he needs to put everything on the line. Accordingly, the following morning he sets to work to tie up the ends of his many business associations. One by one, he proffers letters of resignation and nominates successors. He also systematically disposes of all of his shareholdings in these corporations.

Needless to say, he encounters considerable resistance. First on everyone's mind is the question "Why?"

One morning, a first cousin, with whom Nakamura has always been close, strides into the house unannounced. He passes Yoshi in the hall without so much as acknowledging her presence.

"What's this I hear about you quitting the bank?" he says, upon barging into Nakamura's study.

"Word travels fast," Nakamura responds.

The ensuing tirade is enough to make him wince. "Are you out of your mind? What of your wife and child? What of your mother? There's more at stake here than your simple-minded fancy. What you're doing is totally irresponsible. Furthermore, there's talk of you pursuing public speaking."

"Yes. That's also true," Nakamura acknowledges.

"In that case, I must insist that you come to your senses and give up on the idea immediately."

The cousin is a licensed physician working in public health, and his field is the treatment and containment of tuberculosis. He knows the full history of Nakamura's bought with and remarkable recovery from TB, and his admiration for that accomplishment is unconditional. But he also knows that the tuberculosis, if in remission, has not gone away.

"Your body," he says, "is like a ceramic bowl with a crack in it. Under stress, it'll break."

He is voicing a legitimate concern. Public address systems are an invention yet to come, and to speak in public, one must have the strength and stamina to make his voice carry to the back of the room. What are the implications of such stress when placed on Nakamura's disease-ridden lungs?

Nakamura listens patiently and politely but will not be persuaded. "You're signing your own death sentence," the exasperated cousin concludes before leaving as abruptly as he has come.

Next to weigh in is Nakamura's brother-in-law, his older sister's husband. The brother-in-law, however, ignoring both Saburō and Yoshi, turns to Nakamura's mother.

"Please stop him. He's not right in the head. What's this talk of teaching people how to live? The idea is preposterous. There's no way he'll succeed. Does he think wealth entitles him to tell people how they should live? It's the wrong line of business. It takes more than money. It takes character. It takes reputation. What has he done worthy of note, other than to have gone off to war for a few years? That's not enough to buy him credibility. Tell him to stop this nonsense before he falls flat on his face."

Nakamura's mother listens quietly until the son-in-law has finished. "Whether he fails or succeeds remains to be seen. It's beyond any of us to predict, and furthermore, it isn't our concern. Saburō is his own man. He's made a decision, and as long as his mind is made up, then it's up to us to stand by him and his decision."

235

"I see. So even you have been infected by his madness. Now he's certain to fail; this is a lost cause."

"Maybe so. But when someone puts his body and soul into an endeavor, more often than not, he prevails. If he were acting under duress or with less than pure intentions, then I might want to discourage him. But he's sincere. As a mother, I couldn't be happier for him."

She pauses and looks directly into her son-in-law's eyes. "What about your intentions? Aren't they less than pure?"

The son-in-law bristles. "My only concern is the good of the family," he responds defensively.

"Is that really so? Perhaps you'd better take another look. Only someone with evil in his heart would attempt to stand in the way of another's well-intentioned efforts to do good work."

The son-in-law is without comeback; his objections may, indeed, have been partially motivated by jealousy. Equally humbled, Nakamura takes the clarity of his mother's moral judgment to heart.[3]

Nakamura gives himself just ten days to settle his affairs. They are a busy ten days. He later remarks that, in these ten days, he put in more hours of honest work than he did during all his previous years in business. But, on June 8, 1919, no longer beholden to financial interests, he steps out of his front door and embarks into a new unknown. He is forty-three years old.

The moment is a watershed like no other in his life. Among other things, it is the moment in which Nakamura Saburō measures up to the bar set for him by Tōyama Mitsuru with his bestowal of the name Tempū, "Heaven's Wind." That other watershed, the awakening he underwent in the foothills of the Himalayas, was of profound personal consequence, bringing him in touch with a deeper level of being and, ultimately, saving his life; but, where the stakes of that game had been his personal survival, those of this new game are considerably higher. When he steps out of his door that morning, he is surrendering to a life of service.

Moreover, he is doing so without a plan. Whereas his life up until this point has always been oriented toward the achievement of some tangible outcome—the vanquish of an enemy, the reinstatement of health, the production of wealth—today, he walks into the daylight with only the most abstract of goals in mind. In a sense, he is like a scientist conducting an experiment: he is out to see what kind of difference one human being, armed with no more than his intentions and a box lunch, handed him by Yoshi at the door, can make toward the worldly advancement of peace, happiness, and well-being.

Yoshi watches his back apprehensively as he disappears around the corner at the end of their street.

Had she asked him where he was headed, Nakamura would have been unable to answer. From Hongō, he walks in the direction of Ueno, coming to the shore of Shinobazu Pond and its floating carpet of lotus leaves. He wanders along the shore and then ascends the stone stairs that lead into Ueno Park. The stairs bring him out in front of the Seiyōken,[4] one of the first restaurants in Japan to specialize in French and other Western cuisine; backed by prominent political figures of the Meiji Restoration, the restaurant first opened in 1876, the year of Nakamura's birth, and Nakamura has dined there with clients during his banking career. But such is hardly his intention today.

On the park grounds directly facing the restaurant, he spots a stone pedestal almost knee-high. Meant to support a stone lantern, the pedestal is bare: either the lantern was never installed, or it has been removed, perhaps due to cracking from long exposure to the elements.

"This will work," he thinks to himself. From the cloth satchel that also contains his lunchbox, he withdraws a hand bell, and this, standing atop the pedestal, he holds above his head and rings. The bell's reverberations dissipate quickly into the open air, but they are enough to catch the attention of several passersby.

"Gather here," Nakamura calls out. "Listen to my story. Don't be afraid; I'm not asking for your money and I have nothing to sell."

Ueno today is still one of the largest parks in metropolitan Tokyo, and as such, it collects a wide variety of human traffic: visitors to any of the several museums housed within the park grounds, suited salesmen passing time in dereliction of their rounds, homeless vagabonds, and foreigners of every nationality hawking various wares when park authorities are not looking. The sounds of the surrounding city permeate the park's innermost recesses, rendering incomplete the respite from the oppressively busy pace of city life that most of its visitors are seeking.

The scene in 1919 would have been both similar and different. Automobile traffic was rare, so the park would have been much quieter than is the case today. Nevertheless, the park stood then, as it does now, as a pocket of serenity within the hub of urban life, and its foot traffic would have included a fairly accurate cross-section of the town's citizenry, including the well-to-do as well as the working classes, and housewives and working women as well as men.

Visit the park now on a Sunday or a holiday and you will not fail to encounter street performers of every description: jugglers, mimes, acrobats, magicians, and musicians. This, however, was not the case in 1919, and to come upon someone ringing a bell would have been rare indeed. To most, Nakamura, in his cleanly pressed haori and hakama, standing atop this stone podium, bell in hand, would have cut a figure too odd for comfort. They would have averted their eyes, turned a deaf ear, and hastily continued on their way.

But for some, curiosity would have won over suspicion. These people would have stopped, looked, listened, and then cautiously approached.

Once he has, in this manner, assembled an audience of six or seven, Nakamura begins. "Listen up," he says. "The only guarantee in life is that each of us will eventually die. Could be tomorrow, could be ten, twenty, or thirty years from now, but sooner or later that day will come. So I suggest to you that we are meant to live life to its fullest and to make every minute count."

With the exception of political rallies, this sort of public audition is without precedent. Christian evangelism is confined within church domains or other private gatherings, and even the followers of Nichiren, the most evangelical of all the different brands of Buddhism, are not given to proselytizing in public places. The closest parallel to Nakamura's performance is that of street-side vendors in mercantile districts like Asakusa, men whose livelihoods revolve around drawing attention to themselves and their wares from among the passing crowd, and for whom the right hooks are the essential tools of their trade.[5]

Speaking out in public is subject to restrictions, and several days later, when his talks in the park have become a regular occurrence, Tempū visits the Ueno police station to ascertain whether or not what he is doing requires a permit. He sits the officers down in their chairs and delivers the same talk he has just delivered in the park. "No. For that, you don't need a permit," the police chief concludes; Tempū asks him for a signed statement to that effect, which he provides. Several of the officers come to the park the following day to hear his sequel.

Later, Tempū will be known to entertain Tempūkai summer retreat participants with his performances of *rakugo,* traditional storytelling. The rakugo performer delivers a humorous monologue, typically thirty to forty-five minutes in duration, while sitting alone in *seiza*—kneeling, with buttocks resting on heels—on a single cushion facing the audience, his only props a folding fan and a hand towel. The art relies almost entirely on the verbal medium: even hand gestures are minimal, and the storyteller pulls his audience into his story and holds their interest until delivery of the final punch line, called the *ochi,* all through oral expression.

A structured discipline, rakugo typically requires years of practice to master. Tempū probably learned it in the teahouses of Shinbashi and Kagurazaka, in which case it would have been a competency already at his disposal by the time he mounted the stone pedestal in Ueno.

Nevertheless, a rakugo audience comes to a performance expecting to be entertained; Nakamura's audience in the park is wary and skeptical, and he has all of three minutes at best in which to capture their interest and to gain their trust. He slips easily and quickly into an account of how he miraculously survived the trials of war, even once facing a firing squad, only to then find he had contracted tuberculosis; how he circled the globe in search of a cure; and how, after giving up all hope, he learned, while under the guidance of a venerable sage and meditating by a waterfall in the shadow of the Himalayas, something about the fundamental nature of life.

Inevitably, he loses most of his audience, as, one by one, they return to their business of the day. But a couple of people remain to hear him through until the story's end. Not a bad beginning, Tempū thinks to himself.

"That's all for today," he announces. "If you want to hear more, come back tomorrow at the same time."

No sooner has Tempū finished speaking than a distant factory siren announces the noon recess. Seating himself on the edge of the stone pedestal, he removes the lunchbox from his satchel and consumes the rice balls and slices of pickled radish contained within. When he has finished, he stands and walks in the direction opposite to that from which he has come. At the far side of the park, he descends a stone stairway toward Ueno Station.

At street level, he is greeted by the bell of an approaching trolley. A sign above the trolley's front window reads Shibazonobashi. "That will do," he thinks. He hops aboard.

The trolley ambles down the middle of city streets, making frequent stops. It travels from Ueno to Kanda, then on to Ōtemachi, Hibiya, and finally Onarimon and Shiba Park. At Shiba Park it passes in front of Zōjōji, the main temple of the Jōdo sect of Buddhism, before arriving at Shibazonobashi and the park's southern entrance. What today is a fifteen-minute journey by subway, with changes, the streetcar travels in close to an hour, and when Tempū alights, the time is already midafternoon.

Entering the park, he wanders back in the direction of Zōjōji, arriving at a copper statue of statesman and Waseda University founder Ōkuma Shigenobu. Erected upon the occasion of the Emperor Taishō's ascent to the throne just eight years earlier, while Ōkuma was serving as prime minister, the statue is one of the park's newer landmarks. It is also destined to be a short-lived one, for it will be carted away during a 1944 metal drive to be melted down and allocated to the manufacture of wartime munitions.

Ōkuma, at this time still living, plays a peripheral role in several events relative to Nakamura's past. It was Ōkuma who, as minister of finance, commissioned Nakamura's father to develop and manufacture the paper used in the printing of Japanese currency. Moreover, since 1889, Ōkuma has sported a wooden leg, the result, as mentioned in chapter 1, of a bomb thrown by a member of the Genyōsha cadre; Tōyama Mitsuru, an outspoken critic of what he perceived to be unnecessary leniency toward Western demands in the negotiation of foreign treaties under Ōkuma's watch as foreign minister, was circumstantially implicated as party to this crime but never charged.

None of this is pertinent to Tempū's current purposes, however. His interest is in the broad, stone pedestal on which the statue stands, for the platform it provides is slightly higher but similar in surface area to his platform in Ueno. More importantly, the statue is situated on a heavily trafficked path between Azabu to the west and the park's main gate to the east.

Standing in Ōkuma's shadow atop the statue's pedestal, he once again takes out his bell and rings it. When several curious pedestrians have gathered, he begins a repeat performance of his delivery that morning.

Thus begins a new routine. Each morning, Tempū returns to the same spot in Ueno Park and speaks to whatever audience he can muster. After lunch, he rides the streetcar to Shiba Park, where, in the shadow of Ōkuma Shigenobu, he recruits a new audience and delivers the same talk he has given that morning.

The colloquial term for someone who rapidly fails in his resolutions is *mikka bōzu*, "a monk for three days," and on the fourth morning, Yoshi asks with hesitation whether or not he will be going out again. Tempū laughs. Just how long he will continue this routine or what it is meant to achieve, he cannot say, but he is not, he assures her, "a monk for three days."

He is having too much fun. He genuinely enjoys telling his story; it is *his* story, after all, and a good one. Hardly is he about to quit. One might be tempted to interpret Tempū's conduct as that of a zealot, a man motivated by a messianic calling, but such was not at all the case. A more fitting likeness might be that of a teenage schoolboy out on a lark.

The fragile attention span of his itinerant and capricious audiences places a limit on how far he can venture into philosophical territory, but perhaps he can, ever so slightly, alter their thinking with regard to the possibilities life affords them. Perhaps he can spark them to question their beliefs. Perhaps he can even poke a hole or two in the deep-seated resignation with which they approach their everyday challenges and concerns.

His reward comes in seeing the numbers at these gatherings increase. Particularly gratifying is the sight of familiar faces: he is developing a small but dedicated group of return listeners.

One of these is a young man, always immaculately dressed in suit and tie. On the first occasion, the man is stopped by the sound of Tempū's voice as he happens past the Ōkuma statue in a jinrikisha. Several days later he returns, again by jinrikisha, but this time, dismounts, telling his driver to wait while he moves closer to the podium. He returns, Tempū notices, several more times during the following weeks, now on foot.

One day, as Tempū concludes his talk and descends from beneath the towering likeness of Ōkuma, the man approaches. "I have enjoyed listening several times now," he says. By way of self-introduction, he hands Tempū a business card, on which is printed, "Chiyoda Paper Corporation, Mishima Miyoshi, President."

"My friends and I have an association we call the Sakura Club. I was wondering if you would be willing to speak at one of our gatherings?"

On the appointed day, Tempū leaves home by jinrikisha. The journey takes him along the moat surrounding the imperial palace and into Marunouchi to a brick building bearing the placard "Japan Industrial Club." This association, under the auspices of which the Sakura Club operates, has been founded two years earlier as an industrial policy lobby and advocacy group; it is made up of some of industry's most powerful leaders, as well as its most powerful political defenders. The headquarters building is so new that its formal opening ceremony has yet to be held.[6]

Inside, Tempū is ushered into a second-story sitting room occupied by some twenty men, most of them in business attire. Seated on cushioned sofas and chairs skirting the room, all jump to their feet when he enters. From among them, an elderly man, dressed, as is Tempū, in traditional haori and hakama, steps forward and introduces himself. Mukai Itsuki is his name. Tempū recognizes him immediately, for his wispy, sloping mustache, as another visitor to his talks in Shiba Park.

Mukai, Tempū now understands, is the instigator behind the invitation, with the younger Mishima acting as his emissary. A former public appellate court prosecutor, Mukai is now consul to the imperial throne.

Mukai and Mishima shoulder considerable personal risk in bringing Nakamura Tempū, known to them only as a man delivering an address in a public park, to this venue. Visionaries and pioneers in their own rights, they will continue to support Nakamura Tempū and to wield their influence in making his teachings known within wider business and political circles during months and years to come.

One by one, the introductions continue, until each of the men in the room has come forward. Tempū is impressed by the professional diversity represented. Among them are not only business leaders and entrepreneurs, like Mishima, but also members of parliament and heads of governmental bureaucracies.

Formalities out of the way, Tempū is invited to a small podium at the front of the room. Much to his delight, his audience warms quickly. This time, unlike his talks in the park, he is appearing by invitation before men to whom he has just been given one-on-one introductions. Confident that he has their attention, he enters directly and more deeply into the heart of what it is he wants to say. When the allotted two hours are up, neither is he done talking, nor is his audience done listening; so, with their permission, he continues for an extra hour. And when he concludes to enthusiastic applause, each of the members comes forward again, this time to express personal appreciation and to implore him to return.

He is also presented with a generous honorarium, which he accepts, upon his hosts' unrelenting insistence, only after he has made it understood that he will not accept any such payment in the future—a travel and meal allowance, yes, but not an honorarium. To the end of his days, Tempū never again accepts anything more than an expense allowance for speaking engagements. The privilege associated with such opportunities to share with others what he has to say is remuneration enough and is not, he is adamant, to be confused with livelihood or personal gain.

And such opportunities now became frequent. A series of lectures at the Japan Industrial Club follows the first, each drawing a larger audience than the last. More importantly, out of these audiences come requests and invitations to address other professional organizations and associations.

Exposure within this elite network quickly brings him to the attention of the top echelons of Japanese society. The following year, Tempū is invited to meet with Prime Minister Hara Takashi. Hara and Nakamura Tempū are acquaintances from an earlier period in Hara's political career, and despite divergences in their political views, they hold each other in amiable high regard. Upon visiting the prime minister at his residence, Tempū neither talks politics nor wastes time in getting to what is on his mind.

"Don't for a moment let authority go to your head," he warns Hara. "Stripped of your title and position, you are no different from the common man. The office of prime minister carries extraordinary responsibilities in addition to its privileges, and your countrymen are watching you closely for what you do and say. So, above all, act with humility. You are expected to serve as an example to the nation and an inspiration to its children."

Out of consideration for the prime minister's schedule, he keeps his remarks brief, but even in the short time allotted him, he is able to deliver the principle tenets of his mind-body discipline. Hara is said to have said, "You don't know how important to me this has been. Most people won't tell me what I need to hear."[7]

Tempū would later say in reference to Hara that truly great men are great because they know how to receive criticism: "When a great man is criticized, he receives that criticism with humility and uses it as an opportunity for self-improvement; ordinary people just puff up with anger."[8]

Hara is assassinated the following year in front of Tokyo Station. The motives of his knife-wielding assailant are never clearly established; however, one of Hara's harshest critics has been Tōyama Mitsuru, and an editorial in the popular press comments that the only two people in all of Japan capable of murder with impunity are the emperor and Tōyama Mitsuru. Largely as a result of this unfounded remark, speculation as to Tōyama's involvement becomes rampant, persisting even among later historians. Tōyama's probable role in the Ōkuma incident many years before is evidence enough to show that he was, at least in his younger days, not above the use of violence to achieve political ends; however, times have changed, Tōyama has matured, and the use of such measures to settle political scores is categorically out of character.

The major point of contention between Tōyama and Hara had been the planned tour of Europe by the crown prince, soon to become the Shōwa emperor, Hirohito. Elders advising the monarchy, as well as Hara, conceived the tour, which would take the prince to England, France, Belgium, Holland, and Italy, including the Vatican, as an essential part of the royal's education and an opportunity for him to observe other constitutional monarchies in action. Tōyama, along with Uchida Ryōhei and several prominent members of the Diet, objected on the grounds that such a visit would constitute a display of weakness and that it would be interpreted by the rest of the world as an homage to the Western powers.

On this matter, Tempū disagrees with his mentor and tells him so: exposure of the future monarch to the royalty of other countries is commendable and will almost certainly benefit Japan in its international relations down the road. His remarks are overheard by some of Tōyama's younger and more zealous protégés, and for a short while, Tempū is persona non grata within Genyōsha circles.

The prince's tour goes ahead as planned and is lauded both at home and abroad. Hirohito's youthful enthusiasm makes a strong impression on the Western press, and he is favorably received by England's George V, Belgium's Albert I, the Netherlands' Wilhelma, Italy's Victor Emmanuel III, and the Vatican's Benedict XV. Copious press coverage at home is also overwhelmingly favorable, boosting the monarchy in public opinion for the first time in years.

Shortly after the prince's return, Tempū is called by Tōyama to dine at an exclusive establishment in Akasaka. The old man looks Tempū solemnly in the eye and then lights up in his characteristically impish grin. "You were right," he says. "I was wrong."

In the fall of 1919, Tempū, with financial and legal help from Mukai and Mishima, establishes the first precursor to the current Tempūkai, a foundation for the purpose of disseminating the principles of his mind-body discipline. This organization he first calls the National Society for the Improvement and Unification of Mind and Body but soon renames the Society for Unity-Based Philosophy and Medicine (Tōitsu Tetsu-i Kai). Its office is located not far from Marunouchi in Uchisaiwaichō. The society is supported by its membership, which grows rapidly, to the point that Tempū can draw a small but adequate salary.

Nakamura Tempū's Sakura Club lecture series continues into 1920 and produces a core group of supporters and benefactors who, in turn, bring Tempū to the attention of a wider circle of influential friends. Many of these men are from provincial cities, and soon Nakamura is being invited to speak at venues in both northeastern and western Japan. Tempū's venture into the field of spiritual education is no longer an experiment but a self-sustaining movement.

For all the hopes and aspirations that movement fosters among its membership, however, it is no match for darker forces of history already subsuming the political landscape.

13.
THE UNIFICATION OF MIND AND BODY

The name Nakamura gave to his practical philosophy is 心身統一道 (shin-shin tōitsu-dō), the "way" (道, dō) of "unity" or "integration" (統一, tōitsu) of "mind" (心, shin) and "body" (身, shin). The English translation of this name that has gained the most cultural traction outside Japan is "mind-body unification," especially as this is the rendering given it by Tōhei Kōichi when he introduced his shin-shin tōitsu aikido, a synthesis of Nakamura Tempū's philosophy with Ueshiba Morihei's martial discipline, aikido, into the United States in the 1960s and 1970s.

That translation, while not incorrect, can also be misleading. Where unification implies a fusing of disparate parts into a new whole, shin-shin tōitsu-dō methodically points toward the discovery of the preexisting, underlying unity of mind and body. Mind and body are distinct in appearance but united in much the same way as are the head and tail faces of a single coin. Minds do not occur in the absence of bodies: every mind requires a physical container in which to operate. Conversely, bodies, to the extent that they are living, are animated by an inherent intelligence, the functioning of which, at least on the human rung of evolution, we attribute with the quality of mind. Minds and bodies are already and necessarily integrated and united.

Not so, however, without qualification. Experience informs us that mind and body behave far more differently and with far more apparent autonomy than do the head and tail sides of a coin. Where mind imagines and often yearns for things or outcomes that are unattainable, the body does not always do what we want it to do but reacts instead in ways that are irrational and unpleasant. We may conceive of mind as a higher function, but why, then, does that "higher" mind, against all better judgment, so often succumb to destructive impulses and physical cravings? Furthermore, where the mind can soar, free of the bonds of even time and space, the body is subject to the real-world limitations of age, strength, environment, and so on. The body obeys many basic commands, but it is also insusceptible to many others: we exercise some measure of control over the breath but considerably less over heart rate or the functioning of the endocrine system.

Awareness of the mind-body dichotomy is nothing new. As an existential problem, it has perplexed and intrigued philosophers of all ages, from Socrates and the Buddha to Descartes and Kant. As these philosophers and others have noted, human suffering is usually the result of either wanting what we cannot have or having what we do not want. Why is it that our wants and desires are so at odds with conditions in the real world?

Tempū is less interested in the grand narrative of this dichotomy than he is in its practical resolution. He describes his approach to answering this problem as follows:

> So, how would I describe my outlook on life? That I can answer in a single sentence, so listen up. My outlook on life has nothing to do with endurance in the face of suffering or perseverance in the face of adversity, but rather—and this is what I want to say, so pay attention—it has everything to do with living as joyfully as possible. My purpose in life is to know the joy of living....
>
> Some of you are looking at me with skepticism written on your faces, so let me say it again. No matter what anyone says, for me, the key to living a meaningful life is not the cultivation of endurance and perseverance, but the cultivation of the ability to discover the joy of living under any set of circumstances.

Is that clear now? It should be obvious. What possible reason could there be for living if there is no joy to be had in it?

That said, there are academics and men of religion who will tell you that joy is a luxury. They will tell you that it is pointless to seek joy, because life is fundamentally hard, and that the essence of living is the overcoming of hardships through perseverance. In fact, such is more or less the predominant attitude toward life in the world at large, isn't it? It's the kind of attitude with which you have been indoctrinated. Haven't you been told, from since you were young—and haven't you been led to believe, since before you can remember—things like, "Anyone can endure the endurable, but only when you have endured the unendurable can you say that you have endurance?" Or, "You should never give up the good fight?"

Some of you are thinking, "What in the world is this Tempū guy talking about?" That's alright. I'm not asking you to take me at my word. But I am asking that you continue to listen. And as you listen, to think about what I am saying....

All of us have desires, and in the course of our daily lives we all go about the business of satisfying those desires. We use our bodies, we use our heads, we work and we toil, all to attain or materialize the objects of our desires.

Of course, not all of our desires are the same. Some of us may be after money. Some, after position. Or fame. Some of us may want, more than anything, to be consumed by the passion of love. Others may be more interested in owning jewels. Or a large house. Or expensive furniture. Or expensive clothes. Or all of the above? No, that's going too far; that's called greed.

The point is, we all want this or that or the other thing, but the reason we want these things is because we want to be happy. What we're really after is happiness. This isn't theory; just think about it in terms of your own experience.

In other words, human happiness is a product of the joy and satisfaction we experience in our lives. Happiness is the name we give to the experience of joy. "If you're happy, clap your hands," the song goes [a Japanese children's song], but you can't obtain happiness by clapping your hands.

In any event, rather than fabricating complicated theories about the meaning of life, I have concluded—I don't know about you people; what you decide is up to you—but I have concluded that the cultivation of the ability to experience, whether mentally or physically, the joy of living in any situation or under any set of circumstances is the whole point of being alive. Especially given that sooner or later we are all going to die, and therefore it makes sense to make every moment count.

Usually, this is the kind of advice you would expect to hear from someone for whom death is imminent. But that's only because most of you complacently assume that you are not going to die any time soon and therefore don't need to think about these things. As the saying goes, "The cherry blossom that believes in tomorrow may be blown away by the evening breeze." The reality is that death is always imminent, that "human is mortal."

So one more time about my outlook on life. One more time because it's worth repeating—twice, three times—how many times doesn't matter to me. Life is not about endurance or perseverance. Life is about the experience of joy. The cultivation of the ability to discover joy under any circumstances is the most valuable of pursuits. I first came to this realization while I was in India, and it has been the guiding principle in my life ever since.[1]

The particular experience that produced this realization, he goes on to explain, was the discovery of how to listen for the voice of heaven.

Mind and body, Tempū is saying, are brought into alignment when in service of a common purpose and seeking to realize a common goal, and the purpose best served and the goal best realized is the cultivation of the capacity to experience happiness, satisfaction, and fulfillment, regardless of the circumstances within which we find ourselves. This is not to suggest that he advocates abandonment of ambition or simple acceptance of whatever circumstances are given to us: to the contrary, his is a philosophy and methodology designed to show us how to confront life's challenges and how to overcome the obstacles life inevitably throws up between us and the fulfillment of our dreams; for the best and most effective way to confront challenges and to overcome obstacles is to do so as an expression of vitality and the joy of living. Only out of that vitality and joy do we discover true faith and confidence in our abilities.

The unity or integration implied by Tempū's use of the term *tōitsu,* written with two characters, 統一, a literal reading of which gives us "all one" or "of a single lineage," is thus, a product of neither mind nor body but of a cohesion of mind and body behind a common purpose. Mind and body are different in constitution and function, but both are brought into play when taking action and seeking to achieve a result, and their respective functions are most effective when united behind a common cause. With this understanding, shin-shin tōitsu might also be translated as "mind-body alignment" or "mind-body coordination."

Whether unifying them or coordinating them, however, Tempū speaks of mind and body as one would of tools, of means to an end. His stated purpose is neither the cultivation of mind for mind's sake, nor the cultivation of body for body's sake, but the cultivation of both for the realization of joy and happiness. Therefore, that which is undertaking to coordinate mind and body in the fulfillment of a unified purpose is clearly neither mind nor body, but a third constituent. That constituent is agency. It is the original face of spirit, the original identity, the listening wherein is heard the voice of heaven.

The great conundrum of human existence is that life seldom works out the way we want it to and that we cannot simply will the world to be the way that we would like it to be. What separates Nakamura Tempū's teachings, I believe, from those of either New Thought or New Age pundits is the depth of his experience and his willing acceptance of the hardness of reality. His is no magic formula for the realization of health, fame, and fortune and no prescription for the materialization of intentions. It is, rather, a wake-up call to reality, beginning with the simple observation that life occurs now, in the moment, and concluding, therefore, that the life worth living is one capable of meeting all challenges, head-on, with confidence and equanimity.

Nakamura was already cognizant of the principles of mind-body unification when he first rang his bell in Ueno Park; however, his articulation of shin-shin tōitsu-dō as a complete system came much later. By Tempū's account, his delineation of the fundamentals of mind-body unity into an organized doctrine was eight years in the making, while the fleshing out of that doctrine into a practical methodology was another eight years. Even then, it was never "finished," for he continued to develop, refine, and elaborate his methodology right up until his death. But by simple arithmetic, eight years invested in delineating the fundamentals plus eight years invested in developing the methodology puts completion of shin-shin tōitsu-dō as a system in or about 1935.

The years in between are busy ones. In 1922, he is introduced to Albert Einstein upon Einstein's visit to Japan. In 1923, at the request of the minister of justice, he goes to Korea to assist, as he had done with the miners in Iwaki, in the settlement of a railroad labor dispute that had spurred riots. During his visit, he is befriended by Saitō Makoto, governor-general of annexed Korea, later to serve as the thirtieth prime minister of Japan, and under Saitō's sponsorship, he establishes a Korean chapter of the Society for Unity-Based Philosophy and Medicine.

While he is away, the Great Kantō Earthquake devastates much of Tokyo; Nakamura's house is spared, but that of his lifelong mentor, Tōyama Mitsuru, is destroyed.

In 1924, he publishes the first issue of the periodical *Jikaku* (Self-Realization). Publication will continue until 1941, when wartime paper shortages force it into suspension.

In December 1924, he delivers a series of talks to three of the five royal households directly descended from the Emperor Meiji. In attendance on at least one of these occasions are Prince Regent Hirohito and Princess Nagako, coronation of whom as emperor and empress will follow twenty-four months later. Tempū presents the young prince with a poem, "Make the world yours by living just as you are and you will know neither fear nor regret." Would that, in the light of later history, this singularly prescient advice had gone better heeded.

Also in attendance on this occasion is the prominent author and educator Nitobe Inazō. Nitobe's classic work *Bushido: The Soul of Japan,* written in English and first published in Philadelphia in 1900, is the first serious attempt by a Japanese writer to explain the ethics of Japan's bygone warrior class; it became an international best-seller following the Russo-Japanese War and is still in print today.

In February 1925, Nakamura lectures again in Seoul, this time at the invitation of the *Keijō Nippō,* an Asahi News–affiliated newspaper. Then in June, he delivers a live talk over the airwaves of Osaka Broadcasting. This in turn leads to issue of three vinyl recordings titled *The Philosophy of Laughter, The Philosophy of Work,* and *The Key to Success.* His lectures are drawing the attention of an increasing roster of nobles, generals, admirals, cabinet members, educators, and leaders of industry. Japan's most celebrated navy admiral of all time, Tōgō Heihachirō, the commander who defeated the Russian Baltic Fleet at the 1905 battle of Tsushima, comes to hear him speak and takes particular interest in Tempū's exposition of kumbhaka. Ishikawa Sodō, head abbot of the Sōtō Zen sect of Buddhism, also attends and discovers in Tempū someone with whom he can converse about the heart of Zen.

Construction of Tempū's training headquarters, his Hombu Dojo, is completed in 1927. His mother, Teu, dies in 1928. The following year, his daughter, Tsuruko, is married to Yasutake Sadao, forty years later to

Nakamura Tempū, late 1920s, seated in front of the scroll he often used as a backdrop for his lectures. The calligraphy is by Tōyama Mitsuru and reads *yamato-damashii*, "the Japanese spirit."

(with permission from the Tempu Society, a nonprofit public interest foundation)

succeed Tempū as the Tempūkai's second chairman. Then, in 1930, the Nakamuras adopt a second daughter, Masako, age sixteen; her birth name is Sugano, and she has attended Tempū's lectures since middle school.

Tempū's success, as measured by the size of his following, was due, in large part, to his personal charisma. He was, in every way, the embodiment of the principles he preached, and he had a presence in front of audiences that quickly put them in the palm of his hand, even as he berated them for the shallowness of their beliefs and the errors of their habits. Many have described him as having radiated a magnetic benevolence and love of humanity.

But charisma alone is insufficient cause for the persistence of his ideas. The better explanation is that they work. Following from his story of how he had survived the ravages of tuberculosis in a day and age when such survival was almost unheard of, not surprisingly, many of those attracted to his teachings were suffering from life-threatening illnesses. Tempū was not a doctor, and he did not dispense medical advice; but he did prescribe a method and a means whereby those so willing could help themselves. As a result, miracles occurred. And they continue to occur among people taking up his prescribed practices today. Persons afflicted by tuberculosis, cancer, polio, trauma, and other maladies have attributed either partial or complete recovery, as well as the return of their ability to lead productive and fulfilling lives, to the teachings of Nakamura Tempū.

As stated in my Introduction, a thorough and complete discussion of Tempū's philosophy is beyond the scope of this book. Furthermore, I cannot overstress the point that his philosophy is a practical one, meaning that its practices are integral to its comprehension and understanding. While some of those practices can be explained through the written medium, others require direct transmission from a qualified instructor.

Nevertheless, having brought you this far in his story, I would be remiss were I not to give at least an overview of his philosophy. Because the territory covered by Tempū's teachings is vast, I will inevitably be guilty of omitting far more than I include, and my explanations cannot help but be colored by personal perspective.[2] With that disclaimer on record, let us begin by looking at the relationship between mind and body.

What, exactly, is meant by "mind?" A first distinction to be made is that of mind and brain: a mind is not the same as a brain. To be sure, if asked "Where does the mind occur?" most of us would ascribe to that occurrence a location inside the cranium. That said, in the history of brain surgery, no surgeon has ever uncovered anything in the brain even remotely resembling a mind.

The modern view would have us believe that the experience of mind is a consequence of physiological processes; that our every thought and feeling is a product of electrochemical activity within the nervous system, and especially within that complex tangle of nerves that makes up the nervous system's command center, the brain. That formulation, if useful in chasing down legions of mental pathologies to physiological sources, also has its limitations. Strictly speaking, it conflates the stuff of the brain with the subjective experience of mind; for, while mental activity is most certainly accompanied by and shows up in the brain as electrochemical activity, the measurement or observation of that activity fails to suggest the experience of smelling a rose or of deducing the solution to a quadratic equation. Moreover, the question as to whether it is the fragrance of the rose that causes certain neurons to fire or the firing of the neurons that causes the rose to be experienced as fragrant is a path of inquiry so circular that it is best left alone.

A more useful way of describing the relationship between mind and brain is as that of an interior to an exterior. At the very least, among animate species, some degree of sentience and subjectivity is present within all biological organisms from the moment of conception, and philosopher Ken Wilber has posited that even the most fundamental building blocks of the physical universe, such as quarks, particles, atoms, and molecules, have some form of interiority, what Albert North Whitehead calls "prehension."[3] Wilber speculates that it is this interiority, the prehension of each subsequent moment, that, through eons of evolution, through the formulation of galaxies to star systems to planetary biospheres and the emergence of amoebas, earthworms, and elephants, has led to the awakening of intelligence and the human experience of mind. The awakening of human intelligence, occurring, as it does, atop the totem pole of biological evolution, appears to be the awakening of the very capacity through which the phenomenon of life—and consequently, the universe that parents that phenomenon—begins to take a perspective upon itself. Mind, the vessel or space within which conscious intelligence occurs, is evolution's new frontier, the frontier of evolution of a higher order.

"Higher" necessarily implies both greater complexity and greater autonomy, for in the ways of evolution, while lower structures determine the openings for greater complexity that give rise to higher structures, it is always the higher structures that exercise dominion over the lower and not the other way around.

In other words, the mind leads the body. Nakamura Tempū is unequivocal on this point.

This is not to imply that the mind is somehow separate from and immune to physiology; we all know something about the effects of physical substances, such as caffeine or alcohol, on awareness and judgment. But the capacity for choice, such as the choice to ingest or not ingest those substances, as well as the capacity to learn from past experience, belongs to the mental domain.

Nor is it to imply that reality is subject to whimsical manipulation. No matter how resolutely he believes he can fly, the psychotic on the rooftop will still hit the ground at the same rate of acceleration as a stone dropped from the same height. While that example is extreme, I submit that many of the doctrines espoused by today's New Age gurus—the notion, for example, that anyone can achieve any result or bring any dream into reality simply through faith and visualization—may be almost as delusional as the psychotic's belief that he can fly.

It is to say, however, that the body, more often than not, responds to mental directions, and, more importantly, that freedom and fulfillment are states of mind, not states of body. For that reason, and as Tempū discovered in India, mental attitude and the imagining of positive outcome is paramount to overcoming hardship and physical affliction. We might call this the bootstrap approach to well-being: when, and only when, the mind drops petty self-indulgences does life show up as miraculous. And only when the mind allows for the miraculous does health over disease and providence over misfortune show up as a possibility. Tempū's breath drills and exercise routine are of no more meaning than any system of physical training in the absence of the intention of the practitioner to improve the quality of his or her life; but, conversely, when practiced with proper attitude, they invariably lead to better health and positive results—which foster greater conviction in the value of these practices, resulting in still better health, and so on. That the attitude one takes toward an activity should influence the outcome of that activity is little more than common sense.

If, however, we could always change the results in our lives by simply changing our attitudes, then life would be easy. The problem is that the part of our minds immediately available to us, the conscious part, is no more than the tiny tip of a huge iceberg, and that most of our attitudes rest on beliefs about the world and how it works that are so deeply submerged as to be hidden from us. These attitudes and beliefs are based on experiences had, information learned, and decisions made, whether consciously or unconsciously, a long, long time ago but that have, nevertheless, through relentless reinforcement, become part of our modus operandi. They are self-fulfilling, and they frame the way we approach life and see the world.

Those underlying attitudes and beliefs can be changed, but to do so requires diligence and some time. The first part of the process involves observing the way one's mind works and recognizing one's automatic and habitual responses when they occur. The second part is to feed the mind positive suggestions, and to do so repeatedly, until these suggestions filter down into the subconscious strata of the mind and supplant negative attitudes and beliefs as the defaults to the ways in which we respond to external stimuli. Tempū breaks this process down into three stages. The first, he calls "reformation of elemental concepts" *(kannen yōso-no kōkai)*, referring to the elemental concepts upon which one's mental outlook is built; we might call this activity "internal remodeling." It means consciously adopting a new set of assumptions about the way life works.

The second, he calls "cultivation of spiritual positivity" *(sekkyoku seishin-no yōsei)*; this is the process of cultivating positivity so that it becomes an automatic and habitual first response to every situation. This, of all the stages, is the most demanding, for it requires vigilance and honesty. It requires that we be willing to catch ourselves in the act of responding to events out of old habits, in order that we can then rewind and replace those old habits with new ones.

The third is "conditioning of nervous reactivity" *(shinkei hansha-no chōsetu)*; this is the physiological side of positivity cultivation, the conditioning of the nervous system so that it can withstand stimuli from sudden, unanticipated, and unpleasant events. It involves some amount of sweat and physical exertion.

Reformation of elemental concepts. However much our thoughts and feelings may appear to be random and spontaneous, they are in fact subject to formation along pathways structured by experience. Lurking beneath our cognitive processes are a host of assumptions about the nature of reality—about what is good and bad, right and wrong, desirable and undesirable, possible and impossible, and so on. Prior to our thoughts and feelings, this structural framework determines our basic attitudes, and it shows up in the ways that we react to what life throws at us, in how we respond to problems, and in what we bring to bear on the business of living. It even shows up in our posture and the way that we carry ourselves physically.

That said, while the evidence of this structural framework is everywhere—in our thoughts, feelings, and demeanor—the structures themselves remain hidden; we are cognizant of our thoughts and feelings but we are not cognizant of the underlying structures that shape them.

Tempū's teachings regarding the reformation of the subconscious mind are replete with prescribed practices. One of these is the Lindler system of autosuggestion described in chapter 5. Another is the recitation of what could be described as the mind-body unification method's basic liturgy, a set of written affirmations meant to be memorized and recited out loud. Most of these were written later than the time period I have covered so far: the first volume of eighteen affirmations, a little black book small enough to fit in a shirt pocket, was first published in 1957. They are, nevertheless, both convenient and directly pertinent to this discussion.

The first of these affirmations is, by far, the best-known among practitioners of Tempū's mind-body system and is meant to be recited each morning, ideally just after completion of his breath drills and exercise routine described later. Something of the original's lyricism is lost in translation, but it goes as follows.

DAILY OATH

I do solemnly swear
That, on this day, and for its duration,
I shall perpetrate neither anger, nor fear, nor regret;
That I shall be honest, kind, and joyful,
Delivering upon the obligations and duties of life
With vitality, courage, and eagerness;
And that, with love and peace in my heart,
I shall live as an exemplary and respectable human being.[4]

The passages in this little booklet address the inherent challenges of living from a variety of perspectives under headings such as "Vitality," "Intelligence," "Language," "Courage," "Imagination," and more. One of my favorites is the following:

POWER

I am power.
I am the crystallization of power.
The crystallization of power stronger than any other force.
That is why I shall never be defeated by circumstances.
Not by illness. Not by misfortune.
Nay, the power that I am is invincible.
That is right!
Mighty, mighty, am I. The crystallization of power.[5]

Cultivation of spiritual positivity. Cultivation of positivity is, in essence, the practice of vigilance—the same vigilance that Buddhist practitioners call mindfulness. In order to effect changes in the way we approach the business of living, we must first become aware of our incumbent attitudes. Mental attitude, especially when unexamined, can be singularly pernicious; it can cloud our vision and warp our perception of the world. Taking inventory of what is so, of separating facts from assessments, is the first step toward renewal of our mental constitution. Only when we recognize

Chikara-no-shōku, the "Power" Verse for Recitation; calligraphy by Nakamura Tempū

(*with permission from the Tempu Society, a nonprofit public interest foundation*)

the extent to which the way we respond to circumstances is shaped by our unexamined assumptions and beliefs are we able to begin the work of reframing those assumptions and beliefs in constructive terms.

The good news is that positivity is self-reinforcing. The place to start is with beliefs regarding your ability to change. When you catch yourself responding to a situation by acting out of some undesirable habit, almost as if switched onto automatic pilot, do you experience inner dialogue of the genus "There I go again," or "When will I ever learn?" If so, you are not alone. Such inner dialogue is symptomatic of a deep-seated belief that we are the way we are and that we are unable to change; unless we first address that belief, then any attempt to change the habit in question will be for naught. On the other hand, changing that belief, once aware of it, is not so difficult. Simply replace it with a new belief, along the lines of "I am master of my own ship; of course I can change." Rewind, take an eraser to the defeatist inner dialogue, and replace it with an observation such as, "Oh, that's interesting. I'm reacting, out of habit. What would I do if, instead, I were acting consciously?"

Choice of words—the way we constitute ourselves internally through our use of language—is all-important. Notice, for example, the word "again" in "There I go again!" and the word "ever" in "When will I ever learn?" Is there really an "again?" Is learning something that "ever" happens? Life occurs moment to moment; everything that occurs is occurring for the first and only time, and nothing ever happens "again." Learning, likewise, is something that occurs in the present moment; to speculate on when learning may occur in the future is meaningless. Simple adjustments in language and word choice make all the difference, so be aware of the language you use and the words you choose. Language governs our behavior: the way we language ourselves ultimately affects how we show up in the world.

Belief becomes reality. In the beginning, the notion that you are capable of change may seem like only a belief, but do not be afraid to believe in it. Beliefs are self-fulfilling; every time you change, that belief will be reinforced, until it becomes unshakably real. When you know you can change your beliefs, you know you can change your habits, and when you know you can change your habits, then you know you can become the person you wish to become.

Conditioning of nervous reactivity. If mind leads body, then that which delivers mind's instructions to the body is the nervous system. Similarly, the information upon which mind acts is delivered from body to mind, in the form of sensory input, by way of nervous synapses and axons. While technically, nervous activity and mental activity are related, as posited earlier in this chapter, in the same way that an outside is related to an inside, we can forgo hairsplitting for the moment and say, as an approximate truth, that the nervous system is where mind and body intersect.

When Nakamura Tempū conceived of his mind-body system, neuroscience was still in its infancy; we now know much more about the electrochemical processes that occur in the brain, and brain science has been described as a twenty-first-century frontier. Given his curiosity and fascination with regard to both physiology and the advances of scientific knowledge, Tempū, were he alive today, would almost certainly take great interest in these developments.

What the medical science of his day did tell him, however, was that most internal bodily functions are activated by the autonomic nervous system. The body takes in oxygen and eliminates carbon dioxide by way of the respiratory system; it ingests nutrients and eliminates wastes by way of the digestive system; and it delivers the oxygen and nutrients acquired by way of respiration and digestion throughout the body by way of the circulatory system. These systems and the organs that compose them, however, would be all but inert were it not for sympathetic and parasympathetic nervous commands. The human body, Tempū liked to say, is like a puppet on strings: the puppet, while appearing to move of its own volition, is in fact controlled entirely by a puppet master pulling its strings. In this analogy, the puppet master is the intelligence of the brain and the strings are the nerves that connect that intelligence with the body.

As its name suggests, the autonomic nervous system is that which operates under its own autonomy: it ensures, for example, that our hearts continue to beat and our lungs continue to breath even in the depths of sleep. In this way, it supports the bodily impetus for physical perpetuation, or survival.

Moreover, not only does the quality of that nervous command system keep the internal clock of life ticking, but it also has much to do with determining our vitality. In common parlance, when we speak of life, we usually mean the business of living and how effective and successful we are at that business, as well as what we leave behind as our mark upon the world. Tempū identifies the following six qualities as essential to health, well-being, and performance:

1. stamina

2. mettle (guts)

3. acumen

4. decisiveness

5. vitality

6. aptitude

Furthermore, all of these, he asserts, can be cultivated through training. And training is nothing more than the cultivation of good habits, especially habits of exercise, breath, and posture, through conscious, somatic stimulation of our nervous infrastructure.

Tempū's physical training program, what he calls "physical positivity training" *(kunrenteki sekkyokuka)*, has two purposes: The first is to attune the body to the natural order and to restore and then maintain biological and physiological balance, so that the body can respond appropriately to instructions given it; in other words, to cultivate and call forth the six qualities of health listed above. The second is to build the nervous system's ability to withstand stress, thereby ensuring that sensory information fed back to the mind is untainted by biases born of systemic weaknesses; that is, that the information received by the mind is accurate and free of negativity born of poor habits and poor health.

The program is both unique and a work of genius. Its practices are also, I believe, best learned through direct transmission from a qualified teacher. Rather than attempt a full verbal exposition of these practices, an endeavor bound to invite more confusion than clarity, I shall limit myself to general descriptions.

Cultivation of the breath. Tempū put together a set of breath drills *(kokyū sōren)* that draw upon the yoga of the breath called pranayama. That said, these drills are unlike any yoga practices with which I am familiar. The term *sōren* (in kokyū sōren) is most frequently used to describe military training routines, and the drills may owe as much to Nakamura's martial arts training as they do to yoga; as mentioned in my Introduction, at least one martial artist, aikido's Tada Hiroshi, has incorporated these breath drills into his teachings.

The drills are nine in number and are meant to be practiced in succession, preferably first thing in the morning. The entire routine can be completed within five minutes. Each drill has a stated purpose: the first is the overall activation and strengthening of the autonomic nervous system through focus of concentration, testing of balance, and lengthening of the spine.

The second is the stimulation of nervous activity and reactivity through flicking of the fingers.

The third is the strengthening of the lungs and physical structure related to the breath.

The forth is facilitation of the breath through strengthening of the rib cage and rib fascia and the stimulation of the alveoli.

The fifth is the strengthening of the rib cage and its fascia where they meet the spine.

The sixth is respiratory fortification through stretching of the chest cavity.

The seventh is stimulation of the circulatory system.

The eighth is the cleansing of the lungs through deep exhalation.

The ninth is the strengthening of the throat and vocal cords.

Cultivation of resilience. Tempū developed a set of physical exercises, the mind-body unification exercise routine *(tōitsu-shiki undōhō)*, to be performed upon the heels of the above breath drills. Here again, the exercises are informed by yoga but dissimilar to popular forms of hatha yoga practiced today. Third-hand observation might mistake them for calisthenics, in that they are performed at a springy, rhythmic pace, but this appearance is deceiving: the routine effectively reaches all of the main muscle sets, and especially those that, with the sedentary habits of modern living, are most prone to neglect. The exercises are also just complex enough to tax average (such as mine) physical coordination. They flow naturally from one to the next, and the entire set of eighteen exercises requires only ten minutes to complete, thus bringing the entire duration of this morning routine, including breath drills and exercises, to just fifteen minutes.

Tempū recognized that neither the harsh martial training he underwent as a young man nor the equally harsh ascetic training he underwent as a student of yoga were appropriate to the lifestyles of people in modern urban societies. He also reasoned that if health and happiness were contingent on one's retreat to the foothills of the Himalayas, then most of humanity would be doomed to eternal misery. This fifteen-minute routine is a distillation of his experience with both yoga and the martial arts into a more sympathetic and less demanding routine that, he asserts, when practiced regularly and diligently, is equally or more beneficial to health and well-being.

Furthermore, in the spirit of Tempū's philosophy of mind-body alignment and unification, the exercises are not just physical: each stance, posture, and movement is to be practiced as an expression of a mental posture or attitude and is accompanied by a verbal injunction. The opening stance, for example, is accompanied by the words, "Here I stand, at the center of the universe"; the second one by the words, "Whatever force is brought to bear, I am unmovable, like a mountain"; the third, the words, "Ready for anything! Whatever comes, I know no fear"; and so on.

Kumbhaka. Kumbhaka was addressed in chapter 8. Rather than a separate and stand-alone practice, it is a fundamental element of the entire mind-body system and integral to both the breathing drills and the exercise routine described above.

A practice useful to the cultivation of one's ability to sustain kumbhaka while also enhancing digestion, respiration, blood circulation, and overall health is that of *yōdō-hō,* the method of "nourishment through movement." Yōdō-hō can be practiced either seated or standing, but most typically seated, either on a cushion or in a chair. While tightening the anal sphincter, describe an ellipse with your naval in a clockwise direction: that is, first back, then to the left, then forward, then to the right, and then to the back again. Head and shoulders will rock slightly but should remain relatively central to the arc being described by the lower midsection.

Yōdō-hō can be practiced while engaged in other activities, such as working at a desk, reading a book, or watching television. It should be continued for at least five minutes and preferably for longer: the longer, the better. It massages the internal organs and promotes blood circulation. Tempū insists, however, that the rotation should always be clockwise, as described above; this, because clockwise is the direction in which the colon and intestines wrap within the abdomen.

Another practice endorsed by Tempū is that of cold water dowsing (cold-water showers serve the purpose) in the morning. He, of course, acquired the habit from his training under Kariappa, but it is also prescribed in Chinese qigong and many martial arts systems. For a long time, it was an enforced discipline in English public schools, as well as American prep schools modeled on the English system. It does wonders for the immune system, greatly reducing the incidence of common colds. I include it under the kumbhaka heading because it also contributes to one's ability to assume and sustain the kumbhaka state.

Diet. Tempū's regime also includes dietary guidelines. These, again, like his other practices, are informed by the teachings of yoga but not entirely beholden to them. The first guideline is that all food should be received with unqualified gratitude, that the food appearing on a plate before us is never to be taken for granted. Food, as a necessity to life, is sacred, and its very appearance before us at mealtimes, evidence of divine providence.

In that spirit, food is to be properly masticated. Each mouthful is to be chewed until nothing solid remains—until, as a saying goes, you can "drink the solids and eat the liquids."

The health benefits of proper mastication are legion and well documented. The mouth is the first stage of the digestive tract, and the enzymes contained in saliva are essential to making many of the nutrients in food available to later stages of digestion. The act of chewing is both an expression of respect and an exercise in efficiency, for the more food is chewed, the more fully it is utilized and the less one needs to eat.

Tempū typically ate only two meals a day, and his summer retreats reflected this practice, serving the first meal at noon and the second in the evening. With regard to how much to eat, one should stop, he advises, when less than full; satiation will follow minutes later as the stomach fills itself through the secretion of gastric fluids.

Tempū provides no strict injunctions with regard to what to eat but does make a number of recommendations. Choose grains, vegetables, and fruits over the flesh of animals. Consumption of seafood is acceptable but should be moderated. Foods should not be overcooked. Avoid extreme flavors.

Tempū's dietary recommendations are not unlike those of Sakurazawa Yukikazu, better known in the West as George Ohsawa, the founder of a philosophy of life and diet he called macrobiotics. Sakurazawa was seventeen years junior to Nakamura; however, the respective spans of their teaching activities overlapped, and it is probable that they knew of each other (I have no evidence to suggest they ever met). In Sakurazawa's macrobiotics, proper diet—that is, proper respect for the natural order in the choices one makes with regard to food and its preparation—is deemed essential to the creation of a happy, healthy, and peaceful humanity. Sakurazawa spent years promoting his philosophy and diet abroad, especially in France, and the macrobiotic movement spawned by his teachings and carried forward by his protégés in Japan, Europe, and North America contributed to the broader growth of the present-day natural and organic food movement.[6]

Tempū would have given Sakurazawa no argument regarding the importance of respect for the natural order, but he would, I speculate, have taken exception to Sakurazawa's apparent fixation on food: respect for the natural order, he would have answered, is certainly important to diet but no more so than it is to breath, posture, physical activity, and the way in which we conduct ourselves in the world. Moreover, even more important than the care and conditioning of the body, he would have insisted, is the care and conditioning of the mind.

The domain of spirit. Mind and body are designed to work in tandem. Positivity of mind is essential to the cultivation of physical as well as mental health, and physical discipline is equally essential to the cultivation of a body that can keep up with mind's positive lead. Thus, to the extent that positivity of mind is conducive to sound physical health, the soundness of the body is conducive to positivity of mind. The emphasis in Tempū's teachings is on neither mind nor body but on their integration, the uniting of each with the other into a cohesive whole.

Although Tempū goes to considerable pains to distance his philosophy from the teachings of religion, that philosophy is also, at its core, profoundly spiritual. One need only reflect that if both mind and body are subject to conditioning and discipline, then something other than either mind or body must be doing the conditioning and disciplining: implicitly, I have a mind but am not my mind; I have a body but am not my body. The integration of mind and body can only occur through the agency of a third aspect of being.

Tempū is not the first person to speak of body, mind, and spirit as a trinity. If mind and body are conceived to be geometrically polar opposites, and if the line between them is conceived to be the base of an equilateral triangle, then that third element may be conceived of as that which completes the triangle at its uppermost apex. That apex is the only point along the perimeter of this triangle that permits a concurrent, equidistant, perspectival view of both mind and body. It is the point described by the agreement of separate and distinct mind and body lines.

Tempū describes the apex of our triangle as the soul *(reikon)*. This soul, in turn, is conceived to be the vessel for the energy of spirit *(reiki)*, the energy of universal creation. His resort to semireligious nomenclature is, in this case, by default, since only in religion does nomenclature for these aspects of being occur. Rational inquiry into the nature of life and being invariably confronts its own limits, and when it does so, it must give way to mystery; one comes face-to-face with the hard yet wonderful reality that what we do not know and cannot understand will always, always be infinitely greater than the tiny clearing of knowledge in which we stand. Religion and religious inquiry is the tradition vested with the task of describing humanity's relationship to that great unknown.

From time to time, to invoke the concept of godhead or first cause, Tempū refers to "the Great Something," using English when he does so. The workings of spirit and the soul are of the same vein: they are not knowable in the way that mind and body are knowable, and therefore, are not given to the same kind of rational explanation. The soul is a place to come from in interactions with the world. It is the ground of being. And it is discoverable through the practice of anjō-daza, the essential mind-body meditative practice described in chapter 7.

Practicing the other precepts of mind-body unification without investing in the practice of anjō-daza will render results. It will improve health. It will even improve positivity of thinking. But it will never allow the practitioner to grasp the full meaning and intent of his philosophy. The reason Tempū can say this with finality is that the positivity of which he speaks, that which he advocates as the key to a fulfilled life, is equivalent to the state of nonattachment and emptiness toward which the practice of anjō-daza directs us. More accurately, anjō-daza *is* that state: it is the name given by Tempū to both his meditative practice and to the state of nonattachment and emptiness to which that practice is designed to lead us.

This is an important distinction and one that is often missed among spiritual doctrines. The ground of being is classically described as a domain of existence that supersedes all duality: it is neither up nor down, right nor left, hot nor cold, and so on. While that description is valid, it also invites misinterpretation when other opposites are added to the list: right or wrong, true or false, is or is not, for example. In a certain, limited and relative sense, it is correct to say that right and wrong, true and false, existence and nonexistence are relative values. But the fundamental quality of the ground of being that muffles all other dualities is that it *is*. The ground of being, by the very nature of its emptiness, is present and real: it is defined not by the absence of form but by its presence as the ground upon which, or the vessel within which, the world of form shows up.

By extension, that ground of being can do no wrong. It is beyond the duality of right and wrong, but that beyond-ness is ultimately and absolutely right. Likewise, it is beyond truth and falsehood, and in that beyond-ness it is ultimately always true; it is, in and of itself, absolute truth.

What we are saying here is that the universe is, at its core and in and of itself, unreservedly and categorically positive. It is positivity beyond all possibility of negativity. And it is that positivity that we tap into and breathe into our relative and finite beings, our minds and bodies, when we practice meditation.

Neither is positivity to be construed as a force counter to negativity, nor is the work of mind-body unification to be construed as either the overcoming of negative thoughts and emotions with positive ones or the defeating of destructive carnal desires with more constructive ones. Rather, it is the return of mind and body to an original state of unity, a state of unblemished innocence and emptiness, so that we may cultivate our ability to come from that place of innocence and emptiness at all times and to manifest joy in our lives and in the world.

* * *

In the 1920s and early 1930s, when Tempū was in the process of piecing together his system while at the same time engaging audiences with his stories and his ideas, nowhere did there exist a practical philosophy so broad in scope. Probably the most complete extant exposition of the relationships between body, mind, and spirit occurred in the Vedic tradition supporting the practices of yoga; but yoga, it is to be remembered, other than in India, was little known outside certain elite intellectual circles, and furthermore, what was known was largely based on misconceptions. Yoga was as much obscured by its ancient canon as it was informed by it. Nakamura owes much to his exposure to that vast, if obscure, treasure trove of ancient knowledge; however, as he points out repeatedly in his talks, the training he received under Kariappa consisted not of intellectual learning but of certain selected practices, from which he was left to draw his own conclusions and synthesize his own understanding.

Nakamura was also, however, influenced by Western science. In particular, his studies at Columbia's medical school gave him a basic understanding of human physiology, and while critical of modern medicine for its limitations—especially given that the medicine of his day, a product of the Cartesian worldview, was largely beholden to linear and mechanical explanations of disease and allowed little room for the influences of invisible qualities, such as mind and spirit—he had a continuing high regard

271

and fascination for its rigor and dedication to discovery. His ability to use both the language of yoga and the language of science to express his ideas was unique among men of his generation.

Finally, as a product of the Meiji era, he was saturated with the traditional culture of his native Japan. This included the warrior's tradition of *bunbu*, "letters (meaning the Japanese and Chinese classics) and martial arts," but it also included spiritual traditions. Tempū was versed in Buddhism, especially Zen. He was a great admirer of Hakuin Eikaku, the eighteenth-century Rinzai school revivalist, and he delivers, in his lectures, one of the clearest expositions found anywhere of the Ten Ox Herding Pictures, a set of verse-accompanied drawings passed down through the Zen tradition from China. The story told by the Ten Ox Herding Pictures is a parable for the path and journey to liberation.

From Zen, Tempū acquired the language of spiritual realization; from Western medicine, the objectivity of science; and from yoga, the all-importance of practice and the necessity of providing his followers with not just a description of an end-state but the practical steps to be taken to attain it. He was a revelation, a breath of fresh air such as not to be found elsewhere at the time. Not only were his teachings novel, bringing with them a new clarity of vision and a reexamination of conventional wisdom, but they were also accessible and produced results. Little wonder, then, that he should have so quickly generated a substantial following.

14.
EVIL CLOSE
TO THE THRONE

On the morning of February 26, 1936, the people of Tokyo awoke to find the city not only under a blanket of snow but also under siege. Some twenty-two young radical army officers had unleashed more than 1,400 pairs of boots, worn predominantly by green recruits, on political targets and governmental institutions. By the time the sun came up, the lord keeper of the privy seal, the finance minister, and the inspector general of military education, as well as five policemen and the prime minister's brother-in-law—an army colonel ill-fatedly lodged for the night at the prime minister's residence and mistaken for the prime minister—were all dead; the grand chamberlain, seriously wounded; the Army Ministry and the Metropolitan Police Headquarters, occupied; and the Imperial Palace, partially surrounded.

In recent years, political assassinations had become almost commonplace. In March 1932, ultranationalists inspired by the Nichiren sect priest Inoue Nisshō targeted twenty political and industrial figures and successfully dispatched two, a former finance minister and the director-general of Mitsui Holdings. Then, in May of the same year, the prime minister, Tōyama Mitsuru's fellow longtime Pan-Asianism advocate Inukai Tsuyoshi, was gunned down by a group of young army officers as part of a wider, would-be coup d'état. Successive coup attempts were thwarted in late 1934 and early 1935. And in August 1935, the Military Affairs Bureau chief, Major General Nagata Tetsuzan, was cut down in his office with a sword, his attacker a junior officer protesting the bureau's policies.

But the scale of the February 26 uprising was unprecedented. It shocked the nation and went down in Japanese history as the 2-26 ("two, two six") Incident. Only when the emperor voiced his unusually outspoken condemnation was the mutiny quelled. Its leaders, deluded by their own rhetoric, had believed that the emperor would tacitly approve of their actions and had even purposefully invoked him by calling their plot the Shōwa Restoration; instead, upon the emperor's blunt reprimand, even the foot soldiers under their command quickly retreated to their barracks, leaving them stranded. The navy, meanwhile, positioned warships in Tokyo Bay, and the city was placed under martial law. It remained so for five months.

The fracture within the military, where both factions favored policies of armament and aggressive expansionism, were drawn less along lines of moderate versus extreme than those of class. The elimination of a hereditary, military elite, the bushi or samurai, and the replacement of that elite with a conscription army and navy was one of the hallmark achievements of the Meiji Restoration and essential to Japan's coming of age as a modern state. Allegiances of class, however, are more easily erased from civil and military code than from the national psyche, and there remained an unspoken but acknowledged division, not only in the military, but also in politics and industry, between those of common and those of samurai heritage. The twenty-two officers perpetrating the February 26 uprising were part of the disenfranchised common class. Many hailed from the poorest rural provinces, hard hit by the effects of global recession, and all had been denied admission to the Army War College, a credential prerequisite to acceptance into the cadre of senior officers pulling all of the army's strings.

Partially because of their common upbringings and inferior access to education, this same group was also more susceptible to simplistically radical ideas. The young officers, who differed widely among themselves over practical questions concerning their doctrine's implementation, coalesced ideologically behind what they called the "Imperial

Way." Drawing on the ideas of National Socialism coming out of Hitler's Germany, their "Way" advocated absolute political alignment under the sacred institution of the imperial throne, coupled with military aggrandizement. In the emperor's army was vested, the young officers believed, the duty and sacred mission to forcefully bring about the realization of an ideal state.

In hindsight, the young officers appear to have been only slightly ahead of their time, for many of the features of their vision, even if thwarted at this juncture, were faits accomplis by the end of the decade. In one interpretation, the victory of militarism in Japanese politics signaled the end of the far-reaching but aristocratic vision of the Meiji leaders and the rise of more radical and short-sighted populist control. But then, that interpretation supposes that the Imperial Way arose in opposition to an incumbent faction of more moderate and noble vision, where in fact the so-called Control faction was equally attached to goals of military aggrandizement; the only substantive difference between the factions' respective agendas was that Control advocates chose to pursue their goals pragmatically, through legislative protocol, whereas the Imperial Way ideologues chose armed insurrection.

Partially to blame for this state of affairs were the framers of the Meiji constitution, for in failing to clearly define control of, and accountability for, the actions of the military, they produced a fatally flawed document. The constitution stated only that the military was to report directly to the emperor and that the emperor was to exercise control over the military under the advice of his ministers. The vagueness of this language was undoubtedly intentional, as it gave the military privileged and coveted wiggle room; the framers, after all, were all former samurai. Furthermore, it also worked at the time. During both the Sino-Japanese War of 1894–1895 and the Russo-Japanese War of 1904–1905, the emperor, his ministers, and the nation at large rallied behind the military in almost unconditional support. But as the fledgling republic matured and more complex political realities emerged, the lack of constitutional clarity precipitated divisions within the military leadership and gave rise to the two opposing factions just described. On the one hand, those who sub-scribed to the Imperial Way ideology saw the emperor as the supreme leader of the state and, conversely, the ideal state as one unified in its subservience to that supreme ruler. The implied function of the mili-tary, they contended, was not only that of the ideal state's guardian but as the plenipotentiary mouthpiece and administrator of their god-like sovereign's will. The Control faction, on the other hand, recognized the political reality that the emperor—just thirty-four years old at the time of the 2-26 Incident—was but a babe-in-arms when it came to affairs of state and no match for the seasoned elder statesmen surrounding him; in their interpretation, the advisory role of the emperor's ministers was the real seat of power, and the "control" they sought, through political influence, was over this body.

What of popular sentiment? As reflected in the popular media of the day, opinion was predominantly sympathetic to the young officers. In the aftermath of the May 15 Incident of 1932 that resulted in the assas-sination of Prime Minister Inukai, prosecution of the four navy officers indicted for masterminding the attempted coup, as well as that of Inu-kai's eleven murderers, all of whom had immediately hailed taxis and gone directly to Military Police Headquarters to turn themselves in, was swayed by an outpouring of public sympathy so massive that the mili-tary tribunals operated under threat of popular unrest, and the sentences they handed down were so light as to be easily mistaken for pardons. The young officers indicted for the 2-26 Incident attracted even more atten-tion. They were romanticized and lauded for what was widely viewed as patriotic courage and heroism. At a time when the nation was suffering domestically from economic impoverishment and demonized abroad for its invasion of Manchuria, these young officers had revolted against the seeming complacency of their elders and brought their idealistic fervor to bear. Even if misdirected in their methods, their patriotism and the purity of their intentions were deemed beyond reproach; the same sort of court leniency meted the May 15 Incident perpetrators was demanded and widely expected.

But such was not to be this time around. The severity of the situation had forced the typically reticent emperor to speak, and once those words were spoken, he made sure his words were followed to their necessary conclusion. By imperial decree, the accused were subjected to special courts martial and thereby stripped of all legal rights, including right to counsel and right to call witnesses. The trials were conducted in secret, and the sentences enacted before word of them was released to the public. Fifteen of the surviving officers—two had committed suicide following the incident—were sentenced to death and executed one week later, and the remaining five were sentenced to life imprisonment. In addition, two more officers, retired, were executed the following year and another twenty-two lower ranked accomplices given prison sentences.

Two civilians, tried separately, were also executed. They were ideologue Kita Ikki and his right-hand associate Nishida Mitsugi, and it is here that the unfolding of this history connects us back to the story of Nakamura Tempū.

The Imperial Way faction's ideology was borrowed almost verbatim from Kita's writings. Nishida discovered Kita and his ideas while attending the Military Academy, and he had aligned himself closely with Kita and had been involved in subversive politics ever since. Both Kita and Nishida, although not Genyōsha initiates, were nevertheless acquainted with, and admirers of, Tōyama Mitsuru. Furthermore, Nishida had called upon Nakamura Tempū late on the evening of February 24, so late that Tempū was roused from bed in order to received him. The two talked—or rather, Nishida talked while Tempū listened—in Tempū's sitting room for over an hour before Nishida went on his way.

What neither Nishida nor Nakamura realized at the time was that Nishida was already under Military Police surveillance. Consequently, following Kita and Nishida's arrest just days later, Nakamura was called in for questioning. What had been the purpose of Nishida's visit and what had the two discussed? The police wanted to know everything.

The summons sent shivers through the community of Nakamura's followers. The Military Police, the Kempeitai, were notorious for their tenacity and the brutality of their interrogations. Nakamura was unperturbed.

On the evening in question, thirty-five-year-old Nishida had prevailed upon the Nakamura's gatekeeper to call for the master of the house, even though Nakamura had already retired. Upon accepting the cushion offered him in the sitting room, and after apologizing for his late night intrusion, Nishida began to expound upon the urgency of the problems facing the nation. Nakamura made no comment but lent the young man his full attention. That attention had the effect of drawing out the man's disaffections with people in power and his prescription for the righting of the foundering ship of state; Nishida became ever more impassioned and animated as he spoke, the volume of his voice threatening to carry beyond the house walls.

All of this Nakamura related to his interrogators in a way that did justice to the young man's passionately patriotic concerns. And what did Nakamura tell Nishida upon the conclusion of his diatribe?

"I said to him," Nakamura responded, "A man of old once said, 'Evil close to the throne must be eliminated.'"

When Nakamura recited this last admission to his associates, they gasped. "Evil close to the throne must be eliminated," everyone knew, was a Chinese saying that had been appropriated by the rebel faction as a call to arms: the evil in question, it was understood, was the views and opinions of the emperor's advisers.

"You can't say that, Sensei," his confidantes insisted. "It is an admission of guilt. Go back tomorrow and retract what you said while there is still time."

Tempū would have none of it. "To say I didn't say it would be a lie. I said it and I take responsibility for what I said. But don't worry; I'll be fine."

Later, when he told this story before a larger gathering, he elaborated.

Never, under any circumstances, will I try to cover up or amend something I've said in the past. Count on me never to say I didn't say something I did or to say I said something I didn't.

Words are a direct revelation, the whisper of the soul, and the reflection of the divine. Speaking is an expression of universal spirit and, as such, is never to be disgraced by the perpetration of falsehood.

That said, what I told the police that day was, "A man of old once said, 'Evil close to the throne must be eliminated.'" They weren't my words; I was just repeating the words of a man long ago. So if they wanted to incriminate someone, they would have to incriminate that man of old.[1]

Nishida's conversation with Nakamura had been purely ideological in content. He had said nothing with regard to either concrete plans or the imminence of their implementation, and consequently, Nakamura's comment can be interpreted not as a provocation meant to incite violence but as an acknowledgment that he understood the young man's moral stance: "What you are telling me is that, in the words of a man of old, evil close to the throne must be eliminated."

Nakamura underwent three separate interrogations in relation to this event. In the end, he was absolved of any wrongdoing, as was to be expected were justice to prevail. It was not, however, the last he would see of the Military Police; nor was it the last of those words spoken by the man of old.

Kita and Nishida, as already mentioned, were not so lucky. Nor was the judgment to which they were subjected altogether fair. While Kita's doctrine did advocate insurrection in the interest of bringing about a more perfect world, neither he nor Nishida had had a direct hand in the planning or implementation of the 2-26 Incident; that was undertaken solely at the initiative of the young officers. Only when the plot was already in motion were they appraised, and only then did they give it their tacit, sidelined nod of approval.

The true purpose of Nishida's visit to the Nakamura residence that night was revealed just as he was leaving. "Please give my regards to Admiral Yamamoto," he said.

Admiral Yamamoto was Yamamoto Eisuke, a former commander-in-chief of the Combined Fleet and a person of influence within the War Ministry. Looked upon as a sympathizer by Kita, Nishida, and the young officers, he was also, incidentally, one of Nakamura Tempū's most ardent followers, one who would continue to be active in the Tempūkai long into the postwar years. Kita and Nishida were dangerous elements; for them to approach the admiral directly would cast him under suspicion. But Nakamura's connection to Yamamoto was known to them, and they were intent upon getting a warning to him ahead of the coming insurrection. Nishida's visit, Nakamura realized, had been that warning.

The 2-26 Incident was a turning point on a road that would ultimately lead the nation to war. While the implosion of Kita, Nishida, and the twenty-two young officers' attempted Shōwa Restoration spelled the end of the Imperial Way faction, if not its ideology, it also effectively delivered up the reins of power to military command.

The military's chauvinism toward constitutional authority found its precedent in the army's unilateral invasion of Manchuria and subsequent encroachments on northern Chinese territory, beginning in September 1931. Japanese Kwantung Army troops, ostensibly charged with guarding the Chinese Eastern Railway, the lease for which had been awarded to Japan under the Treaty of Portsmouth, took over Mukden, the primary seat of Chinese administrative authority over the three northeastern Chinese provinces, in response to an act of sabotage purportedly perpetrated by Chinese dissidents. It was a ruse; the weakly charged explosion, which did little damage, had been planted and detonated by the Japanese lieutenant in charge of the Mukden garrison. News of the incident cabled to other garrisons along the railroad line instigated troop movements far too well orchestrated and carried out with far too much efficiency to have been spontaneous. Within twenty-four hours, the Japanese Army held most of the strategic ports and railroad interchanges throughout southern Manchuria.

The entire affair was initiated and completed locally, its leaders seeking approval from central command in Tokyo only after the fact. The excuse given by the Kwantung Army officers was that they had responded to an emergency, the seriousness of which did not allow them time to request and wait for instructions from central command. But then, ten days later—again, without sanction from Tokyo—reinforcements arrived from Korea.

In Tokyo, the emperor and his ministers were dismayed. They were incensed by this abject breach of authority by lower-level army officers and aghast at the repercussions the incident was likely to have on the nation's international relations. At the same time, however, they were reluctant to admit to the world that their army harbored renegade elements over which they exercised almost no control. In the end, they chose to stand by the Kwantung officers' story, even when it became known within official circles, as it did soon after the incident, that the original railroad bombing near Mukden was conducted by the army for the explicit purpose of providing them with a pretext. The emperor, in January, mildly rebuked the officers for overstepping authority, only to follow up four days later with an unequivocal commendation of the Kwantung Army for its courage and distinction.

International condemnation was immediate. It was also toothless: the other Great Powers were too preoccupied with economic woes to become embroiled in, or to devote resources to, sorting out local disputes in the Far East, and the Chinese Republic, now under the leadership of Chiang Kai-shek, was too weak to respond forcefully on its own.

With no one to challenge them, the Japanese quickly became enamored of their new, virtual acquisition of territory on the continental mainland, and bad went to worse. On March 1, 1932, a proclamation, thinly disguised as the work of Manchurian separatists, announced the formation of the independent state of Manchukuo. In February 1933, when the League of Nations voted to disallow the new state's recognition, Japan withdrew from the league.

At the same time that Japan was turning its back on world opinion and leaving the League of Nations, the Kwantung Army invaded the adjacent

province of Jehol, just north of the Great Wall, claiming that it was tradi-
tionally part of Manchuria (Manchuria had no tradition, as it had never
existed as a polity prior to the creation of Manchukuo). Then, in April, the
army crossed the Great Wall, bringing it within striking distance of Beijing.

Throughout this proliferation of events, the vast majority of the Japanese
public was easily led, by nationalistic propaganda, to believe that the army
was acting in self-defense and in the interest of national security, and that
all its actions were morally justified. The army, after all, was the emperor's
army and therefore had the gods on its side. And as is usually the case
with conquest, the justness of the cause was soon conflated with the value
of the gain: what better evidence did one need for divine sanction of the
nation's right to empire than these successes?

Nakamura Tempū disagreed and he said so. He called the actions of
the Kwantung Army a disgrace, a statement that failed to endear him to
the Military Police.

Likewise, Nakamura's lifelong mentor, Tōyama Mitsuru, was crest-
fallen. The creation of the Manchukuo state on the back of unilateral military action was a perversion of the Asia-for-Asians vision for which he had
worked so hard. In 1935, when the deposed Qing emperor, Pu Yi, made a
diplomatic visit to Japan in his new capacity as the emperor of Manchukuo, a title that afforded him no authority and that he had accepted under
Japanese duress, Tōyama declined an invitation to meet with him.

These were tough years for Tōyama. His third son, Hidezō, was serving out a three-year sentence for his involvement in the 1932 assassination of Prime Minister Inukai. This pill was especially bitter to swallow,
given the depth of Tōyama's relationship with Inukai: they had worked
closely together in support of Sun Yat-sen and had traveled together, just
four years prior to the assassination, to Nanjing to attend the consecra-
tion of Sun Yat-sen's mausoleum. Hidezō's role in the incident appears to
have involved procurement of the murder weapon; whether or not he was
aware of its intended use is not clear, and in either event, he acted without
his father's knowledge.

Following his release, and after Japan's 1937 declaration of war on China, Hidezō would assume his father's banner and devote himself to the cause of ending the conflict and restoring peaceful relations between the two nations. In 1944, he moved his entire family of four to Japanese-occupied Shanghai to better pursue these activities. In a eulogy for his father, who died later that same year, broadcast over Shanghai radio, he recalls his father saying to him on the morning the news of war with China broke in Japan, "This is madness. It can only lead to the loss of many precious lives and much needless destruction, and it is sure to continue until both sides are exhausted. Chiang Kai-shek fully understands the need for China and Japan to work together; this I know better than anyone."

Chiang had been educated in Japan and had even served for three years, from 1909 to 1911, in the Japanese Imperial Army. His acquaintance with Tōyama began after his flight from China, together with Sun Yat-sen, following the failed 1913 Second Revolution. Then, in 1927, during a setback in his political fortunes following Sun's death, Chiang was taken in by Tōyama and given temporary residence in the house next door. With Tōyama's encouragement, he returned to China and completed the military expeditions that put the splintering republic back together again. After the outbreak of the war, Chiang was said to have said on several occasions that Tōyama Mitsuru was the one Japanese with whom he would be willing to meet, and several attempts to arrange such a meeting were made by Tōyama's allies; the intensity of the conflict, however, precluded their plans' fruition.

According to his son, Tōyama continued, "Chiang and I agreed that no matter how big the problems or what the difficulties that come between our countries, it was absolutely essential that a cooperative relationship between Japan and China be maintained. This we promised to each other just before he departed." Hidezō reports that while his father moderated this last statement with his impish grin, he was clearly crying on the inside.[2]

In 1935, Tōyama turned eighty. He went out less, choosing instead to spend time with his grandchildren. The Genyōsha ceased operations as a political organization in 1936, reincorporating as an association for the public good, the only significant activity of which was the continuing operation of the Meidōkan Dojo in Fukuoka. In many ways, the times had caught up with and passed by both the Genyōsha and its central figure, Tōyama Mitsuru. The rise of the military, its invasion of China, and finally, its recklessly conceived aggression against the Western powers—all were grossly inconsistent with the Genyōsha's values.

Tōyama Mitsuru was widely considered by men of his day to have been spiritual successor to Saigō Takamori, the Satsuma statesman who played a leading role in toppling the Tokugawa Shogunate and the conception of the imperial monarchy. Saigō had also been passed by the times in which he lived: he recoiled in response to the pace with which the country was modernizing and, as touched on in chapter 1, died by his own hand when his bloody, doomed-from-the-start revolt failed. Like Saigō, Tōyama understood that acquisitions of modern technologies were necessary and essential to national survival. But also like Saigō, he was deeply suspicious of Western ethics. One needed only to look at the European powers' record of duplicity and wanton bloodshed perpetrated on Asian civilization to call into question the extent to which they were really informed by the Christian values they preached. Japan's one strength, he was absolutely sure, was its moral and spiritual fiber, the ethic cultivated by the astute, educated, and disciplined guardians of culture and preservers of the peace—the military, or samurai, class. Nothing, then, could have been so painful for him as to watch, in his later years, the country travel down a path of moral compromise, including the perpetration of crimes against its Asian neighbors every bit as horrific if not more so than the European precedent. The path could only lead to commensurate destruction of the homeland.

In retrospect, that the role of Tōyama Mitsuru and the Genyōsha in prewar history should have been misconstrued by the postwar offices of the Allied Command is hardly surprising. It was not within the victors' purview to appreciate either the nuances of the losers' history or the roots of the losers' culture. Distanced from these events by the passage of time, however, we of later generations can afford to exercise a wider perspective.

The war years were hard on Nakamura as well. When news broke that Japan had attacked and all but decimated the American fleet at Pearl Harbor, he took no part in the revelry and giddy outpouring of public elation that followed but instead was beset by prescient feelings of loss.

Tempū's troubles with the Kempeitai, the publicly dreaded, secret Military Police Corps modeled after Germany's Gestapo, were reignited in 1937 in the wake of the Marco Polo Bridge Incident, when he rented a hall in the Aoyama district of central Tokyo and delivered a scathing indictment of the Konoe government. The incident—involving a skirmish on the outskirts of Beijing between Japanese soldiers ostensibly in China to protect Japanese interests under terms reached after the Boxer Rebellion and local Chinese soldiers—was being seized upon by the Japanese military, with the full support of their government, as an excuse to increase Japan's military presence in China and to accelerate the descent of both nations along a slippery slope toward full-scale war. These implications, thinly veiled under government claims that its goals were "containment" and "keeping of the peace," were lost on neither Nakamura nor most other adequately informed citizens. Tempū even went so far as to call Prime Minister Konoe a liar. He was arrested and jailed for one week.

The arrest did not slow him in his opposition to what he considered insults to the national dignity and reckless gambles with the nation's future. When, four years later, the war with China escalated into a war with the United States and Great Britain, he continued to use the podiums afforded him by his teaching venues as vehicles to call Prime Minister Tōjō Hideki and the national leadership criminal. "This is not a just war," he would say. "It is not a war that will be looked upon favorably by history. It needs to be ended, and it cannot be ended soon enough. Every day this war continues, we risk the future of the nation. Continue it long enough and we will forfeit our national sovereignty."[3]

The Military Police watched his every move. He was assigned two Kempeitai goons, who accompanied him everywhere and listened to every word said by him to anyone outside his immediate family. Even so, Tempū would not be deterred, and the goons, rather, became traveling companions with whom he chatted freely during long train rides; the men were soon deferring to Tempū as "Sensei," and from time to time, being treated by him to dinner. Not once did they ever report anything damaging about his activities.

Fellow Tōyama Mitsuru protégé and Genyōsha sympathizer Nakano Seigō, who had actively advocated the brokering of a peace agreement on favorable terms with Great Britain in 1942, and who, like Nakamura, was an outspoken critic of the Tōjō regime, was arrested and so severely persecuted by the Kempeitai that he committed suicide in 1943. Nakamura, but for one high card that trumped even the Kempeitai's authority, was just as likely a target for persecution as was Nakano. That high card was his relationship with the imperial family.

Since his initial visits to the palace in 1926, Tempū had continued, at the request of those within, to deliver moral and spiritual counsel to the extended family of princes and princesses, and consequently, neither the civilian government nor the Military Police were very well going to malign the reputation of the throne by naming one of its educators an enemy of the state. The Kempeitai were first enlightened by powers above as to who they were dealing with during Tempū's 1937 internment; he was promptly released, issued a formal apology, and beseeched by Kempeitai command not to disseminate the story of his arrest.

Furthermore, the chief of the Imperial Palace Police, Ōtani Kiichirō, was one of Tempū's most ardent disciples, and with the impending appearance of enemy warplanes over Tokyo's skies, Otani called upon Tempū for counsel upon how best to discharge his office's solemn duty to safeguard the monarch and his household. In January 1945, Tempū, at the Palace Police chief's invitation, began making weekly visits to the Palace grounds, while the Kempeitai's goons, denied entry at the gate, waited outside in the winter cold until he reappeared.

But if the Kempeitai could not arrest him, they could still hound him and inhibit his movements, and this they continued to do. In early March 1945, the Kempeitai issued what they called a "special removal order" against Nakamura Tempū—the only such special removal order ever issued, he was later told—under which his residence in Hongō, the same house that had survived the 1923 Great Kantō Earthquake, was condemned and razed to the ground. Tempū packed up the household and moved his family to the town of Ichikawa in Ibaragi Prefecture.

Only days later, American B-29 bombers dropped incendiary bombs on Tokyo, sending wide swaths of the city up in flames and killing over 100,000 people. This was the beginning of the end, and the end came quickly. Germany capitulated and surrendered in early May, and the Allied Powers, now free to fight just one war instead of two, turned all of their attention to the Pacific, issuing, in July, their Potsdam Declaration, dictating terms under which they would accept Japanese surrender.

On August 6, the United States punctuated that declaration with the release of an atomic bomb over Hiroshima. Less than three days later, during the early hours of August 9, the Russians, who until then had pragmatically continued to observe the terms of the Soviet-Japanese Neutrality Pact of 1941, descended upon Manchuria. And that same morning, a second atomic bomb fell, on Nagasaki.

Six days later, on August 15, a pre-recorded address by the emperor, titled "The Imperial Rescript on the Termination of the War," was broadcast by radio to the nation, announcing the nation's unconditional surrender.

Behind those events, however, lies another story, but for which the emperor's broadcast, known popularly as the Gyokuon-hōsō, the "Precious Sound [the emperor's voice] Broadcast,"—the first time the emperor had ever spoken over the radio and that most of his subjects had ever heard the sound of his voice—might never have aired.

Back in April, the emperor had asked Suzuki Kantarō, a former grand chamberlain he had called out of retirement one year earlier to appoint privy councilor, to assume the office of prime minister. This was a strategic decision: the emperor needed someone of mettle at the helm, someone who could stand up to the military leaders in his cabinet, and Suzuki qualified.

Suzuki was the same grand chamberlain who had been mortally wounded in the 2-26 Incident. On that fateful morning, a young officer and his men broke into the grand chamberlain's residence; the officer, upon confronting Suzuki, announced that he and his men bore Suzuki no personal grudge, but that they were there to "eliminate the evil close to the throne."

"We haven't time. I am going to shoot," the officer continued.

"If you must, then shoot," Suzuki responded.

The officer fired three shots, striking the chamberlain in the left groin, the left chest, and the left side of his head, bringing him to the floor in a pool of blood.

"Finish him off," one of the soldiers yelled. The officer pointed his revolver toward the back of the chamberlain's skull.

"Stop!" The cry came from Suzuki's wife, who had been in the room the whole time. "He's as good as dead already. Spare him the last shot."

Out of deference to her, the officer lowered his pistol; a final shot to the skull would have disfigured her husband's face beyond recognition. Bowing once, he led his men out of the room.[4]

Suzuki lived, saved by his wife's last-minute intervention. Now, nine years later, confronted with the terms of the Potsdam Declaration, the emperor needed someone of rational and moderate judgment to whom he could entrust the task of leading the Supreme Council for the Direction of the War to consensus.

The Supreme Council comprised the prime minister, the foreign minister, the army minister, the navy minister, the chief of the Army General Staff, and the chief of the Navy General Staff. Of these six, five—including Suzuki, who was also a former commander in chief of the Combined Fleet—were current or former military men. Only the foreign minister, Tōgō Shigenori, came from a civilian background. A Foreign Service man, Tōgō had served in Manchuria, Switzerland, the United States, and Germany, where he met his German wife. In 1941, as foreign minister to Tōjō Hideki's cabinet, he had voiced vehement opposition to the decision to go to war but, nevertheless, signed the war declaration as an acknowledgment of responsibility for the failure of his diplomatic efforts. Just as Suzuki had been called out of retirement by the emperor, Suzuki called Tōgō out of retirement to reassume that post; he was thus to be remembered as the foreign minister in office at both the beginning and the end of the War.

By July, the Supreme Council was unanimously reconciled to the reality that victory was no longer achievable but split with regard to the Potsdam Declaration. The army, as represented by the army minister, General Anami Korechika, was unwilling to concede defeat; as seen from the perspective of his office, to make such a concession would be a sacrilege, for it would dishonor the spirits of the hundreds of thousands of gallant soldiers who had given their lives in the emperor's name. Anami advocated the continuation of the struggle and the defense of the homeland in the belief that the enemy would eventually back off of the "unconditional" demands of the Potsdam Declaration and agree to a negotiated armistice that recognized at least some of Japan's territorial gains.

Tōgō was far more dispassionate and calculated in his persuasions. The time for negotiations, he argued, was long past, and every day of delay only inflicted greater pain and suffering on the nation's population. Furthermore, if they acted quickly, they might be able to squeeze through a single condition. Tōgō proposed immediate acceptance of the Potsdam Declaration, but with the stipulation that the Kokutai, the national polity, be allowed to continue to exist; the preservation of the Kokutai, in practical terms, meant the continuation of the imperial household and the institution of the throne.

The navy supported Tōgō's position, while the army remained adamantly opposed. Following the devastation of Hiroshima, the emperor called a series of meetings of the Supreme Council, while Suzuki lobbied unsuccessfully for consensus. Finally, Suzuki, resorting to tactical use of parliamentary procedure, made an unprecedented move. At around two o'clock in the morning of August 10, at a Council meeting convened just before midnight, after first declaring that the Council was at an impasse, he referred the decision directly to the emperor.

The emperor had agreed to this plan of action in a private meeting with Suzuki and Tōgō the previous afternoon. Under the Meiji constitution, the emperor was absolved from all responsibility for acts of state: no recourse, it was ordained, could be brought against the monarch for any outcome of his actions. In practice, this meant that imperial decree was conducted with utmost discretion; policy and governance, and the accountability for policy and governance, were left to his ministers. To give the decision with regard to surrender back to the emperor was the equivalent of asking him to take final responsibility for both the war and the national defeat.

To his credit, the emperor accepted this responsibility. Hirohito had proposed to his ministers the commencement of armistice negotiations as early as January, but his proposals had been met with tacit resistance. Now, after whatever bargaining power Japan once held had slipped away, he, as the figurehead in whose name war was being waged, lives lost, and atrocities committed, saw no other recourse but to exercise his above-the-law authority and to overrule his ministers. Citing the preservation of the nation and the end of the people's suffering as his main concerns, he approved Tōgō's proposal.

In the end, even Japan's one condition of the preservation of the national polity never received official Allied concession. But having, in communicating this condition, already expressed to the Allies its decision to capitulate, Japan moved irrevocably in the direction of surrender, and on August 14, even Army Minister Anami signed the cabinet's joint resolution.

Ultimately, as was well understood by the other cabinet members, Anami's opposition to Tōgō's proposal derived not from personal conviction but from concern for the orderly submission of the military command. For Anami, as the army's chief representative and spokesman, to voice anything but total commitment to the war was to invite mutiny, and consequently, he had purposely withheld his true intentions right up until the signing. That evening, he called on Suzuki at the prime minister's residence. He had, he assured Suzuki, been in favor of the

Tōgō proposal from the start, and he thanked Suzuki for his leadership through this difficult time. The real but unspoken purpose of this visit, they both understood, was to say good-bye. Anami committed suicide the following morning.

Anami's apprehensions proved to be only too well founded. In the late hours of that same night of August 14 and into the early hours of the next day, rebel troops surrounded the Imperial Palace, cut its telephone lines, and made a desperate but unsuccessful attempt to locate and take possession of the emperor's recording before it could be released over the airwaves.

Nakamura Tempū was there. His weekly visits to the palace had continued even after his removal to Ichikawa, and following a second major air raid on May 25, these visits, again at the chief of the Palace Police's request, became both more frequent and of longer duration, until, by late July, he had been provided with living quarters inside of the deputy chamberlain's residence and was spending more time there than in Ichikawa.

Furthermore, based on his comments regarding the unfolding of events during the final weeks and days of the war, he had some knowledge of the proceedings going on within the Supreme Council's chambers. Just what the source of that information was, he does not say; however, circumstantial evidence points in the direction of Yoshizawa Kenkichi, the distant relative and career diplomat who had helped him during his sojourn in New York some thirty-seven years earlier, now serving as a member of the emperor's Privy Council. Yoshizawa was unequivocally of the opinion that the Potsdam Declaration was the best deal that Japan could expect—that it represented the Allies final offer and that further delay in its acceptance could bring the next atomic bomb down on Tokyo. And while propriety would have prevented him from revealing details of the discussions then under way, he would almost certainly have known that Nakamura was sympathetic to his views. In lieu of better evidence, I imagine them exchanging words in quiet voices, perhaps under a shade tree somewhere within the palace grounds.

Unlike Yoshizawa, however, Tempū's station at the palace removed him from most immediate, worldly concerns and left him with time on his hands. Tempū divides his time between leisurely strolls in the gardens, reading in the palace library, and playing go with his friend and follower, Imperial Palace Police Chief Ōtani.

Nakamura first infers that something out of the ordinary is afoot when, on August 14, during their after-lunch go game, Ōtani says to him, "I have a favor to ask. Could you stay here this evening?" By "here," the chief means the Palace Police Headquarters.

"Why? Are you lonely?"

"Haven't you heard? There may be trouble this evening."

"What kind of trouble?"

"There are rumors circulating that some of the young officers of the Imperial Guard may try to prevent the broadcast of the emperor's announcement tomorrow." It is the first Nakamura has heard of either an announcement or a broadcast. "Hopefully I am wrong," Ōtani continues. "But I have a feeling that we may be in for some commotion."

The content of the announcement to be made is unknown to even Palace Police Chief Ōtani, but what he does know, Nakamura learns, is that it has already been recorded, for the Police Headquarters under Ōtani's command has been charged with its protection.

"And where is the recording now?" Nakamura asks.

"That is a secret. But I'm going to let you in on it anyway. It is locked away in the grand chamberlain's safe."

"That's no good," Nakamura responds. "That's the first place they'll look for it. The best place to hide something like that is to put it somewhere in plain sight, like on an ordinary shelf."

"But it's the emperor's voice. It's in a paulownia-wood box wrapped in silk carrying the imperial crest."

"Take it out and put it in an ordinary container. If you don't want people to know what it is, you don't advertise it; you want to make it look as plain and ordinary as possible. And you want to hide it in the least likely place, which is somewhere it can easily be seen."

Ōtani is cognizant of Nakamura's expertise as a spy in the arts of keeping and discovering secrets, and he takes the advice to heart. By telephone, he relays it to Grand Chamberlain Tokugawa. What, ultimately, is done with that advice, neither of them ever learn, but when the grand chamberlain's safe is indeed later searched, the recording is not found.

Ōtani reiterates his original request. "Won't you please stay here with me until noon tomorrow?" It's not that he is afraid, he assures Nakamura. It's that the responsibility he shoulders is large, and he can use Nakamura's help in seeing it through.

Where he spends the night makes little difference to him, Nakamura assures him, and the two of them, seated in Ōtani's second-story office, continue their go game late into the evening.

The office is located on the second story of the Headquarters building at the top of the stairs. It is minimally furnished with a worktable that serves as the chief's desk and a second round table with four chairs for receiving guests, the table upon which their go-board now rests. A far corner has been cordoned off with screens, and behind the screens is a cot. At ten, Nakamura sends Ōtani off to get some sleep on the cot. "I'll take the first watch," he says. "We can switch at two."

If something is going to happen, Tempū is thinking, it will probably happen before two; and furthermore, if something does happen, it will be better if he, an ordinary civilian, and not the chief of the Palace Police, who will almost certainly draw fire, deals with it. Ōtani, should he make a wrong move or say something that produces unfortunate consequences, must answer to the Ministry of the Imperial Household, if not to His Majesty, the emperor; Tempū is accountable to no one. "You carry the weight and responsibilities of your office, while I can say and do whatever I want. So leave it to me; if something happens, don't come out."

Ōtani retires and Tempū sits at the desk, reading a book.

All is quiet until shortly before two, when one of the Palace policemen, urgency in his voice, calls up through the open office windows from the outside pavement. He is calling for his chief.

"The chief is sleeping," Nakamura calls down. "What do you want?"

"An officer of the Imperial Guard is headed in this direction with a group of soldiers."

"Soldiers? How did they get into the Palace?"

"Haven't you heard?" the policeman responds. "The Palace is surrounded. The Imperial Guard is controlling the gates."

The imperial family, as well as the grand chamberlain and the keeper of the privy seal, have taken refuge in the underground chambers, he goes on to explain. As he is speaking, he is drowned out by the sound of marching boots, and an officer, in the company of some fifteen of his men, barrels into the building, stomps up the stairs, and bursts into the room, brandishing a drawn saber.

He is greeted by a glaring gentleman, dressed not in uniform but in kimono and neatly pressed hakama. "What do you want here?" Nakamura asks in a voice filled with indignation. "Can't you see this is my room? Who do you think you are to come barging in without so much as knocking?"

The officer comes to a full halt. "My apologies," he replies, acknowledging both the seniority and apparent authority of the man before him, as well as the impropriety of his entry. "But we are searching for something."

"Whatever your purpose, you're a soldier, aren't you? When you enter a room, you first state your name and your rank. My name is Nakamura Tempū."

The young officer snaps to attention. "Major Ishihara of the Imperial Guard, sir. We are here to find the recording of the emperor's precious voice."

"I wouldn't know anything about that. But first, put that piece of tin away." Nakamura is pointing at the major's saber. "You're acting as if the enemy has already come ashore. In our culture, the sword is a symbol of the warrior's soul and is only to be drawn in circumstances of life and death. A warrior never draws his sword as an act of provocation. You're a warrior, so you should know that. Put that thing away, immediately."

Ishihara acknowledges the rectitude of this admonishment and returns the saber to its sheath. At the same time, he is heartened to learn that he is dealing with someone who understands the warrior's code; surely, this man, Nakamura, will be sympathetic to their cause. He explains the purpose behind the siege, the same purpose that has brought him now to the Palace Police Headquarters.

"As a soldier in the emperor's army, defeat is unacceptable." The major's eyes glisten with moisture as he says this.

"Of course." Nakamura understands the young officer's sentiments. "No good soldier charged with preserving the nation is going to willingly accept defeat. But if the emperor has committed words in his own voice to a recording, then those words carry the full authority of the throne. 'Imperial mandate is no more retractable than sweat that has passed through the pores.'" Tempū is quoting a Chinese proverb. "It's not for the military to question the wisdom of the emperor's decision. It's for the military, no matter how heart-breaking that decision, to carry out the emperor's will."

"But that isn't so," Ishihara retorts. "The words on the recording don't reflect the emperor's will; they reflect the collective will of his ministers who have pressured him to take this action. It is the work of evil close to the throne."

"Fool! You call yourself a soldier?" Nakamura's voice contains all the fury of a thunderbolt. "Do you really think that His Majesty is so devoid of dignity that he would allow himself to be swayed by his ministers against his will? If not the emperor, then who has the authority to decide something like this?"

It is not the answer Ishihara expects. He stands, frozen, for some time, virtually immobilized by the weight of this response.

Until this moment, Ishihara has been operating under written orders he and his men believe to have come from their direct superior, the commander of the Imperial Guard's first division, Lieutenant General Mori Takeshi. In fact, however, Mori is dead—murdered by the principle perpetrators of the rebellion. Ishihara's orders, affixed with the deceased Mori's seal, are forged.

Now, for the first time, he questions the authenticity of those orders. Moreover, regardless of their authenticity, should he follow them when they contradict the imperial will? The more he reflects upon this conundrum, the more he finds irrefutable the argument that, ultimately, the emperor has the last word.[5]

The major's confusion is reflected in the even greater confusion of the nation at large when the emperor's voice is heard over the radio just ten hours later. For what and for whom have they been fighting? For what purpose has an entire generation of young men died and most of the nation's major cities suffered massive destruction? Many of the military leaders, like General Anami, as well as the leaders of the siege conducted on the palace the night before, have already committed suicide.

Major Ishihara, after withdrawing his men from the palace, is shot dead while attempting to bring around to reason a group of rebel Army Air Corps officers ensconced behind barricades in Ueno Park. Ultimately, he has been just one more soldier seeking an honorable cause for which to die.

15.
A NEW BEGINNING

In the wake of the emperor's broadcast, thousands knelt in front of the Imperial Palace with bowed heads and cried. At home and abroad, hundreds of military officers, and even some civilians, atoned to their sovereign and the nation by committing ritual suicide. The chanting of Buddhist monks in city temples performing endless successions of funerals wafted through the quiet streets and neighborhoods, where they were heard as last rites on the nation.

A palpable uncertainty descended over the city. What would happen next? The victors had yet to come ashore, but years of propaganda had painted them as wicked and barbarous, and among those who had witnessed or taken part in the subjugation, rape, and plunder of peoples in conquered territories, leniency—now that the tables had been turned—was unimaginable.

The moment passed, however, like the pause between two breaths. Regardless of circumstance, life must go on, and people soon set about picking up the pieces. Shantytowns sprouted out of the rubble, and impromptu markets peddling anything saleable sprang up in the streets. A cardboard sign, a chair, and a pair of scissors was all that was needed to open a barber shop; a wrench, resource enough to go into the business of bicycle repair. In one sense, life had been simplified since the future had been taken away: unable to plan, people lived one day at a time. Furthermore, when they looked into the sky, the sun was still shining. No more B-29s flying, no more nighttime terror. The worst, they realized, was over.

Memories of air raid sirens and fire bombings would surface in the nightmares of many for years to come. Conventional bombing had caused wider devastation and more civilian deaths in each of Japan's three largest cities, Tokyo, Osaka, and Nagoya, than had either of the atomic bombs dropped on Hiroshima and Nagasaki. Sixty-six cities in all had been subjected to such bombings, and on the order of one million civilians killed, millions more injured, and many, many more rendered homeless.

To this wasteland, soldiers and expatriated civilians, all traumatized and many sick or wounded, returned in droves from the would-be empire's far-flung reaches. When the war ended, more than 10 percent of Japan's citizenry (excluding the native populations of Formosa and Korea, then under Japanese dominion) were stationed or living beyond the archipelago's shores, and of that diaspora, more than five million returned to the homeland within the first twelve months after surrender.

Food shortages, extreme in wartime, became only more acute, and many who had managed to survive the war succumbed to malnutrition during the months following. Were it not for massive distributions of rations by the occupying American forces, their number would have been much, much higher.

For Nakamura Tempū, the hardest part of the war had been seeing off many of his younger students. The most he could wish for them was their safe return. But then, because the best strategy for survival, he well knew, was to throw caution to the wind and to dedicate oneself fully and wholeheartedly to the fulfillment of one's mission, he was also beholden to dispatch each of them without hint of reservation or anything less than patriotic fervor; thus, while publically advocating Japan's early withdrawal from the conflict on the one hand, he stood in unity with these young soldiers on the other.

Some of these young men did return and credited their survival to habits cultivated under his tutelage, especially those of clarity of judgment, through anjō-daza, and calm resolve, through the practice of kumbhaka. Many, however, did not; and regardless of his political opposition to the wartime Japanese leadership, as a member of the Japanese nation, Nakamura felt a deep and lasting sense of responsibility and remorse for the war and its consequences.

Just as he had predicted it would, the war had proven to be a stain on history and a wound to national dignity. Unprecedented destruction and suffering had been perpetrated on China, where best estimates put the number of directly attributable deaths at fifteen million. Indignity, pain, and suffering had been inflicted on the people of Korea, of whom, under their annexed status as Japanese nationals (but not citizens), as much or more in the way of sacrifice had been demanded than was of the homeland's population. And in Indochina, Malaya, Singapore, Burma, Indonesia, and much of the South Pacific, the empire's yoke had left a virtual trail of tears. For all this, Nakamura understood, as did most of his countrymen, the Japanese had nobody to blame but themselves.

Culpability for the succession of poor decisions leading to this outcome becomes almost a moot point in light of the magnitude of the harm done; no individual or group of individuals could possibly shoulder so much blame. Nevertheless, the sort of complete and unqualified admission of guilt the victorious nations thought they were due from the Japanese was never forthcoming. Wars are only fought because each side is intractably in the right, and this war was no different; where the prevailing Western narrative would have it—naively, I might add—that the War had been one of unilateral aggression provoked by sociopathic fanaticism,[1] the Japanese could cite a litany of injustices perpetrated against them, not the least of which were British and American oil embargos that threatened them with economic strangulation.[2] In the popular imagination, the Pacific War had been primarily a defensive one (that the best defense is a strong offense is a basic tenet of Japanese military strategy), albeit a defense that had failed, and while "what if" speculation is neither here nor there in the court of historical opinion, a reasonable argument can and has been made for the case that war was not only the option seized upon by Japan's overzealous military leadership but also the one that, placed under similar circumstances and provided with commensurate military resources, most other developed or developing nations would probably have chosen.[3]

Even Nakamura Tempū, in objecting to the war, did so not out of sympathy for what appeared to be Anglo-American belligerence but out of dissension with regard to the solution. One does not wage a war that cannot be won, and this war was, at best, a gamble not worth the bet: Japan stood to lose far more than it could possibly gain.

If his opposition to the War was now vindicated, however, Nakamura, outside his most private conversations, uttered not a word to the effect of "I told you so," nor did he accuse or assert blame. In war, he understood, there is no vindication, only loss, and all had lost—conquered and conquerors alike. The only sensible course was to acknowledge that loss and to move on, to move forward, to rebuild.

Tempū may also have harbored some sense of personal responsibility for his part in the shaping of the policies that led Japan to war. In his dedication to the principles and nationalistic ideology of Tōyama Mitsuru, he had played a consequential role in the fostering and strengthening of the national identity. Likewise, as an advocate of pan-Asianist ideals, he had directly participated in events precipitating Japan's intrusions into the affairs of its neighbors. And while neither was the nationalism envisioned by Tōyama and Nakamura of the narrow-minded, delusional vintage that had carried the nation to war, nor did their commitments to pan-Asianism agree with the annexation of Korea, the creation of Manchukuo, or the invasion of China, it was difficult to argue that, no matter how pure their motives and intentions, they had not in some way contributed to the generation of those results.

Be that as it may, what we do know is that, from the day the war ended, Tempū never again used the podium afforded him by his teaching activities to voice his political views. Instead, he focused exclusively on the spiritual rejuvenation of a traumatized nation and its people.

Just one month after the armistice, Nakamura delivered his first postwar lecture in Tokyo's Toranomon district. Wartime attrition of much of the city's able and better-to-do population to the countryside made for poor attendance, but the event nevertheless marked a new beginning.

Only a short distance from Toranomon, General Douglas MacArthur, Supreme Commander of the Allied Powers, and his General Headquarters

(GHQ) were installed in the Daiichi Life Insurance Building, facing the Imperial Palace from just across the Palace moat, and from this make-do castle, McArthur dispensed his orders with the authority of a surrogate emperor. First to warn Tempū of the impending wave of incriminations was the prominent historian and intellectual Tokutomi Sohō. No victory would be replete without its remonstration of the enemy's sins, and suspects, to include not only military and political leaders but also intellectuals and ideologues, were already being lined up for questioning and eventual showcase prosecution by kangaroo-like tribunal. Tokutomi, although never brought to trial, was charged and held under house arrest for two years. He reached Nakamura, who was still in temporary residence within the palace walls, by telephone: "Be prepared. With your history of patriotic activism, you'll be next on their list."[4]

Sure enough, not long afterward, on November 2, Nakamura and Palace Police Chief Ōtani are interrupted at their game of go by a panicked officer who has just answered the telephone. "He's speaking English! The only thing I can understand is 'Tempū, Tempū,'" he says.

Ōtani goes to the phone and, after a short exchange, employing the few words of English he knows, looks over at Nakamura. "It's come," he says. "It's the GHQ. They are asking for Mr. Tempū Nakamura."

"Nakamura speaking," Tempū says into the receiver after wresting it from Ōtani. The American voice on the other end is deferential and courteous: "If you are available, we would like for you to come over at nine tomorrow morning. We will send a car to pick you up."

Nakamura, after reiterating the caller's request to be sure he has understood correctly, thanks him and hangs up the phone. "It doesn't sound like trouble to me. They just asked me to come by at nine tomorrow."

Alarm bells are sounding louder than ever inside Ōtani's head. "They're only being polite in order to entice you into their lair. Once they've got you there, they won't let you go."

Maybe so, but Tempū has given his word. The car picks him up as agreed the following morning, and he is ushered into the GHQ building, seated in the number one meeting room on the second floor, and served with coffee and coffee cake. Such luxuries, within the confines of the war-ravaged and undernourished capital, are the stuff of dreams, and as Nakamura savors the coffee's aroma and the cake's sweet flavor, he wonders at just how different life on the inside of the GHQ must be.

After a short wait, Lieutenant General Robert Eichelberger, Commander General of the American Eighth Army, enters the room. The general is smiling broadly—"Not the countenance to be expected of an interrogator," Nakamura thinks.

"Thank you for taking the time to come by," Eichelberger says. "Ordinarily we would've dispensed with this matter by messenger, but I wanted to meet with you in person."

Just over five months earlier, on the evening of May 25, B-29s had again appeared in the skies over Tokyo, targeting areas missed during the air raid of March 9. Nakamura was in Ichikawa, and he and his family heard planes passing overhead during the night; Ichikawa, it seems, was on one of the approaching flight paths used by the American squadrons.

He was awakened the following morning by loud voices coming from the fields behind the house. Sometime during the night, Nakamura learns when he goes outside to investigate, an American pilot has parachuted from his burning aircraft and landed in a neighbor's rice field, and farmers, upon discovering him at first light, have set upon him with bamboo poles and farm instruments. The pilot is now hogtied and hooded, and the farmers are taking turns on him with sticks as they tow him to the local police station.

When Nakamura catches up with the party, it has reached the police station, and a patrolman and his sergeant are attempting to interrogate the soldier in Japanese. Failing to elicit a response, they raise their voices and move closer, until they are yelling directly into the man's ear.

"Yelling louder isn't going to help," Nakamura says impatiently. "He doesn't understand a word you're saying."

The men step back. Tempū has already established a reputation in the village, and his immediate neighborhood has appointed him its civic leader.

"Untie him and take off that hood," he commands.

The policemen untie the man's hands and feet but object to uncovering his eyes. "He'll be able to see. What if he has a way of passing valuable information back to the enemy?"

"Don't be ridiculous. What could a man who has just dropped out of the sky into totally unknown surroundings possibly see? Especially here in this tiny police station. Or do you think your police station is of strategic military value?"

Once his blinds have been removed, Nakamura speaks to the young pilot for the first time in English. "Please sit down. You've been through a lot. Are you hungry?"

The man is delighted by this abrupt change of fortune. No, he had been carrying his army rations and had consumed them after he landed, before he was caught. But he has not had anything to drink for hours and would appreciate a glass of water.

Tempū looks over at the patrolman. "Make this man some tea, and use the tea you keep for guests."

While this is transpiring inside the station, a crowd has formed outside and is clamoring to have a go at the prisoner: not every day does heaven deliver up an enemy combatant for the spanking. Nakamura rebukes them from the doorway.

"Listen to me. You want me to send the man in here out so you can have your way with him, but if I were to do that, I'd be making common criminals out of all of you. This man is a lieutenant. He's an officer. The army will decide what to do with him. In the meantime, leave him alone.

"And while we're at it, let me ask, is there anyone here who has a son, or a nephew, or a neighbor who has gone off to war?"

Every hand in the crowd goes up.

"I see. So let me ask those of you who raised your hands: What would you think if you learned that that son or cousin or neighbor had been captured by the Americans and that he'd been tied up and beaten with sticks until he couldn't stand? Would it make you happy? If you say it would, then I'll turn the prisoner over to you right now. But just bear in mind that, when this war is over, and when word gets out that this is the way war prisoners were treated by Japanese civilians, you're going to have to answer for your actions and the shame you've brought on the nation. What do you say?"

The farmers are quiet. Eyes averted, several heads nod in consent.

"Do you think that raising a ruckus over one poor pilot is going to determine the outcome of the war? Go home and get back to your work. Go tend your fields."

The mob now dispersed, Nakamura steps back inside and places a telephone call to the mayor's office. Soon after stating his name and purpose, he has the mayor on the other end of the phone. "We have a downed American pilot in our custody and wish to turn him over to the Military Police. The policemen here are saying we can transport him in the back of a farm truck, but the man's an officer and deserves better treatment. Please send over your car. Or, if that's not convenient, then talk to the Military Police chief and have him send over his car."

In the end, both cars show up—the mayor's car and driver and the Military Police chief's car and driver with the chief in the passenger seat. Tempū shows the pilot into the back seat of the Mayor's car and slides in beside him. With the Police chief's car leading and the mayor's car following, they drive to the Military Police's Ichikawa bureau.

Before turning over his charge, Nakamura turns to the Military Police chief and says, "You're a soldier, so you understand *bushidō*, the warrior's code, right? You know, then, that to be true to the way, the warrior is always to have compassion for his enemy."

"Yes," the chief responds. "Of course."

"In that case, for as long as this young man is in your charge, please treat him as if he were a guest in your house. What happens to him after you turn him over to your headquarters, neither you nor I can control. But at least leave him with one favorable impression of the Japanese soldier's conduct."

Next he turns to the pilot and extends his hand. "The time has come for us to part ways. Should fortune permit, perhaps we'll meet again sometime."

"Pardon me," the young pilot answers. "But please tell me your name."

"We've spent several hours in each other's company. Yet, during that time, I haven't asked you your name. I haven't asked you out of respect for your dignity. Unfortunately, our respective countries are at war. But that's not reason enough for you and me either to bear ill will or to feel obligation toward each other. To ask for your name under these circumstances would not be gentlemanly, and there's no reason for you to ask mine. Neither of us is likely to forget this meeting, so let's leave it at that. That way, if it so happens we meet again under happier circumstances, we can talk about these events as we would, about old times. Until then, I wish you all the best."

Evidently, following the pilot's release and his return to the United States at the end of the War, *Stars and Stripes*, the army newspaper circulated overseas to servicemen and governmentally employed civilians, has gotten wind of his story and has dispatched a reporter to Tokyo to track down the English-speaking Japanese man in the rural countryside who had intervened on the pilot's behalf. The story has filtered up to Eichelberger by way of his staff. Identifying Nakamura Tempū and finding him has not been difficult; the story had also circulated within the Military Police, and a former Military Police officer has directed the Americans to the man for whom they are searching.

"What is it that you do?" Eichelberger asks, after the story of what led him to Tempū is out of the way. "Are you a Christian?"

"Why do you ask?"

"Because the kind of charity you showed toward an enemy combatant is a model Christian act."

"I don't know that Japanese Christians would act that way," Nakamura responds.

"Then what motivated you to do what you did for an American soldier?"

"My humanity," he answers.

Eichelberger is visibly surprised. All too familiar with Japanese ferocity on the battlefield, the answer is one he least expects.

"Tell me more. Have you always thought that way?"

"Not always. I spent a long time in the dark. But it's the way I've felt and acted for the last thirty-five or so years."

"What changed?"

"I encountered the teachings of yoga."

The conversation changes abruptly. Interest in yoga among the American public has proliferated far in excess of the availability of qualified teachers, and that interest extends to members of Eichelberger's staff. Would Nakamura be willing to present his teachings to the Tokyo foreign community?

The logistics take more than a year to work out, but a venue is eventually secured and a date set. And in the spring of 1947, Nakamura Tempū delivers a three-day series of lectures, in English, at the International Press Club, then located in the Mainichi Newspaper building in Yūrakuchō. More than 250 people, most of them foreign civilians and servicemen, attend.

In the hall, unbeknownst to Nakamura, is forty-two-year-old John D. Rockefeller III. Rockefeller, in Tokyo as part of a postwar tour of China, Korea, and Japan, happens to be staying within easy walking distance at Tokyo's premier hotel, the Imperial, designed by Frank Lloyd Wright in the 1920s.

The Rockefeller Foundation has been active in East Asia, especially in China, since the early part of the century, and a grant from JDR III's father, John D. Rockefeller Jr., funded the construction of a new library at the Imperial University, to be renamed Tokyo University, after the destruction of the old library in the Great Kantō Earthquake of 1923. JDR III visited Japan for the first time in 1929 as a twenty-three-year-old just out of college and was smitten by the depth and refinement of the country's culture. Seventeen years later, he is visiting a second time, now on behalf of the Rockefeller Foundation and for the purpose of shaping the foundation's philanthropic strategy with regard to Japanese reconstruction. The foundation will, of course, enact its strategy in coordination with American diplomatic policy, and Rockefeller's stay in Tokyo includes several lengthy interviews and discussions with General Douglas MacArthur.

After Nakamura's lecture, Rockefeller seeks him out, and the two converse for more than an hour. The upshot of this conversation is an invitation to New York: Nakamura would be assured, Rockefeller tells him, of an audience to include persons of power and influence in the United States.

Tempū politely but firmly declines. His responsibilities to the reconstruction of Japanese civil society take precedence over whatever prestige the New York offer might afford him.

This, however, is not the last of Rockefeller and his offer. Four years later, he comes again to Tokyo, this time as an official member of a U.S. State Department delegation led by John Foster Dulles. The delegation is charged with negotiating terms of a peace treaty to end the occupation and to reinstate Japanese sovereignty, and its inclusion of John D. Rockefeller III, whose express assignment is to pursue future possibilities for U.S.-Japan cultural and intellectual exchange, is an anomaly. The State Department, under the auspices of the United States Information Service (USIS), operating out of U.S. embassies around the world, has discovered that cultural exchange is an effective instrument for disseminating propaganda; that discovery notwithstanding, however, the elevation of cultural interests to a position just one step below political ones is unprecedented in U.S. foreign relations, and the Rockefeller name, as well as JDR III's personal affection for, and interest in, the Far East, has recommended him to the position.

Nakamura, upon invitation, joins Rockefeller and his wife, Blanchette, for dinner one evening at the Imperial Hotel. Tempū's is the only account we have of this meeting, but it seems that, this time, with the weight of his mission also on his shoulders, Rockefeller is even more forceful in his attempt to allure Nakamura to the United States, making a considerable monetary reward part of his offer.

Tempū is not to be swayed. Moreover, out of genuine curiosity, he asks the Rockefellers, given how wealthy they were, if they have any worries—and if so, what those are. Their biggest worry, he is surprised to learn, is money: not lack thereof, but overabundance. They are so well endowed, they confide in him, that they are never really sure how much money they have; furthermore, they are consumed with concerns about what to do with their wealth and how to use it responsibly. The response elicits in Nakamura both surprise and compassion: the worries of the wealthy are not the same as the worries of the common man, but worries all the same.

Within eighteen months of his return to New York, JDR III funds the creation of the Intellectual Interchange Program in partnership with Columbia University's East Asia Institute, then under the leadership of the foremost Western scholar of Japanese history and culture, George Sansom, as well as the restitution and revitalization of the Japan Society, while Blanchette prevails upon the Museum of Modern Art to import and erect a traditional Japanese house in its sculpture garden. The Rockefeller Foundation also funds the construction and opening of the International House in Tokyo.[5]

Tempū, not only exonerated from the purge but also recognized by the occupying regime as a positive force for social rehabilitation, is thus given free rein to travel and teach. This he does with singular focus and energy. After ceasing its activities during the last two years of the war, the Tempūkai (Tempu Society), the name assumed in 1940 for his Society for Unity-Based Philosophy and Medicine, is revived. Membership is opened and made affordable for the first time to not just the socially elite but also the general public. The first of his monthly lecture series at Gokokuji, a prominent Shingon-sect temple in Tokyo's Bunkyō Ward, is delivered in April 1948. The monthly Gokokuji lectures became a tradition that continues up until his death.

Nakamura turned seventy in 1946. In April 1947, he publishes *Shin-jin-sei no Tankyū*, "The Search for an Authentic Life," the first of his three-volume formal treatise on mind-body unification; in it, he delineates the broad principles of his philosophy. The following year, he publishes the second volume, *Kenshin Shō*, "Abstract of the Polishing of Mind," an examination of the principles of mental discipline. And in 1949, the third and final volume, *Renshin Shō,* "Abstract of the Training of the Body," examining the principles of physical health and rejuvenation. Also published in 1949 is the first issue of the Tempūkai periodical *Shirube* (the name can mean both "guidepost" and "friend or companion in a mutual undertaking").

* * *

Most everyone expected some form of retribution as a consequence of surrender and thus were not surprised when the Allied Command began rounding up and prosecuting a hastily assembled roster of "war criminals." Many Japanese even openly supported these actions as a means to closure on what they considered to be their leaders' crimes against the people. Indeed, had those leaders been court-martialed and summarily executed, it would have probably prompted little public outcry: local trials conducted in the lands of Japan's former empire proved this point by delivering more than 900 quickly forgotten executions, predominantly of minor officers and enlisted men made to answer for atrocities committed against civilians and prisoners of war. In Tokyo, however, the Allies, in an attempt to give their proceedings legal propriety and an appearance other than that of acts of vengeance, convened a multinational military tribunal and conducted a series of long, drawn-out showcase trials, the hypocrisy of which was readily apparent to most astute observers. The defendants were predominantly found guilty under ex post facto law. They were also ascribed personal culpability for having carried out acts of state. And by the time the trials ended, in 1948, most of the Western powers were engaged in acts of extraterritorial aggression—the British in Malaya, the Dutch in Indonesia, and the French in Indochina (American involvement first in Korea and later in Vietnam would soon follow)—altogether similar to those on which the trials hinged.

Even those Japanese most sympathetic to the occupation and its effort to assign blame for Japan's transgressions were baffled, however, when the Allied Command fingered Hirota Kōki. The crux of Hirota's crime seems to have been poor timing: both the outbreak of war with China and the rape of Nanjing had occurred under his watch as foreign minister. Among combatant nations in the eastern half of World War II, China had suffered most by far, and if anyone was out for blood at the tribunal, it was the Chinese delegation.

Nakamura's acquaintance with Hirota, as mentioned in chapter 1, went back to their days together at the Shūyūkan and the Meidōkan in Fukuoka. As a career diplomat and politician, Hirota had been anything but anti-China: he had advocated Chinese-Japanese alliance as a deterrent to Soviet incursions and the spread of communism (his prescience in this regard had been borne out by the time of his trial by the beginning of the Cold War and the rise of Mao Zedong), and he had been a strong and vocal critic of Japanese military escalation in China—so vocal that the military-dominated cabinet took away his appointment and expelled him from their body in 1938.

The subject of Nanjing is more contentious. In December 1937, after the capitulation of the "southern capital," as its name implies, Japanese troops ran amok, perpetrating unspeakable atrocities against the civilian population. Hirota was almost certainly privy to reports on this development soon after it took place, as was the emperor. That said, neither did he condone what was revealed in these reports, nor was his authority such that he could have either reined in the military or demanded accountability: as noted above, he was already out of favor with the military elite and just six months away from forced resignation from the cabinet.

Moreover, the information that was returned through those initial reports was spotty at best. What exactly happened in Nanjing, even after more than seventy-five years of exhaustive research—and even though the city of Nanjing has invested heavily in the perpetuation of the massacre's memory through the construction of a huge and elaborate memorial, not the most insignificant feature of which is the giant, bold carving in stone of the number 300,000, their estimate of fatalities—is still difficult to say definitively. The People's Republic of China has a record of constructing history through persistent repetition of claims until these claims become fact, and in this case, challenges to their estimate of the body count are easily deflected as arrogance and reluctance on the part of the Japanese to confront their past. Furthermore, while some of the best research on this sordid event has come out of Japan, no sensible Japanese spokesperson is going to be drawn into a dispute over the actual scale of the massacre when, at any scale, it is so inexcusable.

Hirota, in his day, may have felt much the same way. While the assertion that he should be held personally culpable for what happened in Nanjing was blatantly spurious, he was, nevertheless, as a citizen of Japan, and as a person of power and influence at the time these events occurred, remorseful for and shamed by the actions of his countrymen. A man of few words anyway, he remained silent throughout most of his trial, leaving the presentation of his case entirely to his court-appointed lawyers.

The Tokyo tribunal's verdicts were decided by a panel of eleven justices, one each from Australia, Canada, China, France, India, the Netherlands, New Zealand, the Philippines, the Soviet Union, the United Kingdom, and the United States. The justices were allowed neither backups nor proxies, and proceedings continued regardless of absences from the bench—which became more frequent as the trials wore on. Only six of the eleven were in attendance for Hirota's trial, two of whom, Justice Pal of India and Justice Röling of the Netherlands, voted for acquittal; but found guilty of Class A war-crimes by the remaining four, the majority in session, he was nevertheless sent to the gallows. In the final tally, just seven men were executed as a result of the Tokyo tribunal. Of these, Hirota was the only civilian.

Nakamura visited Hirota in Sugamo Prison following the Tribunal's verdict. Man's fate, he was made acutely aware, is ultimately not of his own making; there are times when all one can do is surrender to the current in which one is carried. "Go quietly," he counseled Hirota. "Anything you say will only detract from your dignity."

For someone who had ventured practically everything on the teaching that circumstance is rendered malleable by the forces of mind, this was difficult advice to deliver, and it could only have been more difficult for Hirota to hear. But then, the course of action it recommended was ultimately consistent with Tempū's unwavering confidence in the nobility of spirit. In the end, Hirota took Tempū's advice to heart: he made no effort to explain himself or to transfer blame, and he issued no parting statement. He did, however, go to his death secure in himself and at peace with the world. Due in part to the dignity with which he accepted his sentence, posterity has ruled in his favor: most historians, Western as well as Japanese, now agree that there was no case against Hirota Kōki, that he was unfairly tried and wrongfully executed.

16.

THE YEARS
OF FULFILLMENT

By the mid-1950s, Nakamura Tempū's way of mind-body unification was
an idea whose time had come. In 1955, the Tempūkai's annual summer
training session, its ten-day summer retreat, was attended by upward of
620 people in Tokyo and close to the same number in Kyoto, Kobe, and
Osaka, bringing the total number nationwide to almost 2,000. And these
numbers would continue to grow. By 1966 and 1967 the numbers were, in
Tokyo, close to 1,000; in Kyoto, 800; in other cities, slightly fewer.[1]

Popular aspirations, bruised and betrayed by the war effort, were now
reasserting themselves with extraordinary vigor in the pursuit of economic gain. Furthermore, by a sardonic twist of fate, the dogs of war that
had proven to be Japan's undoing were now encouraging its recovery.
Beginning in 1950, its former enemy now guardian, the United States,
was engaged in an undeclared proxy war against communist Russia and
China on the Korean peninsula. This time, Japan, for whom the contest
was of utmost concern, was spared the pain of direct involvement and
allowed, instead, to stand back and watch others wage war on its behalf.
Japan served as the launching pad for the American offensive, and Japanese factories were hastily engage to churn out equipment and supplies
at full capacity, its maritime industry to transport those goods to the war
zone, and its technicians and mechanics to do maintenance and repair.
The brutal conflict ended in stalemate in 1953, marking a change in the
tide of American fortune in Asia, and its sides, failing to resolve their
underlying difference in vision for the future of the Korean peninsula,

continue to this day to glare at each other from behind concrete walls and barbed wire across the demilitarized thirty-eighth parallel.

Not only did the Korean conflict stimulate Japan's economic recovery, it also hastened the restitution, in 1951, of Japanese sovereignty and the end of the American occupation. For many in the prime of life, these were heady times, and in 1956, a political mantra claimed "We are no longer in the postwar era." Fast-forwarding to the first decade of the twenty-first century, popular Japanese culture, as reflected in its movies, television dramas, and novels, has seen a wave of nostalgia for the 1950s as a time of naive unbridled optimism, and in many respects, this characterization is not inaccurate. Nevertheless, the shadow of the nation's inglorious recent past still lingered, and the real work of reconstruction had only just begun. Not until the middle of the next decade would Japan's resurgence begin to assume, in the eyes of international observers, the semblance of an economic miracle.

The heroes of Japan's reconstruction and that economic miracle are many, and to credit Nakamura Tempū over and above all others would be to overstate the case. That said, the surge in Tempūkai membership, especially among people of influence, is indicative of his reach. The society's archival membership rosters contain a virtual who's who of postwar industry, among them Kurata Chikara (1886–1969), president of Hitachi; Iida Seizō (1894–1976), president of Nomura Securities; Echigo Masakazu (1901–1991), president of Itochu; and Isano Masashi (dates unknown), president of Kawasaki Heavy Industries, to name but a few. Even among such company, however, one name stands out.

Matsushita Kōnosuke, founder of today's Panasonic Corporation, first met Nakamura Tempū in the early 1930s. Born in Wakayama Prefecture in 1894 into a family impoverished by his father's poor business speculations, Matsushita was sent away to Osaka at an early age to apprentice in a bicycle shop. His entire formal education consisted of four years of primary school and several years of night school classes in electrical science, but through a combination of diligence and good fortune, he stumbled into the burgeoning electric appliance industry.

At twenty-two years of age, with savings of 100 yen, the equivalent of about three months' salary, he left his employer to start his own company, converting his 4.5-mat—roughly, eighty square feet (7.5 square meters)—living room into a workshop; there, he and two employees manufactured light sockets, while he and his wife lived out of the flat's remaining, 2-mat room. The hardships of these early years now the stuff of legend, his business somehow survived and eventually began to prosper, and by 1922, at the age of twenty-seven, he owned his own factory and had fifty workers in his employ. The company was called Matsushita Electric and its registered brand name was National. One of its first commercial successes was an electric bicycle lamp that burned for thirty to forty hours, replacing conventional candle- or petroleum-lit alternatives. National soon became synonymous with affordable, durable hand-held electric devices, such as battery-powered lamps and electric irons. Then, in 1931, Matsushita Electric won a government-sponsored competition for innovation in radio design, propelling the National brand to a place of dominance in what proved to be the first generation of consumer electronics.

Somewhere around this time, Matsushita met Nakamura Tempū. The details of that first encounter are lost, but given that Matsushita had a weak physical constitution and was plagued by periods of sickness throughout his life, health concerns may have been what first attracted him to Tempū's teachings. The effect of his exposure to those teachings, however, is dramatically evident in a radical change in his focus as a business leader. To the astonishment of employees and customers alike, he declared "Harmony between corporate profit and social justice" to be Matsushita Electric's corporate slogan and issued a corporate mission statement: "Recognizing our responsibilities as industrialists, we will devote ourselves to the progress and development of society and the well-being of people through our business activities, thereby enhancing the quality of life throughout the world."[2] Then, in 1932, he called a company-wide meeting to reveal a 250-year corporate plan. The plan was divided into ten phases, each phase subsequently broken down into construction, application, and fulfillment subphases, and its intended purpose and goal was "to remove poverty from the earth."[3] Profitability as a force for justice and social good was to be made a core objective of Matsushita's management philosophy.

The war years, beginning with Japan's invasion of China in 1937, interrupted Matsushita's plans just as it did the nation's. Matsushita Electric, by now a multidivisional enterprise of almost 4,000 employees, was first conscripted to manufacture wireless and radar equipment for aircraft. Before long, however, the military's demands almost entirely subsumed the company's operations and extended even to wooden ship and airplane building. These wartime concessions were made under duress and went largely uncompensated, leaving the company saddled with staggering debt when the war ended.

Adding insult to injury, the American-led occupation then proceeded to freeze all of the company's remaining assets and to purge its management. The GHQ, in an unintended but perverse expression of praise, afforded Matsushita Electric—the company started out of Matsushita's living room on a song and a prayer just shy of thirty years earlier—status as a *zaibatsu*, an industrial conglomerate of the order of Mitsui, Mitsubishi, and Sumitomo, and added the Matsushitas to a list of zaibatsu families. Over the following four years, Matsushita made more than fifty trips from Osaka to plead his case at the GHQ offices in Tokyo, while his second-in-charge made an additional one hundred visits to submit supporting documents. Matsushita was willing to accept personal culpability and to relinquish management if that would allow the company to survive, but the company's labor union began its own supplications to the GHQ, collecting over 15,000 signatures in his defense. Ultimately, the decisions against both Matsushita and his company were rescinded.

In the heat of these developments, in November 1946, Matsushita founded the PHP Institute. PHP, the acronym standing for Peace and Happiness through Prosperity, took up the work of cultivating visionary and morally accountable leadership in industry, the work for which Matsushita is now best known. The closeness in timing between Matsushita's launch of PHP and Tempū's resurrection of the Tempūkai could not have been entirely coincidental. PHP began publication of its monthly magazine the following April, and the magazine became a vehicle for the exposure of Tempū's teachings as well Matsushita's. Matsushita would publish some forty-five books and become a major figure in the world of business leadership philosophy. Not to diminish Matsushita's brilliance as an original thinker, Nakamura Tempū's influence is nevertheless visible throughout his writings, including, for example, Matsushita's emphasis on the importance of spiritual growth and the cultivation of the quality of *sunao*, original or unbiased innocence, translated on the PHP Institute's website as "the untrapped mind." PHP also became and continues to be a major publisher of transcripts of Nakamura Tempū's talks and of other books about Nakamura Tempū and his teachings written by his students.

The story of Matsushita Electric's comeback and the subsequent phenomenal success of first the National brand and later the Panasonic brand is tantamount in many ways to the story of Japan's postwar recovery. Living and working in Osaka in the 1970s, I was always struck by the reverence with which the name Matsushita Kōnosuke was spoken by all, even by ordinary people. The town's most favored son, he was commonly referred to as *shōbai-no kami-sama*, "the (living) patron god of trade."

Matsushita lived to the age of ninety-five, dying in 1989. Matsushita Electric is now known the world over as the Panasonic Corporation, and the PHP Institute continues to thrive. Consistent with Matsushita's ideals, PHP, nonprofit by charter, operates on the proceeds from its publications and programs and without subsidy from Panasonic.

By the 1950s and 1960s, Matsushita Electric, employing tens of thousands of workers, was one of the largest employers in Osaka. To be a Matsushita employee was to be part of the founder's extended family and to be familiar with his philosophy; from lower-level managers on up, anyone with any level of authority, as well as many without, read his writings and strove to emulate his ideals. Inevitably, many of these same people were drawn to the teachings of Nakamura Tempū, for whom Matsushita Kōnosuke reserved the title "great teacher," and consequently, Matsushita

Electric was prominently represented in not only the Osaka Tempūkai but also neighboring Kobe and Kyoto chapters.

Small in stature, Nakamura Tempū projected a larger-than-life presence that filled whatever room he spoke in. His authenticity and energy were infectious, while his distinctive, gravelly voice carried through walls and closed doors. In his seventies in the early 1950s, he was widely acknowledged to be the living incarnation of everything he taught—not just the promise of what was possible through practice of his methods but the proof of it.

The Tempūkai's main venue, Gokokuji, has a spacious, gravel-covered ground that allowed for large outdoor assemblies and outdoor training sessions. It also has a separate hall, the Gekkōden, that could accommodate crowds of several hundred, and here, during the first week of every month, Tempū conducted a five-evening seminar. Sessions would begin promptly at six o'clock and go until eight. The first evening consisted of an introductory lecture, in which he would give an overview of the principle concepts of his mind-body system; this was his invitation to first-timers to pursue his teachings to their practical application. Those who returned— and most did—would then, on the second, third, and fourth evenings, be taken into the heart of his teachings, the "how to do" of mental and physical positivity. The final evening would consist of a lecture on a theme of his own choosing, usually one pertaining to some facet of his current research or thinking.

This lecture series was held month after month throughout the year, always with new faces as well as regular repeaters. The Tempūkai neither advertised nor engaged in publicity, and as a matter of policy, newcomers were required to show sponsorship from a current member; Tempū was adamantly opposed to any method of solicitation other than word of mouth, that word to be disseminated only by those who valued his teachings and who had been significantly affected by them. Once inside, however, people of all walks of life mingled freely, people of power and distinction sitting beside and brushing shoulders with ordinary citizens.

Furthermore, anomalous to chauvinistic societal norms, a quarter to a third of the participants were women.

Soon, Tempū was also delivering this weeklong seminar at regional Tempūkai chapters, requiring that he be away from Tokyo for the better part of the month. Kyoto, Osaka, and Kobe chapters dated from before the War; Nagoya and Kamakura, from the 1950s; and Fukuoka, from the early 1960s. All still active, the society, according to its website, has an aggregate of some twenty chapters today.

The preeminent event on the Tempūkai calendar, however, was the summer intensive training session (shūrenkai), or, as I have chosen to call it, the summer retreat. Held at the height of summer heat in August, it was a twelve-day affair, beginning with three evening sessions followed by nine straight days of full immersion in the theory and practice of shin-shin tōitsu-dō. In Tokyo, it was held at Gokokuji, and of the hundreds of participants, many came from too far away to commute and slept at the temple on futons laid out side-by-side in orderly rows in the temple's large halls. Culturally, Japan and the Japanese have a special proclivity for group endeavors, but the summer retreats took that proclivity to new heights, everyone pitching in under the direction of the Tempūkai's seniors with merriment and can-do optimism.

The summer retreat was also conducted in multiple locations, including Kyoto, Osaka, Kobe, and Nagoya, and Tempū's summers, from the

Nakamura Tempū, in 1962 at age eighty-five, leading summer retreat participants at Gokokuji in tōitsu-shiki undōhō, the mind-body unification exercise routine

(with permission from the Tempu Society, a nonprofit public interest foundation)

second half of July through August, were consumed by these camps and by travel from one to the next.

Dress code at these retreats was white. At a glance, and but for the absence of tennis courts, they might have been mistaken for tennis camps, with the men in white shorts and white short-sleeved shirts—the shirts, they would remove to go bare-chested during the day—and the women in white skirts and blouses. Outside, under the hot sun, all would affix white headbands bearing the Tempūkai insignia to keep sweat out of their eyes. Period photos show the hundreds of participants standing in perfect formation in rows separated by two arm-lengths laterally and one arm-length front and back; in these formations, they would practice Tempū's breathing and exercise routines in unison under the direction of leaders—often Tempū himself—standing in front.

The retreats were both intense and high-energy, beginning first thing in the morning with Tempū greeting the assembly outside in a piercing voice from the temple deck with, "Is everyone well?" To which the only acceptable answer was "Yes" in an equally loud and vigorous voice. Tempū would then lead in the recitation of his "Declaration of Rebirth," a statement of commitment to actualize joy, gratitude, and conduct worthy of humanity in one's daily life, followed by his "Daily Oath" (see chapter 13) and his "Pranayama Invocation":

> *I recognize that my vitality as a living human being is impregnated by the vast and supreme universe's all-pervasive, singularly creative energy. In taking up this privileged and closely guarded practice of pranayama, I willfully but gratefully partake of this energy through my breath. May it fill me from my internal organs to my extremities.*[4]

The Pranayama Invocation would be immediately followed by kokyū sōren, Tempū's "breath drills," and tōitsu-shiki undōhō, his "mind-body unification exercise routine" (both described in chapter 13). He would finish with *sekkyoku taisō*, his physically demanding "positivity exercise routine," by the end of which all would have broken into a strong sweat.

The morning outdoor assembly then moved indoors. Tempū's morning lecture series was titled "Meditations on Truth." As always, he spoke spontaneously and without script, drawing on his vast repertoire of stories, especially those from his years in the Himalayan foothills under the tutelage of Kariappa, and exploring questions of man's place in the universe and the imminence of universal truth and spiritual reality in human life. He would then lead the group in the practice of anjō-daza (chapter 7), followed by simple but powerful exercises demonstrating, while also allowing participants to experience, the power of will; one of these, for example, involved striking a wooden chopstick, held in one hand by a fellow practitioner, with a six-inch (fifteen-centimeter) strand of twisted tissue paper in such a way that the chopstick was broken into two.

The morning would end with Tempū's self-massage, a brilliantly effective, self-administered therapy that relieves tensions and enhances mental alertness.[5] Participants would then break for lunch, all seated at long tables set out in the temple's hall. Lunch was followed by skits or comedy routines performed by Tempūkai volunteers, more often than not with Tempū taking the lead. Tempū was a great believer in the restorative power of laughter, and these skits inevitably challenged members of the audience and worked to the regalement of all.

The afternoon sessions would typically begin with a second anjō-daza session. This would be followed by sensitivity training or "telepathy" exercises, about which I will say more below. All would then spill out into the temple yard for practice and coaching in the execution of the breath drills and exercise routines, ending with the assembly jogging in mass around the perimeter of the temple grounds, the joggers chanting *"wasshoi, wasshoi,"* an invigorating but meaningless refrain typically heard at Shinto festivals.

Thus ended the day's official activities, but following the evening meal, participants would often congregate in discussion groups or breakout into study sessions.

As well as very full days, the retreat promised a complete introduction to Tempū's system: by the last day, every participant would have received everything he or she needed to continue the system's practices—and, as Tempū would say, to continue to reinvent his or her health and happiness—after returning to normal life. And as well as turning out hundreds of new initiates each year, these retreats also brought together many long-time practitioners; Tempūkai veterans, people who had already proven to their satisfaction the efficacy of Tempū's system, would return year after year to review and deepen their understanding, as well as to come together with like-minded people.

Stories abound of Tempū's uncanny abilities of second sight. Sasaki Masando told me that Tempū-sensei would sometimes, as a source of amusement, guess the amount of loose change Sasaki was carrying in his pocket, stating both the number of coins and their denominations. He would counsel businessmen on whether or not to go forward with a particular business venture, and he would alert expectant mothers to the sex of their unborn with unfailing accuracy. Many people have stories of Tempū predicting the arrival of unanticipated visitors or of saying, out of the blue, that so-and-so just passed away. All these abilities, he insisted, were available to him not because he was special but because he was ordinary; they were available to anyone and everyone. All that was required was that one slip easily and effortlessly into the quiet space of no mind; in that quietude, such abilities, he said, would automatically appear.

Cultivation of the ability to access that space, through the practice of anjō-daza, was the retreat's most central purpose and feature. Spiritual schools the world over will attest to the increased efficacy of meditation when practiced in groups, and the Tempūkai retreats were no exception: a kind of self-reinforcing resonance is established between meditators in a group, and the larger the group, the more powerful that resonance becomes. Attendance at summer retreats I attended in 2004 and 2005, while not of the order of 1950s and 1960s numbers, was upward of 200, and when engaged in anjō-daza together, that resonance was palpable. I recall, upon opening my eyes after anjō-daza, a sense that the air in the room had been purified; it was imbued with a crispness and seemed to sparkle with energy. "This must be," I remember thinking, "what the Indians mean by the word *prana*."

At the retreats anjō-daza is often followed by game-like exercises intended to demonstrate and to allow participants to experience the extra-sensory dimensions of human perception. Tempū used the English word "telepathy" to describe these phenomena, but "extrasensory perception" is perhaps more accurate. As an example, in one of the practices, the room is broken into groups of about eight, each group, by simple rearrangement of cushions, sitting in a circle. Next, members of each group produce small objects they have on their person—a ball-point pen, a wristwatch, car keys, a pair of glasses, and so on—until a collection of seven or eight such objects has been assembled and laid out, usually on a cloth or towel, on the floor in the center of the circle. One person then chooses or is chosen to be "it" and turns his or her back to the group, while the other members nonverbally select and agree on one of the objects on the floor in front of them. "It" is invited to turn around and to rejoin the circle. He or she sets about identifying the object chosen, simply by passing his hand over each. If so inclined, he may also pick up an object and hold it briefly in hand. When he thinks he knows the correct answer, he holds the object up and shows it to the group, who either nod or shake their heads.

The other members of the group are, of course, to deliver no verbal or visible signals while that person is at work; in any event, he or she is focused on the objects on the floor and is not watching their facial expressions. The other members are, however, to react internally. When "it" passes a hand over any object other than the one chosen, they are not to register any emotion, either positive or negative; they are to remain stone cold. But, when his or her hand passes over the object chosen, they are to light up inside. They are to elicit feelings of rosy delight. They may wish to accompany the feeling with verbal thoughts, such as "That's it! That's it!" but such verbal reinforcement is not necessary; the emotional component of the response is the key ingredient.

"It" is allowed unlimited attempts and continues until he or she correctly identifies the object chosen. Then the role of "it" passes to the next person in the circle. The exercise is repeated and the role of "it" continues to pass on around the circle until each participant has taken a turn. Thereafter, the exercise continues, the role of "it" circulating as many times as can be accommodated before time is called from the front of the room.

What of the results? The first time I participated in this exercise, the initial run around the circle served as something of a warmup; one or two people identified the object correctly on the first try, others, on the second or third. From then on, however, we were on a roll. We went around another four or five times with about ninety percent accuracy on the first try and 100 percent by the second. As "it," my personal experience was not of any particular sensation or cognizant recognition of clues; rather, I would find my hand moving toward a particular object and picking it up almost without conscious direction. One of the main factors contributing to the improved rate of success was, after one or two correct selections, the boosting of confidence and trust in one's instincts; the more detached one became from conscious attempts to either "sense" or "figure out" which object your fellow group members had chosen, and the more one allowed oneself to be guided by impulse, the better the results. I for one came away with a new appreciation for the potential of the mind: it is capable of far more than we normally assume.

Another exercise performed at summer retreats runs as follows. A pre-selected demonstrator—in this case, an experienced Tempūkai member—is led out of the room. Inside the room, the remaining several hundred participants move to the room's periphery, creating a large open space in the middle. Then, by consensus, they script a list of injunctions—something that might look like this:

1. Go to the right side of the room, take one cushion from the stack of cushions in the corner, and place it in the center of the room.

2. Go to the left side of the room, take a chair from the stack of chairs, and place it approximately a yard (one meter) away from the cushion facing away from the cushion.

3. Go to the left side of the room, stand in front of Ms. Nishibei, seated in the front row, and motion to her to come forward. Lead her to the cushion. Have her sit on the cushion, facing away from the chair.

4. Go to the right side of the room, have Mr. Matsuoka come forward, and lead him to the chair. Seat him in the chair.

5. Have Mr. Matsuoka stand up again and lead him over to where Ms. Nishibei is seated.

6. Have Ms. Nishibei stand up.

7. Have Mr. Matsuoka and Ms. Nishibei shake hands.

The injunctions are written out on an easel pad or whiteboard placed at the front of the room where it can be seen by all. The demonstrator is then led back into the room, blindfolded. A second demonstrator, also someone with a solid history of Tempūkai experience, acts as demonstrator one's eyes; he or she makes light hand contact with the demonstrator's hand. The leader may, by touch, turn the demonstrator in a certain direction or coax him or her when he or she gets stuck; but for the most part, other than light hand contact, the demonstrator is on his own. He sets about, based solely on powers of intuition, to reconstruct the planned scenario according to the script.

I have seen this demonstrated on two separate occasions with different scripts and different participants. Inevitably, false steps occurred along the way, but when they did, the demonstrator soon realized he or she had made a mistake and corrected it. On each occasion, in the end, the scripted scenario was faithfully enacted in the order recorded.

The purpose of these demonstrations is not to convince the skeptical—there are too many obvious opportunities for rigging to satisfy a totally disinterested observer, not the least of which is the leader's hand contact and what information might thus be communicated—but rather, to tease and challenge the beliefs of an already receptive audience. Performed in a space of mutual trust, the demonstrations' success is due as much to the alignment of the audiences' intentions as to the demonstrators' sensitivity.

Another exercise performed almost as a rite of passage and quintessential to the summer retreat experience is the breaking of green bamboo. This is less a demonstration of extrasensory powers than a test of will. When I attended, it was performed on the last day of the retreat, but I understand that in Tempū's day, in order to accommodate the larger numbers of participants, it may have been broken into multiple sessions over several days. Bamboo, and especially green bamboo, is extremely strong and pliable; by way of example, it is used (although not so often now as in days past) all over Asia to build scaffolding around constructions sites. The point is, not only does it not break easily, but more importantly, everyone knows that it does not break easily, and consequently, to tell someone to break it is to challenge their beliefs.

Those beliefs and not the bamboo, Tempū would have us understand, are all that is in the way. Bales of green bamboo sticks, 1 to 1.5 inches (three to four centimeters) in diameter, pre-cut into lengths of about four feet (130 centimeters), are brought into the hall, and one at a time, with all of the other participants watching, each participant is given the opportunity to break one of these sticks in half using a wooden sword. The setup may occur in any one of several variations, but a typical one is as follows:

Strips of paper, perhaps three inches (eight centimeters) wide and ten inches (twenty-five centimeters) long are prepared, each with a slit in the middle; the slit does not extend to the paper's edge on either end, so that the paper constitutes a fragile ring or band.

Two volunteers stand facing each other about five feet (1.5 meters) apart, each holding a cleaver-like Japanese kitchen knife in front of him or her at about chest height, the edge of the blade pointing up.

Over each of the two cooking knives is hung one of the slit pieces of paper, the upper end of the slit resting on the cutting edge of the knife.

The ends of one of the bamboo sticks are then inserted into the same slits. The stick now hangs in suspension between the two knife-holding volunteers at about waist height and secured only by two flimsy pieces of paper, each supported by the cutting edge of a sharp kitchen knife.

With these preparations complete, a participant is handed a wooden sword of the type used in Japanese martial arts training. The wooden sword, for those unfamiliar, is a blunt instrument: without an actual blade capable of cutting, it amounts to little more than a hardwood stick.

Mention of wooden swords may suggest that, since it is Japan, most of the people participating in this exercise will know something about how to use the implement they are handed. More often than not, however, this is not the case: at the retreats I have attended, the vast majority of participants have had little or no martial arts experience, and many were apparently holding a wooden sword in their hands for the first time. Furthermore, I was told by one of the retreat organizers, people with some kendo or other sword-art experience are apt to have more difficulty than those who have not.

Directly under the suspended bamboo stick is placed a sitting cushion to catch the falling bamboo stick, whether broken or whole. The instructions I was given the first time I engaged in this exercise, and which proved effective, were to ignore the bamboo stick and to think about striking the cushion beneath it.

There is, of course, nothing mystical about this exercise. The laws of physics will tell you that the force generated by the end of a swinging wooden stick, the sword, when delivered to a single point in the middle of the bamboo, is more than sufficient to break that bamboo in half. The paper strips and the cooking knives are, from the physical perspective, red herrings, since the bamboo exerts little force against them when it receives the blow.

The variable, however, is the person behind the sword delivering the blow. The least hesitancy on his or her part will result in a strike that is less than clean and that does not deliver all of its force to a single point of contact. If the line of the falling sword is not the perpendicular line of gravity, then its force will transfer to one or the other end of the stick, causing the paper strips supporting it to tear. Likewise, if there is any uncertainty in the strike, if it reflects any hesitancy on the part of the striker, then it may either bounce slightly or slide slightly on contact, thereby distributing its force and causing the stick to tear free at one or both ends.

Conversely, over-confidence or false-confidence will have much the same effect. The person with prior sword experience may be overly concerned with technique and more intent upon executing proper form than upon actually cutting the bamboo. Or he may be so sure of himself, given his years of sword training, that his focus is compromised.

Even those who fail on the first try can usually be coached to a place of successful completion by the second or third. Collective willpower also plays a large part, for with each turn, the level of confidence increases among the observers whose turn has yet to come, as the thought that "if everyone else is doing it, then certainly I can do it too" gains ever more traction inside the room. Of the hundreds I have watched perform this exercise, most for the first time, only two failed to complete it within three attempts.

The summer retreats were, in this way, robust in both experiential practice and theoretical teaching. They were also uplifting and joyful, prompting comradery and much, much laughter. Those in which I have participated were, in concession to the demands of modern, working life, of shorter duration than in Tempū's day, occurring over five days spread over two successive weekends, and from period photographs, I can see that the earlier ones were richer in their range of activities, including the likes of pickup baseball games, slapstick performances, and, of course, Tempū's demonstrations of his formidable skill at drawing and cutting with a live blade. Nevertheless, the modern-day retreats in their abbreviated format still successfully convey the essence of Nakamura's teachings, and I count my participation in them to have been among the most richly rewarding and transformative experiences of my adult life.

Nakamura Tempū turned eighty in 1956, a milestone that, he concluded, gave him permission to address the topic of longevity. "Yes," he could now legitimately say for the first time, the practice of mind-body unification was conducive to the extension of life-span.

Toward the other end of the age spectrum, the first of the generations to be educated postwar were just coming of age. In a society whose elders were predominantly carrying scars and vestiges of trauma, the optimism and vitality of this up-and-coming new generation was a breath of fresh air. High school and college students destined, later in the century, to lead in a variety of fields, were attracted to his lectures in number.

Among this generation was Matsubara Naoko (Naoko Matsubara), an internationally acclaimed woodcut artist now living outside Toronto, Canada. Matsubara was born in 1937 in Kyoto, where her father served as head priest to the Kenkun Shrine, a major Shinto shrine established by the Emperor Meiji and dedicated to Oda Nobunaga, the seminal, sixteenth-century military ruler.

As a child of ten, Naoko was deeply affected by the death of her little brother just four months shy of his fourth birthday; like many, her family suffered severe food shortages during and after the War, and the adorable little boy, chronically malnourished, succumbed to the measles. Naoko, the second of four siblings, visited the boy's grave hundreds of times and avowed to live to the limits of her potential as a way to compensate for his loss.

Even more devastated, however, was her mother, who fell into a depression so deep that she lost her will to live. Fortunately, an understudy to her husband recommended that she attend a lecture being given by a man named Nakamura Tempū; this, she did, taking her three remaining children with her, for the first time in 1947. Naoko was too young to understand what was being said, but she could not help but notice the presence of the man behind the words and also felt a sense of sanctuary within the gathering. The family continued to attend as time would permit, and gradually, her mother turned herself around and regained her health.

As a student at the Kyoto Academy of Fine Arts from 1956 to 1960, Naoko was attracted again to the Tempūkai and began attending its events and gatherings regularly on her own. Intrigued by Tempū's stories, explanations, and humor, she applied herself to the study of his methods and integrated their practice into her daily routine. She now counts Tempū's insistence upon the importance of mental positivity as among the most significant influences on her life.

Matsubara remembers Tempū above all for his powers of concentration, powers that gave him the ability to do almost anything he put his mind to do. Retrospectively, she also appreciates him as an artist—not just in his calligraphic works, several of which hang in her house today, but also in the way he dressed and the way he conducted himself and manifested order and aesthetic sensibility in every aspect of his life.

After graduation, Matsubara traveled on a Fulbright Scholarship to Carnegie Mellon University in Pittsburgh, Pennsylvania. While there, she identified and consciously chose, out of all the many directions she could have pursued among the art, craft, and design fields, the wood-cut medium as that most conducive to her creativity. It was an inspired choice. She credits the prescience with which she was able to determine, at the age of just twenty-four, the entire future course of her artistic career to the mental and spiritual clarity she had cultivated under Tempū-sensei's tutelage.

One of her professors at Carnegie Mellon was Arnold Bank, an internationally acclaimed calligrapher of lasting influence on the art of letter design, and Naoko recalls being called upon by him to demonstrate Japanese calligraphy before the class. Taking up a large brush, she wrote out Tempū's Daily Oath (see chapter 13) in bold letters on an enormous piece of paper and then explained the meaning, line by line; teacher and students were deeply moved by both the demonstration and the message.

After obtaining her Master of Fine Arts degree from Carnegie Mellon in 1962, Matsubara returned to Japan by way of London and other points in Europe and renewed her association with the Tempūkai. Two years later, however, she traveled again to the United States to accept a teaching position at the Pratt Institute in New York. There, she also served as an assistant to Fritz Eichenberg, a leading denizen of the New York graphic arts community. One of the projects Matsubara worked on with Eichenberg was the publication of a comprehensive reference volume on the art of prints for Abrams Books; her association with this project, as well as a teaching engagement at the Graphic Art Centre, a Manhattan institution hosting exhibitions and lectures and promoting the exchange of ideas between visiting artists, immersed her in the world of prints and exposed her to many of the major international figures in the field. One of her first major successes was a UNESCO commission to create a woodcut print, *Inner Strength,* for the Geneva Peace Conference in 1967. Then, five summers spent working on Eichenberg's reference volume out of his residence on Nantucket gave rise to the publication of a book titled *Nantucket Woodcuts;* this was followed by *Boston Impressions* and *Solitude,* her acclaimed pictorial response to Henry David Thoreau's *Walden.* Between 1965 and 1971, she published a total of five books and one portfolio and held numerous solo shows in the United States, Holland, and Germany.

Professor Eichenberg, Matsubara says, was the only person during this period to take an active interest in her shin-shin tōitsu-dō practices, and he questioned her persistently about Nakamura Tempū; evidently, he sensed in her a spiritual substance that set her apart from his other students and wanted to know where it came from. Matsubara's explanations were subject to both her youth and her still limited command of English; "I could not fulfill his desire to know about Tempū's teachings," she says. Eichenberg died at age eighty-nine in 1990.

In 1972, Matsubara moved with her English husband, David Waterhouse, to Toronto. Then, in 1973, she suffered severe physical and emotional postpartum complications after the birth of the couple's first and only child. One of the manifestations of this distress was an unbearable homesickness for her native Kyoto. She found restitution, first, by falling back on Tempū's teachings, his words returning to her like an old friend, and second, in her art: she sharpened her woodcutter's blade and produced a series of exquisitely nostalgic images of her childhood, including Kyoto shrines, temples, gardens, street scenes, and artisans, such as Noh and Kabuki performers and dancing Maiko.

In 1986, a trip to Tibet precipitated both a new direction in her printmaking, characterized by a new and liberated sensitivity toward the use of color, and a ten-year project to express her experience of Tibet's natural beauty and spiritual heritage. The project culminated in the 1997 publication of twenty-seven prints under the title *Tibetan Sky,* to which the Dalai Lama contributed a forward.

Arlene Gehmacher, a curator at the Royal Ontario Museum, says "Matsubara continues to this day to challenge herself in her printmaking both technically and emotionally, her use of color, gesture, design, texture, and choice of paper all wedded for a superb aesthetic event forever suspended in the moment." Her works now belong to permanent collections in some of the world's most prestigious museums: the Albertina in Vienna, the British Museum, the Museum of Fine Arts in Boston, the Philadelphia Museum of Art, the Fogg Art Museum at Harvard University, the Haifa Museum in Israel, the Kyoto National Museum of Modern Art, the Royal Ontario Museum, the White House in Washington, DC, the Tokyo National Museum of Modern Art, and the Museum für Asiatische Kunst (Asian Art Museum) in Berlin, to name but a few.[6]

In 1962, the Tempūkai was formally recognized by the Japanese government as a nonprofit public foundation. The year before, in February, Yoshi, Tempū's wife of fifty-eight years, died at the age seventy-eight. Her gravestone stands beside his on the Nakamura family plot within the Gokokuji cemetery, and to its side is a stela inscribed with a verse in classical Chinese *(kanbun)* composed by Tempū:

The singular movement antecedent to heaven, the origin of spirit,
Is that without prior cause or intent which impels all of nature.
Human life and everything within its purview
Ultimately reduces back to this one great essence.[7]

Omi Kōji joined the Tempūkai at age thirty in January 1962. Omi, as the oldest of eight children in a Gunma Prefecture family living hand-to-mouth off of his father's manufacture and sale of wooden clogs, had surprised everyone in his second year in high school, just after the end of the war, by declaring he wanted to go to college. His family's objections were financial—they could not pay his tuition or support him—while those of his teachers were academic: Omi had shown little in the way of scholastic promise. But he threw himself into his studies with singular determination and successfully passed the entrance examination to the prestigious Hitotsubashi University in Tokyo. He also secured scholarship funding and worked part-time to earn living expenses. Then, after graduation, he married, secured a position in the Ministry of International Trade and Industry, and settled into a comfortable career as a civil servant.

In May 1961, just months after the birth of his first child, Omi developed tuberculosis. On extended leave from work and distraught with concern for his family's future, he was told by his herbalist to go to Gokokuji that evening to attend a lecture. There, the man at the front of the room told his audience, "The book of life has only one page; there is no page two. This is the first thing we need to consider. Death is human destiny, so it's up to us as humans to live, not in fear of death, but with gratitude for the gift of life, right now in the present, and to make that life meaningful and productive while it lasts."[8] The words were a wake-up call; Omi had never considered life from this perspective. Tempū went on to say, "Some people act as though, if things don't go well for them this time around, they will be given another chance in the Great Beyond. But even if there were a Great Beyond, were you to get there, it would no longer be the beyond. It would be the here and now. So there is no Great Beyond. The only chance we get is right now. If you are going to find answers to the challenges facing you, you need to do so right here, in this present life."[9]

Omi threw himself into the practice of Tempū's philosophy with the same singularity of purpose he had shown toward his studies for the Hitotsubashi entrance exam, but with greater urgency. Following the summer retreat in August, he returned to his physician for a checkup. His tuberculosis had disappeared. "Come back again in three months so that we can be sure," the incredulous doctor said to him. "To this day, I have never been back," Omi says with delight.

He also returned to work and, no longer content to take a back seat in matters of public policy, rededicated himself to civil service, taking on more and more responsibility and moving up through the ministry's ranks. Typical of Japanese institutions, public and private, during these years of accelerated economic growth, the typical workday extended from early morning to late at night, often beyond midnight. Even so, during all of the remaining seven years that Tempū was alive, Omi never once missed a monthly evening seminar series; he would skip out of the office at five-thirty to make it to Gokokuji by six and then return to work after the session ended at eight. He also attended the summer retreat without fail, a commitment he has continued to fulfill: with the exception of three summers during which he was posted to New York, Omi has, he says, made at least a one- or two-day appearance at every summer retreat since 1962 until the present.

In 1982, after serving in a variety of posts, ranging from consul general in New York and the Trade Policy Bureau's South Asia and Eastern Europe section chief to Science and Technology Agency Secretariat chief of general affairs, he resigned from the Ministry of International Trade and Industry to run for a lower house seat in the National Diet. The move was counter to the advice of almost everyone he knew in government, let alone family and friends. By now, a twenty-six-year veteran of civil service, Omi was a rookie politician, and furthermore, he was running as an independent. Yet, after mounting an underfunded but intensely feet-on-the-ground, door-to-door campaign in his native Gunma, he staged an upset victory. He went on to serve a distinguished twenty-six-year career—a duration equal to that of his time at the ministry—during which he held cabinet positions under several prime ministers, including that of minister of Science and Technology under Koizumi Junichirō and minister of Finance in Abe Shinzō's first administration in 2006–2007. In 2004, he founded the Science and Technology in Society forum, an international organization for the advancement of technological solutions to global problems, and continues to serve as its chairman. And in 2010, he was awarded the Grand Cordon of the Order of the Rising Sun by Emperor Akihito.

Omi is a frequently featured speaker at Tempūkai events, and he is apt to say at the beginning of his address, "I am not a politician who just happens to be a member of the Tempūkai. I am a Tempūkai member who became a politician. I owe everything to my acquaintance with Nakamura Tempū and his teachings." After leaving politics in 2008, he served for several years as Tempūkai chairman.

Among the few—perhaps only two[10]—Westerners to study directly under Nakamura Tempū was American Robert Frager. As a twenty-five-year-old student at Keio University in the spring of 1965, Frager first attended one of Tempū's lectures at the recommendation of a fellow aikido practitioner (Frager was also practicing aikido at the Aikikai's Hombu Dojo). He recalls taking a seat in a hall of about 500 participants and engaging in conversation, prior to the beginning of the program, with an elderly gentleman seated next to him; the man, he learned, had been a follower of Tempū's teachings since before the War. And incidentally, he said, he was also the aeronautical engineer who had designed the Japanese Zero.

When, upon the second evening of his attendance, Frager took a seat near the back of the hall, he was approached by one of the ushers and told that Tempū had asked he be moved forward to the front row. From then on, Frager always sat near the front of the room. Several months later, when presented with the opportunity, he asked Tempū why it was that he had had him moved to the front. Because, Tempū explained, as a young man, he had himself studied in the United States and Europe and understood that, compared to everyone else in the room, Frager was working doubly hard to understand what was being said; only natural, therefore, that he should be allowed to sit as close to the source of those words as possible. "Easy come, easy go," he said in his gruff voiced English— meaning that the converse was also true: the harder one works to acquire something, the more he is likely to take away in the end.

Frager became a regular attendee of Tempū's monthly lecture series and summer retreats, which he attended in 1966 and 1967. On several occasions, he traveled together with Tempū-sensei to other cities and also participated in a summer retreat in Kyoto. Or was it Nagoya or Kobe? He is not sure. He also read Tempū's writings, participated in smaller study and practice groups led by Tempū's senior students, and practiced what he was taught. On several occasions, he had the privilege of being a guest in Nakamura's home.

Frager returned to the United States early in 1968. Prior to his departure, however, Tempū authorized him to teach and disseminate shin-shin tōitsu-dō, making him, probably, the only Westerner to hold that distinction. Over the years, he says, he has taught elements of the shin-shin tōitsu-do system to his aikido students and even, early on, conducted shin-shin tōitsu-do retreats, feedback from which was overwhelmingly positive.

Frager remembers Tempū as the embodiment of shin-shin tōitsu-do, a man who absolutely practiced what he taught and who was the living, breathing evidence of his methods' efficacy. Then in his nineties, he had a vitality that defied conventional wisdom. One of his favorite tricks was, upon entering a restaurant, to ask the waitress to guess his age: answers sometimes placed him in his mid-forties, other times in his sixties, but never older. During the summer retreats, demandingly busy events that accounted for almost every moment of everyone's time, he would often go directly from several hours of lecturing to answering a long line of requests from attendees for calligraphy; these he would fulfill on the spot, taking but a split second to reflect upon what had been requested before executing it in deliberate, impeccable brush strokes.

In 1975, Frager was a frustrated junior faculty member at the University of California, Santa Cruz, attempting to generate enthusiasm for the new field of transpersonal psychology. In its traditional guise, psychology, the study of mind and behavior, takes the position that spiritual and transcendent aspects of human experience, since they do not lend themselves to empirical research, fall outside its purview; transpersonal psychology seeks to reclaim those aspects as legitimate domains worthy of study. Or, to put the case more assertively, it contends that any study of mind and behavior exclusive of those aspects is incomplete. The Santa Cruz psychology department, like those of most contemporary institutions, was unsympathetic to this contention, and Frager could see he was never going to be granted tenure.

"Maybe what you need to do, Bob," a fellow professor suggested, "is to start your own university." But for his exposure to the teachings of Naka-mura Tempū, Frager says, he would never have taken the suggestion seriously. He had no training or experience as a school administrator, nor did he have the entrepreneurial skills that go along with starting and financing a new institution and then attracting students to it. But then, he had been told, over and over, by both Tempū and his senior students, that all human beings are endowed with more or less the same basic mental and physical faculties, and that, therefore, there is no reason any human being should doubt his or her ability to do something another human being has already proven possible. Forty years later, transpersonal psychology is a recognized academic discipline; Frager is regarded as one of its pioneers; and the school he founded in Palo Alto, California, originally called the Institute of Transpersonal Psychology, now, Sofia University, considered its leading graduate institution.

What he had not been told, Frager acknowledges, was how much hard work and heartache he would encountered along the way. But even then, amid the work and heartache, the power to conceive of eventual success, a power cultivated largely through his exposure to the person of Nakamura Tempū and to his teachings, was what carried him through.

In April 1968, the Tempū Kaikan, a newly constructed multistory head-quarters building standing to the left of the entrance to Gokokuji, was inaugurated. Then, in November of the same year, the Tempūkai commemorated its fiftieth anniversary. Nakamura announced at the ceremony that he was stepping down as chairman; his son-in-law, Yasutake Sadao, was named his successor. "To use the heavens as an example," Tempū told his audience, "the earth turns but the sun and moon remain the same. I taught you to look at the moon by pointing to it. Tell this to all our members throughout the country: Don't look at the finger, look at the moon. Whether it's me doing the pointing or Yasutake, the moon is the same."

Twenty days later, on the evening of November 30, he said to his daughter and son-in-law, "I'm going to sleep now. Please watch over me." While the Yasutakes sat in vigil, massaging his feet, he drew his last breath at 1:55 in the morning. The date was December 1, 1968. He was ninety-two years old.

EPILOGUE: THE LEGACY

In 1968, at the inauguration of the newly constructed Tempūkai head-quarters building, the Tempū Kaikan, Tempū told those gathered, "No one has been a more earnest practitioner of the mind-body unification method than me. That's the only reason why there is no one abler than me to communicate these teachings in a way that moves people. Therefore, since there is no Tempū heir apparent, it's my desire that you make of this Tempū Kaikan a hall of learning to which people can come to study the mind-body unification method, each on his own."[1]

His words were heard by many as an admission of defeat. More than one attendee has described Tempū as appearing more dejected on this occasion than on any other. After all, he had bet everything on the proposition that his mind-body unification method was practical and accessible in a way that other spiritual teachings were not, and he had done so with the expectation that someone—perhaps even several—among his many enterprising and highly intelligent younger students would seize the moment, take advantage of the head start he was giving them, and overtake him, both in understanding and in passion for making these teachings known to the world. But now, in the face of the imminent reality that he was not long for this life, when he turned around to look behind, he saw no one bringing up the rear. Just what, he had to wonder, had he achieved? Were he and his teachings to be remembered only for this handsome building, one among many on Tokyo's busy streets?

The problem is classic among pioneers of human knowledge. Those who blaze new paths of inquiry and establish new domains of under-standing—new frontiers of possibility—often enter very lonely territory.

By venturing out in front of the pack, they sometimes disappear from it over the horizon. Moreover, they often end up objects of idolization rather than emulation. This was certainly true of Moses, the Buddha, the Christ, and the Prophet Muhammad. It could also be said of any number of other luminaries: Sophocles, Plotinus, Leonardo da Vinci, William Shakespeare, Ralph Waldo Emerson, Jiddu Krishnamurti, and Nelson Mandela are but a random few of the names that come to mind.[2] All died with little assurance their works had served humanity or would long survive them, and not one of them left behind a successor adequate to the role of filling his shoes.[3]

The point to be made is that, in the light of posterity, of course their works have survived them. These men have, each to a greater or lesser extent, affected the shape of the world as we currently know it. But they have done so in ways they themselves would find surprising if not unfathomable. Such is the nature of human progress.

Based on its records, the Tempūkai cites the round figure of 100,000 as the total number of persons instructed directly by Nakamura Tempū during his lifetime. Among them were members of the imperial family, sitting parliamentary ministers, entrepreneurs and leaders of industry, cultural "living treasures," Order of Cultural Merit Award recipients, sumo champions, professional athletes, and Olympic gold medalists, as well as doctors, lawyers, entertainers, actors, writers, and martial artists. So, while the world has yet to, and may never, see another teacher quite the likes of Nakamura Tempū, his work has survived him in that of his many protégés—in the writings of writers like Uno Chiyo, in the management philosophy of entrepreneurs like Matsushita Kōnosuke, in the public service of political leaders like Omi Koji, in the art of artists like Naoko Matsubara, in the martial arts of teachers like Tōhei Koichi and Tada Hiroshi, and so on; the examples are legion.

Furthermore, the allure of Tempū's philosophy did not wane in the years following his death. In the 1980s, edited transcripts of his talks published by the Japan Management Consultants Association under the title *Seikō-no Jitsugen* (The Realization of Success) became a best seller. And in 1988, seventy years after its inception, the Tempūkai added the one-millionth name to its cumulative membership roster.

Among those to cite Nakamura Tempū's teachings as a major influence is Inamori Kazuo, the charismatic founder of the Kyocera Corporation. Inamori's example is especially notable because, even though he was born in 1932 and consequently came into his prime while Tempū and his Tempūkai were at the peak of their activity, he never met Tempū nor ever heard him speak in person: his acquaintance with the philosophy and practice of mind-body unification came entirely through Tempū's writings.

Like Matsushita Kōnosuke (see chapter 16), a personal mentor, Inamori came from disadvantaged beginnings and rose through diligence and hard work, facing one challenge after another, to become one of Japan's most successful entrepreneurs. And like Matsushita, he has written prolifically and has contributed to management philosophy through the exposition of his Amoeba System of management. In 2010, at the age of seventy-seven, he was drafted by leaders in government, finance, and industry to assume the reins of Japan Airlines, then under court bankruptcy protection; within two years, he successfully engineered the company's turnaround and relisting on the Tokyo Stock Exchange.

Human knowledge is not, as it is sometimes described, a fixed repository—not a library where new titles are constantly added to old ones already on the shelves—but rather, a living, breathing social and cultural phenomenon. Like history itself, knowledge is subject to constant revision, reinterpretation, and reframing within the context of the present; for evidence, one need only look to the Bible and Shakespeare's plays and then consider the extent to which they have morphed in meaning and significance under the weight of countless generations of interpretations placed on them. Such is the nature of transmission.

Like all things human, transmission is messy. Parts get lost, parts get added, mistakes are made, new insights emerge, new teachings supersede old. But on the whole, just as wisdom, as a product of maturity, almost always eventually supersedes impetuosity, so humanity as a whole becomes ever more knowing and enlightened. It is useful to remember, as we take stock of the confusion and chaos that reigns in the current day, that we are living in an age and at a point in time better informed and more enlightened than any so far in history, and that, barring a nuclear winter or total ecological collapse, the present, as the sum total of all that has gone before, will always be fuller than the past.

Nakamura Tempū's teachings, I would argue, have become part of the modern Japanese cultural fabric. The idea that positive attitude should contribute to positive results is certainly not unique to Nakamura Tempū; it long predates him in Japan, just as it does internationally. However, it is also true that Nakamura's particular expression of that idea has had far-reaching effects. My wife and I keep abreast of popular Japanese culture through Japanese television (available to us in the U.S. through cable subscription), and optimism in the face of adversity is a common theme propagated in popular drama. Again, to point to Nakamura Tempū as the unique source of that theme would be to claim too much; however, its expression in television drama, even if watered down and sentimentalized, often reflects language first used by him more than fifty years ago.

Past precedent lives on and affects the present, biologist and author Rupert Sheldrake says, through what he calls "morphic resonance," the enactment of morphogenetic fields. A biological morphogenetic field is one that retains imprints of biological form and structure and imparts them to subsequent generations. In much the same way, human culture is also morphogenetic: our thoughts and ideas are shaped and influenced by the culture we inhabit, and we are susceptible to ideas and beliefs depending on their resonance. Ideas of greater integrity—those that cover more bases and are more inclusive—it would seem reasonable to presume, resonate at a higher frequency and therefore have a deeper and more lasting effect on collective memory. But regardless of the exact nature of the phenomenon or the words used to describe it, Tempū's teachings, fair to say, have had a subliminal but lasting effect on the hearts and minds of many more people than those who ever knew or know of him by name.

On March 11, 2011, northeastern Japan was rocked by a magnitude 9.0 earthquake. A massive tsunami, topping 130 feet (40 meters) in some locations, destroyed much of the northeastern coast, killing close to 20,000 people. It also disabled a nuclear power plant, causing meltdown in two of its reactors and the propagation of lethal levels of radiation over a wide area.

Natural disasters are nothing new in Japan. The Japanese archipelago sits on the Ring of Fire, atop numerous major fault lines, and in the natural path of the typhoons that come spinning up out of the tropics every autumn; volcanic eruptions, earthquakes, tsunamis, and typhoons have been constants throughout Japanese history, their effects on cultural memory having done much to foster resilience and an adaptability among its inhabitants. Just sixteen years prior to 2011, the city of Kobe and much of Osaka were decimated by the Great Hanshin earthquake, and as I write these words, Kumamoto Prefecture is reeling from a continuing succession of severe tremors. There have been no fewer than twenty-five major earthquakes (magnitude 7.0 or greater) in Japan within the past twenty years.

But the 2011 Tōhoku earthquake and tsunami was a disaster of a different order, one of sufficient magnitude to bring most modern nations, economically and socially, to their knees. The World Bank has declared it the costliest natural disaster in world history to date. It paralyzed the Tokyo metropolitan area, the largest in the world, for several days, sending shock waves into global markets, and it generated an evacuee population numbering in the hundreds of thousands that needed to be immediately housed, fed, and cared for. In a nation of 127 million, everyone was affected; those who did not experience the tremors firsthand had relatives, classmates, or coworkers who either did or had immediate family or associates who did.

Vivid video footage was televised worldwide, garnering international sympathy and support, and also spotlighting the orderly determination of the Japanese people. But long after the short span of public attention had been appropriated by the unfolding of the Arab Spring and other world events, the hardships associated with this disaster continue. Five years later, the people of northeastern Japan are still dealing with the repercussions of that fateful day. Many tens of thousands continue to live in cramped, temporary housing; hundreds of thousands continue to mourn and to cope with the trauma of loss—of parents, of grandparents, of siblings, of spouses, of children, of friends and neighbors and teachers and students. Centuries-old social support systems were swept away when entire villages were carried out to sea. The plant at Fukushima is still burning, still leaking radiation.

Despite all of this and more, northeastern Japan is coming back. The recovery is, in many ways, more extraordinary, both in speed and in scale, than the nation's phoenix-like rebirth after World War II. Massive amounts of rubble and debris has somehow been dealt with. Entire towns are being reengineered and reconstructed, some in new locations. Infrastructure is being repaired and has been restored to provisional functionality; municipal services resumed; and schools and hospitals put back in service, even if out of temporary facilities.

Even the much maligned Fukushima disaster is gradually—step by step—being brought under control. This, in and of itself, is no small miracle. The meltdown brought a large portion of the Japanese archipelago within a hair's breadth of being rendered uninhabitable for many hundreds of thousands of years, and in the aftermath, fingers have been pointed every which way to assign blame for the plant's malfunction—not to mention questions concerning the wisdom of building nuclear reactors in regions prone to seismic activity in the first place—as well as for mistakes made during the initial days of the response. But confronting the impossible circumstances created by this disaster has demanded extraordinary courage and resolve; to those who are critical—and there is a plethora of uninformed opinions and holier-than-thou criticisms running around on the internet—I would only offer a challenge to walk a mile in the others' shoes.

When put to the test, we humans are surprisingly resilient. Humanity has survived ice ages, droughts, famines, epidemics, and countless rounds of war, genocide, and persecution. Coming back is what we do best. Were that we were better at seizing the opportunities of the future and generating our fate rather than simply reacting to it.

The Japanese response to the 2011 Tōhoku earthquake, tsunami, and nuclear disaster provides valuable lessons, in terms of both what worked and what did not work, for the rest of the world. Many of these lessons are purely tactical and logistic. But to the extent that Japan's comeback has been remarkable for its speed and efficiency, that nation's cultural and spiritual constitution needs also to be taken into consideration. The past lives only in the present, and the present vestiges of Japan's past have everything to do with how it operates and performs in the world today. That past includes a rich and highly sophisticated religious history and tradition. It also includes one of the most morally astute and aesthetically refined warrior traditions of any society anywhere. And while hard to see through its current glittery, cluttered cloak of modernity, the imprint of that past continues to affect and inform its people.

So too with the teachings of Nakamura Tempū. To credit Tempū with the resilience of the communities in northeastern Japan all but destroyed by the 2011 disaster would be inappropriate; no line connects the dots. At the same time, to say that Tempū's teachings have had no effect on the nation's psyche or on its political leadership would be to withhold credit where credit is due, and one might make a reasonable claim that the spirit of Nakamura Tempū lives on—through morphic resonance and as a morphogenetic field—and that it watches over those who help themselves.

The world is going through some of the most radical changes it has ever known. On the one hand, we are beset by ideological wars, environmental crises, political discord, and civil unrest. But on the other, rapidly accelerating technological innovation and the consequent ease of access to information, coupled with humanity's innate desire to know, is driving us toward a more integrated understanding of the relationships between the arts, ethics, and the sciences. Whether these evolutionary forces of light win out over the entropic forces of darkness remains to be seen, but there is cause for hope.

Less than fifty years after Tempū's death, it is impossible to read his writings without discovering antiquated observations and outdated philosophical arguments, but that is only to be expected; far more important are the aspects of his teachings that are timeless and therefore have immediate applicability to the here and now of this complicated age. Certainly, the most timeless and most important tenet of his teachings is that human intentionality is a genuine force with a real effect, and that by living fully in the present, we have at our disposal the means to create our future.

The case needs also to be made that, rather than a teaching left behind by progress, Tempū's is one still ahead of the curve. In a world suffering from social, economic, political, and even intellectual and philosophical fragmentation, what is ever more clear is that any vision of a future that is sustainable involves more integration and more wholeness. Right and Left must learn to function as nonexclusive, mutually informative political perspectives; Good, True, and Beautiful must be treated as qualitatively distinct but equally valid determinants in the assessment of ideas; and mind and body, in the interest of health, vitality, and spiritual fulfillment, must function as one.

Truth comes in two flavors: that which is absolute and enduring, and that which is ephemeral, subject to time and circumstance. Tempū's teachings contain healthy doses of both. Neither are his to be interpreted as final words on how to live, nor were they ever so intended; he often spoke of a future wherein his teachings, or some version of them, would become part of early education—implying that later education would be given to ideas of even greater insight. But surely, at this stage in humanity's journey, his teachings are wanted and needed more than ever, for they illuminate the path from which those greater insights will inevitably arise.

All of human achievement, fulfillment, joy, and understanding comes out of the present moment. It behooves each and every one of us, Tempū declares from beyond the grave, to bring ourselves to that moment with passion and vitality. That passion and vitality, he also declares, is accessible to each and every one of us. It is our birthright. When mind and body are in agreement, humanity stands tall, in perfect alignment with the forces of heaven and earth, and filled with the breath of heaven's wind.

NOTES

1. Third Male Child

1. The story appears in Ōi Mitsuru's *Senjō-to Meisō* (The Battlefield and Meditation).

2. By some accounts, Nakamura did not take up residence in the Tōyama household until after his expulsion from the Shūyūkan. I defer here to Ōi's account in *Senjō-to Meisō*.

3. Cited by British Journalist Hugh Byas in *Government by Assassination*, a fascinating first-hand account of pre-War Japanese politics. Byas devotes a whole chapter to Tōyama Mitsuru.

4. Quoted by Byas, *Government by Assassination*. The English translation, I assume, is Byas's.

5. Kanō, in an interview conducted and published in the 1920s by Ochiai Torahei, translated and published in English by Brian Watson as part of his *Judo Memoirs of Jigoro Kano,* says there were only four Kōdōkan branch dojos in existence at this time, and lists them; the Meidōkan is not among them. Kanō, however, spent two years as the principal of a junior high school in neighboring Kumamoto in 1891–1893, planting the seeds of judo in Kumamoto while he was there. It is possible—even likely—that his dojo in Kumamoto is the one that figures in this story.

6. Or so I was told by Sasaki Masando. The biographical information I have seen on Yamaza makes no mention of his judo ranking.

7. Uchida's father and grandfather were both masters of several arts and fully transmitted instructors of *shintō musō-ryū jōjutsu*, a traditional heirloom of the Fukuoka fiefdom. His father, Uchida Ryōgorō, taught the art in Tokyo and moved his family there while Ryōhei was still small. He also contributed to shintō musō-ryū jōjutsu a set of short-staff forms that bear his name. The art is still taught and practiced, both in Japan and internationally. Uchida Ryōhei was tutored in martial arts by his father from an early age.

8. That Nakamura should have mastered zuihenryū-battōjutsu in the short time (three years) he was at the Meidōkan is unlikely, and I surmise that he must have received continuing instruction through his late teens and

early twenties in Tokyo. Zuihenryū has since been lost, having died with its last practitioner, and Nakamura Tempū, who is known to have taught it to a small group of Tempūkai members in the 1920s and 1930s under strict injunction that they neither disseminate nor demonstrate it, may well have been its last instructor.

2. In Service of Country

1. Terauchi's address is recorded anecdotally in Ōi Mitsuru's *Senjō-to Meisō*. Ōi's account, I assume, is based solely on Nakamura Tempū's recollections of the event.
2. In keeping with a precedent set by Ōi Mitsuru in *Senjō-to Meisō*, this narrative combines two stories into one: the meeting with the highwaymen and Kondō's paralysis are based on the transcript of a talk from February 18, 1967, while the story of Nakamura's sudden recall of the old man and of his admonition, "not skill but guts," is from a talk delivered one day earlier, on February 17, 1967; both are published in *Seikō-no Jitsugen* (The Realization of Success). The "not skill but guts" incident, Nakamura says, occurred during his first assignment to Manchuria under Kōno Kinichi, but he does not describe the actual encounter; I have chosen, as a matter of convenience, to stick with the version of the story told by Ōi Mitsuru.

   The story of the highwaymen encounter is also told by Tempū in a recording given to me by Sasaki Masando of a talk delivered to students at the National Defense Academy in 1966; this rendition differs in several minor details from Ōi's account, including the time of year in which it occurred (in the 1966 talk, Tempū says it occurred in August).

3. Harbin

1. The Nicholaevsky Cathedral, not to be confused with St. Sophia Cathedral, the present-day city landmark completed in 1932, was destroyed during the Cultural Revolution.
2. Bertram Lenox Simpson, *Manchu and Muscovite* (London: Macmillan, 1904), 138–39. The book is a fascinating Manchuria travelogue written on the eve of the Russo-Japanese War.

3. In 2013, during one of my visits to Harbin, I discovered an early-twentieth-century photograph of this building on display at the historical photographic archive housed in St. Sophia Cathedral. The photograph shows a long two-story structure with sloping roofs and ornate eaves. Notes to the photograph indicated that it was still standing, but when I looked for the building at the address given on West Dahzi Street, the site was occupied by rubble. The old Chinese Eastern Railway headquarters building, just down the street, however, was intact and looked much the same as it does in period photos.

4. From transcript of a talk delivered in 1957 and published in the June 2009 issue of *Shirube*.

4. War's Toll

1. From the transcript of a talk delivered on June 10, 1958, and published in *Seikō-no Jitsugen*.

2. Ibid.

5. A Crisis of Mind

1. The interpretation of the three causes of Nakamura's mental and spiritual decline that follows is based on Tempū's iterations as they occur in both his *Kokoro-ni Seikō-no Honō-wo* (Mentally Kindling the Flame of Success) and Uno Chiyo's *Tempū-sensei Zadan* (Talks by Tempū-sensei). He is more succinct in his explanations than I am here but calls upon the use of terms that demand prior familiarity with his teachings; I have undertaken to unpack those terms in a way that is more generally intelligible.

2. Tsuruko's observations appear in the Tempūkai's *Zusetsu, Nakamura Tempū* (Nakamura Tempū, a Pictorial Guide).

3. In the transcript of a talk delivered on September 24, 1968, Tempū quotes, in English, the sentence, "Unfortunately most of us measure ourselves by our weakness, instead of by our strength." It was, he says, one of the first of Marden's sayings to catch his attention. He also says that it occurs at the beginning of the book. In the 1917 edition of *How to Get What You Want*, the sentence does occur, but not until page 118. The most likely explanation for this discrepancy is that there was an earlier edition, now lost.

This seems especially likely given that 1917 is also the year that Marden reestablished his once-failed publishing business.

4. The story of New Thought and the philosophy of positive thinking, and of their substantial influence on twentieth- and even twenty-first-century American culture, is artfully told by Mitch Horowitz in *One Simple Idea: How Positive Thinking Reshaped Modern Life* (New York: Crown, 2014). Horowitz, however, mentions Marden only once, and only in passing.

5. Yoshizawa died in 1965, just three years before Nakamura, at the age of ninety-one.

6. What the source of Yoshizawa's familiarity with Carrington was, we are not told.

7. Nakamura does not mention the date of issue, but presumably it was either late 1909 or early 1910.

8. Quoted by Arthur Gold and Robert Fizdale, *The Divine Sarah: A Life of Sarah Bernhardt.* (New York: Random House, 1991).

9. Or so we are told by Tempū; Driesch, in his writings, calls this force *entelechy.* The term *vril,* which derives from a novel by Edward Bulwer-Lytton published in 1871, was in popular usage at the time of Tempū's first meeting with Driesch, and Driesch may have used it conversationally with Nakamura in place of the more formal entelechy.

10. I have been unable to discover background or biographical details with regard to Lindler. But then, my resources have also been limited; someone with access to the University of Lyon's archives may do better. Nakamura gives us only Lindler's last name.

11. While Emile Coué's ideas became something of a sensation throughout Europe and the United States beginning in the 1920s, they were still relatively unknown outside the city of Nancy, the site of Coué's clinic, at the time of Nakamura's visit. They were, nevertheless, already in formulation, and given the circumstances of Lindler and Coué's concurrent activities within reasonable proximity of each other, the similarity between their respective teachings are almost certainly more than coincidental.

12. My exposition of the autosuggestive command method in this and the following paragraphs is a compendium of several sources: the instructions of my aikido teacher, Tada Hiroshi, in the 1980s (in particular, it was Tada-sensei who impressed upon me the importance of addressing

oneself by name); the teachings of the Tempūkai; and Nakamura Tempū's explanations as contained in *Shin-jinsei no Tankyū* (The Search for an Authentic Life).

6. "Certainly"

1. Nakamura did visit the pyramids of Giza, he says, prior to leaving Cairo.
2. From Uno Chiyo's *Tempū-sensei Zadan*.
3. The 1966 recording in which Nakamura Tempū says that Kariappa is alive at over 200 years of age is on a CD issued by the Tempūkai. What was Tempū's source for this information? Did he have either some continuing means of contact with Kariappa or some other form of access to information regarding him since returning to Japan? We do not know.

7. The Voice of Heaven

1. From transcript of a talk delivered on October 15, 1965, and published in *Seidai-na Jinsei* (A Prodigious Life).
2. From transcript of a talk delivered in August 1956 and published in *Seidai-na Jinsei*.

8. Kumbhaka

1. Kariappa's comments are adapted from Ōi Mitsuru's *Yoga-ni Ikiru* (Living in Yoga).
2. Nakamura pronounces it "kumbahakka"; the spelling *kumbhaka* is consistent with that used in most yoga texts.
3. The story is adapted from Ōi Mitsuru's *Yoga-ni Ikiru*.
4. From Patanjali and Charles Johnston, *The Yoga Sutras of Patanjali: The Book of the Spiritual Man* (Auckland, New Zealand: Floating Press, 2009).
5. From Swami Krishnananda, *The Study and Practice of Yoga: An Exposition of the Yoga Sutras of Patanjali*, chapter 78: "Kumbhaka and Concentration of Mind," http://www.swami-krishnananda.org/patanjali/raja_78.html.
6. Ibid.
7. Did Nakamura, perhaps, first encounter this teaching in his martial arts training? He is not on record as having indicated this to be the case.

8. From the transcript of a talk delivered on January 19, 1967, and published in *Kokoro-ni Seikō-no Honō-wo*.

9. China

1. Opinions regarding Sun Yat-sen expressed herein are influenced by Marie-Claire Bergère's biography, *Sun Yat-sen,* translated by Janet Lloyd (Stanford, CA: Stanford University Press, 1998).
2. Fitting two full months into a timeline bordered by his late May or early June arrival in Shanghai and his participation in the events of the Second Revolution beginning in mid-July is problematic; the actual duration of his stay in Beijing may have been closer to five or six weeks.
3. From "The Emptiness Chapter" in Miyamoto Musashi's *The Book of Five Rings*. The English translation is mine, based on the modern Japanese translation by Matsumoto Michihiro.
4. The photograph appears in *Zusetsu, Nakamura Tempū*.
5. The details of Nakamura's departure from China at the side of Sun Yat-sen are opaque. I have pieced together from a variety of sources what appears to be the most accurate scenario. Chen Qimei and Chiang Kai-shek were either on the same vessel with Sun and Nakamura or on another arriving soon after.
6. Hasegawa's biography is titled *Yamaza Enjirō, Tairiku Gaikō-no Sakigake* (Yamaza Enjirō, Pioneer of Continental Foreign Policy).

10. The Prodigal's Return

1. Tōyama's words appear in the transcript of a talk delivered by Nakamura Tempū on June 8, 1967, and published in *Kokoro-ni Seikō-no Honō-wo*.

11. Tigers and Miners

1. From transcript of a talk delivered October 12, 1965, and published in *Seidai-na Jinsei*.
2. The phonetic rendering of the animal trainer's name is "Kōn"; this could be something like Cohen or Cone or even Corn. I have been unsuccessful in my attempts to identify an animal trainer from this period with a name to match.

3. Kaneko says he searched for Tempū for twenty-five years after seeing the photograph; the Tempūkai was inactive during the war years, so he must have seen it five or more years after it was taken.

4. From transcript of a talk delivered October 12, 1965, and published in *Seidai-na Jinsei.*

12. The Turning Point

1. *Sensei* is "teacher"; *ō-sensei* is "great teacher."

2. From transcript of a talk delivered on June 8, 1967, and published in *Kokoro-ni Seikō-no Honō-wo.*

3. Some fifty years later, Tempū repeats his mother's words verbatim when reprimanding some of his students for disparaging comments made with regard to an early attempt to build a Tempūkai headquarters building. He tells the story in a 1964 talk, the transcript of which is published in the March 2014 issue of *Shirube.*

4. The Ueno Seiyōken still operates in the same location and under the same name, but in a newer and enlarged edifice.

5. The pageantry of the street vendor's sales pitch is portrayed by the character of Tora-san in the immensely popular, 1970s and 1980s film series *Otoko wa Tsurai yo!* (It's Tough Being a Man).

6. I used to visit this building regularly in the 1980s (a business client had his office there). When I looked for it in or around 2013, however, it had been replaced by a modern, much taller structure.

7. Quoted in *Zusetsu, Nakamura Tempū.*

8. Ibid.

13. The Unification of Mind and Body

1. From transcript a talk delivered October 15, 1965, and published in *Seidai-na Jinsei.*

2. For another perspective, as well as detailed explanations of a number of shin-shin tōitsu-dō practices, see H. E. Davey, *Japanese Yoga: The Way of Dynamic Meditation* (Berkeley, CA: Stone Bridge Press, 2001) and H. E. Davey, *The Teachings of Tempu: Practical Meditation for Daily Life* (Albany, CA: Michi Publishing, 2013).

3. See Ken Wilber, *Sex, Ecology, Spirituality: The Spirit of Evolution* (Boston: Shambala, 2000), especially chapter 4, "A View from Within." Whitehead advances his concept of prehension in his *Process and Reality* (New York: Macmillan, 1957).

4. From *Tempū Shōku-shū (Kuro)* (Tempū's Collected Verses for Recitation [Black]), published by the Tempūkai. In 1967, the Tempūkai published an English translation of this collection that was evidently handed out to members at the summer retreat; it is long since out of print, but I am indebted to Robert Frager for providing me with the English version used in that translation, which he says he still remembers by heart. I have adopted that translation here with only minor modifications.

5. Ibid.; the translation is mine.

6. I was a student of macrobiotics during the 1970s and 1980s and worked for twenty years in the natural foods industry.

14. Evil Close to the Throne

1. Quoted by Ōi Mitsuru in *Shinki-wo Tenzu* (To Start Anew).

2. Hidezō's recollection of his father's words, contained in his eulogy, are recorded in Ikawa Satoshi and Kobayashi Hiroshi, *Hito Arite: Tōyama Mitsuru-to Genyōsha* (A Man Such as He: Tōyama Mitsuru and the Genyōsha).

3. From transcript of a talk delivered by Tempū on August 13, 1960, at the Tempūkai summer retreat in Kobe and posted on the website http://tempu-online.com.

4. A recording of Suzuki's wife's account of the incident was discovered several years ago; I have heard it played a couple of times in NHK historical documentaries.

5. The story of Nakamura Tempū's connection to events at the palace in the early hours of August 15, 1945, including dialogue, appears in the transcript of the August 13, 1960, talk at the Tempūkai summer retreat in Kobe and posted on the website http://tempu-online.com. It also appears in Ōi's *Shinki-wo Tenzu*.

15. A New Beginning

1. Not all Western narratives, of course. A number of Western historians have delivered far more nuanced accounts, among the best of which, in my opinion, is S. C. M. Paine's *The Wars for Asia, 1911–1945* (New York: Cambridge University Press, 2012).

2. Ostensibly, the embargos were levied in response to Japan's incursions into China. But then, from the Japanese perspective, given the weight of the United States and Great Britain's influence in China, not to mention their respective records of imperialism, the objections to Japan's actions appeared not only grossly hypocritical but also aimed only at preserving regional Anglo-American hegemony.

3. Not the only person to make this case but perhaps the first was Helen Mears in her unsparing 1948 criticism of American chauvinism titled *Mirror for Americans: Japan* (Boston: Houghton Mifflin, 1948).

4. Tokutomi's warning, as well as the subsequent story of Tempū's meeting with Eichelberger, is found in the first half of the transcript of one of Tempū's talks published in the July 2009 issue of *Shirube;* the recording from which the transcription is derived is apparently undated.

5. The story of Tempū's intervention on behalf of the downed pilot and how this incident eventually led to his encounter with John D. Rockefeller III, as well as his account of what transpired in his two meetings with Rockefeller, is contained in the second half of the transcript cited in the previous note, published in the August 2009 issue of *Shirube.* A similar but slightly abbreviated version of the story also appears in the transcript of a December 7, 1957, talk published in *Kokoro-ni Seikō-no Honō-wo.*

16. The Years of Fulfillment

1. The 1966 and 1967 numbers are as recalled by Robert Frager.

2. From PHP Institute, "Milestones," in *Matsushita Konosuke (1894–1989), His Life & Legacy: A Collection of Essays in Honor of the Centenary of his Birth.* (Tokyo: PHP Institute, 1994).

3. Ibid.

4. From *Tempū Shōku-shū (Kuro)* (Tempū's Collected Verses for Recitation [Black]), first published by the Tempūkai in 1957.

5. H. E. Davey gives an easy-to-follow pictorial description of this routine in *Japanese Yoga.*

6. For more information on Matsubara and to view samples of her work, see her website, http://naokomatsubara.com, and the Abbozzo Gallery website, http://abbozzogallery.com.

7. 先天一気即霊源　無作為而行自然　人生亦此制疇中　一切還元帰大霊.

8. Quoted by Omi in his *Tempū Tetsugaku-no Jissenki: Jinsei-wo Kirihiraku* (Practical Application Journal of Tempū Philosophy: Pioneering Human Life).

9. Ibid.

10. Frager tells me that fellow aikido practitioner Terry Dobson was also a member of the Tempūkai, but that, at least during the years that Frager was in Japan, he attended only sporadically. Dobson died in 1992.

   The Polish-French artist Balthus (Balthasar Klossowski de Rola) met with Tempū on several occasions in the 1960s and was an ardent admirer. He did not, however, speak Japanese and, to my knowledge, did not actively pursue Tempū's teachings. Balthus was introduced to Tempū by a charming young woman named Ideta Setsuko, one of Tempū's students; she became Setsuko Klossowska de Rola in 1967 and survives her husband, who died in 2001.

Epilogue: A New Legacy

1. Quoted in *Zusetsu, Nakamura Tempū.*

2. Nakamura's contemporary, Ueshiba Morihei, founder of aikido, is another case in point. Ueshiba, who died just five months after Nakamura, was, in the estimation of many, one of the greatest martial artists of the modern era and the inspiration for several generations of instructors to train under him. While his legacy is secure in the respective lineages of those he mentored, none of his protégés nor anyone among their students have yet to approach his level of skill.

3. This is especially true of men and women working in aesthetic, spiritual, and humanitarian domains. Not insignificantly, it is less true among pioneers in the sciences. Albert Einstein is a good example. Einstein's theory of general relativity is a work of genius unmatched by most thinkers of his age; yet, because that theory is supported by mathematics and subject

to objective verification, his work was easily picked up and furthered by other geniuses. The theory of general relativity is now the stuff of pre-graduate college physics, accessible even to high school students, while the cutting edge has advanced to places far beyond—even though what has been done with that understanding and the technologies it has subsequently spawned sometimes merits pause for reflection.

The difference between objective and subjective disciplines, as well as the dissimilarity in their relative ease of transmission, appears to derive not from the sophistication or level of complexity of the knowledge in question but the nature of the injunctions through which that knowledge is realized. The sciences, as an example, are available to anyone able and willing to put in the necessary hours to learn the math and theoretical hypotheses upon which they are built, a learning for which an academic infrastructure is in place. On the other hand, contemplative wisdom, as another example, is equally available, I would assert, to anyone willing to put in the time and effort necessary to search his or her soul, to confront the indignities of his or her own character, and to pierce the veil of personal arrogance. This is a taller order to fill, and it is also one for which the supporting infrastructure, while it does exist, in the form of monasteries, convents, ashrams, retreats, and so on, is predominantly antiquated and of marginal social relevance.

When Tempū asserts that the only reason he lacks a successor is that no one has applied himself to his teachings with as much dedication as he, he is only saying what was true. While dedication of the same order as Nakamura Tempū's is hard to come by, part of the responsibility for the human project rests with our institutions and societal norms; until moral and spiritual development are valued at least as highly as scientific, technical, and economic understanding, the paucity of genuine seekers in those domains will persist. But then, all the signs tell us that day is coming, that a renewal of interest in not just physical health but the wholeness of being is on its way. Nakamura Tempū, I believe, deserves credit as one of that new dawn's pioneers.

BIBLIOGRAPHY

Japanese

井川 聡、小林 寛『人ありて、頭山満と玄洋社』(有)海鳥社、2003年

稲盛 和夫『成功への情熱』PHP研究所、2007年

宇野 千代『天風先生座談』廣済堂出版、1987年

大井 満『戦争と瞑想、若き日の天風 中村三郎の軌跡』(株)春秋社、1989年

　　〃　〃『ヨーガに生きる、中村天風とカリアッパ師の歩み』(株)春秋社、1988年

　　〃　〃『心機を転ず、中村天風激動の生涯』(株)春秋社、1997年

尾身 幸次『天風哲学実践記、人生を切り拓く』(株)PHP研究所、2010年

沢井 淳弘編著『心を空にする、中村天風「心身統一法」の真髄』[監修]財団法人天風会[発行](株)飛鳥新社、2009年

東亜同文会『続対支回顧録 (下)』原書房; 覆刻版、1981年

中島 岳志『中村屋のボース：インド独立運動と近代日本のアジア主義』松岳社(株)青木製本所、2006年

中村 天風『真人生の探究』財団法人天風会、2002年

　　〃　〃『研心抄』財団法人天風会、2004年

　　〃　〃『練身抄』財団法人天風会、2004年

　　〃　〃『成功哲学三部作(成功の実現、盛大な人生、心に成功の炎を)』日本経営合理化協会、2008年

　　〃　〃『天風誦句集(黒)』財団法人天風会

中村天風財団月刊誌「志るべ」1993年 7、8、9月号、2004年－2016年毎月号。公益財団法人天風会発行

中村天風財団編『図説、中村 天風』(有)海鳥社、2005年

長谷川 峻『山座園次郎、大陸外交の先駆』時事通信社、1967年

芳澤 謙吉『外交六十年』中公文庫、1990年

読売新聞西部本社編『大アジア燃ゆるまなざし、頭山満と玄洋社』(有)海鳥社、2001年

English

Bergamini, David. *Japan's Imperial Conspiracy*. London: Panther Books, 1972.

Bergère, Marie-Claire. *Sun Yat-sen*. Translated by Janet Lloyd. Stanford, CA: Stanford University Press, 1998.

Bix, Herbet P. *Hirohito and the Making of Modern Japan*. New York: Harper-Collins, 2000.

Brooks, C. Harry. *The Practice of Autosuggestion by the Method of Emile Coué*. New York: Dodd, Mead and Co., 1922.

Byas, Hugh. *Government by Assassination*. New York: Alfred A. Knopf, 1941.

Connaughton, Richard. *Rising Sun and Tumbling Bear: Russia's War with Japan*. London: Cassell, 2003.

Coué, Emile. *My Method, Including American Impressions*. Garden City, NY: Doubleday, 1923.

———. *Self Mastery through Conscious Autosuggestion*. New York: American Library Service, 1922.

Davey, H. E. *Japanese Yoga: The Way of Dynamic Meditation*. Berkeley, CA: Stone Bridge Press, 2001.

———. *The Teachings of Tempu: Practical Meditation for Daily Life*. Albany, CA: Michi Publishing, 2013.

Deguchi, Kyotaro. *The Great Onisaburo Deguchi*. Translated by Charles Rowe. Kanagawa, Japan: Aiki News, 1998.

Dormandy, Thomas. *The White Death: A History of Tuberculosis*. London: Hambledon, 1999.

Dreisch, Hans. *The History & Theory of Vitalism*. Translated by C. K. Ogden. London: Macmillan, 1914.

Dubos, René J., and Jean Dubos. *The White Plague: Tuberculosis, Man, and Society*. Boston: Little, Brown, 1952.

Duus, Peter. *The Abacus and The Sword: The Japanese Penetration of Korea, 1895–1910*. Berkeley, CA: University of California Press, 1995.

Gold, Arthur, and Robert Fizdale. *The Divine Sarah: A Life of Sarah Bernhardt*. New York: Random House, 1991.

Goldberg, Michelle. *The Goddess Pose: The Audacious Life of Indra Devi, the Woman Who Helped Bring Yoga to the West*. New York: Alfred A. Knopf, 2015.

Gordon, David B. *Sun Yatsen: Seeking a Newer China*. Upper Saddle River, NJ: Prentice Hall, 2010.

Guha, Ramachandra. *India after Gandhi: The History of the World's Largest Democracy*. London: Macmillan, 2007.

Harr, John Ensor, and Peter J. Johnson. *The Rockefeller Century: Three Generations of America's Greatest Family*. New York: Charles Scribner's Sons, 1988.

Horowitz, Mitch. *One Simple Idea: How Positive Thinking Reshaped Modern Life.* New York: Crown, 2014.

Hotta, Eri. *Japan 1941: Countdown to Infamy.* New York: Alfred A. Knopf, 2013.

———. *Pan-Asianism and Japan's War, 1931–1945.* New York: Palgrave Macmillan, 2007.

Iriye, Akira. *The Origins of the Second World War in Asia and the Pacific.* London And New York: Longman, 1987.

Krishnananda, Swami. *The Study and Practice of Yoga: An Exposition of the Yoga Sutras of Patanjali.* Rishikesh: Shivanandangar, India: The Divine Light Mission, 2006. www.swami-krishnananda.org.

Loebl, Suzanne. *America's Medicis: The Rockefellers and their Astonishing Cultural Legacy.* New York: Harper Collins, 2010.

Marden, Orison Swett. *How to Get What You Want.* New York: Thomas Y. Crowell, 1917.

———. *Pushing to the Front, or, Success under Difficulties.* Boston: Houghton, Mifflin and Co., 1895.

Matsusaka, Yoshihisa Tak. *The Making of Japanese Manchuria, 1904–1932.* Cambridge, MA: Harvard University East Asia Center, 2001.

Mears, Helen. *Mirror for Americans: Japan.* Boston: Houghton Mifflin, 1948.

Mitter, Rana. *Forgotten Ally: China's World War II, 1937–1945.* New York: Houghton Mifflin Harcourt, 2013.

Miyamoto, Musashi. *The Book of Five Rings.* Modern Japanese translation by Matsumoto Michihiro. English translation by William Scott Wilson. Tokyo: Kodansha International, 2001.

Paine, S. C. M. *The Sino-Japanese War of 1894–1895: Perceptions, Power, and Primacy.* New York: Cambridge University Press, 2003.

———. *The Wars for Asia, 1911–1949.* New York: Cambridge University Press, 2012.

Patanjali and Charles Johnston. *The Yoga Sutras of Patanjali: The Book of the Spiritual Man.* Auckland, New Zealand: Floating Press, 2009.

PHP Institute, comp. *Matsushita Konosuke (1894–1989), His Life & His Legacy: A Collection of Essays in Honor of the Centenary of His Birth.* Tokyo: PHP Institute, 1994.

Prange, Gordon W., Donald M. Goldstein, and Katherine V. Dillon. *Pearl Harbor: The Verdict of History.* New York: McGraw-Hill, 1986.

Sheldrake, Rupert. *Morphic Resonance: The Nature of Formative Causation*. Rochester, VT: Park Street Press, 2009.

———. *The Presence of the Past: Morphic Resonance and the Habits of Nature*. Rochester, VT: Park Street Press, 1988.

Shiba, Ryōtarō. *The Clouds Above the Hill: A Historical Novel of the Russo-Japan War*. 4 vols. Translated by Juliet Winters Carpenter and Paul McCerthy. Edited by Phyllis Birnbaum. New York: Routledge, 2014.

Silbey, David J. *The Boxer Rebellion and the Great Game in China*. New York: Hill and Wang, 2012.

Simpson, Bertram Lenox. *Manchu and Muscovite*. London: Macmillan, 1904.

Siniawer, Eiko Maruko. *Ruffians, Yakuza, Nationalists: The Violent Politics of Modern Japan, 1860–1960*. Ithaca and London: Cornell University Press, 2008.

Slattery, Peter. *Reporting the Russo-Japanese War, 1904–5: Lionel James's First Wireless Transmissions to the Times*. Folkestone, Kent: Global Oriental, 2004.

Stevens, John. *The Way of Judo: A Portrait of Jigoro Kano and His Students*. Boston: Shambhala, 2013.

Stinnett, Robert B. *Day of Deceit: The Truth about FDR and Pearl Harbor*. New York: The Free Press, 2000.

Thompson, Robert Smith. *Empires on the Pacific: World War II and the Struggle for the Mastery of Asia*. New York: Basic Books, 2001.

Victor, George. *The Pearl Harbor Myth: Rethinking the Unthinkable*. Washington, DC: Potomac Books, 2007.

Victoria, Daizen. *Zen at War*. New York: Weatherhill, 1997.

Washington, Peter. *Madame Blavatsky's Baboon: A History of the Mystics, Mediums, and Misfits Who Brought Spiritualism to America*. New York: Schocken Books, 1995.

Watson, Brian N. *Judo Memoirs of Jigoro Kano: Early History of Judo*. Victoria, Canada: Trafford, 2008.

Weale, B. L. Putnam [Bertram Lenox Simpson]. *The Truth about China and Japan*. New York: Dodd, Mead and Co., 1919.

Wilber, Ken. *Sex, Ecology, Spirituality: The Spirit of Evolution*. Boston: Shambala, 2000.

Whitehead, Alfred North. *Process and Reality*. New York: Macmillan, 1957.

Yogananda, Paramahansa. *Autobiography of a Yogi*. 13th ed. Los Angeles: Self-Realization Fellowship, 1998.

Recordings (Compact Disc)

『神人冥合、中村天風』財団法人天風会

『哲人 中村天風先生、心について(昭和41年防衛大学校にて)』平成17年5月29日、
　　山陰神道上福岡齋宮大祭記念

『中村天風講話録「心身統一法入門編」第1～7巻』財団法人天風会

『中村天風講話録 真人生の創造、第1巻「生きがいある人生」』[監修]財団法人天
　　風会　[制作・著作]PHP研究所、2008年

『中村天風講話録 真人生の創造、第2巻「人生成功の秘訣」』[監修]財団法人天
　　風会[制作・著作]PHP研究所、2008年

『中村天風講話録 真人生の創造、第3巻「六つの力」』[監修]財団法人天風会[制
　　作・著作]PHP研究所、2008年

『中村天風真理瞑想シリーズ第1巻、思考作用の誦句』財団法人天風会、2003年

『中村天風真理瞑想シリーズ第2巻、運命の誦句』財団法人天風会

Recordings (VHS)

『映像シリーズ第1巻、夏期修練編』財団法人天風会

Websites

International Japanese Yoga Association: http://japanese-yoga.com

Sennin Foundation: http://senninfoundation.com

Swami Krishnananda, The Divine Life Society: http://swami-krishnananda.org

Tempūkai: http://tempukai.or.jp

Tempu Online: http://tempu-online.com

INDEX

Page numbers in italics indicate photos.

Kyoto, 311, 319

Kyushu, 10, 13

L

Lepcha, 125–26

Liaodong Peninsula, 26, 28, 31–32, 34, 71

Liaoyang, 73

Lindler, Professor, 96

Li Zongshun, 88–89, 90

London, 90–92

Lushun, 31, 32, 45, 54, 74, 84

M

MacArthur, Douglas, 300–301, 307

Manchukuo, 38, 85, 212, 281, 282

Manchuria, 10, 13, 26, 30–33, 35, 37–38, 47, 51, 54, 67–68, 70, 71, 73, 74, 113, 156, 212, 276, 280–82, 287

Manebhanjang, 120–21, 123, 136

Mangaldas, 130, 135

Manshū Gigun, 73

Mao Zedong, 310

Marco Polo Bridge Incident, 285

Marden, Orison Swett, 63, 80–82, 85–87

Marseilles, 98

Masamune, 183

Matsubara Naoko, 329–32, 340

Matsushita Electric, 315–18

Matsushita Kōnosuke, 314–18, 340, 341

May 15 Incident, 276

Mayung Kara, 129

Meckel, Jacob, 26

Meidōkan, 17–20, 24, 284, 310

Meiji, Emperor, 5, 10, 32, 203, 253, 329

Mencius, 200

mind-body unification (shin-shin tōitsu-dō)

affirmations and, 259–60, 261

breathing and, 179, 258, 264–65

conditioning of nervous reactivity, 258–59, 262–64

cultivating stillness and, 150–64

desires and, 247, 249–50

diet and, 267–68

distinctive character of, 252

history of development of, 252–54

influences on, 86–87, 91, 95, 271–72

Japanese name for, 247, 251

joy and happiness and, 248–51

kumbhaka and, 179–86, 266–67

longevity and, 328

overview of, 255–71

positivity and, 258, 260–62, 270–71

reformation of elemental concepts, 258, 259–60

resilience and, 258, 265–66

spirit and, 268–71

success of, 254–55

Mishima Miyoshi, 242, 243, 246

Miyamoto Musashi, 194

Miyazaki Torazō, 190–91

Mongolia, 70, 71

Mori Takeshi, 295

Mudan River, 70

muga-munen, 158

ABOUT THE AUTHOR

STEPHEN EARLE has been a student of Japanese language and East Asian culture and history for almost fifty years. He lived and worked in Japan continuously for sixteen years during the 1970s and '80s and has visited frequently since. He has also lived and worked in China and Singapore and travelled extensively in East, Southeast, and South Asia. He estimates he has crossed the Pacific Ocean more than 250 times.

Following a forty-year career in international business, during which he served in executive capacities and on the boards of several Japanese and U.S. corporations, Earle retired in 2015 to write. *Heaven's Wind* is his second book. His first, *Words Characters and Transparency: An Introduction to the Art and Science of KOTOHA,* was self-published in 2003. He is also co-translator, with Josh Drachman, of *A Light on Transmission: The Teachings of Morihei Ueshiba, Founder of Aikido* by Mitsugi Saotome.

Earle and his wife, Akemi, live in Richmond, Virginia, where he teaches aikido and she teaches Japanese language. They have two children and three grandchildren.